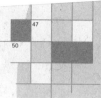

Random House

Casual
CROSSWORD OMNIBUS

edited by *Mel Rosen*

Random House
Puzzles & Games

NEW YORK   TORONTO   LONDON   SYDNEY   AUCKLAND

Visit the Random House Puzzles & Games Web site: www.puzzlesatrandom.com

First Edition

Printed in the United States of America

10 9 8 7 6 5

ISBN: 978-0-375-72244-8

WHAT ARE *CASUAL CROSSWORDS*?

Welcome to this omnibus collection of *Casual Crosswords*.

When new acquaintances find out that I write and edit crossword puzzles, inevitably one of them will say something like, "Oh, I can never do those things. They're always filled with stuff I've never heard of, and even when I look at the answers I can't make sense out of the clues." My standard response to those folks is, "You're attempting the wrong puzzles." If their eyes don't glaze over immediately, I go on to explain that we crossword editors want to challenge, as well as entertain, our audiences.

It turns out that there are lots of ways we do that: We publish puzzles with subtle or gimmicky themes (unifying aspects of the long answers); we permit unusual answer words in the grid, with phrases, Roman numerals, words in other languages, proper names from fields with which you may have less familiarity, and, frankly, words not in everyone's typical vocabulary; we employ vague, encyclopedic, or misleading clues, or clues relying on uncommon meanings of words. We hint at abbreviations without openly telling you that they're present. In books, we write blurbs or subtitles that may appear mysterious or unhelpful. We even publish puzzles with very few short words, so there is no good place for your mind to get a foothold, if you'll pardon that goofy mental image.

Finally, those of us who prepare puzzles for your daily newspapers often increase the overall difficulty through the week, so that if your first sally into the crosswords arena unluckily falls on a Friday or Saturday, you'll face a considerable challenge that incorporates all of the above hurdles.

Let's return to the original question: **What are *Casual Crosswords*?** Simply put: This book contains crosswords for casual—even novice—solvers. The themes are straightforward, with no gimmicks or wordplay. The answer words are almost exclusively (can you say *disclaimer*?) words or names of people you will know or recognize quickly. The clues are likewise uncomplicated, with some imagery (for example, "Swimmer's place" for POND) for variety.

To give your mind another leg up, so to speak, we've supplied each puzzle with a subtitle to help you catch on to its theme. We've also reached back to former times, when a clue had the tag "(2 words)" to tell you that its answer was a 2-word phrase. Then, we've put a "solving tip" on each puzzle page. It provides specific information for the particular puzzle, but we think you'll find many of the tips useful for other puzzles you may encounter. Finally, we've added an outright giveaway answer for every puzzle...but it's upside down and on a different page to remove some of the temptation.

Periodically throughout this volume we've dispensed with that "(2 words)" tag, and added a little more spice to some of the clues to provide a little more challenge.

Relax, learn something about how to solve crossword puzzles, and have fun.

Thanks to Sandy Fein, Oriana Leckert, and Helena Santini at Random House, to test solvers Bob Louty, Francis Heaney, Doug Fink, Adam Cohen and Peggy Rosen, and especially to the puzzle creators. Writing easy puzzles is not easy!

Mel Rosen, editor

Starting Off   by Mel Rosen

This puzzle's theme relates to where it is in the book. The box to the left of every diagram has information you may find helpful.

ACROSS

1 Neck wrap
6 Read a bar code
10 "Think nothing ___" (2 words)
14 Scarlett ___ (Gone With the Wind character)
15 "So what ___ is new?"
16 Stack
17 Where the expensive airline seats are (2 words)
19 Lake that's north of Ohio
20 Spigot for maple syrup
21 Detain
22 Got uptight
24 Animal doctors
25 Premiere appearance
26 Silicon slices for electronic integrated circuits
29 "The ___" (New York City's nickname, 2 words)
32 Beneficiaries of wills
33 Like some barbecue sauce

34 Eliminate
35 Gauzy
36 Jabs
37 Short skirt
38 Pages in a calendar (abbr.)
39 Intimidated
40 Composer of the opera Carmen
41 Declared illegal
43 Marshal Dillon's portrayer, James ___
44 Used a beeper
45 Bundled up
46 More daring
48 Filmdom's Rowlands
49 Pasture call
52 October's birthstone
53 Right away (2 words)
56 Pleasant
57 College credit hour

58 Jazzy singer Lena ___
59 Homeowner's proof of ownership
60 Kenny Rogers hit
61 Swords used in Olympic fencing

DOWN

1 Cushy
2 ___ Pet (novelty gift item)
3 Org. for people over 50 (abbr.)
4 Four Monopoly properties (abbr.)
5 Dads
6 Works in retail
7 Dressed
8 Braying beast
9 Rainy day reserves (2 words)
10 Speak freely (2 words)

11 Award that might be a blue ribbon or a gold medal (2 words)
12 Retired tennis player ___ Nastase
13 ___ up (prepared to drive a golf ball)
18 Barracks beds
23 On-line auction house
24 Quite a bit
25 Ate supper
26 Company that introduced the Frisbee
27 The five vowels
28 Champion's finishing location (2 words)
29 Cooked in the oven
30 Actors' words
31 Reworks text
33 Pulled with a rope or chain
36 Strong

37 Intellectual ability
39 Actor Nicolas of Adaptation and Leaving Las Vegas
40 Inhale and exhale
42 Dished out some soup
43 "It ___ Necessarily So"
45 Peevish
46 Ian Fleming's agent James ___
47 Ron Howard's role on The Andy Griffith Show
48 Crossword diagram
49 Bog down, as in a swamp
50 Author ___ Rice, who writes about vampires
51 Mellows
54 One ___ million (2 words)
55 Jump on one foot

HINT: If 1 Across doesn't immediately make sense, start someplace else. A "fill-in-the-blank" clue, such as 54 Down or 14 Across, is often an easier place to get started. For more help, see the box to the right of puzzle 7.

#43: 15A = IN RE

2

$4.00   by Norma Steinberg

In this puzzle a word that can mean "dollar" occurs in every long answer.
That's the title's hint. Easier puzzles often have "repeated word" themes.

ACROSS

1 Himalayan country
6 Abbreviation for a mandated pay deduction
10 Make beer
14 Expensive Honda brand
15 Confidently declare to be so
16 Actress Olin
17 Summary
18 Gave temporarily
19 Elliptical
20 Sound of disapproval
21 Refuse responsibility (*3 words*)
24 "___ Boots Are Made for Walkin'" (Nancy Sinatra oldie)
26 Unexpected game results
27 The one you date exclusively
29 Actress ___ Hatcher
31 Has creditors
32 Director Kazan
34 Handled some difficulty well
39 Fielder's glove
40 City in Oklahoma
42 The guy in the white hat, stereotypically
43 Early anesthetic
45 Shea Stadium pros
46 Prepare, as a hook
47 Bandstand blasters
49 Mushroom reproductive bodies
51 Tennis star Andre
55 *Out of Africa* star Streep
56 Raw army recruit (*2 words*)
59 Tavern
62 Rachel's baby, on *Friends*
63 "Thanks ___!" (*2 words*)
64 Choreographer Abdul
66 "Wanna make ___?" (*2 words*)
67 Slalom course opening
68 Fancy tie
69 Got up from a seated position
70 Potato outgrowths
71 "Holy moly!"

DOWN

1 Little fruit pie
2 Sherbets
3 Overbite cause
4 Pitcher's stat
5 Touched lightly
6 Not true, in a 50-50 quiz question
7 Singer Burl
8 Penny
9 Camelot's king
10 Clumps
11 Variety show
12 Make a law
13 Strolls
22 To date (*2 words*)
23 Heroic in scope
25 Rush
27 A few
28 Fool
29 Mosaic parts
30 Compass point
33 Sugar cube
35 "Whoopee!" (*2 words*)
36 *The Good Earth* author (*2 words*)
37 Cleveland's lake
38 Connect-the-___
41 Money in the bank, for example
44 Grate
48 Desert traveler's illusion
50 Send the money in advance of shipping
51 "Fuzzy Wuzzy was ___" (*2 words*)
52 Creole soup
53 Summits
54 Play hockey
55 Spouses
57 "Now ___ me down to sleep..." (*2 words*)
58 Participate in a democracy
60 Skin cream ingredient
61 "Phooey!"
65 "___ live and breathe!" (*2 words*)

HINT: In 6 Across, think "Social Security." For a bigger hint, see puzzle 14.

#36: 12A = GARP

Starting Positions   by Diane C. Baldwin

Themes often rely on words or phrases describing related, but not synonymous, activities.

ACROSS

1 Put in jeopardy
5 Three-alarm dish
10 Parts of a play
14 Opposed to
15 One who reacts to the alarm clock
16 Had on
17 Show some backbone (*5 words*)
20 Big pig
21 Ready for picking
22 Takes a gander
23 Engaged in work
24 Chatter on
26 Available to receive visitors (*2 words*)
29 Domestic help
30 Rich soil
31 Paris's river
32 Vegetable that may be split for soup
35 Take a break (*4 words*)
39 Grand ___ Opry
40 Churns up
41 Ringlet
42 School dances
43 Use mouthwash
45 Large primates
48 Restaurant selection list
49 Metal compound
50 Clammy
51 Fuss
54 Be a slacker at work (*5 words*)
58 Make airtight
59 Color of some eyes
60 Maybe-true story
61 Poker player's starting bet
62 Way overweight
63 Pretentious

DOWN

1 Impulsive
2 Division word
3 Bambi, as an adult
4 Family reunion attendees
5 Ocean voyage
6 Commune member, maybe
7 Isolated land
8 Welcoming gift on Hawaii
9 Annoy
10 Anticipates
11 One of Santa's reindeer
12 Fish for cod
13 Have a hunch
18 Oil container
19 Someone who won't answer a direct question directly
23 Explosive weapon
24 Twinges
25 Lemon zest, for example
26 Likewise
27 Hard work
28 Negative emotion
29 Breakfast, lunch, and dinner
31 Just brushes the surface
32 Advertise
33 English nobleman
34 Wheel shaft
36 Water-carved gully
37 Masked critter
38 Hosiery shade
42 French ___ (curly-haired dog)
43 Docile
44 Egyptian cross with a loop
45 Model-maker's wood
46 Green-card holder
47 Sheep's call
48 Lions' ruffs
50 Nod off
51 Somewhat open
52 Blockhead
53 Do as directed
55 "___ goes there?" (sentry's question)
56 Collar
57 Zeta's follower

HINT: The answer to 4 Down is a synonym for "relatives." For an even bigger hint, see puzzle 21.

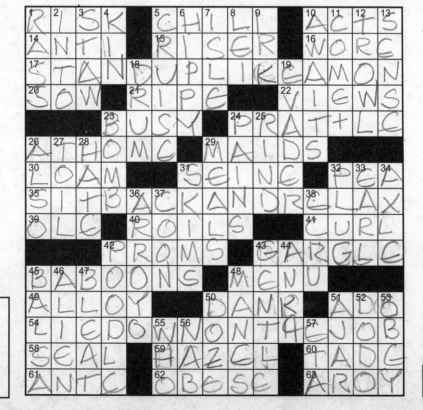

handwritten notes: psychopath, charming, way, manipulate, egocentric, grandiose, callous, emotional, devoid of feelings, emotionally detached, cold blooded, fearless

Come By Any Time! by Bernice Gordon

The first two words of this puzzle's title are a synonym for the important word in *each* of the thematic phrases.

ACROSS

1 Hairless on top
5 Poker necessity
9 Little Bo Peep's lost animals
14 Lake, canal, or city
15 John-Rice-Disney retelling of a Verdi opera
16 Deputies out west
17 Dollop
18 Meat-and-potatoes dish
19 "Do you come here ___?"
20 Catch on to (*4 words*)
23 One with "high hopes," in song
24 Avail
25 Geographic landmass from Portugal to Korea
29 Kingdom
31 Hard to find
33 Decal on Buckeye rooters' cars
34 Baking chambers
36 Repress, as a sneeze
39 Become badly involved (*4 words*)
43 Laundry worker
44 Computer printer brand
45 ___ de Janeiro
46 Clearasil target
48 SLR camera setting (*hyphenated*)
52 One of the Great Lakes
55 *Norma* ___ (Sally Field film)
57 Call ___ day (*2 words*)
58 Surprise with a gun (*4 words*)
61 Have food at home (*2 words*)
64 Lug
65 "This must weigh ___!" (*2 words*)
66 Weighing device
67 "*¿Cómo ___ usted?*"
68 Part in a play or film
69 Scatter about
70 Not imaginary
71 Tournament ranking

DOWN

1 Panhandler
2 ___ Francis of the old *What's My Line?* show
3 Actor Ray of *John Q*
4 Outstanding credit card balance
5 Examples
6 Until now
7 "What's the big ___?"
8 One who uses a ring as security for a loan
9 Tracker's trail
10 Labor leader Jimmy ___
11 Winter clock setting for the east coast (abbr.)
12 Wind direction (abbr.)
13 Prison, informally
21 Kind-hearted
22 Invited partygoers
26 Subdued
27 Speck of land
28 Violinist who taught Heifetz
30 Cut of veal
32 Pale
35 Country singer George ___
37 Half-price offer, slangily
38 McEwan and McKellen
39 Helicopter's forerunner, briefly
40 Actress Moran
41 Horn sound
42 *The Student Prince* or *The Pirates of Penzance*
47 Machine pin
49 Walk very cautiously
50 *Lawrence of Arabia* star Peter ___
51 Gave a thumbs-down review
53 Spry
54 Extend a magazine subscription
56 *Let's Make* ___ (*2 words*)
59 Hydrant hookup
60 Rower's needs
61 Letter before tee
62 Part of a play
63 Roofer's goo

HINT: Regarding 8 Down: A clue with the phrase "one who" often leads to an answer in which the last two letters are ER. See puzzle 28 for more help.

#22: 63A = IDIOM

Some of the Hard Stuff   by Mary Brindamour

The title refers to the hard stuff that ends each long answer. Once you discover what that ending is, you'll have a big head start.

ACROSS

1 Sleeve endings
6 Engine sound
10 Floor or desk lighter
14 Shoelace tip
15 Top-notch (*hyphenated*)
16 TV actress McClurg
17 Carpenter's tool
18 Semi-transparent gem rock
20 Lit with a match
22 Parent, during a child's childhood
23 George of TV's *Just Shoot Me*
24 Fast plane
25 Hospital trauma centers (abbr.)
26 In-house electrical supply
28 Endures
30 Greek letter after pi
31 Original *Who Wants to Be a Millionaire?* host Philbin
33 Expressed surprise
37 Departed
39 Cut the grass again
41 "___ Ha'i" (*South Pacific* song)
42 Seashore find
44 Underwater detection apparatus
46 "A mind ___ terrible thing to waste" (*2 words*)
47 Frontier posts
49 Expensive furs
51 *Bad Behaviour* star Stephen ___
54 Owing
55 Peruvian mountains
56 Says "yes"
58 Manet and Monet
60 The Biblical name for sulfur
62 Coral island
64 Smile broadly
65 "Sweater Girl" ___ Turner
66 Taboos
67 ___-bitsy
68 Adds to (with "out")
69 Bird's sound

DOWN

1 Baseballer's topper
2 Tangelo variety
3 Walkway paving slab
4 Herb similar to celery
5 Rod of *In the Heat of the Night*
6 Dromedary
7 Gangster
8 Popular card game
9 Artistic categories, as of novels or paintings
10 "I ___ Song Go Out of My Heart" (*2 words*)
11 Put on a pedestal
12 Coal digger
13 Equals
19 Spat (*hyphenated*)
21 Spud
24 ___ Alexander (George on *Seinfeld*)
26 Associations (abbr.)
27 Klutz's comment (*hyphenated*)
28 Prom vehicles
29 Weep and wail
32 *Beau ___* (1939 Gary Cooper French Foreign Legion film)
34 Ice pellet
35 Or follower, in a threat
36 "¡Buenos ___!" ("Good day," in Spain)
38 Santa's helper
40 Never existed
43 Ore deposits
45 All aglow
48 Steal cattle
50 Endow
51 Synagogue leader
52 Plumed bird
53 Operatic solos
55 Spaces
57 Television award
58 Diarist ___ Frank
59 ___ gin fizz
61 ___ leaf cluster (decoration for valor)
63 D-Day vehicle (abbr.)

HINT: That actor at 51 Across was also featured in the gender-bender film *The Crying Game*. There's another hint for you in the box alongside puzzle 35.

#15: 24A = ALCOA

A Tense Situation   by Manny Nosowsky

6

This puzzle and #19 (by the same writer) are clearly related to each other. Enjoy them both.

ACROSS

1 Carriers for schoolchildren
6 Wowed
10 Ripped
14 Strong glue
15 Stretched car
16 Cleveland's state
17 Relic (*5 words*)
20 Shout "Yay team!"
21 Sacagawea denomination, coinwise
22 Broadcaster
23 Plant supported by a trellis
25 Ovisac deposited by a spider or whelk (*2 words*)
27 Step in road building
30 Mountains crossed by the Trans-Siberian Railroad
31 Are
32 Become accustomed (to)
33 Has been
36 Like some danger, in a Tom Clancy title (*3 words*)
39 London's ___ Gardens (Royal Botanic Gardens locale)
40 Resident of the western Alaska Peninsula
41 1945 Allied conference site
42 Dagwood's "SKNXX-X"
43 Guy, informally
44 Record player (*2 words*)
47 One of six on a die
48 Saudi neighbor
49 French holy woman (abbr.)
50 Student exams, briefly
54 Sci-fi comedy of 1985 (*4 words*)
58 "Garfield" dog
59 Hapless
60 Plastic food wrap
61 Fortuneteller
62 Small city
63 Precise

DOWN

1 Symbol on California's flag
2 Capable of performing (the task, *2 words*)
3 Area of London or Manhattan
4 Okay-to-leave stamp (*2 words*)
5 Antonym's opposite (abbr.)
6 Unaccompanied
7 " ... had a ___ and couldn't keep her"
8 Ambulance worker (abbr.)
9 Homer Simpson's shout
10 Subject matters
11 Tara's owner
12 Levitates
13 ___ Dame
18 Big bell in a pagoda
19 Keen-sighted (*hyphenated*)
24 On the way (*2 words*)
25 Have an outburst
26 Teri in *Young Frankenstein*
27 "A Bushel and a ___"
28 Part of a drive train
29 Look at
30 Excessive, as force
32 Just lying there
33 In good shape
34 Entry fee for a poker hand
35 Asterisk
37 Lip-balm ingredient
38 Add-on to a purchase (*2 words*)
42 Doughnut, slangily
43 Feudal lord's land
44 Depression-era rail riders
45 "___ you what you are today!" (*2 words*)
46 Prima ___ evidence
47 Unforgiving
49 Exhibition
51 Pre-migraine sensation some people experience
52 ___ II (razor brand)
53 FedExed
55 Choose, with "for"
56 As well
57 Get something out of

HINT: Those mountains at 30 Across are usually considered to be the boundary between Europe and Asia. There's another hint for you to the right of puzzle 42.

#8: 25D = GUILDS

Bleached!   by Norma Johnson

Just like your laundry after adding bleach, everything's the same color. Well, at least the long entries are.

ACROSS

1 Desensitizes
6 Stingy person
11 Took first place
14 Be in sync
15 ___ Oyl
16 Tint
17 Kind of clerical worker (*hyphenated*)
19 The "I" in TGIF
20 Deposed Russian ruler
21 Yoko ___
22 Vietnamese New Year observation
23 "It's the truth!" (*2 words*)
26 Apartment building custodians
28 To the ___ degree
29 Power rating word on a light bulb
33 Toothbrush brand
34 ___ chi (martial arts discipline)
35 Plant with fronds and no flowers
36 Dada artist Max ___

39 1992 Rock and Roll Hall of Fame inductee ___ James
41 Internet communications technique (*hyphenated*)
43 5,280 feet
44 *Entertainment Tonight* host ___ Gibbons
46 Gas or water tube
47 "Skedaddle!"
48 Play on words
49 Big Bend National Park's Santa ___ Canyon
51 Medical group (*abbr.*)
52 Jaunty
55 Protein in flour
57 Light tap
58 Sam-___ (Seuss character, *hyphenated*)
60 Abbreviation on a business mailing

61 ___ moment's notice (*2 words*)
62 Elderly, perhaps (*hyphenated*)
67 Pose for a photograph
68 Certain Internet subscriber
69 Rapscallions
70 Guernsey's greeting
71 Cowboy competition
72 Hägar the Horrible's dog

DOWN

1 Slangy turndown
2 Exclamation of disgust
3 Hospital scanning test (*abbr.*)
4 Moviedom's Midler

5 Teeter-totter
6 Robin Hood's beneficiaries, so the stories go
7 Feeling under the weather
8 Prefix meaning "1,000"
9 Cowgirl Dale ___
10 Set up a detour
11 Savior in shining armor (*2 words*)
12 Peripheral
13 Bird houses
18 Sangria decanter
23 Company that makes the Pentium chip
24 North Dakota or Arizona
25 The common spud (*2 words*)
27 Salon offering, commonly

30 Arizona city
31 Hiker's path
32 Shoot from ambush
37 Goo in *Ghostbusters*
38 Wyoming's Grand ___ National Park
40 Côte d'___ (fashionable Mediterranean region of southeast France)
42 Pant leg measurement
45 Like a pacifist
50 Sacred stands
52 Muscle twitch
53 Place for a cookout, maybe
54 Popular Internet search engine
56 Foe of the Confederacy
59 Salsa style
60 Prefix meaning "gas" or "aviation"
63 Golfer's need
64 Regret
65 Suffix with chariot
66 Reason for clock changing (*abbr.*)

HINT: There are only a few ways to clue the answer at 49 Across, including a TV actress best-known in the 1970s. See puzzle 49 for more.

#1: 61A = EPEES

In Living Color   by Sarah Keller

Three films that prominently feature a color in their titles—a different one each time arrayed like an upside-down stop light.

ACROSS

1 Thick slices of cheese
6 Play opener (*2 words*)
10 Become liquid
14 "Delta Dawn" singer Tucker
15 Drug buster, for short
16 Aroma
17 The little mermaid
18 *The* ___ (colorful 1999 Tom Hanks film, *2 words*)
20 Mouse's cousin
21 Double agent
23 Medieval fortification
24 Dream up
26 Make an effort
27 Family card game
28 Book, as a hotel room
33 Cow in Borden ads
36 China's continent
38 Stink
39 Colorful 1968 Beatles' film (*2 words*)

42 "Gee whiz!"
43 Ireland, to the Irish
44 Comes down to earth
45 Husky's load
47 Choose
48 Eisenhower's nickname
49 Add to the value of
53 Like much junk mail
57 La ___ Tar Pits
58 Gershwin or Levin
59 Colorful 2002 Anthony Hopkins film (*2 words*)
61 Works in the ring
63 Country which was once Persia
64 Cosmonaut Gagarin

65 Run off to wed
66 Sammy of the Chicago Cubs
67 "Auld Lang ___"
68 Revival spots

DOWN

1 "...first ___ see tonight" (*2 words*)
2 Former NFL team member, now playing in St. Louis (*2 words*)
3 Ekberg of *La Dolce Vita*
4 Tournament sit-out for a seeded player
5 *Exodus* actor (*2 words*)
6 Geometry calculation
7 Give a hoot
8 Three, in Italy

9 Cone contents (*2 words*)
10 Dads' partners
11 Work on a manuscript
12 Loaf about
13 Oak or elm
19 Not ayes
22 John Lennon's Yoko
25 Trade unions' relatives
26 Apache or Arapahoe
29 List of printing mistakes
30 Bridle attachment
31 Sell
32 ___ out a living (makes do)
33 Got a glimpse of
34 Child's toy block brand
35 Smelting residue
36 Out of the way

37 Big ___, rugged California resort region
40 When public school is in session
41 Preschool subject
46 Teller of tall tales
47 *A Chorus Line* showstopper
49 Tennessee ___ Ford
50 President in 1972
51 Moved on hands and knees
52 Lightens
53 *Exodus* novelist Leon
54 Pianist Peter
55 Suggestions on food labels (abbr.)
56 Author Ferber
57 "___ in the USA"
60 Gal's counterpart
62 Encouragement at the bullring

HINT: Regarding 5 Down and 53 Down, which refer to the same book/film: If one name comes to you, the other probably will. This technique of using one reference in two or more clues is sometimes called "echoing." Puzzle 6 has another hint for you.

#44: 18D = HACEK

Somewhat Racy   by Norma Steinberg

Each long answer in this puzzle begins with the same word. Oddly enough, that word can mean either puritanical or indecent.

ACROSS

1 Part of the leg
5 Test tube
9 "___ was that lady I saw you with last night?"
12 Woodwind
13 Cove
15 Cartoon character Betty
16 Working class (*hyphenated*)
18 Actor Rob, formerly of *The West Wing*
19 Fourposter
20 "Bummer!"
21 Took advantage of
23 Make beer
24 "...with the rope in the library" board game
25 Billfold
28 Magnificence

32 *All ___ Eve* (1950 Bette Davis film)
33 "Nifty!"
34 Lower than soprano
35 Bad habit
36 "The March King" John Philip ___
37 "___ creature was stirring..." (*2 words*)
38 Dutch cheese
39 Labels
40 Played for a fool
41 Move
43 Cavalry swords
44 Convent residents
45 Horse hair
46 Swapped
49 "Surely you ___!"
50 Tundra wanderer

53 Hawaiian dance
54 "I'm happy in my ___" (*2 words*)
57 TV's "Oscar"
58 Blabbermouth
59 Sink one's teeth into
60 Ecological watchdog organization (abbr.)
61 Snoopy
62 Otherwise

DOWN

1 Ty ___ (baseball's "Georgia Peach")
2 Competent
3 Of great volume
4 Price for services
5 Rainbow stripe
6 Relative by marriage

7 ___ *Well That Ends Well*
8 Meadow
9 Tries to endear
10 "Battle Hymn of the Republic" songwriter Julia Ward ___
11 Newspaper opinion page
14 Singing syllables (*3 words*)
15 Strauss waltz (*2 words*)
17 Editor's insertion symbol
22 Hamburger roll
23 Weekend comedown (*2 words*)
24 Cranky
25 Vacillate
26 Put up with
27 Dietetic, in ads (*hyphenated*)

28 Way overcharge
29 Run off to marry
30 Say
31 Highways
33 Layers of paint
36 One who'll be on the flight, with any luck
40 Florentine poet
42 Pool stick
43 Stroll ostentatiously
45 Bumps into
46 Amish "you"
47 Type of roast
48 ___ mater
49 Jupiter's wife
50 Preacher's subject
51 "Oh, why not?"
52 Leg joint
55 Author Deighton
56 Mary Lincoln's husband

HINT: If the clue about songwriting didn't help you at 10 Down, a Hall of Fame hockey star has the same last name. For more help, see puzzle 13.

#37:
46D = LARSEN

In the Dairy Section　by Manny Nosowsky

10

The phrase entries involve some items you might select at the dairy counter.

ACROSS
1 "Immediately!" in the ER
5 Ding-a-___
9 Country singer Brooks
14 Operatic solo
15 Woodwind instrument
16 Boise's state
17 Baby's temporary chompers (2 words)
19 Taken-back autos
20 Olympic fencing competitor
21 Provokes (2 words)
23 Corrects text
24 Uproars
25 Title for a head honcho (3 words)
31 Charioteer Ben-___

34 Goofs up
35 Crossbreed
36 Throat-clearer's interruption
38 Wood used in baseball bats
40 Fearless
41 Return (2 words)
44 Snaky swimmers
47 Chicken Little thought it was falling
48 Lather for a razor (2 words)
51 Not messy
52 Runs at an easy pace
55 Unwelcome report (2 words)
59 Uses semaphore
61 Truism
62 Kind of squash
64 Volkswagen model

65 Oman resident
66 Gumbo pods
67 Wood-shaping tools
68 Derisive remark
69 Catch sight of

DOWN
1 "I'll have the ___" (bar order)
2 "Rubbish!"
3 Felt poorly
4 "___ easy" (relax) (2 words)
5 Songwriter Frank of Guys and Dolls
6 Skeptic's scoff (2 words)
7 ___ cricket (unfair)
8 Baseball great Lou
9 1924 Harold Lloyd comedy classic (2 words)

10 "Zip-___- Doo-Dah" (hyphenated)
11 Entertains like Eminem
12 Biblical pronoun
13 Medical building (abbr.)
18 10% for the church
22 Foot fraction
24 Analyze in detail, as in anatomy class
26 Lingerie buy
27 Go out, like the tide
28 Greek god of love
29 Natural chiffon fabric
30 Whirling water
31 Witches
32 "Here comes trouble!" (hyphenated)
33 Country queen McEntire

37 Dallas hoopster, for short
39 That woman
42 Movie houses
43 Grasped in the mind with certainty
45 Beatles movie (3 words)
46 Snorkel, to Beetle Bailey
49 Chatterbox
50 The Seven Year Itch star Marilyn
53 Armored military vehicles
54 Drink without couth
55 ___ California
56 Fired
57 Airhead
58 Musical tone
59 Pierce with a dagger
60 Stick around
63 Spoon-bending Geller

HINT: 1 Across sounds like a technical word, but it's common in medical dramas. See puzzle 20 for another, bigger hint.

#30: 38D = CREDO

The Secret's Out by Diane C. Baldwin

11

The three long phrases that make up this puzzle's theme all pertain to revealing confidential information.

ACROSS
1 Smile broadly
5 Library volume that usually has large pages
10 Nimble
14 Wheel shaft
15 "Six ___ a-laying..."
16 Bona fide
17 Told all (*3 words*)
20 Currently popular, slangily
21 Final curtains
22 Fix a knot
23 Having a lot of frills
24 Damsels
26 Charlie Brown's dog
29 Gets thin on top
30 Aquatic bird
31 Faithful to duty

32 Resort sometimes referred to as a "fat farm"
35 Broke silence (*3 words*)
39 Word with "whiz"
40 Church official
41 Destructive emotion
42 Nestles closely
43 Story's turning point
45 Astronomy rarity
48 Encourage an encore
49 Bout site
50 Fedora feature
51 Tantrum
54 Blabbed everything (*4 words*)
58 Satan's specialty

59 Abandon
60 Out of control
61 Contradict
62 Tent peg
63 Chromosome bit

DOWN
1 Gala event
2 Montreal baseballer
3 Came to earth
4 Gibson in films
5 The "A" of C.I.A.
6 Nickname for "Theodore"
7 Permits
8 Wood used to make baseball bats
9 "Get it?"
10 Knights' mounts

11 Talk, talk, talk
12 Argument (*hyphenated*)
13 Favorable responses
18 Clear, as a hurdle
19 Rein in
23 Actress Anderson
24 City official
25 Economist ___ Greenspan
26 Snail's cousin
27 Zilch
28 Slimy stuff
29 Foreshadows
31 Rocky shelf
32 Cutting criticism
33 Pocket bread
34 Peak
36 Distant correspondent (*2 words*)

37 Positive factor
38 Ark or sloop
42 One by one
43 Overused expression
44 Tibetan monk
45 Slacked off
46 Yearn for
47 Founder of Bolshevism
48 Sound of a whip
50 ___ blocker (hypertension medication)
51 Notoriety
52 Golf bag item
53 Youngster
55 Drivers licenses, passports, and so on (abbr.)
56 The whole ___ and caboodle
57 Old horse

HINT: In the clue for 47 Down, the word "Bolshevism" means Majority Party. In 1917 they were, in fact, in a minority position right after the Russian Revolution, but led by the answer to this clue, they overthrew the provisional government in the October Revolution and ultimately became the Communist Party. See puzzle 27 for a giveaway answer.

#23: 14A = HAMEL

Shawls and Such   by Mary Brindamour

12

This straightforward puzzle offers four varieties of head covering for women. You should come out on top this time.

ACROSS
1 Bit of snow
6 Do something
9 Fray, as material
14 Title bird in Poe poem
15 In favor of
16 Martini additive
17 Above-board
18 Playground game
19 Bumped off, as a dragon
20 Automobile's fuel tank topper (2 words)
22 Lacy headwear
24 Employs
26 Raw metal
27 Blond Monroe
30 Smeared
34 Lotion additives
35 Water vapor

37 Actress ___ Dawn Chong
38 House top
39 Pertaining to the moon
40 Restrain, as breath
41 Junior naval officer (abbr.)
42 Borscht vegetables
43 Assigned a number to
44 Medium sized sofas
46 First-day baseball games
48 Circle section
49 Prepare dough
50 Peasant's headwear
54 New York's Lake ___
58 Make very happy

59 Look over
61 "___ ear and out..." (2 words)
62 Serious
63 Guy's companion
64 Sleep noisily
65 Barren
66 Use the slopes
67 Manufacturer

DOWN
1 Kermit, for one
2 Mt. Etna's output
3 City roads (abbr.)
4 Windy day headwear
5 Involves
6 Likely
7 Stuffs, as luggage
8 Loose robe

9 Speaker's platform
10 Affiliated
11 Small vessel for liquids
12 Very bad
13 Horne of song
21 Ask too many questions
23 Baseballer Garciaparra
25 Follows
27 Female horses
28 By oneself
29 Henhouse rod
30 Add salt and pepper
31 Barbecue grill
32 "Peter, Peter, pumpkin ___..."
33 Monopoly player's papers
36 Dynamite, for short

39 Bloodsucker
40 Colorful headwear
42 Frenzied or crazed
43 Inclination toward natural truth without embellishment
45 Tighter
47 Vitality
49 Canoe relative
50 First lady Truman
51 "Thanks ___!" (2 words)
52 Rum cake
53 Beer containers
55 Make dinner
56 "Pertaining to," on a memo (2 words)
57 "Caught in the headlights" animal
60 Yale graduate

HINT: The clue at 43 Down might look daunting, but the answer is a perfectly ordinary word. See puzzle 34's page for another hint.

#16: 5D = MACROS

Quite "Suit"-able by Alan Olschwang

Besides the four theme answers, the shorter answers at 23 Across and 50 Down are also relevant.

ACROSS

1 Actor Sean who was once married to Madonna
5 Bear whose bed was too hard
9 Make a solemn promise
14 Offshore
15 Cooling citrus drinks
16 Young person, slangily
17 Preparatory activity
19 Company that makes Pentium computer chips
20 Damascus citizen
21 Involving people of the highest office (*hyphenated*)
23 Highest cards in the deck
25 Internet address, briefly
26 America's Uncle ___
29 Compassion, figuratively speaking (*3 words*)
35 Controversial orchard spray
37 Take to court
38 Entertainment bigshot Ted ___
39 Prom transports, informally
41 Sitter's creation
43 "Mule Train" singer Frankie ___
44 Monastery leaders
46 Beat walker
48 Short Morse code clicks
49 Oahu promontory (*2 words*)
52 1, 2, 3, etc. (abbr.)
53 Recline
54 High school math course, briefly
56 Retired but holding an honorary title
61 Where the trash goes
65 Powered bicycle
66 Golf course building
68 Utopian
69 English nobleman
70 Revue component
71 Suspicious
72 "Auld Lang ___"
73 English afternoon refreshments

DOWN

1 Quarterback's option
2 Catch sight of
3 Approach
4 First name in Olympic gymnastics
5 Warriors who fought against the Sioux
6 Bother
7 Saucy
8 Invite on a date (*2 words*)
9 Showing expert ability
10 Zinfandel, for example
11 1999 film directed by Ron Howard
12 "Zip-___-Doo-Dah" (*hyphenated*)
13 Croissant, for one
18 Per unit
22 Follower of Martin Luther (abbr.)
24 *Herzog* author ___ Bellow
26 Dieter's choice
27 Suspect's "I couldn't have done it" story
28 Venomous arboreal snake
30 Extend
31 Diploma getter, commonly
32 Vidalia ___
33 Slowly, in music
34 Put some clothes on
36 Capacity
40 In an impassive manner
42 Bard
45 State of irritation
47 Simple story with a lesson
50 Low cards in the deck
51 Part of a table setting
55 Spirit
56 ___ *and the Detectives* (1964 Disney film)
57 Method
58 Fencing weapon
59 Raise
60 Delight, as a comedy club audience
62 Ingredient in a 26 Down, informally
63 Nepal's continent
64 Takes home
67 Coffee server

HINT: In a clue such as 62 Down, look at the *answer* of the cross-referenced clue, not the clue itself. There's another hint for you at puzzle 41.

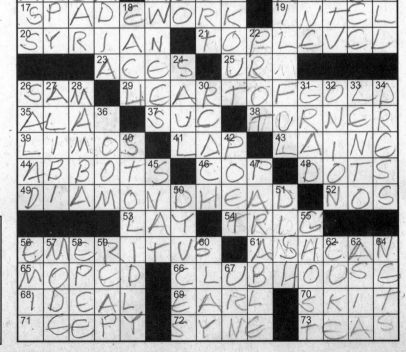

#9: 58A = YENTA

(handwritten notes: PA _ NEES, PAR _ _ LE, STOLID)

Just Say the Word   by Norma Steinberg

14

Each long theme answer begins with a word that is a synonym for "speak." That should be enough for you to go on this time.

ACROSS
1 Item in Tiger Woods's golf bag
5 Foundation
10 Diminishes
14 Tardy
15 Backspace over, on a computer screen
16 Toss, as a coin
17 Card player's stake
18 Civil rights landmark Alabama city
19 Greek salad cheese
20 Dwight Eisenhower's nickname
21 The bluebonnet in Texas, for example (*2 words*)
23 Ties the knot
25 Ventilate
26 Case of the sniffles
27 Elastic
32 Sneeze sound
34 Felt concern
35 Shade of color
36 Sailing vessel
37 More faithful
38 Corridor
39 They sang "Evil Woman"
40 "Ode on a Grecian Urn" poet John ___
41 Calculator button
42 Smith or Jones (*2 words*)
44 Coin factory
45 Skirt edge
46 Staff members
49 "10 items or less" super-market queue (*2 words*)
54 Salesperson, briefly

55 Andean nation whose capital is Lima
56 Tease
57 Muffin spread
58 Grandson of Adam and Eve
59 *Love Story* author Segal
60 In case
61 Direction of dawn's arrival
62 Ascends
63 Recolors

DOWN
1 Insurance form
2 Sri ___ (new name for Ceylon)
3 Complete disorder (*2 words*)
4 Hive resident
5 Went one better
6 Neighborhoods
7 Pretzel topping

8 "Woe ___!" (*2 words*)
9 Sailor
10 Endeavor
11 Huffed and puffed
12 Fisherman's wake-up call, perhaps
13 Practice boxing
21 Farm tower
22 Fibbed
24 The edible part of a radish or potato plant
27 Fry
28 "___ chic" (very fashionable)
29 Titular lady in a then-shocking D.H. Lawrence novel
30 Dance on Maui
31 Holler
32 Cain's brother
33 Soft drink
34 Study the night before

37 Truck driver
38 Beep
40 "...with a banjo on my ___"
41 Grow weary
43 Attack movement, in fencing
44 Parts of a trimester
46 Flinch
47 Actress ___ Witherspoon
48 Espies
49 Fencing weapon with a blunted point
50 TV's warrior princess
51 Highly trained workers
52 New Delhi dress
53 Hall of Fame shortstop Aparicio
57 Antique

HINT: You may know that English rock band at 39 Across by a longer name. They performed "Xanadu" with Olivia Newton-John on a hit 1980 recording. See puzzle 48 for a give-away answer, if you need it.

#2: 6A = FICA

High and Low   by Mary Brindamour

Two of the long entries pertain to one of the title words; the other two, to the other.

ACROSS
1 Shade of hair
6 Half a quart
10 Baseball hats
14 Broadway show
15 Cruising
16 Ready for business
17 Without stop (*2 words*)
18 Tidy
19 Aloe ___ (lotion ingredient)
20 Major armed conflict
21 Where unpleasantries might be swept, figuratively speaking (*3 words*)
24 Siding firm that uses a lot of bauxite
26 Hearing organ
27 Turned down

29 Destroyed by fire (*2 words*)
33 Totaled
34 Gathered leaves
35 Opposite of "con"
37 Life stories, for short
38 Relaxed, as tension
39 Stash away
40 R-V fill-in
41 Exaggerated ad claims
42 Call a friend
43 Elm and Main, to name two
45 Slanted away from vertical
46 Frequently, to poets
47 Pass up
48 Realistic (*hyphenated*)
53 Wrigley product

56 "What's the big ___?"
57 "Are you coming, yes ___?" (*2 words*)
58 Alternative to Shell, at the gas pumps
60 Window ledge
61 Muffin pans
62 Backyard attractions
63 Hugged
64 Warm up, as food
65 Colas

DOWN
1 Forehead
2 Horne of song
3 Radio operator's signoff (*3 words*)
4 Convent dweller
5 Figured out
6 Black and white bear

7 "Is this a dagger which ___ before me...?" (*Macbeth, 2 words*)
8 Close in on
9 Worn and torn
10 Secretive
11 Mimic
12 Lima's country
13 Hosiery problem
22 Give the ___ to (endorse)
23 Arm extremity
25 Some are white
27 Small amounts
28 Alters text
29 Fenway spots
30 Maui music makers
31 Heading for mischief (*4 words*)
32 Facedown on the floor
34 Enthralled
36 Was indebted to

38 Canine in your mouth
39 Rug type
41 Try out for weight
42 Maybe
44 President between Jimmy and George
45 Sodom survivor
47 Ice a cake
48 Satellite TV receiver
49 Dog in "Garfield" comics
50 Water source
51 Lake represented by the "E" in HOMES
52 Kournikova of tennis
54 School whose athletes call themselves the Bruins
55 Shade of green
59 Farmyard sound

HINT: The clue at 40 Across uses the word *fill-in* instead of showing you a fill-in-the-blank. Other words you might see in this kind of clue include *bridge* and *connection.* Puzzle 5's page has more assistance.

#45: 14A = HIREE

ORER__OOY
D_DU_ED
overanoOUT

Crossword grid (handwritten answers):
Row 1: BLOND / PINT / CAPS
Row 2: REVUE / ASEA / OPEN
Row 3: ONEND / NEAT / VERA
Row 4: WAR / UNDERTHERUG
Row 5: ALCOA / EAR
Row 6: DENIED / BURNTUP
Row 7: ADDED / RAKED / PRO
Row 8: BIOS / EASED / STOW
Row 9: STU / HYPES / PHONE
Row 10: STREETS / EANED
Row 11: OFT / FORGO
Row 12: DOWNTOEARTH / GUM
Row 13: IDEA / ORNO / AMOCO
Row 14: SILL / TINS / POOLS
Row 15: HELD / HEAT / SODAS

16 Scary Stuff   by Ed Early

In this puzzle, the four long answers each begin with a word that means "fear." You shouldn't be afraid, however.

ACROSS

1 Small bundle of straw or hair
5 Dwight Eisenhower's wife
10 Skedaddled
14 Ms. Krabappel (teacher in *The Simpsons*)
15 Without help
16 Have faith (in)
17 Sleep disturber (*2 words*)
19 First Russian tsar
20 Beer container
21 Sports facility
22 Nimble
23 Devious maneuver
24 Topic of a PTA meeting (abbr.)
25 Sings jazz like Ella Fitzgerald
27 17 Across, if you're sound asleep
32 Reads in, as a bar code

33 Harry Houdini, to Erich Weiss (*2 words*)
34 Mata ___ (World War I spy for Germany)
35 Bungles
36 Shah's land, once
37 Democracies hold them to pick leaders
39 Longhorn's sports foe
40 Surgeon, slangily
41 Song belter ___ Merman
42 Ash holder
43 Homer-hitter's gait around the bases
44 Clunky car
47 Slobber (over)
49 Letters on a battery
52 Persevere

53 Rastafarian hair style
55 Sandwich cookie
56 Ouzo flavoring
57 Setting on a blender
58 Campus official
59 No-nos
60 Kodak "eye"

DOWN

1 Lacking muscle power
2 Wait for the green light
3 Hosiery rip
4 Golf course standard
5 Computer key-stroke savers
6 Narrow street between buildings
7 Earth satellite
8 Peruvian of yore
9 "A mouse!" shout

10 1985 Sarandon horror flick (*2 words*)
11 Strauss of jeans
12 Airline to Israel (*2 words*)
13 Unit of force
18 Soda shop orders
22 Farm unit
23 Emergency signal (*2 words*)
24 Yields to gravity
25 Milan's La ___ (historic opera house)
26 Seven-time batting champ Rod ___
27 Wows
28 File folder projections
29 Sweatshirt size
30 One way to pass along a joke, nowadays (*hyphenated*)

31 ___ Russo of film
32 "___ a Lady" (Tom Jones hit)
33 Plumlike fruit used for flavoring gin
35 Helsinki citizen
38 Raced
39 Coral island
41 Creates, as a gorge
43 Pre-dinner announcement
44 Lummox
45 Hard to find
46 Perplexed
47 James Bond film (*2 words*)
48 Jockey's control strap
49 Twinge
50 Related by blood
51 Nile cobras
53 Family figure
54 Nocturnal predator

HINT: 39 Across refers to two Texas universities. There's another hint alongside puzzle 12.

#38: 6D = ALLELE

On Hand   by Nancy Kavanaugh

You won't need an iron fist to solve this one. That comment, plus the title, should reveal a lot about this theme.

ACROSS
1 Boxer's moves
5 Lyric poet
9 Expand
14 "Waiting for the Robert ___" (*2 words*)
15 Busy as ___ (*2 words*)
16 Spooky
17 ___-bitten (dilapidated)
18 Girls in gowns, informally
19 Audacity
20 Upstate NY resort region (*2 words*)
23 "___ the land of the free..."
24 Speed skater's track shape
25 Stone pit
27 Oscar winner Meryl ___
30 Customary
32 Rose stickers
33 Carpenters' tools (*2 words*)
37 Slithery swimmer
38 Toward the back, on a ship
39 Nothing
40 Cooonut source (*2 words*)
44 Sign after Taurus
47 Piece of wood
48 Like violent movies (*hyphenated*)
49 Someone from Mogadishu
52 Transgressions
53 Time period
54 Fool
60 Boredom
62 Ice shower
63 Dot of land in the sea
64 Watery fabric finish
65 Eyeball impolitely
66 Church area
67 Discoloration
68 Comforted, in a way
69 US territory in the Pacific

DOWN
1 NASCAR racer Gordon
2 "___ want for Christmas..." (*2 words*)
3 "___ there, done that!"
4 One who enjoys open-water sailing
5 Raw deals (*2 words*)
6 Clear as ___ (*2 words*)
7 Country singer McEntire
8 Piece of office furniture
9 Sultry
10 Very small
11 Mistake
12 "What am I, chopped ___?"
13 Suspicious
21 Roulette bet
22 Lead-in with "distant" or "lateral"
26 Math subject (abbr.)
27 Part of a procedure
28 "___-Team" (TV series staring Mr. T, *2 words*)
29 Turn over and over
30 Hungry, perhaps
31 Took a chair
34 Group of soldiers
35 ___ *to Five* (Fonda–Parton–Tomlin–Coleman film)
36 Skidded
38 Ireland's ___ Lingus
41 CEO's degree, perhaps (abbr.)
42 *The Lord of the Rings* writer
43 Watery precipitation
44 Cooked on the hibachi
45 White-tailed sea eagle
46 Preparing potatoes, perhaps
49 Appears to be
50 "To be ___ to be..." (*2 words*)
51 Craze
52 Ability acquired through experience
55 "Oops!" (*hyphenated*)
56 Pet bird's enclosure
57 Jacob's twin
58 Thomas Edison's middle name
59 Regard
61 Geller the spoon-bender

HINT: In 22 Down: The word "lead-in" is often used in place of "prefix." You may also see "intro" in harder puzzles. See puzzle 19 for more help.

#31: 53D = MAHRE

Grid (handwritten answers):
1 JABS / 5 BARD / 9 SWELL
14 ELEC / 15 ABEE / 16 EERIE
17 FLEC / 18 DEBS / 19 NERVE
20 FINGERLAKES / 22 OER
24 OVAL / 25 QUARRY
27 STREEP / 30 USUAL
32 THORNS / 33 NAILGUNS
37 EEL / 38 AFT / 39 NIL
40 PALMTREE / 44 GEMINI
47 BOARD / 48 RRATED
49 SOMALI / 52 SINS
53 ERA / 54 KNUCKLEHEAD
60 ENN / 62 HAIL / 63 ISLE
64 MOIE / 65 OGLE / 66 NAVE
67 STAIN / 68 HELD / 69 GUAM

(handwritten margin notes: -ENSUA- / ENSUAL)

18 Fundamental Elements by Norman Wizer

Empedocles, a Greek philosopher who lived about 2,500 years ago, believed these were the fundamental substances of the universe.

ACROSS
1 Group of bees
6 Scarlett O'Hara's plantation
10 Direction 90° clockwise from south
14 Exclamation of surprise (*2 words*)
15 Highways (abbr.)
16 Bullets
17 R2-D2, for one
18 Cheers in the bullring
19 Even-steven
20 Nature's rumbling
22 Jazz singer Fitzgerald
23 Solar system centers
24 With energy
26 Bit of greenery
30 Hockey rink surface

31 Attack command
32 "___ Need is the Girl" (*2 words*)
33 Della's role on *Touched by an Angel*
35 Upper body
39 More intelligent
41 Bomber's cargo
43 Book of the Old Testament
44 Brit's neighbor
46 Roman poet
47 Trains in the city
49 Move like a kangaroo
50 Warren Beatty movie
51 Monopoly square
54 Medical school course (abbr.)
56 Pealed

57 Quick delivery system (*2 words*)
63 Prefix meaning "opposed to"
64 Seating section
65 So long, in France
66 Natural satellite
67 Suit to ___ (*2 words*)
68 Famous person, commonly
69 Tree with cones
70 The ___ of Avon (Shakespeare)
71 House passageways

DOWN
1 Tender
2 Command to Dobbin

3 Shortened form often seen in crossword puzzles
4 Plant part
5 Legends
6 Decisive victors
7 Books of maps
8 Smell horribly
9 Put a value on
10 Artist's medium
11 Post or Dickinson
12 "I ___ a rat!"
13 NBC's long-running morning show
21 Considerably
25 Feel sorry for
26 Whip
27 Pollster ___ Roper
28 Expression of concern
29 Emergency vehicle (*2 words*)

34 Pamper (*hyphenated*)
36 Meander
37 Uttered
38 Probabilities
40 Soft mineral
42 How some securities are sold (*2 words*)
45 San Diego NFL player
48 Site for experiments under the ocean's surface
51 Muscle spasm
52 Capital of Vietnam
53 Russian author Chekhov
55 Instruct
58 Small amount
59 Brainstorm
60 Fish's breathing apparatus
61 Shoe part
62 Vats

HINT: 42 Down has to do with selling stocks, bonds, or other negotiable investment instruments exactly as the face value specifies. If you'd like another hint, see puzzle 26.

#24: 46A = SERAPHS

Another Tense Situation   by Manny Nosowsky

19

Take a look back at puzzle 6 to see how one idea can inspire more than one puzzle.

ACROSS

1 Surgical memento
5 "See ya!" (*2 words*)
10 Shrink-___
14 Impulse
15 Changes places
16 Boat body
17 ___ off (miffed)
18 Grownup
19 No more than
20 Reo Motor Car Company founder (*3 words*)
23 "Are not!" rebuttal (*2 words*)
24 Big show, commonly
25 ABC rival
28 Comics hero (*hyphenated*)
31 Like two-day-old bread
33 Fireplace remains
36 Blood fluid
40 Monopoly placeholder
41 Kevin Spacey film based on a Pulitzer-winning novel by E. Annie Proulx (*3 words*)

44 "The Crimson Tide"
45 "Old Rough and Ready" Zachary ___
46 Hairwash coloring additive
47 Oven brand name
49 Fight dirty
51 Basic unit of currency in Japan
52 Lhasa ___ (dog breed)
56 Superfluous
60 Play the commodities market (*3 words*)
64 "Now, that's funny!" (*2 words*)
66 Assumed name taken by criminals
67 Camera part

68 Suave actor ___ Sharif
69 Shoots (by)
70 "Cheerio!" (*hyphenated*)
71 Puppy feet
72 Host of E!'s *Revealed*, Jules ___
73 Corset stiffener

DOWN

1 *Kama* ___
2 Alfredo sauce ingredient
3 Go-between
4 Fenway Park players (*2 words*)
5 Mosque leader
6 Pie à la ___
7 Small egg
8 ___ the Cat (cartoon character since 1919)

9 Photographer's setting (*hyphenated*)
10 "___-a thunk it?"
11 Worry about defeat (*2 words*)
12 Each and every one
13 Word on a tissue box
21 Pizzazz
22 ___ Alamos, New Mexico
26 Windy
27 Have a hunch
29 Came down to earth
30 California wine valley
32 Sardine holder
33 Cornered (*2 words*)
34 Loss of face
35 Waffle verbally (*3 words*)

37 Le Carré character
38 "Got ___?" (Dairy Council ad slogan)
39 Before long, in older literature
42 ___ Quentin prison
43 Say "hi" to
48 Letters on a small battery
50 Jumps for joy
53 Public square
54 Rural skyline sights
55 Pizza topping
57 Pick up the tab
58 Fashion designer Oscar De La ___
59 Subject to chemical analysis
61 Dumbo's "wings"
62 Celeb's quality
63 Outdated atlas abbreviation
64 "At the ___" (Danny and the Juniors hit of the 1950s)
65 Authoritative doctors' group (abbr.)

HINT: It may help you to know that the person who answers the clue at 20 Across used his own initials in deciding on the car company's name. See puzzle 33 for another hint.

#17: 49A = SOMALI

20 On Two Wheels   by Raymond Hamel

There are five two-wheeled vehicles for you to find in this one. Have a smooth ride.

ACROSS

1 Measure of heat (abbr.)
4 Head on a glass of beer
8 Beetle considered sacred in old Egypt
14 Coffee dispenser
15 At ___ (military command)
16 From Cuba, perhaps
17 TWO-WHEELED VEHICLE
19 Chant
20 Go separate directions (2 words)
21 TWO-WHEELED VEHICLE
22 Fan of Justin Timberlake, most likely
23 Cake maker
24 Welcome Back, Kotter star Gabe
28 Almost, to a poet
32 "Many moons ___..."
35 Lo ___ (Chinese restaurant dish)
36 Frankfurter
38 TWO-WHEELED VEHICLE (2 words)
41 Reveal
42 Word following steam or bubble
43 Ate
44 Borscht ingredient
45 Big brand name in salt
47 The finger next to your thumb
50 What the "A" in UAE stands for
54 TWO-WHEELED VEHICLE
57 Goulash seasoning
60 Give up, as a job
61 TWO-WHEELED VEHICLE
62 Up and about

63 Semisoft, white cheese
64 Preschooler
65 More often than not
66 Chopped cabbage side dish
67 "...have you ___ wool?"

DOWN

1 Exploded
2 Edible stomach lining
3 Parent's brother
4 Joyous gathering
5 Diamond Head's island
6 "Right away!" (abbr.)
7 Kitten's call
8 Floating film of oil
9 Kayak's kin
10 Court representative
11 Take part in public disorder
12 Diary keeper Frank
13 Dutch South African
18 Muscle cramp
21 ___ José, California
23 Lightweight cylindrical clothing container
25 Concert blasters
26 Cheat in hide-and-seek
27 Stretch the truth
29 Move slowly
30 ___ monster (poisonous lizard)
31 Do not ignore
32 "...three men in ___". (2 words)
33 Film star Wilder
34 "The joke's ___!" (2 words)
36 Olympic skater Katarina
37 Sonic phenomenon
39 Writer of spoofs
40 Tavern
45 Shea Stadium player
46 Drug dealer's nemesis
48 ___ Bruce of Sherlock Holmes films
49 Marie Osmond's brother
51 Steer-stopping rope
52 City where tires are manufactured
53 Nuts
54 Study hard
55 The guy in the white hat, stereotypically
56 Garage sale caveat (2 words)
57 Kind of stitch used in knitting
58 Continent with the most people
59 "What a relief!" sigh
61 Sesame Street network

HINT: The clue at 53 Down has nothing to do with, say, walnuts. See puzzle 40 for more help if you need it.

17A = MILK TEETH
#10:

21

It's a Guy Thing   by Norma Steinberg

The theme answer phrases either start or end with a word for a male animal. Not the same animal each time.

ACROSS

1 Started off
6 Food fish
10 Actress Ward
14 Decide against a big wedding
15 Role model
16 Sound of a horse's step
17 Former *NYPD Blue* star Jimmy
18 Parched
19 Halo
20 "___ of a gun!"
21 Look (*3 words*)
24 "Gee whiz!"
26 Full range
27 "It's the ___ truth!"
29 Singer/ songwriter ___ Simon
31 Poker game input
32 Husband or wife

34 Football scores (abbr.)
37 Reads a bar code
39 Feedbag grain
40 ___ the works (risk everything)
42 Wooden nail
43 Rock guitarist Santana
46 Poet ___ Lazarus
47 Window sections
48 Port
50 Bodyguard
53 Trunk of the body
54 Informal discussion (*2 words*)
57 "That's all ___ wrote!"
60 Close tightly
61 "I ___ a hug!"
62 ___ Island, NY

64 ___ Falco of *The Sopranos*
65 Nominate
66 Oozes
67 Bookworm
68 Author Kingsley
69 "If I do ___ myself..." (*2 words*)

DOWN

1 Mrs. Truman
2 Ticklish Muppet
3 Attending without a date (*2 words*)
4 Likely
5 Snuggle
6 Iffy
7 Response to a roll call
8 Operatic showstopper
9 Los Angeles ballplayers
10 Sparse

11 Sidestep
12 Film celebrity Sophia
13 Separated
22 "___ fair in love and war"
23 Rods between wheels
25 Accepting customers
27 Sudden inhalation
28 "I'll try anything ___!"
29 Embers
30 Sedan
33 Read closely, with "over"
34 He played Mr. Cunningham on *Happy Days* (*2 words*)
35 Major-___ (chief butler)
36 Constellation component

38 Indelible marks
41 Mommy's
44 Rabbit ears
45 "Beat it!"
47 Got the public's opinions
49 James of *Gunsmoke* fame
50 Buddy of *The Beverly Hillbillies*
51 Like Elvis's blue shoes
52 Debussy's ___ de Lune
53 Oceanic movements
55 Stitched line
56 Large truck
58 Pelvis-femur joints
59 Sinclair's gas pump rival
63 Thompson of *Caroline in the City*

HINT: The clues at 10 Across and 68 Across appear to be parallel. Each has an occupation and a proper name. In one case, though, that name is the last name and in the other it's the first name. That's where the puzzle comes in—you have to decide which name is sought. Puzzles with proper names often have clues like these instead of 46 Across. See puzzle 47 for more help.

#3: 44D = ANKH

22 Ways to Go by Nancy Kavanaugh

In this theme, the important words are at the end of the long answers instead of the beginning.

ACROSS

1 Floor model
5 Hindu religious teacher
10 Suitcases
14 Racetrack shape
15 Pilot's place
16 Dismounted
17 Nail shaper
18 "___ we a pair?"
19 Small, medium, or large
20 Trajectory (2 words)
22 Big rig
23 News article
24 Kind of patch (hyphenated)
26 Did some office work
30 Genetic code letters
31 ___-than-thou
32 Ethical course (2 words)
37 "Tickle Me" doll
38 Very long time
39 Formerly
40 Reckless, self-indulgent lifestyle (2 words)
43 Make certain
45 Miners dig it
46 Piece of bedroom furniture
47 Some family members (hyphenated)
51 Huge boats
52 Lunch or dinner
53 Condition of financial security (2 words)
59 Mexican coin
60 Rocket fuel ingredient, for short
61 Wheel shaft
62 Biblical garden
63 Dialect
64 Town with the Leaning Tower
65 Old Greek harp
66 À la ___
67 Wineglass part

DOWN

1 Briefly tip, as a hat
2 Wicked
3 West African republic
4 Designer Cassini
5 Spread around
6 Bent out of shape
7 At right angles to the keel
8 Toothpaste flavor
9 Popular fad (2 words)
10 Lowest singing voice
11 One from outer space
12 Gadget
13 Beer mug
21 Walk in the woods
25 Cheer from the stands
26 Restaurant employee
27 Hit song by the Kinks
28 Shade trees
29 Public disturbance
30 Noisy clamor
32 Gardener's tool
33 Flag maker Betsy
34 Responsibility
35 4,840 square yards
36 Does and bucks
38 Compass heading
41 Near the ground
42 ___ and Old Lace
43 Annoying
44 Hatchling's home
46 Lumber crumbler (2 words)
47 Drive forward
48 Impoverished
49 Modern-day surgical tool
50 By oneself
51 Up and about
54 Opera by Verdi
55 Knocks on the door
56 Sign over some doors
57 Other than
58 Sports group

HINT: You might be tempted to take the clue at 45 Across figuratively, but that's not the case at all. If you still need some help, see puzzle 4.

#46: 27D = IMAC

Un-Cover Story   by Elizabeth C. Gorski

23

Don't let those parallel 7-letter words in the southwest and northeast corners of the grid intimidate you. The unvarnished truth will emerge.

ACROSS
1 Put on a happy face
6 Spheres
10 ___ time (never, *2 words*)
14 Veronica ___ of *Hill Street Blues*
15 Stead
16 Trim, as a photograph
17 It will ruin a picture (*2 words*)
20 Have the flu
21 Embassy leader (abbr.)
22 Erie Canal mule, in a song
23 Storage area
24 Genetics lab molecule
25 Derek and Jackson
27 Cut back
29 Capitol Hill legislator (abbr.)
30 Aspirin bottle name
32 Microsoft mogul Bill ___

33 Drop from a duct
35 Never used
37 Bullet-proof item
38 With "The," old television show starring James Franciscus (*2 words*)
41 Tarot deck unit
44 Abbreviation on a bottle of skin-safety lotion
45 House in a tree
47 Keats' "___ a Grecian Urn" (*2 words*)
49 Main artery
51 Nile reptile
54 Blew hard, like the wolf in a child's tale
56 Be sorry about
57 African antelope
58 Pub purchase
59 "...man ___ mouse?" (*2 words*)

61 Oldest high schoolers, gradewise (abbr.)
63 Wimbledon call
64 Food, clothing, and shelter (*2 words*)
68 List component
69 "Me, Myself, ___" (*2 words*)
70 ___ scheme (investment swindle)
71 Casual Friday tops
72 Flat land
73 Dutch painter Jan

DOWN
1 Wool gatherer's tools
2 Tyne's role on *Judging Amy*
3 False tooth, perhaps
4 Late July baby

5 Literary lioness
6 Type of network (*2 words*)
7 ___ Tin Tin
8 Hive dwellers
9 Coffee sweetener
10 Play the part
11 Compliment
12 Mother Superior's charges
13 Least secretive
18 Begins, as a cruise
19 Shake ___ (hurry, *2 words*)
26 Summon (*2 words*)
28 Jones and Crockett
30 Noise of the lambs
31 Legend on a VCR button
34 Graham Greene's *The ___ the Affair* (*2 words*)

36 Cold seasons
39 Smog watchdog (abbr.)
40 Afternoon brew
41 Share quarters (with)
42 Worship
43 One who whistles while he works
46 Ad slogan (*2 words*)
48 Marquee light
50 Moscow's land
52 It precedes "Gesundheit"
53 Plants, as a garden (*2 words*)
55 Word with pipe or day
60 Prom night woe
62 Drinks slowly
65 Agency featured in *Third Watch* (abbr.)
66 Norton and Wood
67 Youngster

HINT: Regarding 33 Across, you need to know that the first word is a noun, even though you might first read it as a verb. See puzzle 11 for another hint.

#39: 14A = CREE

Terms of Endearment by Bernice Gordon

24

This puzzle features four words or phrases that you might call your darling.

ACROSS

1 Eliot Ness, e.g. (*hyphenated*)
5 Square or circle
10 Food fish
14 Effortlessness
15 Stereotypical name for a parrot
16 HBO gangster ___ Soprano
17 Term of endearment (*2 words*)
19 Put chips in the pot
20 Swap meet participant
21 Altruistic
23 Stretched out
25 Posturepedic mattress maker
26 21st president ___ Alan Arthur
29 "That's a real shame!" (*2 words*)
32 "The Gold Bug" author
33 Sees
35 Undressed
36 A jillion
38 "Rope-a-dope" boxer
39 Communist party developer
40 Aching
41 Heavy hammer
43 Playing hard to get
44 Snitch
46 Angels with six wings
48 Streetcars
50 Latvia's capital
51 Calls a place a home
54 Quick thrusts
58 Undercover cop
59 Term of endearment
61 Deliberate string snarl
62 ___ nous ("just between us...")
63 Length x width
64 Underwater boats, commonly
65 Reserved
66 Used E-mail

DOWN

1 Examination
2 Bryn ___ College
3 Off shore
4 Sewing instrument
5 Supernatural beings
6 Garden tool
7 Swiss peaks
8 Carries on, as a business
9 Shoelace holes
10 *Rocky* star Sylvester
11 Term of endearment
12 Picnic pests
13 Hair salon liquids
18 Back-combs
22 Toy retailer ___ Schwarz
24 Himalayan kingdom
26 Chocolate-y beverage
27 Term of endearment
28 Annoys to the point of anger
30 "So long, señor"
31 Contradict
32 Attention-getter
34 Duck that's a source of comforter down
37 Takes away (from)
39 Sports association
41 Many Middle Easterners
42 Cooked on the patio, perhaps
45 Where experiments may take place
47 Black-and-white bamboo eaters
49 Feat of physical daring
51 Printing fluids
52 When doubled, Mork's good-bye
53 Miss, in Madrid (abbr.)
55 Clinton's vice president
56 Roulette bettor's choice
57 Stock exchange position
60 Prefix meaning "three"

HINT: The answer to 30 Down is common enough that you should have no trouble. The tip is: A clue with a foreign word or name usually leads to an answer in that same foreign language. Also, while it was originally French, the dictionary says the answer at 62 Across is now considered part of the English language. See puzzle 18's page for more help.

#32: 1A = KIEV

25

A Time for... by Manny Nosowsky

This theme will take you on a journey through life. As a side note, this grid contains every letter of the alphabet.

ACROSS

1 City where *The Scarlet Letter* is set
6 Little device for gathering a throat culture
10 Blue hue
14 Accused's defense
15 Thanksgiving day (abbr.)
16 Do an about-face
17 Jingle creator
18 Man Friday
19 Hourglass filler
20 Infant transportation (*2 words*)
23 Make a mistake
24 Mild cusswords
27 Take into custody
31 Stuff to the gills
33 Boo or yoo follower
35 Writer/cartoonist Silverstein
36 Teenager's association (*2 words*)
39 Living room pieces
41 Remote
42 California missionary Junipero ___
43 Grown-up entertainment (*2 words*)
46 The chemical formula for ordinary table salt
47 Ouija board answer
48 Go like goo
49 Microsoft gaming consoles
51 Japanese watchmaker
53 Automobile
54 Temporary lapse, humorously (*2 words*)
61 Magic African amulet
64 One and only
65 At no time
66 From ___ (the gamut, *3 words*)
67 Line-___ veto
68 Largest Greek island
69 Dish list
70 Anecdote
71 Just know

DOWN

1 Swedish 9000 Turbo, for example
2 Alan of *M*A*S*H*
3 Arm or leg
4 Popular on-line auction site
5 Chops finely
6 Longtime Green Bay Packer quarterback Bart ___
7 Buzzing sound
8 Autobahn auto
9 Scope
10 Confounded (*2 words*)
11 Sine ___ non (essential element)
12 Thirty-cup container
13 "Go on..."
21 Too-too
22 Diver Louganis and golfer Norman
25 The part of an insect's body to which the legs and wings attach
26 Informant
27 Test for gold content
28 ___ Scholar (student attending Oxford University with financial aid)
29 Just say "no"
30 Israeli airline (*2 words*)
31 Polished
32 "The Bell of ___" (Longfellow poem)
34 October birthstones
37 *The Wizard ___* (*2 words*)
38 Attorney General during the Clinton administration
40 Use a poker
44 Like a romantic evening, maybe
45 Reason to hit the books
50 Rodeo horses
52 Mazda rival
53 ___ de menthe
55 Scintilla
56 "The ___ lama, he's a priest" (line from an Ogden Nash poem, *hyphenated*)
57 Little more than
58 Fifty-fifty
59 Profits
60 Picnic shade
61 Toast topper
62 Athlete from Salt Lake City
63 Garfield owner ___ Arbuckle

HINT: In any clue like 22 Down, the answer should always be a pluralized name. There's a bigger hint for you at puzzle 50.

#50:
37D = TEMERITY

26 End-to-End Entertainment   by Norma Steinberg

In which the first and last parts of each long answer are the same. If you get either part, you're on your way.

ACROSS
1 Striking worker's replacement
5 London streetcar
9 Onetime Hollywood gossip columnist Hopper
14 ___ over (read closely)
15 Went by bus
16 "The hunter" constellation
17 Competent
18 Actor Sharif
19 ___ bag it (take your lunch to work)
20 007's self-introduction (*3 words*)
23 Campaigned for office
24 Cartoon frame
25 Kramden's neighbor
29 3 Musketeers parent candy company
31 Baby wear
34 ___ rings (side dish)

35 List of choices
36 Japanese wrestling form
37 Endlessly improving (*3 words*)
40 Commits perjury
41 Not at all good-looking
42 Coffee shop order
43 Printing spaces half as wide as ems
44 Advertising award
45 Irish singer O'Connor
46 Word alphabetizers ignore
47 Parcel of land
48 "It could possibly happen" (*3 words*)

55 Uptight
56 Go bad
57 Lie adjacent to
59 Command
60 Pennsylvania port city
61 Identical
62 Fence uprights
63 Treaty
64 Use a keyboard

DOWN
1 Hot tub
2 Ty of baseball's Hall of Fame
3 Woody Guthrie's son
4 ___ there, done that
5 ___ horse (sneaky gift)
6 Brutus or Caesar
7 Eden dweller
8 Insignificant

9 Calvin's sometimes-alive stuffed tiger
10 Actor ___ Flynn of *Captain Blood*
11 "Abraham, Martin and John" artist
12 Mamie ___ Eisenhower
13 New England's Cape ___
21 Male bee
22 Call off, as a mission
25 Of high integrity
26 ___ a million (*2 words*)
27 Ceremonies
28 Day care charges
29 ___ Park (Edison's workplace)
30 Commentator Rooney of *60 Minutes*

31 Southwestern land formation similar to a mesa
32 "...___ man with seven wives" (*3 words*)
33 World-weary
35 Biblical travelers
36 Jazzman ___ Getz
38 King or emperor
39 Crème de la crème
44 Sam Malone's bar, in a sitcom
45 Poetic form
46 Boob tube (*2 words*)
47 Song's words
48 Stepson to Claudius
49 Concludes
50 Pace
51 Ambience
52 Immense
53 Internet auction site
54 Beef cut
55 Pinnacle
58 Golfer's peg

HINT: At 13 Down, your first guess might be Cape Cod. That's the wrong one. This is a little north of Cape Cod, but still in Massachusetts. There's more help for you near puzzle 32.

#18: 46A = OVID

House-Raising   by Randall J. Hartman

27

In order from bottom to top, the theme entries in this puzzle go from bottom to top. Make sense? It will.

ACROSS

1 *Iliad* and *Odyssey*
6 Alan who portrayed "Hawkeye" Pierce
10 Lug
14 Pond scum
15 Salon wave
16 Stratford-on-___
17 Green space atop a building (*2 words*)
19 Refuse to recognize
20 Trail of light
21 Catholic prayer (*2 words*)
23 Broadway hit of the 1960s
25 Prefix meaning "equal"
26 Long, easy stride
30 Room cooler (*2 words*)
36 NYSE competitor
37 Novak of *Vertigo* and *Picnic*
38 Bacterium that needs air
39 Percolate
41 Young man
43 *The Canterbury ___* (Chaucer classic)
44 Comes to terms
46 Astronaut Grissom
48 Actor Brad
49 1987 Michael Douglas film (*2 words*)
51 One of the Cartwright boys
52 ___ Lanka
53 Posed
55 Brainy types
60 Government in power
65 *The Twilight ___*
66 Appliance often sold at a discount (*2 words*)
68 Wander about
69 Morays
70 Use an iron
71 They live in colonies
72 Colors
73 Pull someone's leg

DOWN

1 Be all ___ (listen)
2 Murder mystery storyline
3 Helicopter pioneer Sikorsky
4 Sidewalk eatery
5 *Love Story* author Erich
6 Busy month for the IRS (abbr.)
7 Mother of Castor and Pollux
8 Foe of Austin Powers (*2 words*)
9 Loss of memory
10 Vocal fanfare (*hyphenated*)
11 Finished
12 *Beloved* writer Morrison
13 New Age vocalist who uses only one name
18 Run ___ (rush about in a frenzy)
22 French impressionist
24 This covers a bride's face
26 1980s TV legal drama (*2 words*)
27 Alpha opposite
28 Oyster prize
29 Stand out
31 Reflection in a mirror
32 Annual report exhibit
33 Shakespeare volume
34 Drives the getaway car for
35 Fits together
40 *Steppenwolf* author Hermann ___
42 Membership fees
45 Attacked from the air
47 Beatles drummer Ringo
50 *Gladiator* director Scott
54 Entice
55 Old Testament book
56 Thug
57 No-see-um
58 Skirt edges
59 Singular
61 He was defeated by Bush
62 Brainstorm
63 Many a teenager's room
64 Otherwise
67 Pre-CIA spy org. (abbr.)

HINT: 51 Across refers to the old TV show *Bonanza.* See puzzle 39 for a blatant giveaway.

#11: 11D = PRATE

28 Rhyme Time   by Norma Johnson

This puzzle has five thematic answers, including the shorter one in the center row. Say them out loud to reveal the theme.

ACROSS

1 Subordinate staffer
5 Poses for a portrait
9 Warmth of color
13 Phone connection
14 Apple center
15 Under-the-table money to an official
16 Sports car, usually (*hyphenated*)
18 Uncompromising
19 Syrup source
20 Dental data
21 Hearth residue
22 Poker "bullets"
23 Light rain
24 Got the normal result on a golf hole
27 Financially worthwhile
31 Specks
32 Milky birthstone
33 Slight
34 ___-mo replay
35 1st bishop of Rome (*2 words*)
38 Decimal system base
39 Scottish berets
41 Natural resources, of a sort
42 *Wheel of Fortune* category
44 Smoker's conveniences
46 Campfire treats
47 Looked over
48 Timely benefit or blessing
49 Piano student's exercise
51 Be skeptical about
53 Clairvoyant's claim, in short
56 "___ I can help it!" (*2 words*)
57 Kitchen tool used in making meringue
59 Prophetic signs
60 ___ Stanley Gardner (author of Perry Mason stories)
61 Wile E. Coyote's supply company in Roadrunner cartoons
62 Bjorn ___ of tennis
63 Purchase for Kenny G
64 "___ ahoy!"

DOWN

1 Alphabetically, it's the first book in the Bible
2 State whose capital is Des Moines
3 Plummet
4 McMahon and Asner
5 Frightened
6 Greek letters
7 Card that beats a deuce
8 Sunday talks in church (abbr.)
9 Early astronaut Virgil "Gus" ___
10 Photographer's gadget (*2 words*)
11 Theater award (but not the Tony)
12 Gets married to
15 Smarty
17 More than enough
22 Extension
23 Double agent, in CIA lingo
24 Linguini or angel hair
25 Book of maps
26 Space warmer (*2 words*)
27 Fencing swords
28 Lions and tigers
29 "Goodnight ___" (Jo Stafford standard)
30 Pennies
32 Grand Ole ___
36 *The Wind in the Willows* character
37 Couch potato's TV control gadget
40 Working in a hair salon, perhaps
43 Ludwig ___ Beethoven
45 Good places to enjoy snorkeling or scuba diving
46 Cried
48 Reveille horn
49 "I'm better than you" person
50 "Catch a Falling Star" singer Perry ___
51 The moose is the largest one
52 Villain in fairy tales
53 Do artistic work with acid
54 Trucker's transport
55 Get ready for surgery
58 Small batteries

HINT: 55 Down's answer is a shorter form of a perfectly ordinary word which you probably hear often on medical dramas. There's another hint for you alongside puzzle 46.

#4: 28D = AUER

29

Attack! by Norma Steinberg

This time, the long phrase entries begin with words involving bodily contact. And not necessarily pleasant contact, at that.

ACROSS

1 Force forward
6 Flower stalk
10 Clothing store framework
14 Loop at the end of a lasso
15 Perspiration opening
16 1975 Wimbledon winner
17 Pizza part
18 Motel room
19 Light carriage
20 Actress ___ "The Oomph Girl" Sheridan
21 Adopt an attitude (3 words)
24 ___ the manger (hindrance of a sort, 2 words)
26 Kicked out
27 Synthetic polyester fabric

29 Work for
31 "Holy cow!" ancestor
32 Chutzpah
34 Candle
39 Lap dog, commonly
40 Napoleon's sentence
42 Whopper
43 Equals
45 ___-back (relaxed)
46 Small land mass
47 Sherbets
49 ___ the dirt (gossips)
51 Engine problem
55 Spotted pony
56 Predictable (hyphenated)
59 Farm doctor, commonly
62 "Step ___!" ("Hurry!", 2 words)

63 Epitome of thinness
64 Norma or Carmen
66 Marathon, for example
67 Role model
68 Utah Senator Hatch
69 Historical periods
70 Long-running musical with the song "Memory"
71 Pasadena float flowers

DOWN

1 Peruvian of olden times
2 Early time
3 Rich dessert (2 words)
4 Slalom turn
5 "Time to leave" (2 words)
6 Pooh-pooh

7 Nobelist Morrison
8 Composer Satie
9 "Visitor" from outer space
10 Rough tools
11 Give it ___ (try, 2 words)
12 Run after
13 ___ up (tense)
22 Hint of color
23 Mom's sister
25 Command
27 Johnny of Edward Scissorhands
28 A Death in the Family writer
29 Inventor Howe
30 "___ want is a room somewhere..." (My Fair Lady lyric, 2 words)
33 Spindle

35 Most important invitees (2 words)
36 Gullible people
37 Model Macpherson
38 Regrets
41 Money or Rabbit
44 Affix one's John Hancock
48 ___ the Entertainer
50 Not al fresco
51 Cross the goal line
52 Of the moon
53 City in New York
54 Goes out with
55 Medicinal tablets
57 Baby's second word?
58 Mob scene
60 Small Great Lake
61 Sunbathes
65 In favor of

HINT: The answer to 48 Down was one of the headliners in Spike Lee's film The Original Kings of Comedy. If you need another hint, see puzzle 3.

#47: 51A = OSAGE

30 Good Advice by Diane C. Baldwin

This puzzle features three phrases that are supposed to have a quieting effect—either on the hearer or the speaker.

ACROSS
1 Outbuilding used for storage
5 Young lady
9 Torn ticket pieces
14 Continental currency
15 Subject for medical students (abbr.)
16 Warming winter drink
17 Paper fastener
18 Not working
19 Mythical strongman
20 Calming advice (*4 words*)
23 *My Fair Lady* star ___ Harrison
24 Spearheaded
25 Atoll feature, often
29 Clothed (in)
31 Gun the engine
34 Trepidation
35 Front of the lower leg
36 Dreadful
37 Soothing instruction (*4 words*)
40 ___ out (barely manages)
41 Disturb the peace
42 On the plump side, and then some
43 "Paint-the-town" color
44 Camera's eye
45 Deep voices
46 Pitiful
47 Long in the tooth
48 Mom's plea to a restless child (*3 words*)
57 Hiawatha's transport
58 Fully satisfy
59 Christmas song
60 Film or stage performer
61 Holiday precursors
62 Director Preminger
63 Wrenches, hammers, and so on
64 Enraptured
65 Hornet

DOWN
1 Religious faction
2 Luau entertainment
3 Estrada in *CHiPS* TV series
4 Dummy
5 Young lady
6 Back-of-the-book list
7 Word that can follow yard, white, or rummage
8 Ladder rung
9 Spooked
10 Lugged around
11 Pacific-10 school letters
12 Skiff or dory
13 Bathrobe tie
21 Bakery come-on
22 Mild-tasting
25 Surgical beam
26 Similar
27 Like exclusive communities
28 Symbols of royal power
29 Wild disorder
30 Dark suit bane
31 Gets one's goat
32 Start a pencil correction
33 Annoys
35 Onion covering
36 Society ingenues, for short
38 Ideology to live by
39 Thoroughfares
44 Cake tiers
45 Most melancholy
46 Thread holder
47 Frequently
48 "Get lost!"
49 Tex-Mex treat
50 Aware of
51 Takes advantage of
52 Spout angry talk
53 Bowl over with charm
54 Tiniest bit
55 Makes after taxes
56 Unappetizing food

HINT: 62 Across directed such classic films as *Laura* and *Exodus*. See puzzle 10 for another hint.

#40: 44A = ONE-L

Four-H Club   by Fred Piscop

31

If you *don't* remember the four pillars of the 4-H Clubs, this puzzle will help.

ACROSS

1. ___ Lee cakes
5. Mild oaths
10. Lecture room
14. Felipe or Moises of baseball
15. Tex-Mex appetizer
16. Emollient-yielding plant
17. Private-school honcho
19. Granny
20. Unaffiliated film company
21. Less wobbly
23. Ring holder, at a wedding (*2 words*)
26. Partner of sciences
27. Leaves out
29. *Golden Boy* playwright
33. Hiker's route
37. "It's ___-win situation" (*2 words*)
38. Unconcerned with right and wrong
39. Double-reed instrument
40. More rational
42. Skid row denizen
43. Aliens with green cards, for instance
45. Mai ___ (cocktail)
46. Robin's residence
47. Like old bread
48. Wounded in the bullring
50. Wedding cake level
52. Peacock's feathers
57. Anti-male sort (*hyphenated*)
61. Billiards bounce
62. Pop singer Tori
63. Object of one's love
66. Talk like Daffy Duck
67. Go in
68. Flower sold by the dozen
69. "What's the big ___?!"
70. Partner of willing and able
71. Washstand pitcher

DOWN

1. "Sir," in colonial India
2. Coeur d'___, Idaho
3. Traffic arteries
4. IRS investigation
5. Genetic letters
6. ___ Tafari (old name of Ethiopian ruler Haile Selassie)
7. Play sections
8. Greek consonants
9. More achy
10. With no trouble (*2 words*)
11. Jai ___
12. Like 28 Down's Ranger friend
13. Shakespearean king
18. Interoffice note
22. Molecule component
24. Accumulate
25. One of Columbus's ships
28. "Kemo sabe" utterer
30. Fourth largest of the Great Lakes
31. Beachgoers' shades
32. Piggy bank opening
33. Veteran campaigners, informally
34. Assist in a crime
35. Roman's garb
36. Fitness place (*2 words*)
38. Israel's Sharon
41. Wyatt of the O.K. Corral
44. *Star Wars* princess
48. Ben Cartwright player Lorne
49. Ventilation conduit
51. Old-time anesthetic
53. Olympic skier Phil
54. Missile from Cupid
55. Bird in a V-formation
56. Glowing bit of coal
57. Timbuktu's country
58. Surrounded by
59. Pinocchio's protuberance
60. Pro ___ (proportionately)
64. Checkers color
65. Make an attempt

HINT: 48 Down refers to the old TV western series *Bonanza*. There's another hint accompanying puzzle 17.

#33: 32A = OLIOS

Count on It! by Holden Baker

32

The pinwheel pattern of theme answers offers a progression with mathematical logic.

ACROSS

1 Ukraine's capital
5 Athletic events
10 Greek letters
14 Morales of *La Bamba* and *NYPD Blue*
15 Cause embarrassment to
16 Minnesota baseball team member
17 Agency that put a man on the moon (abbr.)
18 Egyptian peninsula
19 La ___ Nostra
20 This, it is often said, deserves another (*3 words*)
23 Sort
24 Tsar or queen
25 Hard chewy candy
27 Hunting expedition
30 Soak up
32 Blood-typing system
33 Cyrano's feature
35 Authority (*hyphenated*)
38 Bordered

41 Places in balance (*2 words*)
43 Wearing less clothing
44 "¿Cómo ___ usted?"
46 Washday alternative to Tide, perhaps
47 White meat, as of turkey
49 San ___, California
52 Lionel's products
54 10-point type
56 Heavy motorcycle, slangily
57 1986 comedy featuring Chevy Chase, Steve Martin, and Martin Short (*2 words*)
62 *The ___ of Night* (TV soap, 1956-84)

64 *Gigi* star Leslie ___
65 Alaska city where the Iditarod Trail Sled Dog Race ends
66 Instinctive ability
67 FBI employee
68 It might bear fruit
69 British loyalist, during colonial times
70 Some works of art
71 Transmit by E-mail, perhaps

DOWN

1 Relative of bingo
2 "This ___ outrage!" (*2 words*)
3 Relax
4 Drug Bob Dole endorsed
5 Auto fuel
6 Put up with

7 Meditation syllables
8 Genesis brother
9 Skins' opponents, in pickup games
10 Abbreviation that's often used to end a list
11 Old North Church warning signal option (*4 words*)
12 Church path
13 Garden of Eden reptile
21 Your and my
22 Hangman's need
26 Pro football Hall of Fame quarterback ___ Tarkenton
27 Volvo competitor
28 "Fernando" group
29 Home run (*hyphenated*)

31 Borscht ingredient
34 Keats specialties
36 "Of course!"
37 Milky birthstone
39 Actress Garr of *Mr. Mom*
40 Senator Lott
42 Differing versions
45 Directed the course
48 Trash barrel
50 Cash dispenser (abbr.)
51 Fencer's moves
52 Larceny
53 The Calgary Stampede, for example
55 Sierra ___ (republic in western Africa)
58 Prego rival
59 Clinton's vice president
60 Augury
61 Apricot pit, for example
63 Ron ___, former emcee of the Miss America pageant

HINT: If the answer to 26 Down doesn't come to you quickly enough, you might think of the woman who played opposite Burr Tillstrom's puppets on TV. Or, you might take a look at puzzle 24 for more help.

#26: 9A = HEDDA

33

Auto Focus   by Norma Steinberg

This puzzle does not involve cameras. Instead, the four theme answers pertain to something else implied by the title.

ACROSS

1 Ferris wheel, for example
5 Prelude to a duel, perhaps
9 In good shape
12 Big birds
13 Whiskers
15 Hubbub (*hyphenated*)
16 Farmer's success (*2 words*)
18 Do some laundry work
19 Poisonous snake of the Nile
20 Competes
21 Once in a blue moon
23 Round of applause
24 Use a stopwatch
25 "Scarface" Al
28 Noblewoman
32 Hodgepodges

33 Yin's partner
34 Etcher's fluid
35 Repair
36 One of Sneezy's housemates
37 Hourglass filling
38 Make tea
39 "Beware the ___ of March"
40 Cut into tiny pieces
41 Exotic dancer
43 Left in a hurry
44 Role for Jodie
45 Title for Godiva
46 Lecture (*2 words*)
49 Seeing red
50 Ballroom dancing move
53 Falco of film and TV
54 Non-stop speaker
57 Come to earth

58 Went up
59 Newspaper page (*hyphenated*)
60 Soap ingredient
61 Was obligated
62 Shortens a skirt

DOWN

1 "I'm a Survivor" singer McEntire
2 Radio shock jock Don ___
3 Jettison
4 Fortune teller's talent (abbr.)
5 Place for relics
6 Tied, as sneakers
7 Affectations
8 Golf course employee

9 Golfer's warning
10 Role model
11 Broadway equivalent of the Oscar
14 Bouncy
15 Have no stamina (*2 words*)
17 Olympic swimmer Janet ___
22 Quantity (abbr.)
23 Deceived
24 Musical sounds
25 Works on ones hair
26 Vigilant
27 Yearning type
28 Adventure
29 Meager
30 From then on
31 Annexed

33 Sing in the Alps
36 School-issued document
40 Internet connection device
42 House animal
43 Excluded
45 Like a caftan
46 Snitch
47 Call it ___ (*2 words*)
48 Opening remark at a singles bar
49 Pack away
50 Fool
51 Part of a list
52 Advanced university degrees (abbr.)
55 Gold, in Mexico
56 "Will ya look at that!"

HINT: 44 Across refers to a Jodie Foster film about a girl raised in the North Carolina backwoods. See puzzle 31's page for a giveaway answer.

#19: 39D = ANON

34

Lights, Please!   by Raymond Hamel

Despite the title's plea, the truth of the matter is that these places are supposed to be dark.

ACROSS

1 Suburban greenery
5 French actress Aimée
10 Old harp
14 *A Death in the Family* author James ___
15 Literary category
16 *David Copperfield* villain Uriah ___
17 It's dark in here! (*2 words*)
19 ___ Domini
20 Order of business
21 Levy added to a purchase (*2 words*)
23 Plane grounded in 2000 (abbr.)
25 By word of mouth
26 It's dark in here! (*2 words*)
32 Oak nut
33 Designer in the Art Deco era
34 Young cow or bull
38 Elisabeth ___ of *Leaving Las Vegas*
39 What you walk on
40 Result of taking a picture with an unstable camera
41 Pay attention to
42 "___ Fire" (Springsteen song) (*2 words*)
43 Dessert plugged by Bill Cosby (*hyphenated*)
44 It's dark in here!
46 Optimistic
50 Prohibiting alcohol
51 Telemarketer's technique (*2 words*)
54 Bassett of *What's Love Got to Do With It?*
59 "Speak softly and carry ___ stick" (Teddy Roosevelt, *2 words*)
60 It's dark in here! (*2 words*)
62 Cinematic beekeeper played by Peter Fonda
63 Come next
64 Passing notice
65 ___ of the manor
66 Tune
67 *Star* ___

DOWN

1 Buddhist title
2 Very excited
3 "___ Only Just Begun" (Carpenters song)
4 Rheinland refusal
5 Shocked
6 Hero in *The Matrix Reloaded*
7 Burden of proof
8 Bear of the sky
9 Faint (*2 words*)
10 Forbidden City of Tibet
11 First movie directed by Barbra Streisand
12 Of the kidneys
13 Powerful adhesive
18 "The Gumps" cartoonist Gus
22 "...___ he drove out of sight"
24 ___ & *Louise* (1991 film)
26 Word after sour or monster
27 Tooth trouble
28 Small grimace
29 TV equine (*2 words*)
30 Sing like Bing Crosby
31 Made amends
34 Truck driver on the radio, in the lingo
35 "___ want for Christmas..." (*2 words*)
36 Humdinger
37 Going ___ bad to worse
39 Like some tap water
43 Blonde bombshell actress ___ Mansfield
44 Fathers
45 English-born comedic actress ___ Ullman
46 Move-it-yourself company (*hyphenated*)
47 Artist ___ Picasso
48 Type of patch in an Uncle Remus story
49 Bordered
52 Actress Anderson
53 Didn't win
55 Give off light
56 Island in the Mediterranean
57 Secret retreat
58 Garfunkel and Carney
61 Egyptian boy-king, commonly

HINT: The answer at 64 Across is a short form of a longer word. See puzzle 38 for more help.

35 Phrases on Location   by Norman Wizer

In this puzzle, the "location" in the title refers to where the theme answers reside in the crossword grid.

ACROSS

1 Thorn
5 Grade school numbers subject (abbr.)
10 *Betsy's Wedding* star Alan
14 Indiana neighbor
15 Proportion
16 Lunch time, for many
17 Irish greeting (*4 words*)
20 African scavenger
21 Marsh gas
22 Great number
25 One who claims to be able to predict the future
26 Nurse a drink
29 Added frosting to a cake
31 Jewish spiritual leaders
35 Pub order
36 Puts chips in the poker pot
38 Word on "shoppe" signs
39 Neither radical nor conservative (*4 words*)
43 Reveal
44 Office copier pioneer
45 "So!"
46 Takes as one's own
49 Gather, as crops
50 Coal measure
51 Sailors' assents
53 Court command
55 Condo "patio"
58 Vents one's anger
62 Loser's place (*4 words*)
65 Sea bird
66 Go on stage
67 Aware of
68 Word with heat or end
60 Snug refuges
70 Direction of the sunrise

DOWN

1 These two
2 Sailor's greeting
3 Ready for plucking
4 Blessings
5 Op or Pop follower
6 Shout from the stands
7 Bit of news
8 New York City newspaper
9 Owl
10 Michigan city (*2 words*)
11 Beef cut
12 Thoroughly cooked
13 *Eat Drink Man Woman* director ___ Lee
18 Beauty parlor offering
19 Rosie O'Donnell's talk-show successor Caroline
23 Teenager's bane
24 First step in rehab
26 Brazilian dance
27 Greek epic attributed to Homer
28 Pitcher Martinez
30 Put off
32 Puff up
33 The Snake River flows across it
34 Car type
37 Scatter
40 Gone
41 ___ frost
42 Run out
47 Beginner
48 Gobs
52 Quickbread served with tea
54 California-Nevada border lake
55 Ripped
56 Volcano in Sicily
57 "Cashless society" money-mover (abbr.)
59 Actress Rowlands
60 Dines
61 Notice
62 Flower plot
63 Vietnamese new year
64 Sixty-minute periods (abbr.)

HINT: When a clue has a word in quotation marks (as in 55 Across in this puzzle), it often means you should not take that word quite so literally. See puzzle 45 for a bigger hint.

#5: 2D = UGLI

36

Neutral Corners by Norma Steinberg

Here's another theme involving colors. This time, though, as the title implies, they're, well, neutral.

ACROSS
1 Opposite of flows
5 Part of a necklace
9 In favor of
12 Early Robin Williams role
13 Sped
15 Radar screen signal
16 Slang for intellect (*2 words*)
18 Lingerie trim
19 Tennis match segment
20 High cards
21 Gave the go-ahead for
23 "Say ___!"
24 Blueprint, in brief
25 Crushes, as potatoes
28 Shines like a star
32 Up and about

33 Word in a comparison
34 Yawn producer
35 Street fight
36 Parts of legs
37 Actress Falco
38 Narrow street
39 Expert, slangily
40 Beeped
41 Here and/or there
43 Unorthodox thinking
44 Model from Mogadishu
45 Round of applause
46 Musical key (*2 words*)
49 007
50 Kook
53 It makes the world go round, so they say
54 Urban building material

57 Woeful word
58 Busybody
59 Poker player's input
60 Chicken coop matriarch
61 Milne bear
62 Shows disapproval

DOWN
1 Omelet ingredient
2 Stripped
3 Someone else's kid
4 *Harriet the* ___
5 Orthodontic appliances
6 Devoured
7 Deeds
8 Billy ____ Williams
9 Broadway offering
10 Pilaf ingredient

11 Newspaper's columnist page (*hyphenated*)
14 Unexpected company (*hyphenated*)
15 English pirate Teach
17 *Politically Incorrect* host
22 Barbie's boyfriend
23 Chardonnay and others (*2 words*)
24 Oscar winner Hilary
25 The Donald's second wife
26 Oriental
27 Unemotional
28 "...for ___ is the kingdom..."
29 Mountain shelter
30 New York Indian tribe
31 Run-down

33 Rose sticker
36 Have total faith in (*2 words*)
40 Awaits settlement
42 Kind of medical provider (abbr.)
43 Hard-hearted "vamp of Savannah"
45 Instructional book (*hyphenated*)
46 Slightly depressed
47 Double agent
48 Terrible Tsar
49 Cher's first married name
50 Forbidden activity (*hyphenated*)
51 "Do ___ others..."
52 Pullover shirts
55 Salesperson
56 Airplane stabilizing airfoil

HINT: 43 Down refers to a 1929 novelty song that was revived and made popular again by Peggy Lee. If you need another hint, see puzzle 2.

#48: 43A = OSIER

37

We Deliver   by Nancy Salomon

This puzzle features three occupations who make deliveries of sorts. The theme is really in the clues, not so much in the answers.

ACROSS

1 "The Divine ___" (Bette Midler album, *2 words*)
6 Urban health hazard
10 Prima donna
14 Pertaining to sheep
15 Rowdydow (*hyphenated*)
16 "Tree of knowledge" garden
17 Evil spirit
18 Santa's landing spot
19 Mass of floating ice
20 We deliver babies
23 Wrestling win
25 ___ Gardner of classic films
26 Prepared (*2 words*)
27 Manager's aide (abbr.)
29 Snowy slopes (*2 words*)
32 Trolley sound, in a Judy Garland song
34 Kind of life insurance
35 Health club
38 We deliver addresses (*2 words*)

42 Alabama and New York (abbr.)
43 Coal carrier
44 Shout that starts a game of tag (*2 words*)
45 With intensity
48 Kind of ranch
49 Geronimo or Cochise
52 Satisfied sigh
54 The "p" of mph
55 We deliver mail (*2 words*)
59 "That ___ you!" (*2 words*)
60 Units of electrical resistance
61 Phil ___ (1980s slalom racing star)
64 Cordelia's father in a Shakespeare play

65 Transport for Tarzan
66 Make amends
67 Häagen-Dazs alternative
68 ___ *Brockovich* (Julia Roberts film)
69 Sherpa's land

DOWN

1 Rocker's foe, in England
2 "___ had it up to here!"
3 Following-directions game (*2 words*)
4 Stuck-up sort
5 Organization for very smart people
6 Run of luck
7 Not worth debating
8 Bad nasal news

9 "No one could have predicted that!" (*2 words*)
10 Moneys owed, as recorded in account ledgers
11 Things to think about
12 *Journey to the Center of the Earth* author Jules ___
13 That sinking feeling
21 Home-entertainment appliances
22 Scam artist (*2 words*)
23 Stuffs a suitcase
24 Land in a lake
28 Cable outlet for C&W music
30 "Who's there?" reply (*2 words*)

31 Sales staff member
33 "Had you going there, didn't I?"
35 Begin a business (*3 words*)
36 Pack of lions
37 Daisylike flower
39 The real deal, romantically speaking (*2 words*)
40 Grab a bite
41 Pasted in the ring
45 Cast members
46 Don ___ (who pitched a perfect game in the 1956 World Series)
47 Shoot the breeze
49 Heaps (*2 words*)
50 Put forth, as a question
51 Measure metal
53 "Mr. Muscles"
56 Sound from a fan
57 Prefix meaning "all"
58 Fixed charge per unit of quantity
62 Virus innards, briefly
63 Sushi option

HINT: At 1 Down: The Rockers were bike-riding, rough-dressing teens in 1960s England. Their fashion-conscious counter-parts answer the clue. See puzzle 9 for another hint.

38 What a Spread! by Nancy Kavanaugh

Presenting a selection of items to spread on your toast. Enjoy!

ACROSS

1 Actress Thompson of *Family*
5 Looked with amazement
10 Some miles away
14 Musical work
15 Popular pain relief brand
16 Corrida bull
17 Wine region of Italy
18 Killed, as a dragon
19 The Dixie Chicks, for example
20 Baby food for bees (*2 words*)
22 Couple, in the tabloids
23 Lamprey and moray
24 With sarcasm
25 Was behind schedule (*2 words*)
29 Footwear
31 Divisions of the mind
32 Partnership
33 Ostrichlike bird
36 Some parks (*2 words*)
41 Chapter in history
42 Channel marker
43 Like a used-up battery
44 Sing like the birdies sing
46 Grassy plain
49 Workout consequences, perhaps
51 Phonograph player, for example (*hyphenated*)
52 Dressed
53 Commuter tie-up (*2 words*)
59 Sound of a little bell
60 Must (*2 words*)
61 Angel topper
62 A single time
63 Aquatic mammal
64 Finished
65 Clarinet mouthpiece insert
66 Total up again
67 Walk nervously back and forth

DOWN

1 Fly like an eagle
2 Lhasa ___ (small dog from Tibet)
3 Obligation
4 Where the Yalu River is
5 Stove part (*2 words*)
6 Alternative gene form
7 Bell sounds
8 Wicked
9 Refuse to accept
10 Clothing
11 Number of states on 1/20/1912 (*hyphenated*)
12 Israeli politician ___ Sharon
13 Spacious
21 Thompson of *Back to the Future*
24 Capitol topping
25 Philosopher Descartes
26 Culture medium in a petri dish
27 "Never!" (*3 words*)
28 Baton Rouge learning institution (abbr.)
29 Notice
30 Owns
32 Make an effort
34 Not very nice
35 Meat-inspecting agency (abbr.)
37 Baseball stats (abbr.)
38 Norway, Italy, etc. (abbr.)
39 Generic soft drink
40 Vitamin bottle letters
45 Bet against yourself to protect some money
46 Passed through a strainer, as flour
47 Be able to manage financially
48 Half of XIV
49 Person with a role to play
50 Patsy of country music
51 "___ la vista, baby!"
53 Norse god of thunder
54 The "R" of APR
55 Lamb serving
56 Coffee, slangily
57 Baldwin or Guinness
58 Additional amount

HINT: Regarding 11 Down: This is a perfect example of an answer that you probably do not know off the top of your head (unless you live in one of two states). If you keep plugging away, however, you can figure it out...and learn something in the process. And check out puzzle 16.

#34: 28D = MOUE

Jam Session by Sarah Keller

39

Sometimes crossword writers hit on related themes. This one has some similarity with the previous puzzle, but the results are quite different.

ACROSS

1 Become liquid
5 Appeared on stage
10 Church recess
14 Native Canadian
15 Blacksmith, at times
16 Evil glance
17 Mama's mama
18 CNN anchor ___ Zahn
19 Author Ferber
20 Prince hit (2 words)
23 Had a bite
24 Word after fire or carpenter
25 ___ With Love (2 words)
27 Stinging insects
29 Cowboy boot attachments
33 C&W cable station (abbr.)
34 Kindled
36 Motorist's org. (abbr.)
37 Scot's denials
38 Fats Domino hit (2 words)
42 Married women of Madrid (abbr.)
43 Boxing biopic that starred Will Smith
44 Movie matinee day (abbr.)
45 Nursery school item
46 Rendezvous
48 Plan a different route
52 Use cuss words
54 Airport abbr.
56 Piercing tool
57 Deana Carter hit (2 words)
62 Trifecta and exacta
63 Clear, as a blackboard
64 Director ___ Kazan
65 Hydrox alternative
66 Does a triple gainer
67 Monthly budget item
68 Organization (abbr.)
69 Prophets
70 Work units

DOWN

1 Quick Draw ___
2 List of printing goofs
3 Car-rental contracts
4 Office sub
5 Rocky Mountain resort
6 They're flipped at a seminar
7 Sightseeing trip
8 Elusive
9 Hardly colorful
10 Oldsmobile model
11 Place for a statue
12 Lookout
13 Long time span
21 Musical Count
22 UFO crew (abbr.)
26 MD's helpers (abbr.)
28 Letter grade add-on, maybe
30 France's capital
31 Egypt and Syria, at one time (abbr.)
32 They're caught on the beach
35 Aid to skiers
37 Nick at ___
38 Window-shoppers
39 Newborns' necessities
40 Tarzan portrayer Ron
41 Laurel's partner
42 Avenue crossers (abbr.)
46 ___ la la
47 More concise
49 Author Norman
50 Canvas shelter
51 Feature of some skirts
53 Fiery crime
55 Lock of hair
58 Marries
59 Relative of Camembert cheese
60 Gutter location
61 ___ No Angels (1935 escape-from-Devil's-Island film)
62 Feathery wrap

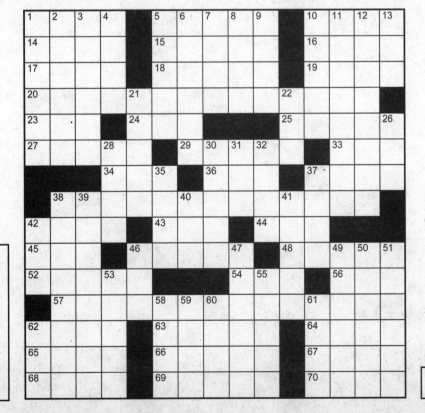

HINT: The answer to 65 Across shows up fairly often in crossword puzzles. Ironically, it is older than the newspaper crossword puzzle. There's another hint for you on the page with puzzle 23.

#27: 7D = LEDA

40

Fun with A-E-I-O-U Sounds — by Norma Johnson

Each thematic answer starts with the same consonants, but the first vowels change.

ACROSS

1 Meander
5 Furnace fuel
9 Mennonite sect in Pennsylvania
14 Teen's skin problem
15 Theater award
16 ___ Park (Edison's New Jersey lab site)
17 Postal substations in large offices
19 Breakfast meat
20 Tall cupboard
21 Fragrance
23 Actresses Rigg and Ross
24 More sincere, as a welcome
27 *A Bug's Life* insects
28 Rules out
29 ___ way, shape or form (2 words)
30 Scottish denial
31 King Kong and Mighty Joe Young

33 "Stand-up" amusement
35 Significant life event
37 One way to get out of jail
40 Homesites
41 Bar bill
44 First-year law student, commonly (*hyphenated*)
45 Russian refusal
47 Lockup room
48 Beholden to another
50 Lisa's role on *Friends*
52 ___ Rebellion (1786 uprising)
53 College graduate
54 Dine at home (2 words)
56 Old West wagon pullers
58 Plant support

59 Where China and Vietnam are
60 *The African Queen* screenwriter James ___
61 Some British noblemen
62 Requirement
63 Watch over

DOWN

1 Month of fasting, in Islam
2 Musical instrument also called the "sweet potato"
3 Draw movie cartoons
4 Honeydews, for example
5 Budweiser rival
6 Double-reed wind instrument
7 "Fire!" preceder
8 Reduce
9 Fossil resin used for jewelry

10 Dining hour
11 Slope
12 ___-mo replay
13 Darlin'
18 River inlet
22 University of Georgia's bulldog, for example
24 Gave a hard time
25 Stopping point
26 Artist Lichtenstein
28 Spelling contest
31 Have the sniffles
32 Completely adequate supply
34 Slip-___ (pullovers)
35 Make a mountain out of a ___ (exaggerate)
36 Youngster
37 Luau dish

38 Landers of advice columns
39 Antares or Betelgeuse, to astronomers (2 words)
41 Approaching twenty, say
42 Egg white
43 Sanctified
46 One who always agrees with the boss (*hyphenated*)
47 Charge (2 words)
49 Savings account institutions
50 Say "not guilty," for example
51 Shack
53 "I cannot tell ___" (2 words)
54 Compass direction (abbr.)
55 Week-___-glance calendar (*hyphenated*)
57 Put to work

HINT: If a clue uses the word "more" (as does 24 Across in this puzzle), the answer is often an adjective ending with the letters ER. See puzzle 30 for another hint.

#20: 8A = SCARAB

Whenever... by Mary Brindamour

41

The three long answers pertain to time periods. It's your job to discover whether they are short or long periods.

ACROSS

1 Eve's mate
5 Phony
9 Cleaned a fish
14 *Sleepless in Seattle* director ___ Ephron
15 Stretch vehicle, for short
16 "Once ___ time..." (*2 words*)
17 All-day-every-day (*hyphenated* and *2 words*)
20 Slow mover
21 Publisher
22 Do something
24 Seeds for flavoring
28 Railroad stops (abbr.)
31 ___ Park, Colorado
34 Experiment
35 Supply weapons to
36 Song by Verdi
37 Game of chance
38 Rest period (*3 words*)
42 Things
43 Dems and Reps
44 AAA suggestion (abbr.)
45 *The Godfather* composer Nino ___
46 Grove components
48 Sugars (suffix)
49 Trap
51 Hearing organ
53 Treats badly
56 Featured half of a 45 rpm record (*2 words*)
60 Two days (*hyphenated* and *2 words*)
64 Great Lakes tribesmen
65 Room access
66 Songbird
67 Proceeds on one's way
68 Spot
69 Lanchester of *The Bride of Frankenstein*

DOWN

1 Picnic pests
2 Direction of this clue's answer
3 Land measurement
4 Excessively intense desires
5 Like a fox
6 Sound system, for short
7 Maker of "Famous" cookies
8 Hair-styling foam
9 Long city transports
10 Telephone company employee
11 Thanksgiving month (abbr.)
12 Wind direction (abbr.)
13 Aykroyd of *Ghostbusters*
18 Pampering, briefly
19 Regrets
23 Actress Garr
25 Sidewalk timers
26 Real ___
27 Tends a fire
28 Columnist William
29 One of Saturn's moons
30 Organization that lobbies for benefits for people who served in the U.S. military
32 Transgression
33 Hosiery shade
36 Mornings (abbr.)
37 Scale figures (abbr.)
39 Came forth
40 Ballerina's balancing point
41 Threat word
46 ___ *Grit* (John Wayne film)
47 Live in a place
48 Baltimore baseballer
50 Deep chasm
52 Shade of blond
54 Swelled heads
55 Store
57 Twofold
58 Makes a mistake
59 "___ silly question..." (*2 words*)
60 Small number of things
61 Raw metal
62 ___ Tin Tin
63 Listen to a case in court

#13:
5D = PAWNEES

42

On Broadway   by Dave Tuller

Each long entry begins with a word that happens to be the name of a hit Broadway show. Don't overlook 25 Across and 51 Across.

ACROSS

1 Large Internet service provider, briefly
4 Help
7 George W. Bush's country
10 2001, to Nero
13 Before (2 words)
15 Letter after upsilon
16 Baseball "point"
17 Policy that keeps housing costs down (2 words)
19 Ingredient in a kid's pie
20 "___ Kick Out of You" (3 words)
21 Winter precipitation
22 Musical based on a Patrick Dennis novel
23 Photographer's device
25 Capone-era weapon (2 words)
27 Burdensome
29 Remove, as a subscription card (2 words)
30 2,000 pounds
31 Noise

33 Plus-shaped symbol
34 Comb alternative
38 Senior
41 The Holy Grail, for example
42 Round shape (abbr.)
45 Rots (2 words)
48 Knotting technique for some wall hangings
51 Taxi that's not supposed to be hailed (2 words)
53 Football Hall of Famer Jim
54 Loser to the tortoise
55 Farmer's yield
57 Jordan's capital
58 Yale graduate
59 Part of a clown's makeup kit
61 Off-road conveyance, for short

62 Groove in the ground
63 Psychologist B.F. ___
64 Yellow No. 5, for instance
65 ___ Speed-wagon ("Keep on Loving You" band)
66 Top of a rating scale
67 Television Tarzan Ron

DOWN

1 Downy peachlike fruit
2 Leafy seasoning used in Italian cooking
3 Tackles and centers, in football
4 Jockey Eddie
5 "How was ___ know?" (2 words)
6 Puts on

7 Displace
8 Phrase associated with Missouri (2 words)
9 Feel bad
10 Myopic cartoon character (2 words)
11 Hawaiian-style dresses
12 Uses the tab key, perhaps
14 Marine mammal with valuable fur
18 Nitroglycerine cousin (abbr.)
22 Gift from one of the three wise men
24 Car imported from Germany
26 Alternatives to PCs
28 Knight's title
32 ER network

34 German state whose capital is Wiesbaden
35 Roast beef chain name
36 Captain Morgan product
37 ___ the crack of dawn (2 words)
38 Brainiac
39 Quality praised by the Mafia
40 Take away from, with "of"
42 Shade of red
43 Place on the jury
44 It's between orbit and splashdown
46 Accumulate
47 "___ be great" (2 words)
49 Singer Mary ___ Carpenter
50 Director Polanski
52 Snake that may have a crush on you?
56 "Hey, over here!"
59 Rover's warning
60 Barely make, with "out"

HINT: At 22 Across: If it helps you, we'll tell you that Angela Lansbury was the star. The box next to puzzle 44 has another hint.

43

The Sounds of Music   by Norma Steinberg

Presenting a quartet of phrases that each offers a style of music, although the important word has another usage.

ACROSS

1 Old McDonald's place
5 Brings to court
9 "___ is my witness!" (2 words)
14 Sheltered, at sea
15 About (2 words)
16 Stockholm resident
17 Ocean's sound
18 Comedienne McClurg
19 Affix, as a corsage (2 words)
20 Former SNL star (2 words)
22 Way in
23 Spring holiday
24 Crooned
26 Stinging insect
29 Matters
33 Squeals
37 A ___ to the wise
39 ___ Stanley Gardner
40 Verdi heroine
41 Donny Oomond's sister
42 Part of a mosaic
43 Usurp
44 Newspaper section (hyphenated)
45 City on the Ruhr
46 Accept a proposal (2 words)
48 Meaningful progress
50 Certain sandwiches, commonly
52 Punctual (2 words)
57 TV angel Reese
60 Football league for kids (2 words)
63 Devoured fully (2 words)
04 Joe Millionaire ___ Marriott
65 Brainstorm
66 Bowling alleys
67 Emperor of old Rome
68 Programming units
69 "How can ___?" (2 words)
70 Carey of Whose Line Is It Anyway?
71 Slack

DOWN

1 Satirical comedy
2 Hi on HI
3 Brings up, as a child
4 Deserve
5 ___ Leone
6 Take back
7 Hockey star Lindros
8 Looks for
9 Quaking trees
10 Sights in suburban yards (2 words)
11 Bloke
12 Bloodhound's clue
13 Refuse to admit
21 Stitches
25 Intern
27 Trade
28 Gazed intently
30 Author Leon
31 Vogue competitor
32 Witnessed
33 Skycap's burden
34 Luigi's money
35 One-___ Vitamins (hyphenated)
36 Sinatra's eyes, so-called
38 Go by bus
41 Lion's share
45 Volcano on Sicily
47 Pass, as time
49 Comforting phrase (2 words)
51 Exhaust
53 Clan
54 Asian country
55 Bumps into
56 Backspace over
57 Spanish surrealist
58 Bibliography abbreviation
59 Letterman's competition
61 CBer's "your turn"
62 Peel

HINT: 64 Across refers to that TV show that turned a blue-collar worker into a seeming millionaire so the viewers could watch a group of women compete for his affections, and later react to the lie. Puzzle 1 has another hint, even if you don't need it.

#49: 7D = GRENADA

44

Guy Flicks   by Randall J. Hartman

Sometimes a puzzle's title makes you put on your thinking cap. In this case the question is, "Who are these people?"

ACROSS

1 There's none of this on a rolling stone
5 ___ as a rock
10 College residence, for short
14 Birthplace of seven U.S. presidents
15 Plural of "that"
16 *On the Waterfront* director Kazan
17 1998 Robin Williams role/movie
19 Super Bowl III winners
20 Spoon-bender Geller
21 Ripened, like cheese
22 Oklahoma Indians
24 Cure-all
26 Abbreviation on a mountain-pass sign
27 1996 Tom Cruise role/movie
32 *Wheel of Fortune* star Pat
35 Family vehicle
36 Feathery fashion accessory
37 Trebek of *Jeopardy!*
38 Deputized group in western films

40 Lubricates
41 "Give ___ rest!" (*2 words*)
42 Garr of *Tootsie*
43 In a peculiar way
44 1997 Johnny Depp role/movie (*2 words*)
48 Places of asylum
49 Nathan Lane's role in *The Lion King*
53 The Gulf of Suez is at its head (*2 words*)
56 Annapolis institute for would-be admirals (abbr.)
57 Emissions-watching org. (abbr.)
58 Former spouses
59 1991 John Turturro role/movie

62 One of Columbus's ships
63 1987 world figure skating champ Brian ___
64 Suit to ___ (*2 words*)
65 "___, Brute?" (question in *Julius Caesar*, *2 words*)
66 City in north-central Florida
67 "Faster ___ a speeding bullet..."

DOWN

1 Post-victory duty (*hyphenated*)
2 Maureen ___ of *The Quiet Man*
3 Campus protest (*hyphenated*)
4 Relative of an assn.

5 One who puts on plays
6 "My goodness!" (*2 words*)
7 Burden
8 Doctrine
9 Like the surface of the moon
10 Feeling of having been there before (*2 words*)
11 Designer Cassini
12 Baptism, for one
13 Sunday service
18 Diacritical mark resembling an inverted carat
23 State flower of Utah
25 Trojan War hero
26 Ostrich relatives
28 Arafat of the PLO
29 In the same place, in footnotes (abbr.)

30 Croissant, for one
31 Effortless
32 Articulated
33 Choir voice
34 The "J" in J. Paul Getty
38 Children's game
39 Peepers
40 Carbon monoxide lacks it
42 Exhaust
43 Symbol of vastness
45 Capital of the Bahamas
46 Beer brewed in the Netherlands
47 Mexican title for a married woman
50 ___ Richards of the Rolling Stones
51 Sleeping disorder
52 Occupied, as a seat
53 Russo of *Tin Cup*
54 Way out
55 Fender bender result
56 ___ Minor (constellation with the North Star)
60 Basketball's path
61 Dieter's no-no

HINT: 4 Down uses an abbreviation in the clue to signal an abbreviated answer. That's typical of harder puzzles...a hint of things to come. See puzzle 8 for more.

#42:
46D = ACCRUE

Nothing Could be Finer   by Nancy Salomon

45

These thematic entries have a little subtle something in common, as any diviner could tell you.

ACROSS
1 Go with the flow
6 Grandchild in the book of Genesis
10 Sing singly
14 Staff addition
15 Barbershop symbol
16 Per person (*2 words*)
17 Cruise ship (*2 words*)
19 Spree
20 Nay counterbalance
21 Game played on horseback
22 Easter animal
23 Prefix denoting "Chinese"
24 JCPenney rival
26 Round-the-clock eatery (*hyphenated and 2 words*)
30 Burn balms
31 Othello's nemesis
32 "Just ___ no"

34 Water lily's home
35 Landing pier
37 Throw for a loop
38 Smallest bill
39 Like the eye of a storm
40 Fat cats' transports
41 Bewhiskered gold seeker (*2 words*)
45 Flabbergast
46 Acorns' offspring
47 Ridiculous blunder
49 Green Gables girl
50 Have bills
53 Gold-medal gymnast Korbut
54 San Francisco football pro (*hyphenated*)
57 Spike and Robert E.

58 Neighbor of Calif.
59 Blow, volcano-style
60 Canadian Conservative
61 Cancún coin
62 Fritter away

DOWN
1 Sailor's hail
2 Casino cubes
3 Length x width
4 Shade of green
5 Bowling game
6 Literary wrap-up
7 Fudge, to a dieter (*hyphenated*)
8 "¡Rah!"
9 Reverend's remarks (abbr.)
10 Ringed planet
11 Storied password (*2 words*)
12 Shark's transaction

13 C&W mecca, with "the"
18 *WKRP...* actress Anderson
22 Scott ___ of *Charles in Charge*
23 Musher's vehicle
24 "Now!" in the OR
25 On pins and needles
26 Go ___ with (agree to)
27 Silver's owner (*2 words*)
28 Order to a blackjack dealer (*2 words*)
29 Stubble shaver
30 Military mail-drop designation (abbr.)
33 "That's a go"
35 Music that developed in New Orleans

36 *Vogue* competitor
37 Salmon stabilizers
39 Business bigwig
40 In near-mint condition (*2 words*)
42 "Makes no difference to me" (*2 words*)
43 "Please stay!" (*2 words*)
44 "...and ___ more"
47 Make a run for it
48 Bread spread
49 Greek god of war
50 Big burden
51 Turned on the waterworks
52 Big name in Art Deco
54 Dandy dude
55 Mine metal
56 The Gershwin who wrote the lyrics

HINT: Regarding 8 Down: That upside-down exclamation point is a clue to the language of the answer. Even so, though, the word is common enough that you should recognize it. Also, see puzzle 15's page.

46

Sounds Like...   by Norma Johnson

For the next five puzzles we'll turn up the heat a notch by omitting "2-word" tags and using some tougher clues. This theme involves three homophones.

ACROSS
1 ___ mater
5 Bal. checkers
9 Threw for a loop
14 Fawns' moms
15 Bruins' sch.
16 Canine from Japan
17 Bank amounts
20 Symbol of strength
21 Go downhill fast
22 "Sure!"
23 Accompany to the airport, perhaps
26 Surrounded by
28 "Hostess with the Mostest" Mesta
30 Sticky campfire treats
34 Soaking spot

37 Org. for 50s-and-up
39 Director Kurosawa
40 Lavender and rosemary
44 Up to the time of
45 Almost forever
46 "Golly!"
47 Washington of *Training Day*
49 Ladder steps
52 Snappy-looking suit
54 Book before Proverbs
57 Nick and Nora's terrier
60 Throw easily
62 Steady boyfriends
64 Talking Heads concert film
68 Indian wraps
69 And others, in a list

70 Meat often used in mock turtle soup
71 Bird houses, often
72 *Nautilus* captain
73 Sicilian peak

DOWN
1 Foots the bill?
2 Pilfers
3 Free-for-all
4 Not yet awake
5 Mixed breed
6 Some may sit on your lap
7 "What a shame!"
8 Decaf brand
9 WWII female enlistee
10 "Sure as shootin'!"
11 Merlot or Madeira

12 Jazz singer ___ James
13 Short sprint
18 Skin soother
19 Turns down
24 Haus keeper
25 React strongly, with "up"
27 Apple for the student?
29 Wrong turn, for example
31 Symbol of commitment
32 Art Deco artist
33 Prepaid mailer
34 Tater
35 Corn ___
36 Business letter abbr.
38 ___ girl
41 Delivered dish, often
42 Butter stand-in
43 Employees' IDs

48 *Damn Yankees* vamp
50 Runs off at the mouth
51 Cheater's place for an ace
53 Just for show
55 Artist who greatly influenced impressionism
56 Contemporary essayist Sontag
57 Gofer, briefly
58 Something to wish on
59 Rushed or ripped
61 Snack
63 Emmy winner Ward
65 Ed.'s workpile
66 *The Deer Hunter* locale, commonly
67 Day-___ paint

HINT: The woman who answers the clue at 28 Across was a Washington socialite and diplomat. She was our ambassador to Luxembourg in the early 1950s. Also, see puzzle 22.

#28: 50D = COMO

47

Skin-Deep Folks   by Randall J. Hartman

Puzzles with quotations or quips are harder because many letters are essentially unclued. It's usually worth the wait...and this is no exception.

ACROSS
1 Decree
5 Greek letter
10 Dick and Jane's dog
14 Site of the Taj Mahal
15 *Silas Marner* novelist
16 Kiri Te Kanawa solo
17 Start of a quip
19 Resist, with "off"
20 "Give it the old college ___"
21 Fencing swords
22 Assignments
23 Actress Joanne of 1950s films
24 Shoots 72 at Augusta
25 Part 2 of the quip
32 Immediately following
33 American songbird
34 Shaving cream style
36 King of ___ hill
37 Relinquish-ments, as rights
39 Dir. from Los Angeles to Chicago
40 Cul-de-___
41 Starred on Broadway
42 Biblical preposition
43 Part 3 of the quip
47 Palm, for one
48 Cool ___ cucumber
49 Public an-nouncer of yore
51 Missouri River tributary
54 Tucked away
57 Vesuvius output
58 End of the quip

60 Scored 100 on a test
61 Nebraska city
62 Its symbol is Fe
63 Military cafe-teria, for short
64 Ed of *Lou Grant*
65 Camp enclosure

DOWN
1 Abstain from food
2 Composer Stravinsky
3 Colin Powell's military branch
4 ___ kwon do
5 "Don't lag behind!"
6 Skin cream ingredient
7 Popeye prop
8 Senators and representatives
9 "It must have been some-thing I ___!"

10 Serengeti expedition
11 Hollywood spokesperson
12 Barnyard grunt
13 Young'uns
18 Andean nation
22 Sonora snacks
23 It ends in Oct.
24 Ship landing structure
25 Picnic pests
26 Restoration, for short
27 Corporate bigshots
28 1996 Madonna movie
29 Steelworker's pin
30 Astaire and Flintstone
31 Slowly, in music
35 Rocker Russell

37 Most of the earth
38 Charley horse
42 Bruce Springsteen's "Born in the ___"
44 Tire patterns
45 Amazon cat
46 ___-friendly
49 Dollar, slangily
50 Daytona 500, for one
51 Resistance units
52 James Bond portrayer Connery
53 Former Davis Cup captain
54 Dupe in an Aesop fable
55 Sacred image
56 Depression
58 ___ man (everyone)
59 Temper tantrum

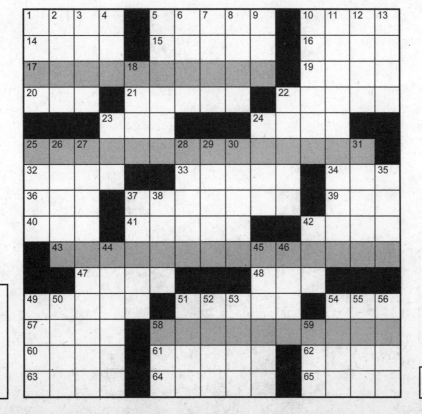

HINT: 10 Across refers to the old elementary school primer that began "See Dick run." See puzzle 29 for more help.

#21: 35D = DOMO

48 Formerly Known As... by Robert H. Wolfe

Each long theme word starts with a prefix that could be interpreted as changing a base word's meaning.

ACROSS
1 Pan Am competitor, commonly
4 Really beat
8 Different
12 Possesses
13 Connect
14 Banish
15 Former boxer?
17 Like 1943's pennies
18 Safe
19 Climbs
21 Get the lead out?
22 Church officer
24 Fax forerunner
26 Impassioned
30 "Long ___ and Far Away"
33 Certain tides
35 Placido Domingo's voice range
36 Swamp area
38 Blocks
40 Wander
41 College boss, slangily
43 Willow tree
45 Speak
46 Skiing locations
48 Computer key
50 1871 Chicago cow owner Kate ___
52 Flat
56 Guard dog, perhaps
59 Playwright ___ O'Neill
60 Nick of *Prince of Tides*
61 Former ironer?
64 Wrath
65 Comes close to
66 Globe
67 Juicy fruit
68 Tacks on
69 Hog's home

DOWN
1 The ones here
2 Floor shiner
3 Humane org.
4 Sup
5 Ink color for debits
6 Certain westerner
7 Cleansing agent
8 Former sheep herder?
9 Legal claim against property
10 Vehicle used in the Iditarod race
11 Snakelike fish
13 Chowder holder
14 Accompany
16 Expel
20 Rwy. stop
22 Defense gp. that disbanded in 1977
23 Former model?
25 Bandleader ___ Brown
27 Son of Seth
28 PBS science series
29 Card that beats the deuce
30 Concert blasters
31 "The ___ From Ipanema"
32 Sandwich cookie
34 Barbed
37 Former train worker?
39 TV, for example
42 One who shouts
44 Variety shows
47 "I told you so!"
49 Cleaning cloths
51 Action site
53 Mexican coins
54 Non-reactive
55 Race
56 ___ up (acquire quickly)
57 Not any
58 Plant organism
59 Goes off
62 ___ out (removed)
63 Mouse's place?

HINT: Solving this puzzle's theme is sorta like playing charades. Once you figure out what's going on, you should have no trouble. On the other hand, see puzzle 36 for an outright giveaway.

#14: 40A = KEATS

Grammatical Pauses by Dave and Diane Epperson

49

Each long phrase starts with a letter sequence that coincidentally spells a punctuation mark. Harder puzzles often use themes similar to this idea.

ACROSS
1 On the rocks, like a bar drink
5 Gymnast Korbut
9 Milky gems
14 ___ me tangere (touch-me-not)
15 Homer and Marge Simpson's boy
16 Cobra toxin
17 Pioneer
19 Disco-era suffix
20 Oldsmobile model
21 Author Bagnold
23 Work like ___
24 Hand holder?
26 Emanations
28 Orbital flight deck
33 Killer whale
34 Where the buoys are?
35 Cadiz coin
37 Hiccup-stopping cry
38 Oft-framed document (abbr.)
39 Dijon denial
40 1" pencil, say
41 Attack quickly
43 ___ Dhabi
44 Computes a total
45 Element chart
48 Up and about
49 ___-Na-Na (Bowzer's doo-wop group)
50 Sunrise
53 "I could ___ horse!"
55 Pond scum
59 Wonderland visitor
61 Auto instrument panel
63 Powered bike
64 Montreal baseballer
65 World's longest river
66 Looks searchingly
67 Light rain
68 James Bond's school

DOWN
1 Ancient Peruvian
2 Nonchalant
3 Model Macpherson
4 Museum exhibit
5 Geisha girdle?
6 Goof off
7 One of the Windward Islands
8 Open courtyard
9 Eggs, to a biologist
10 Winged horse of Greek myth
11 "And giving ___, up the chimney he rose"
12 Corporate symbol
13 Bad air
18 Standard
22 Quitters
25 Flirtatious letter
27 Yemen port
28 Hoarse cough
29 "___ All Ye Faithful"
30 ___ Flanders (*The Simpsons* character)
31 Ivan of tennis
32 Musical form developed by Chopin and Liszt
33 Goal, briefly
36 Tummy muscles
38 Pasty Hawaiian finger-food dishes
39 *Dateline* network
42 One of Santa's reindeer
43 Short-hop commuter plane
44 Mother-of-pearl source
46 Royal crown
47 *Moby Dick* captain
50 Humid
51 Lotion additive
52 Rub dry
54 Nile vipers
56 Canter or trot
57 Singer Guthrie
58 Snake-infested garden
60 Asner and McMahon
62 All the rage

HINT: Some clues in harder puzzles use alliteration with imagery to evoke a mental picture with few words. An example is 5 Down. See puzzle 43 for another helpful hint.

#7: 69A = ROUES

Critical Review   by Ed Early

50

Presenting a short criticism by the author of *The Devil's Dictionary*. We hope you don't think it applies to this collection.

ACROSS

1 "___ the Season..."
4 Made a grating sound
10 Make a scene
13 MD mil. inst.
15 Breathe out
16 Promissory note of a sort
17 With 37 Across and 61 Across, terse criticism by 48 Down
19 Hold up
20 Former *SNL* player Cheri ___
21 Beatles song
23 Seldom if ever
25 MS-___ (Windows precursor)
26 Skunk's defense
29 S.A.T. takers
30 Porky or Petunia of cartoons
32 Ruling, as a queen
34 Chicken buy
36 U.S. Grant's adversary
37 See 17 Across
40 Mr. ___ (man of unquestioned integrity)
42 They just barely beat deuces
43 Rodent used as a pet or in research
46 *Golden Girl* Arthur
47 Org. for lawyers
50 Watch for the cops, maybe
51 Wyo. neighbor
53 Early boxing-card bout, commonly
55 Exerted a counterforce
58 Colorado's ___ Park
59 Hawaiian food made from taro
61 See 17 Across
63 Dracula's alter ego
64 Reach a destination
65 Resort on the French Riviera
66 Farm enclosure
67 Took home
68 Syst. of faith

DOWN

1 Private teachers
2 Hoffman–Beatty film flop
3 Contemptuous looks
4 Gun the engine
5 ___ Foley (Eddie Murphy's *Beverly Hills Cop* role)
6 Reduce to tatters
7 Congregation leader
8 Kay Thompson's brat, in a 1955 story
9 Adroit
10 Big terrier
11 Pigeon English?
12 Place for a rubber duckie
14 Zoning unit
18 Medium for Matisse
22 Major errors
24 Sharp barks
27 Showstopper in the show *A Chorus Line*
28 Map abbr.
31 Sailor, slangily
33 Uncertainty
34 Morally pure
35 "___ to worry!"
37 Recklessness
38 Eyeball, for example
39 Hold on to
40 When doubled, a dance
41 Testing place, familiarly
44 Audience request
45 Conversational comeback
47 Bright star 16 light-years away
48 Quoted cynical author Ambrose ___
49 Lager-style beer from Holland
52 Prove appropriate to
54 Basic Cable sports channel
56 ___ end (finished)
57 Humor columnist Barry
59 *Nova* outlet
60 Bit of horse feed
62 Blushing

HINT: Clues such as 11 Down, that end in a question mark, often signal a mild pun or other misleading idea. If you think about the clue long enough, the intention should become clear. See puzzle 25 for another hint. We hope you enjoyed this volume of *Casual Crosswords*.

#25: 61A = JUUU

51 Self-Description   by Mel Rosen

It's all about...itself! Have fun.

ACROSS

1 Major armed conflict
4 Reacts to a pun, perhaps
10 Nothing more than
14 Pie ___ mode (2 words)
15 Band with a heavy beat
16 Highest cards
17 The answer you're filling in right now (2 words)
20 Twelve or under
21 Actor Patrick ___ (John Steed on The Avengers)
22 Homer hitter Sammy
23 "___ Freedom Ring"
24 "That hurt!" shouts
25 First Greek letter
29 Sleeve filler
31 The Drew Carey Show network
34 Plastic food wrap brand
35 Self-confidence
38 What you're solving right now (2 words)

41 Nescafé rival
42 "...to fetch ___ of water" (2 words)
43 Hurricane center
44 Airline to Sweden
45 Sermon on the ___
46 Prior to, poetically
48 Family nickname
50 Ambassadorial fashion accessory
54 Checkpoint Charlie city
56 Two Kettles in rural films of the 1940s and 1950s (3 words)
59 What this 38 Across has, overall (2 words, hyphenated)
62 Roulette bet

63 Land, as a fish (2 words)
64 Back muscle, for short
65 Hornet's home
66 Threatening phrase (2 words)
67 Do one's best at something

DOWN

1 Slender-waisted insects
2 Oldsmobile introduced in 1999
3 Four-star reviews
4 Vanished
5 Mechanical learning process
6 Warning sign
7 Tarzan, the ___ Man

8 One of the Bobbsey twins, in children's literature
9 Embarrass
10 "I Need to Know" singer ___ Anthony
11 Scrimp
12 Fix an open seam
13 Curvy letters
18 Airport listing, for short
19 Launch
23 Oscar winning actor Martin ___
25 Hired killer
26 What a criminal breaks
27 Charity golf tournaments, commonly (hyphenated)
28 Horn-honking Marx brother
30 Peri Gilpin's Frasier character

31 Their capacities are measured in BTUs (abbr.)
32 Lingerie purchase
33 Saves
36 Like a fox
37 Wide shoe designation
39 Jamaican music
40 Seamstress's fastener
46 Buddy ___ of The Beverly Hillbillies
47 Superman portrayer Christopher ___
49 Emcee's task
50 NBC comedy skit show, briefly
51 One never seen in "Peanuts"
52 Javelin or harpoon
53 Reckless
55 Ash Wednesday follower
56 Building where grain is ground into flour
57 Baseline on a graph
58 Reason to use Stridex
60 "___ dern tootin'!"
61 "Get it?"

HINT: If the answer to 1 Across doesn't come to mind when you first look at it, start somewhere else. An easier place to get started is often a "fill-in-the-blank" clue, such as 42 Across or 45 Across. For a free answer, see the box alongside puzzle 57.

#93: 50D = ECOLE

52

Applause! Applause!   by Fran & Lou Sabin

Once you spot the important word that is repeated in all the long answers, you should be well on your way.

ACROSS

1 Israeli dance
5 Ancient Celtic priest
10 Seaweed
14 Sermon closing
15 "Whoopee!"
16 Barker with flippers
17 Item of clothing passed from older to younger children (*hyphenated*)
19 Minor tantrum
20 Nighttime noise-maker
21 Presented (*2 words*)
23 Actress ___ Lanchester
25 Chows down
26 Times gone by
29 Shoshonean Indian
32 Russian rulers
35 Be next to

36 "Superstition" singer ___ Wonder
38 ___ Haw (corny variety series)
39 ___ Garr of *Tootsie*
40 Leading
41 ___ Modern (new London gallery)
42 Follower (suffix)
43 DiCaprio and Redford
44 Bagnold who wrote *National Velvet*
45 Actor Milo ___
47 Deli bread
48 Yields
49 Actor ___ Alda
51 Read quickly
53 Boxers' trainers
57 Lassoes
61 Merry ___ England

62 Distributing (*2 words*)
64 AOL subscriber, for example
65 ___ Janeiro (*2 words*)
66 Singer ___ James
67 Gats, in corny gangster films
68 Without a wife or husband
69 Fans do it

DOWN

1 Words of surprise
2 Sultanate whose capital is Muscat
3 Nevada gambling city
4 Mario of auto racing fame
5 Hair colorists
6 "Real cool!"

7 "Here comes trouble!" (*hyphenated*)
8 Neighbor of Nebraska
9 Poet who wrote "Death be not proud"
10 Good looks, brains, money, and so forth
11 Helps with work (*3 words*)
12 Gallop or canter
13 Chorus voice
18 Brooks and Gibson of film
22 June 25, for example
24 Book writer
26 Barbecue setting, perhaps
27 Helps pull a heist
28 Like a Gold Glove fielder (*hyphenated*)

30 Mighty small
31 Gets away from
33 Fix a knot
34 Bird food
36 ___ Mineo of *Exodus*
37 Dogtags or name tags (abbr.)
41 Adolescent
43 False god
46 Senior citizens
48 No. 1 son
50 India's first prime minister, Jawaharlal ___
52 Shed a tear
53 3600 seconds
54 In addition
55 Game delay cause
56 Winter forecast
58 Dorothy's dog
59 Family vehicle
60 RBI or ERA
63 Ike's initials

HINT: At 60 Down: An abbreviation in a clue is likely to signal an abbreviation or a short form of a word in an answer. Puzzle 64's page has another answer for you.

#86: 20A = NIM

No Theme   by Gail Grabowski

53

Not every puzzle needs a theme. This one relies on words and phrases you probably know.

ACROSS

1 Filmdom's ___ Sharif
5 Authoritative decree
10 Potato, slangily
14 Tardy
15 Manly, in Mexico
16 In addition
17 "Separate checks, please" date (*2 words*)
19 Beyond
20 Madonna film role
21 ___ St. Vincent Millay
22 Ancient Greek instrument
23 Narrate
25 Gold Rush stake
27 Panther or puma
30 Sleeper's sound
33 Imitate
36 Heckler's holler
37 Filet ___
38 Abbr. on a "Wanted" poster
39 Tennis game
41 Inventor ___ Whitney
42 Slim, like shoes
44 Rock's ___ Zeppelin
45 Colored, as hair
46 Little kids
47 Small woman's size
49 Military Academy freshman
51 High-priced appetizer
55 Jazz singer ___ Fitzgerald
57 Picnic pests
60 Vocalist ___ Ronstadt
61 Persuade
62 Airhead (*2 words*)
64 Pilaf ingredient
65 Really worry (*2 words*)
66 Prefix with phone or marketer
67 Secondhand, as a car
68 Shuts forcefully
69 Previous partners

DOWN

1 More mature
2 Purple color
3 Homeowner's storage area
4 Make right
5 CPR pro
6 Have the nerve
7 Chilled, as champagne
8 By ___ (accidentally)
9 Add up
10 Young tree
11 Cash for 35 Down
12 Khrushchev's country (abbr.)
13 Be overly affectionate toward, with "on"
18 Abhor
24 Arm joint
26 Garage sale words (*2 words*)
28 Debtor's letters
29 Stately
31 Actor's part
32 Author ___ Bagnold
33 "I ___ Stop Loving You"
34 Give a thumbs up
35 $350 Monopoly property
37 Military first-aid staffer
39 Prescription quantity
40 Allow
43 Laid-back
45 Wander off the beaten path
47 Someone to write to regularly (*2 words*)
48 Locker room powder
50 Military installations
52 Alphabetical list in a book
53 Fred Astaire's sister
54 Fixed charges
55 Beige color
56 Dot and Ditto's mom, in the comics
58 "Goodbye," in London (*2 words*)
59 Confidence game
63 Sci-fi invaders

HINT: Regarding 1 Down: If a clue starts with the word "more," chances are good the answer ends in ER. For an even bigger hint, see puzzle 71's page.

54A = ABSCAM
#79:

54 Little Poems   by Norma Steinberg

A common type of puzzle theme involves phrases with rhyming words. Here's a case in point.

ACROSS

1 Explorer Vasco da ___
5 One way to pay
9 Chevrolet van brand
14 Second word in many fairy tales
15 "Do ___ others as..."
16 AFL-CIO member
17 Etna outpouring
18 AAA offerings (abbr.)
19 "The Inferno" poet
20 Major evening television programming period (2 words)
22 Religious ceremonies
23 Navigates
24 Alexander Hamilton's downfall
26 Pitcher Nolan ___
29 Logo
33 Most Bahrainis
37 Merchandising event
39 Intern
40 Determination
41 Puts in the bank
42 Nuptial vows (2 words)
43 ___ mater
44 Unwrap
45 Warning signal
46 Unquestioningly obedient followers (hyphenated)
48 Profit and ___ statement
50 Therefore
52 Miffed
57 Last Greek letter
60 Everyone's ethical contribution (2 words)
63 Lorenzo ___ of Final Impact
64 Conflagration
65 Singer-songwriter ___ Redding
66 Dirt
67 Actress ___ Falco
68 Choose
69 Behaved
70 Grate
71 Black and Caspian

DOWN

1 Swallows whole
2 Separated
3 Flick
4 "What's in ___?" (Juliet's question, 2 words)
5 Girl's bow
6 Against
7 Flower support
8 Watered the garden
9 ___ Hepburn of film fame
10 Letters through the Post Office (2 words)
11 Color
12 Memorization by repetition
13 Singles
21 Goofs up
25 Functions
27 "NOW!" (abbr.)
28 Belly-button
30 Wait
31 Fragrance
32 In case
33 Out of town
34 Annoy
35 Charity
36 Mutual finger-pointing (2 words)
38 Letterman's contemporary
41 Melody
45 Seller's warning (2 words)
47 Backspaced over
49 Adaptation co-star Meryl ___
51 Proposal
53 Words that follow karate and pork
54 Newscaster ___ Couric
55 ___ Kane (Susan Lucci's longtime soap role)
56 Cubicle furniture
57 Gymnast ___ Korbut
58 Artist ___ Chagall
59 Give forth
61 Verdi heroine
62 Spring flower

HINT: At 71 Across: If a clue includes two proper names, the answer is probably a plural proper name that either goes before or after the names in the clue. In this case, it goes after. There's a giveaway answer alongside puzzle 78.

#72: 37A = BAER

Relatively Speaking   by Bernice Gordon

55

In this puzzle the long answers all involve family members.

ACROSS

1 ___ Raton, Florida
5 Storage buildings
10 Remote
13 Commotions
14 Slip-on garment
15 Town in Texas
16 Abundant supply (2 words)
18 Volcano in Sicily
19 Weapon stores
20 Large bird whose mate has eyespots on its tail
22 "___ the season to be jolly"
23 Look (at) with purpose
24 Item of value on a balance sheet
27 Sacrificed oneself for a cause
30 Monastery officer
31 Where to gather honey
32 Menlo Park inventor's monogram
33 Organization (abbr.)
34 Discloses everything
35 Get out of bed
36 Sodom survivor
37 Funnyman Soupy
38 More sporting
39 Unfair (hyphenated)
41 Like many modern stadiums
42 All prepared
43 ___ Paulo, Brazil
44 "What ___!" ("Too bad!"; 2 words)
46 Savior-kings
51 Weaver's apparatus
52 1938 film with Ronald Reagan (2 words)
54 Devious maneuver
55 Rich cake
56 Dull throb
57 The opposite of "even"
58 Mister, in Madrid
59 "Begin the Beguine" clarinet player Artie

DOWN

1 The Crimson Tide, familiarly
2 Aroma
3 Barracks beds
4 Tennis's Arthur ___ Stadium
5 Country singer George ___
6 Boat bodies
7 Grandchild in the book of Genesis
8 Accomplished
9 Symbols of royalty
10 Old man, symbolically (2 words)
11 Teenager's skin problem
12 Multihued horse
15 Tired to the point of exhaustion
17 Come into a room
21 Enjoys a meal
23 Puts money away for a rainy day
24 Firebug's crime
25 Ladies' group
26 Junior
27 Bogged down
28 Alleviated
29 Bambi, for one
30 ___ Alto, California
31 Author of Roots
34 Uncollectable IOUs (2 words)
35 Ewe's mate
37 The King and I country
38 Layer of golden eggs, so the story goes
40 Sordid
41 One of Santa's reindeer
43 Altercation (hyphenated)
44 Ken-L Ration alternative
45 Auctioneer's final word
46 Break of day
47 Gershwin and Levin
48 St. Louis landmark
49 "Now, that's funny!" (2 words)
50 Fret
53 Fish eggs

HINT: That inventor at 32 Across is probably the best-known of all American inventors. See the box next to puzzle 85 for a free answer.

#65:
50A = HARRIMAN

A Sense of Direction   by Alan Olschwang

56

The long across answers contain words describing their locations in the grid.

ACROSS
1 Radiate
5 Farm measure
9 Accumulate
14 About 1/6 inch, to a printer
15 Yuletide refrain
16 Ship of 1492
17 False god
18 Featured comics, in burlesque (2 words)
20 Movie theater
22 Deliver from sin
23 Antiquated (abbr.)
24 The Big Apple (abbr.)
25 Direction from Iowa to Illinois
27 Offensive hockey player (2 words)
33 Conflicts
36 "Float like a butterfly" boxer
37 Bedecks
38 Provo's state
39 Tropical eel
41 Concept embodying yin and yang
42 ___ acid
43 Early characters in *2001: A Space Odyssey*
44 Cloaklike raincoat
46 Corporal, for one (abbr.)
47 Autumn month (abbr.)
48 Having the support of law (3 words)
50 Desolate
52 Lawyer (abbr.)
53 General Lee's government (abbr.)
55 Versatile trucks, for short
58 Sprints
62 As low as one can go (2 words)
65 James ___ Jones
66 Utopian
67 Salad fish
68 Capital of Peru
69 Apply juice, as to a turkey
70 Middle East gulf
71 Weakness

DOWN
1 Like *The Iliad* in scope
2 Calf-length skirt
3 Double-clicked desktop item
4 Stars have it, presumably
5 Stomach aid
6 Dove sound
7 Workout tallies
8 Exile island for Napoleon
9 Sleep disorder
10 Soccer star ___ Hamm
11 Adding explanations to a text
12 Pierce with a dagger
13 Impudence
19 Declares
21 How Sinatra "did it," in a song (2 words)
26 Dog-paddled
27 Tibetan monks
28 Decide against a big wedding
29 Room warmers
30 "___ your life!" (2 words)
31 Endowment
32 Methuselah's father
34 Cowboy's milieu
35 Fire a derringer
40 Concerning (2 words)
42 Main artery
44 Kind of bean
45 Village leader
49 In a class by ___
51 Moscow monetary unit
53 Infant's bed
54 Soft drink
56 1993 Rock and Roll Hall of Fame inductee James
57 Kind of poker
59 Ice shower
60 Humor columnist ___ Bombeck
61 Chopped cabbage side dish
63 Krazy ___ of the comics
64 Indivisible

HINT: You might initially write the wrong third letter in the answer at 26 Down, but the answer for 38 Across will set you straight. The tip here is: Don't fixate on what might be a wrong entry. See puzzle 92's page for another hint.

Tootsy Talk   by Diane C. Baldwin

The title refers to baby talk for a certain part of the body.

ACROSS

1 Most worthwhile
5 Barbershop item
9 Some baseball sacrifices
14 Limburger cheese characteristic
15 All done
16 Chemically nonreactive
17 Husband's spouse
18 Light green legume
19 Lined up the cross hairs
20 Keeps alert (*4 words*)
23 Indignation
24 Two-finger sign
25 Tungsten and nickel, for example
29 Trudge wearily
31 Wisecracking sitcom waitress at Mel's Diner
34 Davy Crockett's last stand
35 Tough journey
36 Opera highlight
37 Arises (*4 words*)
40 Broad-minded
41 Knocks one's socks off
42 Comic's reward
43 Actor ___ Beatty
44 Become insipid
45 Multitudes
46 "The Greatest" boxer
47 Tumbling cushion
48 Is stubborn (*4 words*)
57 Make a speech
58 Dozes off
59 Colonel Mustard's game
60 African country or river
61 Hard work
62 Word before "Who goes there?"
63 Former Russian despots
64 In the past
65 Burden

DOWN

1 Gift-wrapping toppers
2 Clean up a manuscript
3 Upholstered seat
4 Low card
5 Marks with crayons
6 Sheeplike
7 Written reminder
8 Cereal fiber
9 Unfair
10 Join forces
11 Finding ___ (animated blockbuster)
12 Shoe preserver
13 Benchmarks (abbr.)
21 Farm storage sites
22 Conjure up
25 Georgia city
26 Get hitched on the sly
27 Domesticated
28 "You said it!"
29 ___ car (police vehicle)
30 Camera's eye
31 Pioneering psychoanalyst
32 Feudal landholder
33 Expletives
35 Hammer or saw
36 Distant
38 Sawyer's creator
39 The sin of laziness
44 Pinching implements
45 Give a hard time to
46 Fall bloom
47 Corpsman
48 "___ Be Cruel"
49 Showy flower
50 Infatuated
51 Aware of
52 Lunch hour
53 Canyon sound
54 Panache
55 Dilly
56 Tennis match divisions

HINT: If a clue is written like a bit of dialogue (as at 28 Down), the answer must also be something you might say. There's a free answer alongside puzzle 99.

#51: 15A = OOMPAH

58

B-Hive   by Norma Steinberg

Alliteration is a common building block for crossword themes. Here's a typical example, with a big hint in the title.

ACROSS

1 Picture book
6 "Eureka!" moments
10 "Oh, why not!"
14 March composer John Philip ___
15 Separate
16 Way out
17 "Rags to riches" author Horatio ___
18 Broadway offering
19 Columbus's smallest ship
20 Faux ___ (blunder)
21 Former senator and retired basketball star (*2 words*)
24 Lowest part of a ship's hull
26 Worry too much
27 Oliver Hardy's film partner, Stan ___
29 Of sound mind
31 Annapolis monogram
32 October birthstone
34 Typical domestic cat
39 Faxed
40 Synthetic fabric
42 Clinton's vice president
43 Isaac who composed the theme from *Shaft*
45 Spreadable substitute
46 Cain's victim
47 Posing no problem
49 Of the clan
51 Soak up
55 Stadium
56 *The Fabulous Baker Boys* co-star (*2 words*)
59 Pioneering color TV brand
62 Garfunkel and Linkletter
63 Fragrance
64 Spoken for
66 Skirt opening
67 Sheryl Crow's "___ Wanna Do" (*2 words*)
68 Happening
69 Egg layers
70 Profound
71 Pub game

DOWN

1 "At once!" (abbr.)
2 *Damn Yankees* heroine
3 Elmer Fudd's quarry (*2 words*)
4 ___ only as directed
5 Michelangelo's sculpting medium
6 Eve's offer to Adam
7 Corridor
8 Saudi, for one
9 *Sophie's Choice* author William ___
10 Gives temporarily
11 Napoleon's sentence
12 Prongs
13 Corset stiffeners
22 Tundra shelter
23 Aid, as in a heist
25 Furious
27 Lavish
28 Sailing
29 Oscar winning actress ___ Field
30 Skin lotion ingredient
33 Experts
35 At least twice
36 *The Price Is Right* host (*2 words*)
37 La ___ Tar Pits
38 Holler
41 ___ Dame
44 Balkan resident
48 In foreign lands
50 Took a breather
51 Embarrass
52 "Uncle Miltie"
53 Lustrous fabric
54 Removes from office
55 "Get ___!" ("Calm down!", *2 words*)
57 Run in neutral
58 Runner-up in 1996
60 Penny
61 Unwelcome houseguests
65 Actress ___ Gardner

HINT: If you don't know an answer from just the given clue (which might be the case at 19 Across), sometimes there is only one possible answer that's the right length to fit in the crossword grid. Puzzle 56 has another hint for you.

59

Crib Notes   by Mel Kenworthy

Here's another example of the common theme idea of repeating a single word in several phrases.

ACROSS

1 Yaks
5 Brainy
10 Touch
14 Where China and Vietnam are
15 Manly, in Mexico
16 Urn
17 Tot minder
19 Mountain goat
20 Letter, in the New Testament
21 Psychiatrist
23 Suffix with "ballad" or "auction"
24 Mideast resident
25 Macaroni noodles
29 "Smooth Operator" singer
31 How some stocks trade (abbr.)
34 Brings up, as a child
35 Sings without backup
36 "So there you are!"
37 Feeling you get about someone, informally
38 Yuletide candy shapes
39 Warning sign
40 Like hazardous winter roads
41 Providing a prompt
42 Reagan confidant Ed ___
43 Old horse
44 Friendly nation
45 Jim ___ of The Mask
46 Ottawa-based law enforcement group (abbr.)
48 Cigarette ingredient
49 Rumor
52 Problem on Florida's Gulf beaches (2 words)

57 Author ___ Rice, who writes about vampires
58 Younger sibling (2 words)
60 Divining devices
61 Alpaca's cousin
62 ___-mell
63 "Hey, there!"
64 Bugs bugger ___ Fudd
65 Henchman to Captain Hook

DOWN

1 ___ Kaplan of old sitcoms
2 Quickly, on memos
3 Netanyahu of Israel, familiarly
4 Comes out with
5 Happy-face features
6 Alma ___
7 Perform
8 Sabrina the Teenage Witch costar Caroline ___
9 Whirlwinds
10 City near Madrid
11 Someone born in the late 1940s (2 words)
12 Applications
13 Sermon source
18 One-dish meals
22 Greek war god
25 Watergate-period senator Sam ___
26 Nikon competitor
27 Some pianos (2 words)
28 Mineral source
29 Kiddo
30 Without ___ to stand on (2 words)
32 "___ Boots Are Made for Walkin'" (Nancy Sinatra oldie)

33 Brooklyn's ___ Island
35 Spinnaker or jib
38 Blameworthy
39 "___ the land of the free..."
41 Engine parts
42 ___ Gras
45 Salad type
47 Wave top
48 Possible answer to a dare (2 words)
49 Angelic instrument
50 The Dukes of Hazzard character
51 Southern plural pronoun
53 Cookbook amounts (abbr.)
54 Agenda part
55 Editor's removal mark
56 Lawyer-author ___ Stanley Gardner
59 Chef Emeril's exclamation

HINT: If the name at 3 Down doesn't pop quickly to mind, it may help to know that Swedish actress Andersson, who appeared in many Ingmar Bergman films, has the same first name. For more help, see puzzle 63.

GABS SMART ABUT
ASIA MACHO VASE
BABYSITTER BEX
EPISTLE ANALYST
EER ARAB
ELBOWS SADO OTC
REARS SOLOS OHIO
VIBE CANES MEN
ICY CUING MEESE
NAG ALLY CARREY
RCMP TAR
HEARSAY REDTIDE
ANNE BABYSISTER
RODS LLAMA PELL
SOT ELMER SMEE

60 Now Playing   by Nancy Kavanaugh

Each long phrase starts with a word that happens to be a film genre.

ACROSS
1 Costa ___
5 *American* ___ (Fox talent-search show)
9 ___ Antoinette
14 Mideast sultanate
15 Opposite of "yep"
16 Bad smells
17 Share a border with
18 Dog pest
19 Carries
20 Child's party game (*2 words*)
23 Catch a glimpse of
24 Some hospital workers (abbr.)
25 Fish eggs
26 Captain Jean-___ Picard (*Star Trek: The Next Generation* role)

27 Never been used (*hyphenated*)
32 Stand-up's milieu (*2 words*)
36 Bullring cheer
37 Have ___ (nibble; *2 words*)
38 "___ in apple" (*2 words*)
39 Rhea Perlman's *Cheers* character
41 "Help!" at sea
42 People wonder about him (*2 words*)
44 Most irritable
47 Word before a maiden name
48 Photographic blowup (abbr.)
49 Roth ___ (nest egg)
50 Stomach muscles, informally
53 Breakfast dish (*2 words*)

57 Find fault with
59 Ballerina skirt
60 Robe for a *Julius Caesar* actor
61 Brimless Special Forces cap
62 Assist a criminal
63 Action-movie star Jackie ___
64 Transmits
65 Singer ___ Lovett
66 Round of applause

DOWN
1 Wanders
2 Permeate
3 Make happen
4 One who is opposed
5 Earliest childhood
6 Barbie and Ken
7 International oil group (abbr.)

8 First wife of Jacob
9 Movement
10 Loved
11 Goes bad
12 Wrath
13 Superman's symbol
21 Unrefined
22 Middle Easterner
26 Tennis server's do-over
27 Explosion
28 Oxidation
29 George Wendt's *Cheers* character
30 Jazz singer ___ Fitzgerald
31 Move to solid food
32 Unfortunate sight at the ski lodge
33 Orchestral "tuning fork"
34 Young lady

35 Small, low islands
39 Fatty part of milk
40 A vote for
42 Become liquid
43 On the way (*2 words*)
45 Was full of, with "with"
46 City maps, often
49 Computer chip maker
50 Hello, at a luau
51 Started
52 Get up from a chair
53 Admonish
54 And others, in a list (abbr., *2 words*)
55 Red gemstone
56 Do artistic work with acid
57 Ammo for some air rifles
58 Golfer ___ Trevino

HINT: Regarding 47 Across: the word is French for "born." See puzzle 70 for another, bigger hint.

#80: 13D = STET

61

A Visit to the Clothing Store   by Diane C. Baldwin

The original title for this puzzle was "Keeping Up Appearances." See which one makes more sense.

ACROSS

1 Computer graphic image
5 Meal, informally
9 Mexican mister
14 Slangy denial
15 Diner food
16 Conjure up
17 Blacken on the grill
18 Bit of sea-bound land
19 Signs of remorse
20 "Prepare for a shock!" (5 words)
23 Buck's mate
24 Make a choice
25 Brandishes
29 ___ out (disappoints)
31 Use an armchair
34 Blacksmith item
35 File for scraping
36 Strong wind
37 "Be patient!" (4 words)
40 Shows fallibility
41 Marina structure
42 Discontinue
43 Sow's shelter
44 Sailboat power
45 Official document seal
46 ___ Francisco
47 Personal enemy
48 "Brace for adversity!" (3 words)
57 Love with a passion
58 Deserve by one's efforts
59 Hawaiian feast
60 More modern
61 Clothed
62 Colored eye part
63 Lillle Orphan Annie's dog
64 Piano ivories
65 Sausage meat, often

DOWN

1 Part of a foot
2 Variety of salmon
3 Translucent gem
4 School misfit
5 Cotton pants
6 Hurriedness
7 Norway's capital
8 Cheesemaking leftover
9 Arrangements
10 Navratilova foe
11 Dictionary writer ___ Webster
12 Gumbo ingredient
13 Musical pause
21 In a strange manner
22 Pizzazz
25 Boats' water trails
26 Unmoving
27 Each and all
28 "Read my ___!"
29 Made public
30 Former superpower (abbr.)
31 Old Nick
32 "How can ___?" (2 words)
33 Belief or dogma
35 Devastation
36 Diver Louganis
38 Speak one's mind
39 More frosty
44 Overly diluted
45 Auditory sensations
46 Tatter
47 Brief invasion
48 Sunbathing mementos
49 Creative spark
50 Ball garment
51 Place for an ascot
52 Ivy League school
53 Radar screen image
54 Continental currency
55 Hibernation spot
56 Walrus tooth

62

Have a Bawl   by Sarah Keller

That's not a typographical error in the puzzle's title. Here are some appropriate songs for you.

ACROSS

1 "Someone's at the door" signal
5 Take it easy
9 Oscar or Emmy, e.g.
14 Dog in "Garfield" comics
15 Reverberate
16 Movie critic ___ Ebert
17 Green citrus fruit
18 Male pig
19 Swap
20 Hit for Little Anthony and the Imperials (*4 words*)
23 No longer an amateur
24 Chianti color
25 Oatmeal cookie bit
29 Wharf's cousin
31 Guitar innovator ___ Paul

34 Grace of *Will and Grace*
35 "What's a girl ___?" (*2 words*)
36 Cotton bundle
37 Hit torch song of 1932 (*4 words*)
40 Loll around
41 Radio operators
42 Raring to go
43 Fast flying plane (abbr.)
44 Young lady
45 Makes changes to
46 Dumbo's "wing"
47 Excitement
48 Hit for Frankie Valli and the Four Seasons (*4 words*)
57 Dress up
58 Country singer ___ Jackson
59 Spread in a tub

60 Mutineer
61 Star of Bethlehem followers
62 Wedding cake feature
63 Disagreeable
64 Chimps and such
65 Shoe bottom

DOWN

1 It comes out of the blue
2 ___ Falco of *The Sopranos*
3 Succotash bean
4 Evil glance
5 Like some Christians
6 ___ Lodge motel chain
7 Not the real thing
8 Conservative Party member in Canada

9 More pretentious
10 Word before Series or Cup
11 "I Got ___ in Kalamazoo" (*2 words*)
12 Upgrade the decor
13 Selected, as straws
21 Nixon's first vice president ___ Agnew
22 Before surgery, for short
25 Lou ___ of blues and pop
26 "So long, señor"
27 ___ ease (uncomfortable; *2 words*)
28 "To thine own ___ be true"
29 Literary verses
30 "Beware the ___ of March"

31 Sweatshirt size
32 ___ Fudd of cartoons
33 Crystal ball consultants
35 " ___ the night before..."
36 Sailing vessel
38 Blender sound
39 Serious offender
44 For the most part
45 Handsome guy
46 Plumed bird
47 Proverb
48 "Were you raised in a ___?"
49 Concept
50 Large sums
51 Buddhist title
52 Kind of shot, in hockey
53 Little tykes
54 Advertising prize
55 Film spool
56 Time long past

HINT: At 37 Across: A torch song is just a sentimental pop love song. You'll find a bigger hint in the box next to puzzle 84.

63 Thoroughfares by Bernice Gordon

The last word in each phrase is the relevant element here.

ACROSS

1 ___ & Span (household cleanser)
5 Devoured fully (2 words)
10 Problematical
14 Opera about an Ethiopian slave girl
15 Inherently (2 words)
16 Anger
17 Thoroughfare in the center of town (2 words)
19 ___ Good Men (2 words)
20 Mimics
21 Hall of Fame quarterback Johnny ___
23 Emphasize
25 Dough filled with potatoes
26 Apply holy oil to
27 Natives of Santiago
30 Clad like a judge
31 Nepalese monks
32 Panel truck's cousin
33 Eon parts
34 Words for actors
35 Toy building brick brand
36 Japanese computer company (abbr.)
37 High temperature
38 Juicy fruit
39 Places for old documents
41 Formal French dance
42 Rowed
43 Made a quick move, as with a sword
44 Tiny amount
46 Spine-tingling
47 Greek Cupid
48 Make-out spot (2 words)
53 Sincere
54 Audrey's character in My Fair Lady
55 Property claim
56 Secret writing
57 Put off
58 Shortstop/slugger, in headlines (hyphenated)

DOWN

1 America's Uncle ___
2 Entertainer ___ Zadora
3 First name in Ugandan terrorism
4 Yellow singing birds
5 Most fitting
6 Districts (abbr.)
7 "___ Tu" (1974 hit by Mocedades)
8 Manipulate
9 Ornamental plants with funnel-shaped blossoms
10 Poker declaration (2 words)
11 Easter Parade locale (2 words)
12 Pet's pest
13 Trees used for archers' bows
18 Throw dough around
22 Guitar star Lofgren
23 One who sleeps soundly?
24 Novel by Erskine Caldwell (2 words)
25 ___ Rouge (Communist force in Cambodia)
26 Sports facility
27 Walking sticks
28 Harped on endlessly
29 Highbrow
31 Dwelt
34 Evened off
35 Stage and film Dracula portrayer Frank ___
37 Arsonist's "creation"
38 Short skirts
40 Argument
41 Bill ___ of Groundhog Day
43 Entertainment Tonight host ___ Gibbons
44 Grand Marquis, in car lingo
45 After-school snack
46 Satanic
49 Corrida cheer
50 Televise
51 Keanu's The Matrix character
52 Stopping point

HINT: The ballplayer at 58 Across is one of the highest paid players ever. In 2004 he began playing for the New York Yankees. See puzzle 91's page for another hint.

64 Now Hear This!   by Diane C. Baldwin

Each phrase answer begins with a word describing a way to utter something.

ACROSS
1 "Oh, dear!"
5 Animal companions
9 Hollywood profession
14 Trouser adjunct
15 Workout memento
16 Beef classification
17 New Haven university
18 Fired off
19 Needed healing
20 Doesn't mince words (*2 words*)
22 Soon-to-be adults
23 Stand in the way of
24 Expressions of delight
26 Steep, rugged cliff
29 Country roads
33 Egg-beating utensil
37 Wan
39 Instrument in the reed section
40 Verdi opera
41 Pass along
42 Gospel writer
43 Western author Zane ___
44 Chops down
45 Chasing
46 Type of ticket
48 Prepare prunes, for example
50 Egg on
52 Reason behind behavior
57 Food from heaven, in Exodus
60 Can't shut up (*2 words*)
63 Vertical
64 Butter substitute
65 Surprise attack
66 Weighing device
67 Shrimp snares
68 Tortoise-hare affair
69 Destroy documents
70 Audible votes
71 Passed with flying colors

DOWN
1 Bottomless pit
2 Moved like a gazelle
3 Bowling place
4 Teakettle vapor
5 Quarterback, often
6 Canyon sound
7 You, to a Quaker
8 Brouhaha (*hyphenated*)
9 Unconcern
10 Gives a false alarm (*2 words*)
11 Shower stall square
12 Foreshadowing
13 Side in the game of checkers
21 Boot a ball
25 Follow orders
27 Zenith
28 Strong winds
30 Share a border with
31 Oxen coupler
32 Visionary
33 Doggie greetings
34 Add to the payroll
35 Creative notion
36 Surrenders (*2 words*)
38 Linger on
41 "You ___?" (butler's line)
45 G.I. on the lam (abbr.)
47 Made a speech
49 Raise in relief
51 Dark, heavy wood
53 ___ firma
54 Sir ___ Newton
55 Diva's pride
56 Through
57 Slob's creation
58 Foot part
59 Close at hand
61 On the safe side, at sea
62 ___ carotene

HINT: There are two logical answers for the clue at 7 Down. If one doesn't work, try the other. The tip here is: Don't be afraid to backtrack and try another approach. There's another hint for you at puzzle 98.

A Bit of S&M?   by Holden Baker

The title refers to the initial letters of the words in the long phrases. Surely you didn't think...?

ACROSS

1 Strikebreaker
5 Wed in secret
10 Now-grounded fast passenger planes (abbr.)
14 Ticklish doll
15 *Everybody ___ Raymond*
16 Persistent pain
17 "Who is buried in Grant's ___?" (consolation prize question on *You Bet Your Life*)
18 Vote into office
19 "Stop, Dobbin!"
20 Where security traders work
23 Hockey Hall of Famer Bobby ___
24 "You ___ So Beautiful"
25 Winter, spring, summer, and autumn
27 Battle scene in 1066
32 Stanley Cup org.
33 Circle segment
34 Pigeon's park perch

37 "Famous" cookie maker
40 Prove durable
42 Separated
43 Pub missile
44 Cabbage kin
45 Renter, perhaps
47 Indianapolis's ___ Dome
48 Starfleet Academy graduate (abbr.)
50 U.S. diplomat and national political figure from the 1940s to the 1980s, William Averell ___
52 Vacation period (*2 words*)
56 College basketball tournament for those that don't make the NCAA (abbr.)
57 Self-importance

58 One-armed bandit (*2 words*)
64 *M*A*S*H* star Alan ___
66 Movie swashbuckler ___ Flynn
67 Served perfectly
68 Like most colleges and some dorms
69 Seat at the bar
70 Apple center
71 Cargo area on a ship
72 Any of eight English kings
73 Unknown writer (abbr.)

DOWN

1 Tennis units
2 Coagulate
3 Bullets and cannonballs
4 Small lynx
5 Pertaining to first principles or forces of nature

6 *Damn Yankees* vamp
7 Finished
8 Quick little kisses
9 First name in cosmetics
10 Tool with teeth
11 Oater love interest, traditionally
12 Garden sticker
13 Scorches
21 ___ Kristofferson of *Lone Star*
22 Beachcomber's shade
26 Roe-producing fish
27 Bird of prey
28 Academic field
29 Toy store airplane kit, maybe (*2 words*)
30 Stare open-mouthed
31 Cache

35 ___ Major (constellation with the Big Dipper)
36 Forever and ever
38 Puget sound whale
39 Laurel or Musial
41 ___ Russo of *Get Shorty*
46 "Tears In Heaven" singer ___ Clapton
49 Maritime distress signal
51 Home of Odysseus or Cornell
52 Instruct
53 Inuit domicile
54 Blood's partner
55 Strong point
59 Disney sci-fi film of 1982
60 Othello, the ___ of Venice
61 Desktop image
62 Sleuth ___ Wolfe
63 Genesis serpent's home
65 Put two and two together

HINT: That doll at 14 Across was highly sought after as a holiday gift a few years ago. Puzzle 55's page has more assistance.

#95: 27D = ATARI

66

F Troupe   by Randall J. Hartman

Here's another alliteration theme for you.

ACROSS
1 Unspecified amount
5 Kid around
9 Cuban export
14 "Once ___ a time..."
15 Skin cream ingredient
16 Carry a major crush on
17 Punjab princess
18 Image on a monitor
19 Mob scenes
20 Bedrock resident (2 words)
23 Hog's home
24 Scarlet
25 Chef's container
26 Newspaper's columnist page (hyphenated)
28 Read a bar code
30 NFL scores (abbr.)
33 Hold the same opinion

35 Marquee name
36 Merit
37 La Dolce Vita director (2 words)
40 Smell to high heaven
41 Few and far between
42 Parcel out
43 Bobby ___ of hockey fame
44 Sharp tug
45 List-shortening abbr. (2 words)
46 Many, many years
47 Winner of the "Thrilla in Manila"
48 401(k) alternative (abbr.)
51 Founder of Boys Town (2 words)
56 Maui greeting
57 Jai ___
58 Marker
59 Closet contents

60 Plant that can grow on trees
61 Suffix many say is politically incorrect
62 Strict
63 Under control
64 Former JFK planes (abbr.)

DOWN
1 Hangs ten
2 Dizzying pictures (2 words)
3 Payment issued by the post office (2 words)
4 City west of Tulsa
5 Locked up
6 1961 Charlton Heston movie (2 words)
7 Before long
8 Camper's shelter
9 Box
10 ___ box (TV)
11 Paid ruffian

12 ___ Johnson of Laugh-In
13 Hi-___ graphics
21 Less reserved
22 Save, as from embarrassment
27 Cheat in hide-and-seek
28 Bird some say brings babies
29 Bistro on the Champs Élysées
30 These turn red in a traffic jam
31 Connery "James Bond" film (2 words)
32 Huffy state
33 Bushy hair style
34 Actor Will ___ of The Waltons
35 Appendectomy reminder
36 Jazz singer ___ Fitzgerald

38 ___ Ryan (actress who played Granny in The Beverly Hillbillies)
39 The language of old Rome
44 Composer ___ Sebastian Bach
45 Julia's role in Seinfeld
46 No-longer-used anesthetic
47 Firebox transmittal
49 Singer Bonnie ___
50 Pays to play, in poker
51 Skim along
52 Top-drawer (hyphenated)
53 Ride for Huckleberry Finn
54 Insect that annoys dogs and cats
55 Unreturnable tennis serves
56 Capone and Hirt

HINT: The answer to 13 Down is a computer term. It's an informal shortening of a longer word, just as "Hi" is short for "High." See puzzle 62's page for a bigger hint.

#88: 48D = MAMIE

67 July Celebration by Mary Brindamour

This theme (or something very much like it) typically appears for a certain holiday. You can enjoy it now.

ACROSS

1 Imitator
5 Wading bird
9 "That's ridiculous!"
14 Libertine, like Casanova
15 Slam ___ (sure thing, especially in basketball)
16 Chopin exercise
17 Measure of firewood
18 ___ 500 Race
19 Fits of wrath
20 Someone who moves at a snail's pace
22 Dense woodland
23 Highly excited (2 words)
24 Crossword entry (abbr.)
25 ___ Hawkins Day
28 Lunch or dinner
30 On ___ with (equal to; 2 words)
34 Move rapidly and with great force
36 Where the United Nations headquarters is (abbr.)
37 Musical tone
38 Singer ___ Brickell
39 Audio complement
41 Per ___ (by the day)
42 Singer with star quality
43 Before, poetically
44 Capital of the Bahamas
46 Observed
47 Used the doorbell
49 Features of wineglasses
50 Period
52 Use crayons
54 Dances that originated in Cuba
57 Later parts of the day
61 Doctoral tests
62 "What's the big ___?"
63 Type of moss
64 Debate topic
65 Cigarette byproducts
66 Roof overhang
67 Minnesota claims to have 10,000 of them
68 "Auld Lang ___"
69 Eject, as lava

DOWN

1 Circle sections
2 Game requiring a cuestick
3 It replaced the lira in 2002
4 "The Fourth" colors (4 words)
5 Dunderhead
6 Foolish talk
7 "The Fourth" (2 words)
8 Upper atmosphere
9 Evita's surname
10 "The Fourth" design (3 words)
11 Enormous
12 Sidewalk stand drinks
13 Leader to the first trick in most bridge columns
21 Banana eater's discard
22 The Maltese ___
25 Storage buildings
26 Actor ___ Murphy of old war films
27 Get behind the wheel
29 Buccaneer's affirmative
31 Self-confidence
32 Col. "Hannibal" Smith's TV group (hyphenated)
33 Romulus's twin
35 Turns inside out
40 Roth ___ (nest egg)
45 "...for unto us ___ is given" (2 words)
48 Rule
51 Desert stopovers
53 Rent
54 Stir up
55 ___ Major ("bear" constellation)
56 Superhero's secret identity preserver
58 One of the tides
59 Donated
60 Do a slow burn
62 ___ a Wonderful Life

#81: 12D = BERET

68

Flag Day   by Norma Johnson

This puzzle uses essentially the same idea as the previous puzzle, but with a somewhat subtler result.

ACROSS
1 Squabble
5 Distress signal
10 Canine cries
14 Roof overhang
15 Storytelling Uncle
16 Ore source
17 Kuwaiti ruler
18 Big occasion
19 Little fruit pie
20 Crimson-cloaked girl in a fairy tale (3 words)
23 Comedienne DeGeneres
24 Stitch
25 Home for 40 Down
28 What a whole season of 24 spans
29 Sunrise direction
33 Accept a "golden handshake"

35 Become visible
37 Freudian subjects
38 Stereotypical useless auction item (2 words)
42 Egg on
43 More sappy
44 Take into custody
47 Eggy beverages
48 Sing-along syllable
51 Garden area
52 Top of a rating scale
54 More ticked off
56 Extremely exasperated (4 words)
61 Jai ___
63 "___ All Ye Faithful" (2 words)
64 Arabian Sea gulf

65 "Got ___?" (Dairy Council ad slogan)
66 Flu symptom
67 Jazz singer ___ Horne
68 Soccer legend
69 Allison and Tarkenton
70 Troop carriers of 6-6-44 (abbr.)

DOWN
1 Do a slow burn (2 words)
2 Actress ___ Anderson
3 In an enthusiastic way
4 ___ Haute, Indiana
5 Golfer ___ Couples
6 Son of Jacob and Leah

7 Prayer closer
8 Ladder steps
9 Queen of Persia, in the Bible
10 Kind of saxophone
11 Driver's aid, perhaps (2 words)
12 President before Truman (abbr.)
13 Firm
21 All thumbs
22 Have debts
26 Race pace
27 "O.K.!"
30 Copycat
31 Put in plants
32 Eagle's claw
34 Eye drop
35 Gofer
36 Seized sedan, briefly
38 Drained, with "out"

39 Newscast hosted by Chris Matthews
40 Resident of 25 Across
41 Steppenwolf author
42 Chatter
45 R-V connection
46 Start on the links
48 Swaps
49 Modern
50 Sports venues
53 More gracious
55 "___ the nerve!" (2 words)
57 Resembling
58 PBS science series
59 The Untouchables extras
60 Towel word
61 Roadie's responsibility
62 Falsification

HINT: At first glance, the clue at 45 Down may look like it involes a motor home, but that's not the case. For another hint, see puzzle 76's page.

#74: 18A = POMP

69 Every Day in Every Way... by Norma Steinberg

The puzzle's title refers to a self-improvement assertion. An implied progression starts each theme answer.

ACROSS

1 Severe
6 Theatrical group
10 Club sandwiches, commonly
14 Nebraska city
15 Saxophone range
16 Thin as a ___
17 Muggy
18 Feed the hogs
19 Intern
20 ___-friendly
21 ___ boy (favorite; hyphenated)
23 Trusted guide
25 Jazz flute player Herbie ___
26 Professional charges
29 Ivory and Eiffel
33 De Niro/ Pesci flick
38 Skin cream ingredient
39 General ___ Bradley
40 "___ of a gun!"
41 Window ledge
42 Richard ___ of Chicago
43 Wife, some say (2 words)
46 Marked down (2 words)
48 Bee home
49 ___ Lisa
51 But (for)
56 Very popular book
61 Angelic headpiece
62 Nobelist ___ Wiesel
63 ___ on the floor (car shift option)
64 Comforter
65 ___ mater
66 Long division word
67 Vicinities
68 Hurt
69 Casual tops
70 Sauce made of basil, garlic, pine nuts, and so on

DOWN

1 "BO-ring!" (hyphenated)
2 Entertain
3 Asian noodle soup
4 Blouse
5 Used to own
6 Hernando's house
7 "That's ___ wanted to know" (2 words)
8 Hurricane, for instance
9 "Stovepipes" (2 words)
10 Convince through repetition
11 Where cubs grow up
12 Oceanic movement
13 Luge, for one
21 Price-less?
22 Purchase from Sajak (2 words)
24 Word before base or kilter
27 Otherwise
28 Laziness
30 On the Waterfront director ___ Kazan
31 ___ with the punches
32 Ego
33 Assertively busy (hyphenated)
34 Fortune teller's clue
35 Rowing team poles
36 Winning combination (2 words)
37 Against
43 Fundraising event
44 At all
45 Actor ___ Harrison
47 ___ Lobos ("La Bamba" band)
50 Solely
52 To-do list item
53 Starting place for icicles
54 Fold in a skirt
55 Trunk of the body
56 Smile broadly
57 Singer ___ Fitzgerald
58 Valley in California
59 Stringed instrument
60 God of love
64 Polar ice ___

HINT: A clue such as 21 Down, with a question mark at the end, is supposed to make you think twice. In this case, you should conclude that the clue's hyphen signals a different interpretation. See puzzle 83's page for a free answer.

#67: 26D = AUDIE

Three Places   by Thomas W. Schier

This puzzle features three locations in the United States whose names have something in common.

ACROSS

1 Herb used in pesto sauce
6 First four alphabet letters
10 Mama's man
14 Make reparation (for)
15 Soccer star known as "The Black Pearl"
16 Mineral usually found in a multivitamin tablet
17 Shaky 600-mile-long zone in California (*3 words*)
20 Locomotive
21 Musical group of three
22 Spelling contest
23 Goes bad
25 Unpaid debts
27 Tin-coated container
30 *To Renew America* author Gingrich
32 Grade-A purchase
33 Whitish, milky gem
35 Roll of postage stamps
37 Posture-perfect
41 Where the Alamo is (*3 words*)
44 Swap
45 Remain undecided
46 Singer Turner
47 Swim-race segment
49 Cooking direction
51 Road paving substance
52 Situated on the side
56 Bathroom bar
58 Actress Gardner
59 Nephew of Abel in the Bible
61 Prepare for a nude beach, perhaps
65 Where Alcatraz is located (*3 words*)
68 Buster Brown's dog, in old shoe ads
69 Unkind
70 Sheeplike
71 Tortoiselike
72 ___ and crafts
73 Smells badly

DOWN

1 Pyramid's bottom
2 ___ end (finished; *2 words*)
3 Billboard Top 40 item
4 "The bombs bursting ___" (*2 words*)
5 John ___ of the Beatles
6 Month after March (*abbr.*)
7 Red vegetable
8 ___ Bow of old movies
9 Wish for
10 Actress ___ Zadora of *Hairspray*
11 Island resort off Venezuela
12 Gondola guider
13 Starts a poker pot
18 Discover
19 Draw a blank
24 Dive
26 Snowy Gulf Coast bird
27 Price
28 On ___ with (equal to; *2 words*)
29 Grandma, by another name
31 Fork points
34 Soup scoop
36 Dryer clogs
38 Roadway turnoff
39 Biblical water-to-wine town
40 Pre-1917 Russian ruler
42 Closer to
43 Hateful
48 Central American country with a canal
50 Deep-seated ill will
52 Wears well
53 Be of use
54 Ballroom dance
55 Solitary person
57 Demonstrate to a jury's satisfaction
60 Wordless singing style
62 Theater award presented by *The Village Voice*
63 Financial institution
64 Organs of sight
66 Not many
67 Fed. agcy. that deals with illegal residents (abbr.)

HINT: If you like, consider the clue "Office holders" for 67 Down. See puzzle 90 for more help if you need it.

#60: 2D = IMBUE

71

Moving Right Along   by Norma Steinberg

The four long answers in this puzzle each begin with a word that has to do with movement.

ACROSS

1 *Mystic River* Oscar-winning actor Sean ___
5 Exaggerates, as an expense account
9 Ark-boarding groups
13 Second-smallest Great Lake
14 Printed sheet
15 Hindu music style
16 Leader, as in a mile race
18 Lloyd Webber's "___ Ask of You" (*2 words*)
19 Internet logon information (*2 words*)
20 Ganged up on
22 For each
23 Skyrocket
25 Involved with, as a hobby
26 Grime
27 Freedom from duties
30 Presidential "no"
33 Be a witness
35 Smidgeon
36 Works for
38 *Dr. No* writer ___ Fleming
39 As a companion
41 Prior to
42 Proverbial incentive for good behavior
45 Ann's raggedy shelfmate
46 Appease
48 Harvest
50 "___ you dare!"
51 *That '70s Show* extra
52 Lobster eater's protection
55 Bivouac spot
58 City in Washington
60 Opera feature
61 Go off in battle (*3 words*)
63 Be sure of, with "on"
64 Cow in Borden ads
65 Autograph
66 Good buddies
67 Apricot pit, for example
68 Golfers' gadgets

DOWN

1 Enliven (*2 words*)
2 Backspace over
3 More pleasant
4 ___-do-well
5 Poker winning
6 Communion table
7 Eat less
8 Fighter plane flights
9 Land parcels
10 Leave in the lurch (*3 words*)
11 Leer at
12 Uttered
14 Stereotypical detective hat
17 Enthusiastic agreement from Manuel (*2 words*)
21 "Giving You the Best That I Got" singer ___ Baker
24 Garb
26 Vito Corleone's title
27 Maiden in Poe's poem "The Raven"
28 Cape Town coin
29 Tense
30 President's second-in-command, slangily
31 Jimmy Carter's middle name
32 Gym machine
34 Black gunk
37 Reads a bar code
40 Portable computer's place, perhaps
43 Occasionally (*2 words*)
44 Cut some canines
47 Insured's contributions
49 Subject for medical students (abbr.)
51 To the point
52 Texan who died at the Alamo
53 Public relations concern
54 Farm structures
55 Nitpick
56 Zone
57 Yarn
59 Buyer's concern
62 El ___ (Spanish hero)

HINT: 47 Down refers to small charges levied against insurance holders for doctor visits and medication. See puzzle 97 for more help.

#53: 49A = PLEBE

72

Doubling Up   by Mel Kenworthy

From the theme, you might think there's an echo in here. As an extra hint, this puzzle contains every letter of the alphabet.

ACROSS
1 Holey cheese
6 Envelope part
10 Slices into
14 "Live Free ___" (New Hampshire's motto, *2 words*)
15 Part of the ear
16 Sweeping story, like Homer's *Iliad*
17 Double-named city in Washington (*2 words*)
19 *You've Got Mail* director ___ Ephron
20 *Admiral Graf* ___ (German warship of the late 1930s)
21 Part of a drive train
22 Lou Grant portrayer Ed ___
23 ___ off (start to snooze)
25 Cheerleading groups
26 Double-named resort hotel/ casino in Las Vegas or Reno (*2 words*)
32 Bridesmaid's counterpart
33 Nebraska's largest city
34 Went first
37 Mid-'30s heavy-weight champ Max ___

38 Large container
39 Game played on horseback
40 Alias indicator (abbr.)
41 Hostile takeover
43 Rodeo rope
44 Double-named sitcom of the 1990s starring Tia and Tamara Mowry (*2 words*)
46 Jar, as in a crowd
49 House dog, say
50 "He's ___ nowhere man..." (Beatles, *2 words*)
51 Wise men of the New Testament
54 "Fancy" singer ___ McEntire
58 *North by Northwest* star ___ Grant

59 Double-named German resort city (*hyphenated*)
61 NFL Hall of Fame quarterback ___ Graham
62 ___ Epps of *The Mod Squad*
63 Have ___ of one's own (be defiant, maybe, *2 words*)
64 Lima ___
65 Poker or Pong
66 Swank

DOWN
1 Scatters seed
2 Bandage
3 At rest
4 Gun barrel attachment
5 Whale's whereabouts
6 Linen source
7 Recline lazily
8 Up to the task

9 Green shade
10 Official count of people and demographic information
11 "Once ___ time..." (*2 words*)
12 Exhausted
13 Surgery reminders
18 Rolls of bills
22 Bluish green
24 Lord's Prayer starter
25 Location for a PTA meeting (abbr.)
26 Castro's country
27 *Out of Africa* writer ___ Dinesen
28 Carla's portrayer on *Cheers*, ___ Perlman
29 Disobey the Tenth Commandment

30 Appearance, as in a mirror
31 Appraiser
34 Didn't win
35 "What ___ is new?"
36 Room access
39 Deli meat
41 Place for a cooling pie
42 British verb ending
43 Stretch the truth
44 Remain in a position (*2 words*)
45 Make yarn
46 Ebenezer Scrooge's ghostly ex-partner ___ Marley in *A Christmas Carol*
47 Make a speech
48 "Perfect Sleeper" mattress company
51 Crib cry
52 ___ Sandler of *Little Nicky*
53 Actor Richard ___
55 Work on a manuscript
56 Mercedes-___ automobile
57 Commentator Rooney of *60 Minutes*
59 Poorly drained area
60 High-jumper's hurdle

HINT: At 5 Down the answer is not POD. If you need more help, see puzzle 54's page.

#96: 39D = ILIAD

73 The Cat's Meow   by Randall J. Hartman

This time, as the title's hint implies, the long phrases start with kinds of cats.

ACROSS
1 Claim
5 Baseball player known as "the Georgia Peach"
9 Places for earrings
14 United Fund slogan
15 Hodgepodge
16 Wear away
17 Chopped down
18 ___ the Merciless (Flash Gordon foe)
19 *Steal This Book!* author ___ Hoffman
20 Arabian Sea arm that goes to southwest Iran (*2 words*)
23 Fourposter, for one
24 Walk onstage
25 Tamale topping
27 More than adequate
31 Eccentric nonconformist
34 Soak up, as gravy with bread
37 *Jeopardy!* host ___ Trebek

38 Risked, as a reputation
39 "Thanks ___!" (*2 words*)
41 Farewell, to Fifi
43 Beverage of fermented honey
44 Big oaf
46 Cut back, as a budget
48 Some hospital workers (abbr.)
49 New York City's Madison, for example
50 Wedding dress fabric
52 Curriculum ___ (list of qualifications, etc.)
54 Birthplace of Muhammad
58 Cause of royal insomnia, in a children's story

60 Shrub with silky catkins (*2 words*)
64 Customary
66 Bangkok resident
67 Detective novelist ___ Paretsky
68 Island south of Sicily
69 Husband of a countess
70 Natural resources, of a sort
71 It can be silly
72 Little whirlpool
73 Singer Graham ___

DOWN
1 Looking stunned
2 Female fox
3 Six-time U.S. Open tennis champ Chris ___

4 It's at one end of the Suez Canal (*2 words*)
5 Deep, deep sleep
6 Long ___ of *Hollywood Homicide*
7 Crooner ___ Crosby
8 Like a three-dollar bill
9 Newspaper insert, frequently
10 Symbol of royalty
11 *The Price is Right* host (*2 words*)
12 She plays Carmela on *The Sopranos*
13 Sunflower start
21 ___ *La Douce*
22 Court case
26 *Anna and the King of* ___
28 Mesa

29 Went first
30 Goes out
32 University bigwig
33 Las Vegas figures
34 Tale of heroism
35 King of Norway
36 Track and field event (*2 words*)
40 *Beloved* writer Morrison
42 Pitcher's stat
45 Perform better than
47 *The Drew Carey Show* gal
51 South Africa's ___ Mandela
53 Cosmetics maker ___ Lauder
55 Santa ___, California
56 Drilling samples
57 Ready to sink
58 The heart, in a sense
59 Jacob's twin
61 Herring
62 Small football gain
63 Cunning
65 ABA member (abbr.)

HINT: The author at 67 Across created private eye V.I. Warshawski, who was the title character of a 1991 film starring Kathleen Turner. See puzzle 61 for another hint.

#89: 40D = URIAH

74

A Race to the Finish   by Diane C. Baldwin

In this puzzle you will be gradually improving your position. We predict you'll eventually be a clear winner.

ACROSS
1 Unruly kid
5 Escapade
9 Make changes to legislation
14 Top-notch (*hyphenated*)
15 Burn balm
16 Eel variety
17 Have status
18 "___ and Circumstance" (traditional graduation march)
19 Social grace
20 Trails (*4 words*)
23 Garnet's color
24 Before, in poetry
25 On the schedule
29 Castaway's locale
31 Chicago ballplayer

34 Hiawatha's craft
35 Add to the poker pot
36 Arm bone
37 Is dead even (*4 words*)
40 Braggarts' problems
41 Food for Miss Muffet
42 Deer hunter's weapon
43 "How come?"
44 Tend the garden
45 Fritter's coating
46 Goof up
47 Maple product
48 Wins handily (*4 words*)
57 Baffled (*2 words*)
58 Figure skater ___ Lipinski
59 Peruvian Indian

60 Title for Peter or Valentine
61 Dutch cheese
62 Molecule piece
63 Drastically reduce
64 Poet ___ Angelou
65 Oodles

DOWN
1 Fishhook feature
2 Niagara Falls noise
3 Debate side
4 Adolescent
5 Backslid
6 Spoken audibly
7 Cavort
8 Withheld for oneself
9 Current measure
10 James Bond portrayer Roger ___

11 Lake represented by the "E" in HOMES
12 Space launch org.
13 Salon employee, at times
21 "Go" color
22 Oscar winner ___ Hunt
25 ___ up (bungle)
26 Comedy club guffaw
27 Ruffle one's feathers
28 Mix, as salad
29 Signed with pen
30 Remain in place
31 Fissure
32 Word of surrender
33 Bread maker
35 Workout memento

36 Army group
38 Washstand pitchers
39 Cover loosely
44 Christmas decoration
45 Grand ___ Island
46 Odds counterpart
47 Alley cat, perhaps
48 Young miss
49 And others, in a list (abbr., *2 words*)
50 India's continent
51 Part of an agenda
52 Nothing at all
53 Tuning knob
54 "Do ___ others..."
55 Edinburgh native
56 Edinburgh caps

HINT: At 31 Across: the clue does not refer to a specific player's name. For more help, see puzzle 69's page.

#82: 2D = TOADY

Getting a Round   by Lee Glickstein & Nancy Salomon

A repeated word in the first three long answers leads to a surprising last long answer. Sing along!

ACROSS
1 Puma or tiger
4 Brand choice for Fido
8 Go from pub to pub
14 One, in Madrid
15 Thug
16 Like baseball, in the Metrodome
17 One in a series of homes (*2 words*)
19 Poem "paragraph"
20 On the bounding main
21 "Don't ___ me!"
23 "The Star-Spangled Banner" author
24 Reese of *Touched by an Angel*
26 Intrinsically (*2 words*)
29 Theatergoer's coup
35 Chess pieces
38 Harbor markers
39 ___ Lederer, a.k.a. Ann Landers

40 Had a humble meal? (*2 words*)
42 Garage door gadgets
44 Facing the pitcher (*2 words*)
45 Charged (*2 words*)
47 Contractor's approximation (abbr.)
48 1927 Yankee lineup, admiringly
51 Loud, as a crowd
52 Cut made on a gunslinger's pistol handle
56 "___ Had a Hammer" (*2 words*)
59 Spills the beans
62 Infiltrating spy
63 Comet's sleigh mate

66 "Whatever floats ___" (*2 words*)
68 The bull, in Barcelona (*2 words*)
69 Pinza of *South Pacific* fame
70 One-man show about Capote that starred Robert Morse on Broadway
71 Like some suckers (*hyphenated*)
72 Pamper, with "on"
73 Bebopper's word

DOWN
1 Band-Aid competitor
2 Win by ___ (*2 words*)
3 After-swim need
4 In the past

5 Big galoot
6 Sit for a photo
7 Risky way to run a car (*2 words*)
0 Intimate cafe
9 Picnic pest
10 Nutritionist's abbr.
11 Sound the horn
12 Move like sludge
13 Talk to God
18 Kennedy coin
22 Individuals
25 Judge
27 Enamored of (*2 words*)
28 *Baseball Tonight* network
30 "___ Day Will Come"
31 Imagined (*2 words*)
32 Fencing sword
33 Makes public
34 Midterm, for one

35 "Just the facts, ___"
36 "___, Brute?" (Caesar's dying accusation; *2 words*)
37 Neighbor of Kansas (abbr.)
41 Infant's "father"
43 What golfers try to break
46 Decked out
49 Scotch cocktail (*2 words*)
50 Embryo's place
53 Part of a comb
54 County of Ireland
55 In a lather (*2 words*)
56 Brainchild
57 TV premiere season
58 Worldwide (abbr.)
60 Lunchbox clown
61 Business attire
64 Fish used in fish sticks
65 Wisk competitor
67 Beluga delicacy

HINT: In 19 Across: A word in quotation marks in a clue may be used in a close, but figurative, sense. There's a bigger hint for you beside puzzle 100.

#100: 2D = AGHA

76 Countdown — by Alan Olschwang

This time, we're asking you to think of phrases in which the first word makes a natural mathematical progression.

ACROSS

1 La ___ Nostra
5 Bad-mouth
9 Famed physicist Enrico ___
14 College graduate, briefly
15 China's continent
16 Egg-shaped
17 Jaunty rhythm
18 With 60 Down, a hard-to-believe yarn
19 Conserve, in a way
20 Finishing position that doesn't earn a ribbon (*2 words*)
23 Ocean
24 Rifle range command
25 Evening meals
27 Host of *The Tonight Show* before Johnny Carson (*2 words*)
32 *Norma* ___ (Sally Field film)
33 Make a mistake
34 TV drama set in New York City (*2 words*)
39 Some sports car roofs (*hyphenated*)
42 Commotion
43 Filched
44 Deserving the silver medal (*2 words*)
47 Fish with long, narrow jaws
48 Number of sides on a snowflake
49 Romantic ballad
52 Fundraising event
56 Spoon-bending ___ Geller
57 *Pulp Fiction*'s ___ Thurman
58 George and Martha, originally (*2 words*)
64 Letterman, to Leno
66 Patron saint of Norway
67 Highlands hillside
68 Piece of china
69 Cash holder
70 "Sweater Girl" ___ Turner
71 Monica of tennis fame
72 Captain Hook's companion
73 Targets for Brett Favre

DOWN

1 Lower leg part
2 Potpourri
3 Enterprise helmsman on *Star Trek*
4 Metroliner company
5 A place to step when you're wet (*2 words*)
6 "Pronto!" to a CEO (abbr.)
7 Door threshold
8 Longtime Chicago Bears coach George ___
9 Animal's leg portions
10 Holiday forerunner
11 Waken
12 Scrooge
13 Conceptions
21 Waitperson's reward
22 Milk component
26 Type of moss
27 Fast planes
28 ___ Johnson of *Laugh-In*
29 Gator relative
30 "___ the Arab" (Ray Stevens novelty hit)
31 Disney World attractions
35 Red, red flower
36 Forum wear
37 Attired
38 Roll call response
40 Model's stance
41 Head cold, some say
45 512, in Roman numerals
46 Cocoa-dusted chocolate candy
50 Washday alternative to Tide, perhaps
51 Agile
52 Post-pablum sounds
53 Author ___ Zola
54 Marine
55 Horses' gaits
59 Slender
60 See 18 Across
61 Middle East country
62 Come down
63 Affirmative votes
65 Consumed completely, with "up"

HINT: 63 Down's clue might lead you to the wrong answer at first. Just backtrack and you'll be fine. There's more help near puzzle 82.

#68: 6D = LEVI

Hold It! by Norma Steinberg

77

If important thematic words appear more or less equally at the start or at the end of the long answers, it's a bit more challenging. That's the case here.

ACROSS

1 House, in Mexico
5 *Julius Caesar* statesman
9 Provide irrigation for
14 Heidi's mountains
15 Elvis Presley's middle name
16 "___ to bed..."
17 Mob scene
18 Cheerful tune
19 Apprehension
20 Move at a good clip (*2 words*)
23 Summer, in France
24 Put away
25 Lecturer's prop
27 Fountain drinks
30 Have on
31 Lobbying organization (abbr.)
34 Businessmen, facetiously
36 Potatoes
39 Sore spot
41 "Guilty" and "Not guilty"
43 *Scary Movie* actress ___ Faris
44 Actions
46 Madrid mister
48 Cosmetics queen Mary ___
49 Croon
51 Accounting entry
53 Closes up, as a shirt
56 "Beat it!"
59 Abbreviation on a cover letter
60 Brand-new (*4 words*)
64 Crouch
66 Janis's comic-strip husband
67 Prosperous period
68 Spanish diacritical mark
69 Bring up
70 Together Krabappel on *The Simpsons*
71 Passover meal
72 Kunta Kinte's slave name
73 What typists tap

DOWN

1 Take in starches before a race, with "up"
2 Info on a "Wanted" poster
3 The S of SUV
4 Houston baseballers
5 Got in touch with (*2 words*)
6 *La Bohème* highlight, for example
7 Bridge fee
8 Leading (*2 words*)
9 Shoes with tapered soles
10 Longest wholly Swiss river
11 Woodpecker's "drum" (*2 words*)
12 Make happy
13 Actress Winona ___
21 Cupid, to the Greeks
22 "Immediately!"
26 California wine valley
28 Feels poorly
29 Knight's mount
31 Cushion
32 Detective Ventura
33 Winter affliction (*2 words*)
35 Rational
37 Forensic clue, briefly
38 Utter
40 Check for typos
42 Tearjerker (*2 words*)
45 Spy
47 Rolling in dough
50 Wildebeest
52 *Jeopardy!* answer man
53 Goes one better than
54 Loosen, as a knot
55 Beginning
57 Home
58 Starry-eyed
61 Popular cookie
62 Extra weight
63 December holiday, commonly
65 Poem of praise

#61: 45A = SIGNET

78 It's Play Time! by Bernice Gordon

Not only that, but where you play is important, too. This puzzle has several cross-reference clues, but the result should not be too difficult.

ACROSS
1 Brand choice for Fido
5 Humane org. since 1824
9 Studies desperately
14 Bluish green
15 Swimmer's place
16 Vietnam's capital
17 Where nine play on a team (2 words)
20 Film or stage performer
21 Propels a lifeboat
22 Classic Jaguar model designation
23 "Show me ___ money!"
24 Server's edge after deuce, commonly (2 words)
27 See 39 Down
29 Photographer's request
30 Deteriorates
34 With 42 Across, where eleven play on a team
37 Mrs. Eisenhower

38 Signs up, as for a class
39 Draw movie cartoons
41 Prolonged gaze
42 See 34 Across
43 Cobbler's item
44 Coins of Cape Town
45 Amount in a Brylcreem slogan
48 Airline to Israel (2 words)
49 January western clock setting (abbr.)
52 Sheepish female
55 Slender
57 Zhou ___ (former Chinese premier)
59 Where five play on a team (2 words)
63 British Prime Minister Tony ___

64 Emmy winner ___ Falco
65 State of the 2002 Winter Olympics
66 Daring film feat
67 Watch readouts (abbr.)
68 "It's ___ of your business!"

DOWN
1 Facing the pitcher (2 words)
2 "Champagne wishes and caviar dreams" guy
3 Kindergarten adhesive
4 Butter substitute
5 Hydrotherapy center
6 Beltway insider, commonly
7 Military rank

8 The Four Seasons director
9 Run after
10 Mate of 52 Across
11 Strong as ___ (2 words)
12 Brother
13 Team
18 Prickly shrub
19 April 15 addressee (abbr.)
25 Passé phone feature
26 Problems
28 Cologne brand for men
29 Kept for later
31 Suave actor ___ Sharif
32 Brother of Jermaine and Michael
33 In the public eye
34 Daniel Boone star ___ Parker

35 Lock ___ (track with technology, 2 words)
36 ___ Roberts University
37 Keyboard center (2 words)
39 Shrinking body of water, with 27 Across
40 1492 ship
42 Small bomb
46 Put on call
47 Play the point spread
49 Disney pooch
50 Kitchen wrap
51 10% for the church
52 Dwindles
53 Mickey Mouse marketeer ___ Disney
54 Biblical birthright seller
56 Adam's second son
58 "Person," "place," or "thing," in grammar class
60 Family reunion attendees
61 Pot top
62 Guitar master ___ Paul

HINT: At 67 Across: A word that appears to be a verb might be a noun. And vice versa, of course. There's another hint for you next to puzzle 96.

#54: 63A = LAMAS

79 State Sights   by Mel Kenworthy

The three long answers involve state names and...something associated.

ACROSS

1 Unwritten
5 Hypochondriac's dread
10 Concerning (*2 words*)
14 Emeril's restaurant in New Orleans' French Quarter
15 ___ cologne (*2 words*)
16 Faculty leader
17 Yellow or orange flower cultivated in the Golden State (*2 words*)
20 Wielder of a blue pencil
21 Strong whirlpool
22 Safecracker
24 Distribute
25 Hat with a visor
28 Elton John's title
29 Pitching statistic (abbr.)
30 Are you a man ___ mouse? (*2 words*)
33 Jai ___
35 Verdi opera
37 The "S" of WASP
39 Cheddar, for example (*2 words*)
42 Gobbled up

43 "Mary ___ little lamb..." (*2 words*)
44 Cereal grasses
45 Rapping "Dr."
46 Seventh Greek letter
48 Scrabble 3-pointers
50 Winter clock setting in NYC (abbr.)
51 Confidence game
52 Bank takeback, for short
54 1980 Congressional scandal
57 Add more seasoning
61 Vista looking west from Denver (*2 words*)
65 "I knew ___ instant..." (*2 words*)
66 State revenue generator

67 River that flooded Florence in 1966
68 Capitol's cap
69 German ironworks center
70 Classic cars

DOWN

1 Fairy tale opener
2 Highway
3 "___ Ask of You" (*The Phantom of the Opera* song; *2 words*)
4 People in the pew
5 Jimmy Carter, for one
6 Attentiveness
7 Seek office
8 1501, in Roman numerals
9 Hall of Fame pitcher Tom
10 Carry a major crush on

11 The start of autumn (abbr.)
12 Scotch or duct follower
13 Black gemstone
18 Enemies
19 Soap and saltpeter ingredient
23 *The Client* author John ___
24 Wander aimlessly
25 Imitated a crow
26 "Are you calling me ___?" (*2 words*)
27 Artificial gem
30 Daisy type
31 Peace and American Beauty
32 "...___ of robins..." (*2 words*)
34 Cola cooler

36 *Sábado* or *domingo*
38 Prefix meaning "gas" or "atmosphere"
40 Like some garages (*hyphenated*)
41 African nation that neighbors Chad
47 Steamed Mexican entrée
49 On ___ (in hopes of a sale)
51 British quick bread
53 Herr Schindler
54 Low-pH stuff
55 U2 lead singer
56 Close with a loud noise
58 Suffix with "million" or "concession"
59 "Headlines" reader on Monday nights
60 General ___ chicken (Chinese restaurant offering)
62 MS-___ (Windows precursor)
63 Bonus NHL periods (abbr.)
64 AAA suggestion (abbr.)

HINT: At first glance you'd expect the clue at 5 Across to lead to a singular answer. In this case, though, "dread" is something plural. See puzzle 53's page for another hint.

#97: 12D = DACHE

80

Chockablock   by Randall J. Hartman

In this case, the long answers all rhyme. With what, you ask? With each other...and the title.

ACROSS

1 "Miracle" baseball team of 1969
5 "Higher and Higher" singer ___ Coolidge
9 A whole bunch
14 Sheltered, nautically
15 *Exodus* author Leon ___
16 Fortuneteller's card
17 Workplace "punch in" device (*2 words*)
19 Shake an Etch-A-Sketch
20 *This Is Spinal* ___ (mockumentary film)
21 Internet reference
22 *Nutcracker Suite*, for one
23 Dean's singing partner
24 Gorilla trained in sign language
25 Butt of a joke (*2 words*)
31 Work groups
33 Follow orders
34 Buddhist movement
35 Washing machine cycle
36 Cool ___ cucumber (*2 words*)
37 Fictional detective Sam ___
39 "Thrilla in Manila" victor
40 Like Scotch whisky
41 Food blender setting
42 Noted baby doctor (*2 words*)
46 Lotion ingredient
47 Genesis boat
48 Bee gatherings
51 Very easy victory
53 Lao-tzu's philosophy
56 Freighter's load
57 Stuff and nonsense
59 "So long," in Sonora
60 Theater award (but not the Tony)
61 Mystique
62 "That's what I ___ to say"
63 Forest resident
64 63 Across, to a hunter

DOWN

1 ___ Damon of *The Bourne Identity*
2 *On the Waterfront* director ___ Kazan
3 One-day replacement, often
4 "Get it?"
5 Judge's decision
6 Word preceding hand and fist
7 Carrier of Rocky Mountain spotted fever
8 "All you have to do is ___"
9 T-bone and sirloin
10 Where you might buy a lemon? (*2 words*)
11 Shrinking inland sea
12 Medicinal quantity
13 Proofreader's "keep"
18 Contract provision
22 Hobgoblin
23 Top-grossing film of 1975
24 Works the dough
25 Leader buried in Red Square
26 Another name for a submarine sandwich
27 *Ghosts* playwright Henrik ___
28 Mountain range of Missouri
29 Give up
30 Patella location
31 Chesapeake Bay catch
32 Stir up
37 Like a Corvette
38 Focus of a poke check
40 Old Testament book
43 Legalese, for example
44 Close, but no cigar
45 Poorhouse resident
48 Shell game, for instance
49 Do more than dip the toe
50 Kiri Te Kanawa solo
51 Dressing gown
52 Mayberry lad
53 "Magical Mystery ___" (1968 Beatles album)
54 Farmland division
55 Give a thumbs-up
57 School of whales
58 Mushroom top

#90: 43D = ARIL

Nice Talk   by Norma Steinberg

That's what the first words of these long phrases imply.

81

ACROSS
1 *60 Minutes* anchor Morley ___
6 Peruvian capital
10 Sheepherding pig, in a film
14 Popeye's better half
15 Bad day for Caesar
16 Height (abbr.)
17 Bowling alleys
18 Dairy farm sounds
19 Ripped
20 "In ___ ear and out the other"
21 Autumn forecast, perhaps (*2 words*)
24 "Officiates" at tea
26 International peace contract
27 Bit of corn
29 Traveler's document
31 Camera diaphragm
32 Fortune-teller's sign
34 Headquartered
39 ___ Inch Nails (rock group)
40 Your sibling's daughter
42 Spiritual teacher
43 Oil billionaire J. Paul ___
45 Mast
46 "...blackbirds, baked in ___" (*2 words*)
47 Film, literature, dance, and so on
49 Feel sorry for
51 Garb
55 California Senator Barbara ___
56 Fireworks show ending, for example (*2 words*)
59 Drink slowly
62 Belgian export
63 Poems
64 Copycat's statement (*2 words*)
66 Bloodhound's clue
67 Kick back
68 Practical joke
69 Adam or Mae
70 Pal, to an Aussie
71 Abrupt

DOWN
1 Alone
2 Thicke or Bates
3 Lease's qualifications (*2 words*)
4 Actress Arden
5 Step in and save
6 VIP wheels
7 Role model
8 Kitten's cry
9 Holdings
10 Ms. Midler
11 Hawaiian greeting
12 Renoir's hat
13 Each
22 Synthetic fabric
23 Bedouin
25 Beginning
27 Important chess piece
28 Pennsylvania city
29 Slangy titles for Gore and Agnew
30 Peruvian native
33 Spray
35 Hanging open
36 Diva
37 Ms. Brookovich
38 Twosome
41 Actor Flynn
44 Three feet
48 Improvement
50 Nontaxable
51 Gleaming
52 Swap
53 Mexican sandwiches
54 Not chemically active
55 Moisten the bird
57 Inventive thinking
58 Goldfinch home
60 Electrified particles
61 Nudge
65 Before

HINT: This puzzle has four different ways to clue a first name (14 Across, 2 Down, 4 Down, and 37 Down), and they're equally valid. There's another hint accompanying puzzle 67.

Let's Get Together

by Nancy Salomon

This time each thematic phrase involves repetition with a common linking word.

ACROSS

1 Even a bit (2 words)
6 Prom vehicle, in common talk
10 "A likely story!" (2 words)
14 Puccini opera
15 List ender (abbr., 2 words)
16 A ___ pittance
17 Like some combat (hyphenated)
19 Smear of ink
20 Keats creation
21 Goofs up
22 Beach toys
24 Hypodermic gadget
26 Sheikdom in an old song
27 Like a sincere conversation (hyphenated)
31 Needing a trim, lawnwise
34 Bonus NHL periods (abbr.)
35 Pool stick
36 Daytime dramas
37 C.I.A. employee
38 Giggle
40 Alfred E. Neuman's magazine
41 "___ lied!" (2 words)
42 Distance runners
43 Like intimate dancing (hyphenated)
47 ___-Kettering Institute
48 Abate (2 words)
52 Sheds tears
53 Lip-___ (pretend to sing)
54 One-man show about Capote
55 Metal used in brass
56 Like a heated confrontation (hyphenated)
59 Helper (abbr.)
60 Jane Austen classic novel
61 Supply new equipment
62 "My goodness!" exclamations
63 Chop ___
64 The Dalai Lama, nowadays

DOWN

1 One of the Three Musketeers
2 Yes-man
3 Mary Tyler Moore's TV boss, Ed ___
4 Digital readout, briefly
5 11 P.M. broadcast, for many (2 words)
6 The MacNeil-___ Report
7 "I'll take ___ a compliment" (2 words)
8 Chess piece
9 Veterans (2 words)
10 Drink, as liquor
11 Gripe, gripe, gripe
12 Statue in Piccadilly Circus
13 Vietnamese New Year
18 Church keyboard
23 Sound of contentment
25 Breakfast chain, familiarly
26 Representative in court (abbr.)
28 Something to talk about
29 Regretful one
30 Souvenir shop tops
31 Gomer Pyle's organization (abbr.)
32 Biblical boat builder
33 Seemed reasonable (2 words)
37 Any minute now
38 Three-three, for example (2 words)
39 Actress ___ Sommer
41 Squirrels away
42 Had in mind
44 Votes into a job
45 Keystone lawman
46 Personal "prime time"
49 Former SNL player Sheri ___
50 Delicate
51 Soft creamy candy
52 Like Solomon
53 Unchanged
55 Second of two sharp turns
57 Outback bird
58 Whammy

HINT: 45 Down refers to the old Mack Sennett comedies. You might take a look at puzzle 74's page for more help.

83 Warning Sign   by Mel Rosen

The first words of each long across answer, taken in order, form a common warning phrase. It was introduced in 1917.

ACROSS

1 Bringing up the rear
5 Huffs and puffs
10 James Bond portrayer ___ Connery
14 "___ the Lonely" (Roy Orbison hit)
15 Central Florida city
16 Circle over a saint
17 Claymation filming technique (hyphenated)
19 Look amorously at
20 Got a look at
21 Banned insecticide
22 Israeli airline (2 words)
23 Nickname for a lanky cowpoke
25 Potpourri bags
27 Touched down
30 Belle of the ball, maybe
32 Jack ___ of Barney Miller fame
33 Fireplace fodder
34 Guitarist ___ Clapton
36 Part of a coat of arms
40 1956 play about a discontented working-class man (4 words)
44 Carousal
45 Hairy Himalayan humanoid
46 "That's incredible!"
47 Chicago's trains
49 Actor Billy ___ Williams
50 Promotional overkill
51 Recited, as a mantra
55 552, to Nero
57 Deserve
58 Former Notre Dame coach ___ Parseghian
60 Yielded to gravity or exhaustion
64 Make better
65 Mother's warning (2 words)
67 "How sweet ___!" (2 words)
68 Bottled water brand
69 Internet addresses, for short
70 Calculator readouts, briefly
71 College officials
72 Cheat in hide-and-seek

DOWN

1 Shake off, as a shadow
2 A Bug's Life insects
3 Swill
4 Pre-computer keyboarder
5 Worthwhile brainstorm (2 words)
6 Part of a play
7 Pronounced
8 Walks laboriously
9 Some December temporary workers
10 Implement you may use to help get your oxfords on
11 Two under par
12 ___ once (suddenly; 2 words)
13 Christmas carols
18 Hall of Famer ___ Ott
24 Lenient treatment
26 ___-Cola
27 "___ fair in love and war"
28 Stunt pilot's maneuver
29 Lab helper in horror flicks
31 Pedaled
35 Wrote up, as a speeder
37 Like a soufflé
38 Ooze
39 Oak or maple
41 Alert quality
42 Pants holder
43 Television ratings, commonly
48 Made airtight
50 Elevated (2 words)
51 Filmdom's ___ B. DeMille
52 ___ cuisine
53 Deodorant choice
54 Impetus
56 ___ McKellen of the Lord of the Rings films
59 Marco Polo's destination
61 Roberts's Runaway Bride costar
62 Lawyer-author ___ Stanley Gardner
63 Work station
66 Respond to UV rays

HINT: There's a giveaway answer on puzzle 81's page. If you don't want to look there just yet, it may help you to know that the answer at 52 Down is another example of a foreign phrase being fully assimilated into English.

#69: 62A = ELIE

84

Do I Hear an Echo?   by Gail Grabowski

Here's another rhyming theme for you. Notice the helpful little entry right in the grid's center. Nice touch.

ACROSS
1 Alma ___
6 Angelic instrument
10 Pipe impediment
14 Marry secretly
15 Toward a boat's sheltered side
16 Impolite
17 1997 Tommy Lee Jones/ Will Smith movie (*3 words*)
19 Scads (*2 words*)
20 Leftover
21 Some baseball calls
22 Happen
24 Twain's tales
26 Alpine apex
27 Colossal coffeepot
28 Rental from Blockbuster, for example
32 Architect's sketch

35 Partially opened
37 Pick up the tab
38 Prudential rival
40 Outburst from Bill the Cat, in the comics
41 DVD player control button
42 Ancient Roman language
43 School orgs.
45 Hollywood canine of yore
46 Chinese seaport
48 *Trading Spaces* TV outlet (abbr.)
50 Singer ___ Campbell
51 Concocts, as an excuse (*2 words*)
55 Form of jazz
57 Long periods of time
58 SSW opposite
59 Mt. Etna's outflow

60 1980 Danger-field/Murray golf film
63 Baldwin or Guinness
64 *The African Queen* screenwriter James ___
65 *Nana* author ___ Zola
66 Become lively, with "up"
67 Bunches, slangily
68 Boot bottoms

DOWN
1 Business notes
2 Wide-awake
3 The Lone Ranger's sidekick
4 Prefix with "cure" or "cycle"
5 French painter Pierre Auguste ___

6 Obeys a stop sign
7 "Woe is me!"
8 Kind of room, for short
9 Black tea varieties
10 Expert
11 Humdinger
12 Aroma
13 "___ off my back!"
18 ___ Vista, California
23 Social system
25 Offensive football player (*2 words*)
26 Hooded garment
28 Prickly plants
29 Pebble Beach pegs
30 Diplomacy
31 Blues singer ___ James
32 Good buddies

33 Reuben's mother, in the Bible
34 United Nations figure Kofi ___ Annan
36 Kyoto's country
39 ___-Saxon
44 Expressionless
47 Jive buff
49 Defeats
51 Ciphers
52 Slow-moving mollusk
53 Male relative
54 Some lap dogs, commonly
55 Hay unit
56 At all times
57 Barbara ___ of *I Dream of Jeannie*
59 Drink like Lassie
61 "Fourscore and seven years ___..."
62 Kind of medical provider (abbr.)

HINT: The alternate clue for 48 Across involves gentle over-sight. See puzzle 88's page for more help.

#62: 58A = ALAN

Group Therapy   by Thomas W. Schier

85

In two of the long phrases, the thematic word is last. In the other two, it's the first word.

ACROSS

1 Allergic reaction, perhaps
5 "Woe is me!"
9 *Green* ___ (old sitcom starring Eddie Albert and Eva Gabor)
14 Eyeball impolitely
15 Colonist loyal to Britain
16 Swell up
17 Vienna choral group (*2 words*)
19 Spicy chip dip
20 "...___ he drove out of sight"
21 Skirt edges
22 "Children should ___ and not heard" (*2 words*)
23 *On the Origin of Species* author Charles ___
25 Roy Rogers' partner Dale ___
27 ___ Lanchester of *The Bride of Frankenstein*
29 Elegant dancer Fred
33 ___ Gras
36 Strong air current
38 Filthy buildup
39 Like two peas in ___ (*2 words*)
40 Evil spirit
41 Zingy taste
42 Highway transport
43 Fit as a fiddle
44 Timid type
45 Hypnotic states
47 Audition tape
49 Chivalrous chaps
51 Malicious troublemaker
55 Take a ___ (try; *2 words*)
58 Neighbor of Cambodia and Vietnam
60 Consumed
61 Actress Turner and singer Cantrell
62 Equine used to carry loads
64 Do penance
65 Robinson Crusoe landed on one
66 Stags and does
67 Relaxes (the rules)
68 Hitting-the-ground sound
69 June 6, 1944 (*hyphenated*)

DOWN

1 Dressed like a judge
2 Public square, in ancient Greece
3 More cunning
4 "___ So Fine" (1963 Chiffons song)
5 The capital of Greece
6 Rug-maker's apparatus
7 Get out of bed
8 Neighbor of Israel (*abbr.*)
9 Not in school
10 Kind of lawsuit brought by a group (*2 words*)
11 Auditioning actor's desire
12 "He flies through the air with the greatest of ___..."
13 Spider-Man creator ___ Lee
18 Tex-Mex dish
22 City in NW Switzerland
24 Ring given for marriage (*2 words*)
26 Highly regarded
28 Horrorstruck
30 Tax deductions for some (abbr.)
31 Scurries
32 Skittish
33 Yacht spar
34 One who mimics
35 ___ Downey of *Touched by an Angel*
37 Part of many e-mail addresses
40 Belgium treaty city
44 Hit hard
46 Breaks off
48 Called up
50 Mark down, as prices
52 Took risks
53 Totally confused (*2 words*)
54 Suspicious
55 Big chunk
56 *Little Man* ___ (Jodie Foster film)
57 In a little while, to Juliet
59 Rights-advocacy org.
62 Casino area
63 Roulette bet

HINT: The answer at 47 Across is really a common shortening of a more formal word. See puzzle 95's page for a bigger hint.

#55: 12D = ROAN

Which Came First?   by Ed Early

Quotations in puzzles are harder because more letters are essentially unclued. Once you get the gist of this one, you should be okay.

ACROSS

1 Q-Tip tip
5 Vexed continually (*2 words*)
10 Piped up
14 "Don't ___ a cow, man!"
15 Boo-boo
16 Air freshener scent
17 Start of an amusing quip by 25 Across (*4 words*)
19 Gather from the fields
20 Matchstick-removing game
21 Covers one's i's
22 Model airplane material
23 Santa ___, California
24 DJ's inventory (abbr.)
25 Samuel ___ (quoted author in this puzzle)
26 War of ___ (psychological conflict)
28 Lambs' mothers
30 Halloween month (abbr.)
31 Home to billions
32 Parts of shoes
34 Part 2 of the quip (*4 words*)
39 Exhilarate
40 Pols' providers (abbr.)
43 Trains in the city
46 Strong as ___ (*2 words*)
47 In an optimistic way
49 Part 3 of the quip
51 Testing ground
52 ___ Tin Tin
53 In ___ (troubled; *2 words*)
54 He loved Lucy
55 Forensic sampling (abbr.)
56 Colored eye part
57 End of the quip (*2 words*)
60 Post-Mardi Gras period
61 Door pivot
62 Amer.-Eur. alliance (abbr.)
63 Droops
64 Chorus members
65 Trudge through sludge

DOWN

1 Bowzer Bauman's "greaser" group (*3 words*)
2 Hawaiian girls
3 Catholic prayer (*2 words*)
4 Michael Jackson's first solo #1 tune
5 ___ Fables
6 Runs at an easy pace
7 Sea eagles
8 Big name on the Internet
9 "You'll never know unless you ___"
10 Nonfat advocate?
11 Danny ___ of *Do the Right Thing*
12 Soon, informally (*3 words*)
13 Go
18 At rest
22 Gary ___ of *The Buddy Holly Story*
25 Composer ___ Bartok
27 Windmill part
28 County in southeastern England
29 Dazzle
33 Soaks (up), as gravy
35 Large antelope
36 Bunch of ruffians
37 One-time Pontiac model
38 Truman's proposal (*2 words*)
41 Rely strongly on (*2 words*)
42 Jewish temple
43 Modern missives
44 Los Angeles's ___ Tar Pits (*2 words*)
45 It's done on water or snow
47 Lotion targets
48 Award presented by *The Village Voice*
50 Technical schools (abbr.)
51 Free
54 "___ you dare!"
57 Solver's shout
58 Zilch
59 MD's helpers (abbr.)

HINT: The clue at 21 Across puns on the word "eyes." Just read it literally and you'll be fine. If you need another hint, see the box beside puzzle 52.

#98: 43A = ORIBI

Four in a Row   by Alan Olschwang

87

This time, you'll discover that every long entry contains four sequential letters of the alphabet.

ACROSS

1 Dilapidated clothes
5 Makes tea
10 Soccer announcer's shout
14 Name of five Norwegian kings
15 Scheduled a show for summer viewing
16 Impolite look
17 "Encore!"
18 Sharpshooter ___ Oakley
19 Algerian seaport
20 Help for some accused felons (*2 words*)
23 Ballerina's perch
24 *Cocoon* director ___ Howard
25 Good ___ (*2 words*)
28 Health resort
31 Preclude
35 Summer zodiac sign
36 Turkey's capital
39 ___ Ward of *Sisters*
40 *The Third Man* or *Notorious*, for example (*3 words*)
43 Entry fee for a poker hand
44 Close again
45 Holiday forerunner
46 Prediction makers
48 Visibly embarrassed
49 Sort of limit
51 Bush Sr.'s former organization (abbr.)
53 Former cable outlet for C&W music
54 17th century director-general of New Netherland colony (*2 words*)
63 Bone dry
64 Lays asphalt
65 Neighborhood
66 Punch-in time, maybe
67 "Flashdance" singer ___ Cara
68 Pugilist's weapon
69 Understands, as a joke
70 Save fuel
71 Let off pressure

DOWN

1 Easy victory
2 Felipe of baseball
3 Apparel
4 Slim and trim
5 "___ yourself" ("Get ready")
6 Tear
7 Sea eagle
8 Street urchin
9 Villain's expression
10 Virtue
11 Fairy tale villain
12 Banned orchard spray
13 Zoom or fisheye
21 Hawkeye state denizen
22 Silent assent
25 Sporty European cars, briefly
26 Paris's river
27 Nick ___ of *48 HRS.*
28 One who enjoys the giant slalom
29 Break down a sentence
30 Moved in a curved path
32 Attack
33 Animated
34 Fast-moving snake
37 Neither's partner
38 State of the Crimson Tide (abbr.)
41 Actress ___ McCambridge
42 Going solo
47 Knight's title
50 Dangerous
52 Meat mold material
53 Electronic babysitter (*2 words*)
54 Twinge
55 Cleveland lake
56 Shade
57 Poi source
58 Eye part
59 Cravings
60 Operatic highlight
61 "Untouchable" Eliot ___
62 Family name on the old *Soap* sitcom

HINT: The answer to 19 Across is an anagram of the word ROAN. See puzzle 59's page for another hint.

At Arm's Length?   by Diane C. Baldwin

88

That's where you'll find the body part featured in this puzzle.

ACROSS
1 Cry loudly
5 Beast of a man
10 ___ Lendl of tennis fame
14 The Buckeye State
15 Place for a boutonniere
16 Chess or checkers, for example
17 Refuses to help (*4 words*)
20 Drain-cleaning substance
21 Film director ___ Preminger
22 Pitcher's place
23 Told-you-so exclamations
24 Sadden
26 Columbus Day event
29 Drive-in offering
30 Mosque leader
31 Carryalls
32 ___ and caboodle
35 Won't applaud (*4 words*)
39 Junk mail, mostly
40 Propelled a small boat
41 Soda pop choice
42 Actor ___ Glover
43 Hard to swallow
45 Disproves
48 Some raincoats, for short
49 Isolated
50 In the altogether
51 Diary of sorts
54 Signals rejection (*3 words*)
58 Cutting part of a knife
59 Hair-raising
60 Geometry calculation
61 Something to sow
62 Goofed up
63 Unsurpassed

DOWN
1 ___ over (stun)
2 Sailor's shout
3 Dark red color
4 Land parcel
5 Merry
6 Swim floats
7 As far as (*2 words*)
8 Word with pot or bag
9 Santa's helper
10 Pay no attention to
11 Ambiguous
12 Tent meeting affirmations
13 Geeky folks
18 Laundromat fill-up
19 Pixie-like
23 Pork products
24 Lavished affection
25 Holiday precursors
26 Leaning Tower city
27 In the thick of
28 "Gosh darn it!"
29 Legal tender
31 Urban settings
32 Sheet bend or clove hitch
33 Put in neutral
34 Despot of the past
36 Makes a moving speech
37 Zilch
38 Pretenses
42 Demanded payment from
43 Like most fishhooks
44 Chills champagne
45 Has status
46 Steer clear of
47 Smithy's shop
48 Ike's First Lady
50 Raymond ___ (*Perry Mason* actor)
51 Folk wisdom
52 Has obligations
53 Tiny flier
55 Links starting place
56 That woman
57 Pat daintily

HINT: 22 Across has nothing to do with washstands. Check out the box next to puzzle 66 for a free answer.

#84: 34D = ATTA

Going to the Front   by Ed Early

89

The relevant word in each of the long phrases (twice at the front, once at the back) has to do with being in front. Just as the title suggests.

ACROSS

1 Shakespearean king
5 Balkan native
10 Eccentric engine parts
14 Strong impulse
15 Take away the Joy?
16 Plant with a soothing extract
17 Former Venezia coin
18 Señora Perón
19 Loon or dodo
20 Make impossible (*4 words*)
23 Cover girl Macpherson
24 Take in or let out
25 Phrase written by hand on a dirty car window (*2 words*)
29 Posed
31 Put ___ to (halt; *2 words*)
32 Explorer ___ Heyerdahl
34 "Don't throw bouquets ___" (*2 words*)
38 1960 Vincent Price horror film (*4 words*)
41 Proofreader's find
42 Chess "soldier"
43 100-dinar coins
44 Inner tube filler
45 Subject to limitations
46 Hornswoggle
50 On an ocean liner, perhaps
52 "Run!" (*4 words*)
59 Paul Desmond's sax
60 Food on a skewer
61 Ham's father
62 Hispanic hurrahs
63 "___ else fails..." (*2 words*)
64 Fewer than twice
65 Carrying a grudge
66 Cosmetics maker ___ Lauder
67 Have an opening for

DOWN

1 Calm interval
2 Canal with one end at the Hudson River
3 Taj Mahal locale
4 Interpret
5 Spicy cuisine from Louisiana
6 Competitor
7 Cat-___-tails (*hyphenated*)
8 Wine district in Italy's Piedmont region
9 Collaborate, with "up"
10 Plotting clique
11 Most important invitees (*2 words*)
12 -- --- --- -- ---- .
13 Exodus commemoration
21 Music pace
22 Nixon or Sajak
25 Unit of power
26 Pale grey
27 Ladder rung
28 "What's this!?" (*2 words*)
29 Any minute now
30 Kennel sound
32 Russian ruler until 1917
33 Knock down with an axe
34 Z ___ zebra (*2 words*)
35 Bangkok voter
36 Use rock salt on ice
37 Gaelic language
39 AP competitor
40 Dickensian clerk ___ Heep
44 Federal law enforcement agcy. (*abbr.*)
45 Lame, as an excuse
46 Wild disorder
47 "Greetings!"
48 "Peter, Peter, pumpkin ___..."
49 Give someone ___ of his own medicine (*2 words*)
50 Facing the pitcher (*2 words*)
51 Oil-yielding rock
53 Merle Haggard's "___ from Muskogee"
54 Gridiron officials, briefly
55 Having a part of (*2 words*)
56 Unaccompanied
57 Boot binding
58 Storage structure

HINT: That capital letter J in 15 Across should warn you that the clue is not what it seems. Look for a free answer on the page with puzzle 73.

#77: 58D = MOONY

Name That Celebrity   by Fran & Lou Sabin

Featuring a lot of show-business people, mostly from days gone by. You'll recognize (most of) them.

ACROSS

1 Hairless
5 Black tea
10 Partly open
14 Sheltered, at sea
15 Madison Square Garden, for one
16 Kind of bag
17 Hollywood's "Sweater Girl" (2 words)
19 Far from fat
20 Barrymore or Hampton
21 He played Gene Krupa in The Gene Krupa Story (2 words)
23 Johnny ___, "The Man in Black"
25 Order to your stock broker
26 Designer ___ de la Renta
29 Sound booster
32 Highlanders
35 West African republic
36 Sorrowful sounds
38 Federal cultural funding organization (abbr.)
39 Pizzazz
40 The Color Purple author ___ Walker
41 Author unknown (abbr.)
42 Bach's language (abbr.)
43 Loved like mad
44 Skeleton segment
45 Answer seeker
47 Card game for two
48 Mammy Yokum's boy
49 Hold tightly
51 Flounderlike flatfish
53 This Gun For Hire star (2 words)
57 Depended (on)
61 Rubik's challenge
62 In Grand Hotel she said, "I want to be alone." (2 words)
64 Bent building extensions
65 Painter's prop
66 Close by
67 Nelson Eddy-Jeanette MacDonald vocal effort
68 Pigpens
69 Crime novelist ___ Buchanan

DOWN

1 Pitch out of the strike zone
2 Jai ___
3 Letterman's #1 rival
4 1993–97 television Superman actor (2 words)
5 Singers Anka and Simon
6 Flub a line, for example
7 Novelists Follett and Kesey
8 Ideal for the draft (hyphenated)
9 Some British noblemen
10 ___ the Hun
11 Yoko Ono's hubby (2 words)
12 End in ___ (require overtime; 2 words)
13 Ashcroft's predecessor
18 Weeper's drop
22 Actresses Tilly and Ryan
24 Jean ___, filmdom's "Platinum Blonde"
26 Alpha's opposite
27 Clearance events
28 Gone With the Wind star (2 words)
30 Dancer ___ Shearer of 1948's The Red Shoes
31 Indiana's NBA team
33 Sierra ___ (African nation)
34 More reasonable
36 ___ about (roam)
37 Waking ___ Devine (1998 film)
41 Singer and onetime wife of Xavier Cugat (2 words)
43 Seed coat
46 "Papa" Hemingway
48 Without ___ to stand on (2 words)
50 Book's contents
52 Doctoral tests
53 Served a winner
54 Beaut
55 "Curses!"
56 Name linked to 1 Down
58 Ticked off
59 Abba of Israel
60 "Dumb ___" (1920s Chic Young comic strip)
63 Golf shop purchase

HINT: 41 Down isn't Charo. It's the other one. Puzzle 80's page has another hint.

#70: 43D = ODIOUS

Gear Shifting   by Bonnie L. Gentry

We're not talking about four-on-the-floor here, just your basic automatic transmission.

ACROSS
1 "Quiet!"
5 Regal headdress
10 "As___ saying..." (*2 words*)
14 Suffix with major or novel
15 Negatively charged particle
16 Waikiki wreaths
17 Invisible emanation
18 Suicide squeeze taps
19 Some cameras (abbr.)
20 Exasperate (*4 words*)
23 Remove, as from a cribbage board
24 Castaway's locale
25 Performed
27 Letter addenda (abbr.)
28 Outback hopper
31 Steak selection (*hyphenated*)
33 Ignore (*2 words*)
37 First-year law student, commonly (*hyphenated*)
38 Where a boxer goes after a knockdown (*2 words*)
41 No-___-land
42 Egg white
43 North Dakota or Arizona
45 Govt. narcotics watchdog (abbr.)
46 Japanese rival of IBM
49 Chewing ___
50 Figure skater Michelle ___
54 Woolly Andean
56 One way to get purified water (*2 words*)
60 University at New Haven
61 Without ___ in the world (*2 words*)
62 Bruins' school decal letters
63 Fashion designer ___ Cassini
64 Father, in refined English society
65 Travel by boat
66 Meat-inspecting agency (abbr.)
67 Parody
68 God of love

DOWN
1 Lead (*2 words*)
2 180-degree maneuvers (*hyphenated*)
3 Takes it all off
4 Throw, in a way
5 Perfume brand
6 ___ to one's neck (*2 words*)
7 "___ a stinker?" (Bugs Bunny line; *2 words*)
8 Authors Henry and Philip
9 Photographer ___ Adams
10 Rick's *Casablanca* love
11 "Bravo!" (*2 words*)
12 Member of the jet set?
13 Draft organization (abbr.)
21 Plumed heron
22 Dripping
26 Neighbor of Penna.
29 "Other," in Oaxaca
30 Lustrous gem
32 Capital of the former West Germany
33 Passionate desire
34 Vatican vestment
35 Gulf War missile
36 Vague amount
38 Rolls of 7 or 11 in craps
39 Painted on metal or glass
40 Domain
41 Chinese food additive
44 ___ out a living
46 Org. for Richard Petty and Sterling Martin, commonly
47 Actor ___ Estevez
48 Cellist Pablo ___
51 Concludes, with "up"
52 Songwriter's org.
53 "Peachy!"
55 Despicable character
57 1970s Chevrolet model
58 Cookie sandwich
59 Peasant worker
60 "___ go, girl!"

HINT: The answer to 28 Across is a common shortened form of a longer word. For a giveaway answer, see puzzle 87's page.

#63: 35D = LANGELLA

92

By the Numbers   by Sarah Keller

In this one, each long answer is a number. That should be all you need to know.

ACROSS

1 ___-ply tire
5 Male turkeys
9 Marina poles
14 Cartoon bear in Jellystone Park
15 Owl's sound
16 "If ___ a Rich Man" (*2 words*)
17 Casino game (*hyphenated*)
19 Like a fair playing field
20 Less demanding
21 Bottom of the boat
23 Sushi option
24 Signs of success, on B'way (abbr.)
26 Sports star ___ "Prime Time" Sanders
28 Rehemming, for example
32 Oscar nominee Diane ___
35 "___, humbug!"
36 Glorifies
38 Promotional overkill
39 From Korea or China, for instance
41 ___-Mart (retail chain)
42 Girl in "Calvin & Hobbes" comics
43 Former territories combined with Russia (abbr.)
44 Help out
46 State that's east of Illinois (abbr.)
47 More blistering
49 Battle weapons used in medieval times
51 Early time of one's life
53 Lacerate
54 Calendar abbreviation
56 Some whiskeys
58 He was Mingo in T.V.'s *Daniel Boone* (*2 words*)
62 Friend, to a Spaniard
64 Caliber of the Colt Peacemaker revolver (*hyphenated*)
66 Incurred, as expenses (*2 words*)
67 Toothpaste container
68 From the top
69 Greek island
70 Lost one's footing
71 Top ratings

DOWN

1 Computer memory measure
2 State whose capital is Des Moines
3 Mellows, winewise
4 Gary ___ of *Apollo 13*
5 Growth gland
6 Winning *Hollywood Squares* line, perhaps
7 Adrian ___ (quirky crime solver played by Tony Shalhoub)
8 Powerful horse
9 Barbara Bush's dog
10 Wonder
11 Number of trombones that led "the big parade" (*hyphenated*)
12 Shade source
13 Peddle
18 Earthling, in sci-fi stories
22 Cartoon cries
25 Winter falls
27 Diamond Head's island
28 Cause embarrassment to
29 Rustler's rope
30 Jack Benny's perpetual age, in a running gag (*hyphenated*)
31 Get a grip on
33 Think out loud
34 Basics
37 *The Untouchables* boss ___ Ness
40 Concerning (*2 words*)
42 Exclusive date
44 Pretentious
45 Came down hard in winter?
48 Copenhagen's continent
50 Palestinian leader
52 Lifts
54 Cleopatra's lover ___ Antony
55 ___ Sharif of *Funny Girl*
57 Music genre
59 Where ore is found
60 Smooth
61 Makes a hem
63 Type of reaction
65 Slugger's statistic, in box scores (abbr.)

HINT: The answer to 7 Down is also a name for a member of a religious order. The box alongside puzzle 94 has another hint.

#56: 50A = LORN

93

"Duh!" by Diane C. Baldwin

Here, the three long phrases are reasons someone might recite the puzzle's title.

ACROSS
1 You, to King James
5 Hawaiian instruments, for short
9 Motown's ___ Ross
14 Really trounce
15 Scruff of the neck
16 Island in New York Bay
17 Enthralled with
18 Was unable to remember (*3 words*)
20 Door spying feature
22 Commotions
23 Neighbor of Lebanon
24 Butter square
25 Honored mid-season athlete (*hyphenated*)
29 Awaken
33 Escalates
36 Venomous snake
37 Supermarket section
38 Tried to think (*3 words*)
41 Applies liquid cement
42 Divided Asian country
43 Ruby's color
44 Television award
45 Least wordy
47 Amusing activity
48 Goofed up
52 Left jolted
56 Chinese food condiment (*2 words*)
59 Was totally unaware (*3 words*)
61 Toot one's own horn
62 Fondly remem-bered song
63 Pervasive glow
64 Leafy greens
65 Puts on the bulletin board
66 Minus
67 Alaskan transport

DOWN
1 Triggers off
2 Pancake topper, for some
3 Exterior
4 Best of all worlds
5 Invalidate
6 Communist ___ Marx
7 Fencing sword
8 Do a tailor's work
9 Introduction into society
10 Ailments
11 "What a pity!"
12 Number of a cat's lives, proverbially
13 Sets a price
19 Distant
21 Divides in two
24 Kitchen gadgets
26 Hat, informally
27 Verbalized
28 Opera voice
29 Knight's title
30 Russian monarch, once
31 Tennis star Nastase
32 Tear violently
33 Hankering
34 Tropical tree
35 Pond covering
37 Humbles
39 Piano ivory
40 "Get it?"
45 Albacore
46 Racecourses
47 Elaborate parties
49 The "R" of RFD
50 School, to a Frenchman
51 Condensed into moisture, on the lawn
52 Look for bargains, perhaps
53 Saintly ring
54 Tacks on
55 Use a purl stitch
56 Swerve
57 What belongs to us
58 Affirmatives
60 Ripken of baseball fame

HINT: You might not have known that the root word in the answer to 51 Down could be a verb. The box next to puzzle 51 has a free answer for you, even if you don't need it.

#93: 59A = OOOLA

94

Way to Go...Not!   by Manny Nosowsky

Sometimes a puzzle's theme links two or more long answers together with a twist. Here's an example.

ACROSS

1 Holder of spectacles
5 Horn-honking Marx brother
10 Make well
14 Boat body
15 "The Hunter" constellation
16 Blues singer James
17 Ring around a pupil
18 Not really the way 27 Across goes (*2 words*)
20 Salary limit
21 ___ well (be a good omen)
22 Paradises
23 Leslie of *60 Minutes*
25 Cake brand "nobody doesn't like"
27 Costumed club employee, 1960–91 (*2 words*)

30 Unsteady
31 Possible reply to "Shall we?"
32 A long way off
35 Woodwind instrument
36 "Blue ___ Shoes"
38 Govern
39 Panhandle
40 Celebrity status
41 Island republic whose capital is Valletta
42 Not really the way 54 Across goes (*2 words*)
45 Educates
48 Chess and checkers
49 First-class, slangily
50 Not good-looking
51 Cornfield comment

54 Hippopotamus (*2 words*)
57 Coffee
58 A.A.R.P. part (abbr.)
59 Local group
60 "Thanks ___!" (*2 words*)
61 Thomas Hardy heroine
62 ___ a clue (doesn't know)
63 Departed

DOWN

1 Swank
2 Particular atmosphere
3 Blunders, perhaps (*3 words*)
4 Golfer Ernie
5 Sound from Santa (*3 words*)
6 In a dry manner
7 Ready to eat

8 Firecracker sound
9 Till bill
10 Great time of life
11 Merman or Mertz
12 Do penance (for)
13 Senior moment, for example
19 Fork-tailed marine birds
21 Kid in a crib
24 Kid
25 Took to court
26 Poker contribution
27 "No ___" ("I can handle this")
28 Earring site
29 Edit out
32 All-out (*hyphenated*)
33 Chorus singer
34 Harvest

36 Breeze (through)
37 Calls a strike?
38 Go quickly
40 Bottom level
41 "Goodness gracious" (*2 words*)
42 Stars of the future
43 Provokes (*2 words*)
44 Natural ability
45 Jack who ate no fat
46 Felony or misdemeanor
47 Itchy rash
50 *The Haj* author Leon
52 Stratford's river
53 Light bulb unit
55 "How's that again?"
56 ___ roll (doing well; *2 words*)
57 Chin bone

HINT: The clue at 42 Down refers to show business, not to astronomy. See puzzle 58's page for more help.

#92: 18D = TERRAN

95

Troubled   by Ed Early

The three long entries in this puzzle are clued in the same way. Coincidentally, they all begin with the same short word.

ACROSS
1 Noah's eldest son
5 Interest charges
10 Reached maturity
14 Bus alternative
15 Ocean menace, once (*hyphenated*)
16 Lymphatic mass
17 In an uncomfortable position (*3 words*)
20 Negligent
21 Thorough auto cleaner
22 Feature of a skirt
24 William Penn title
25 Health resort
28 English nobleman
30 Necktie

35 Nullified tennis serves
37 Finalize (with "down")
39 Sheeplike
40 In an uncomfortable position (*5 words*)
43 Measure of gold purity
44 Where "the buck stops"
45 It's found on a witch's nose
46 In-groups
48 Ump's cousins
50 Guitar innovator ___ Paul
51 ID document (abbr.)
53 Breakfast reading, perhaps
55 Conditionally released prisoners
60 Crib toy

64 In an uncomfortable position (*3 words*)
66 Mountain climber's challenge
67 Mousy color
68 Café au ___
69 Like most of the puzzles in this book, we hope
70 Roll-on buy
71 Gaelic laguage

DOWN
1 Something to wish upon
2 More than dislike
3 Purpose of a visit to the doc's office
4 Skirt types
5 Putin's constituents
6 Lawyers' org. (abbr.)

7 *Sweeney* ___ (Sondheim musical)
8 They are rimmed by gutters
9 Noise
10 Con
11 Objective
12 Beat by a hair
13 A lot of bucks
18 Capri, for one
19 Wide's opposite
23 Something to carry out
25 Relieve, as thirst
26 Rose part
27 Big name in video games
29 Permanent prisoner
31 Acknowledge
32 Like the flu
33 Agassi of tennis
34 Experiments
36 Bedframe segment

38 Grant's costar in *Houseboat*
41 Verdi opera
42 Turned (to), as lecture notes
47 Nap after noon
49 Trade
52 Farm labor leader ___ Chavez
54 Winter evening wear
55 Velocity
56 Trac II alternative
57 Some TVs and VCRs
58 Wild party
59 Railway siding
61 Ivan the Terrible, for one
62 Arrival gifts in Honolulu
63 Tivoli's Villa d'___
65 Wire service inits.

HINT: The answer at 43 Across can be spelled with a different first letter, but that variation usually concerns weight, not purity. Also, see puzzle 65's page.

#85: 22D = BASEL

Mixed Priorities

by Diane C. Baldwin

For the next five puzzles, we'll turn up the heat a little by omitting "2-word" tags and using some tougher clues. Not too tough, we hope.

ACROSS
1 James in *Giant*
5 Tot transport
9 Sesame Street grouch
14 Derby contest
15 Indian royalty
16 Stifle, perhaps
17 Sonic boomerang
18 Russian version of the name John
19 Secretary of State Powell
20 At a convenient time
23 Warning hue
24 Perform diligently
25 Little seedling
29 Letter opener's mark

31 Corn holder
34 Boy scout unit
35 First word of many Commandments
36 "Heart and ___"
37 "Now!"
40 Dangerous time for Caesar
41 Subtle suggestion
42 Sweater size
43 ___ se (in itself)
44 Up in smoke
45 A-one
46 Paver's gunk
47 Flock call
48 Occasionally
57 Hair-raising
58 Take a stroll
59 Libertine

60 Jaunty tunes
61 If not
62 Makes a blunder
63 Nasty weather
64 Sweetie
65 Lumber flaw

DOWN
1 Attracted
2 Apiece
3 Workout memento
4 Sign enhancement
5 Prickly hedge
6 Waxed enthusiastic
7 Partly open
8 Numerous
9 Mystical
10 Flamboyant

11 Caffeinated quaff
12 Related
13 Landlord's due
21 Flare up
22 Poppy derivative
25 Piece of bacon
26 Lion group
27 Pilot's affirmative
28 Expressions of delight
29 Polish up
30 Forfeited
31 Where suits are settled
32 Expenditure
33 Edit an expletive
35 Scanty
36 Go berserk

38 Brier feature
39 Homer classic
44 Most merry
45 Oil-carrying ship
46 Cliched
47 Model-maker's wood
48 "Shocking" swimmers
49 Part of a bride's attire
50 Writer ___ Stanley Gardner
51 Saw red?
52 Corduroy ridge
53 Arduous journey
54 Rhino's weapon
55 Cash on the continent
56 Biddy's abode

HINT: Regarding 1 Across: Sometimes it's difficult to tell whether a proper name in a clue is a first or last name. In this case, it's a first name. Also, see puzzle 72's page.

#78: 44A = RANDS

97

Chronometry 101   by Bernice Gordon

Each of the four long answers refers to a chronometer. That should keep you going for a second or two.

ACROSS

1 Tennis's Arthur ___ Stadium
5 Schoolroom group
10 See 41 Down
14 Reading material
15 Desert watering hole
16 Supplemental mil. org. estab. in 1942
17 "...with the rope in the library" board game
18 Product introduced in 1892 by Ingersoll
20 Sunday speech (abbr.)
21 *Gone With the Wind* plantation
22 Nouveau ___
23 Old ___ (United States flag)
25 Dressed
27 Bermuda is one
29 "That was ___, this is now"
30 "___ all, folks!"
31 Great ape from Borneo
36 Eject
37 Odds' opposites
38 Evening, in ads
39 Changing the tripmeter back to zero, for example
41 Own up to
42 Deliver a tirade
43 Is in dreamland
44 Argue about
48 Like a tack
49 John who played Gomez Addams on TV
50 Spider-Man creator Lee
51 Intense wrath
54 Seth Thomas, for one
57 "___ there, done that"
58 Slugger Aaron
59 In existence
60 Scored high on, as a test
61 Irving and Carter
62 Wrote up, as a speeder
63 NFL officials

DOWN

1 Kindergartner's recitation
2 One and only
3 Instrument containing sand
4 ___ out a living
5 Fraidy-cat
6 One of the Three Stooges
7 Largest continent
8 Family nickname
9 Sonic boom source (abbr.)
10 Anticipate
11 Screen door closer
12 Swanky hat designer Lilly
13 Rued the aerobics
19 Erroneous
21 Heavy weights
24 Coffee shop choice
25 Retired tennis star Michael
26 Eye part
27 "Ripley's Believe ___ Not"
28 Elisabeth of *Leaving Las Vegas*
29 Senator Lott
31 Sheeplike
32 Beneath
33 Chronometer
34 "Take ___ from me..."
35 New Jersey NBAers
37 Coup d'___
40 Tree part
41 With 10 Across, *M*A*S*H* star
43 Split up
44 Country house in Russia
45 Allah's religion
46 Hard and cold
47 Makes a selection
48 Apple creator Jobs
50 Funny sketch
52 Underwater obstacle
53 Extremes
55 PC alternative
56 "Sting like a bee" boxer
57 Tavern

HINT: In a pair of clues such as those at 10 Across and 41 Down: The answer to the clue containing the word "with" comes before the other one, and neither can be an incomplete word. See the box next to puzzle 79 for more help.

#71: 8D = SORTIES

Making Progress by Randall J. Hartman

98

The "progress" in this puzzle depicts a growing sense of confidence that comes with maturity.

ACROSS

1 Rapper born Tracy Marrow
5 Gene Krupa played them
10 Clean up
14 Agcy. head-quartered in Brussels
15 Weird
16 Capital of Norway
17 Storage access under some homes
19 Angler's gear
20 Napping
21 ___ Misérables
22 Alan of Shane
23 Rise on the horizon
25 Young 'un
27 Sounds of relief
30 Assume responsibility, symbolically
36 Burden
38 Pub choice
39 Rod of tennis fame
40 Boston airport
42 Hydrogen or nitrogen
43 Graceful antelope
44 Chicago airport
45 UFO passengers
46 Tennis pro Nastase
47 Home buyer's inspection
51 Sum up
52 Suffix with Siam or Japan
53 Shoot, in B westerns
55 Penn on film
58 Capp and Capone
61 Entertained
65 Contrarian
66 Jog without going anywhere
68 Cosmetics brand
69 Plunge into boiling water
70 Trout temptation
71 Hockey's Lady ___ Trophy
72 Does data entry
73 Disparage

DOWN

1 Machu Picchu inhabitant
2 Railroad crossing parade
3 Catchall abbr.
4 Throw in the ___ (give up)
5 Ivan the Terrible, for one
6 Salesman, briefly
7 Eurasian river
8 They became Cinderella's horses
9 Takes care of
10 Conflict that ended with the collapse of the Central Powers
11 Bewildered
12 Luge, for instance
13 Omit, in diners
18 Many August births
24 Too little
26 Guthrie of "Alice's Restaurant" fame
27 Permit
28 Uproar
29 8 Simple Rules star Katey
31 Student of Socrates
32 Admit, slangily
33 Walled city near Madrid
34 Two spades, perhaps
35 Evaporated, with "up"
37 Heading toward nightfall
41 Makes after taxes
48 Real-life model for Citizen Kane
49 Pituitary and adrenal
50 Camel feature
54 Scavenging seabirds
55 Volvo rival
56 One of the seven deadly sins
57 "This must weigh ___!"
59 Mrs. Ricky Ricardo
60 Crisp cookie
62 Humboldt's Gift writer Bellow
63 Light beige
64 Bambi and kin
67 French island

HINT: The answer to 31 Down is the classic philosopher who wrote The Republic. See puzzle 86's page for an outright giveaway.

#64: 57A = MANNA

Spoonerisms   by Randall J. Hartman

Spoonerisms are swaps of initial sounds of words (for example, "why hay" for "highway"). The results can be amusing.

ACROSS

1 He lost to Dwight in 1952 and 1956
6 "Toodle-oo"
10 Shoemaker's holemakers
14 Steady boyfriends
15 Secondhand
16 Casual talk
17 Thanksgiving dessert shortfall?
19 *Gone With the Wind* plantation
20 Before, poetically
21 Loamy soil
22 Fussy
23 Former Chief Justice Warren
24 Peter Pan's foe
25 1920s boxer Gene's quickness?

30 "___ diem" ("seize the day")
31 Out of kilter
32 Bambi's mother, for example
34 Cover up
35 Apportion
37 What an adjective modifies
38 ___-mo (replay technique)
39 The "E" in CEO
40 Becomes bitter
41 Singer Midler's Stockholm sweethearts?
45 Call a cab
46 Top-notch
47 Prolonged attack
49 Trade association
51 Chinese food additive, for short
54 Israeli airline

55 More than enough adventure for Goldilocks?
57 Not narrow
58 Hollywood's Heche
59 Alley Oop's girlfriend
60 Robin's residence
61 Turnpike
62 Handled the oars

DOWN

1 "___ to leap tall buildings..."
2 First word in a diary entry
3 Lingerie trim
4 Arctic diving bird
5 Set apart
6 Birthplace of Elvis
7 Garage sale warning

8 Pullover shirts
9 Classified items
10 Movie director's cry
11 Really weird
12 Brownish songbird
13 "Don't leave"
18 Golfer's shout
22 Youngster's equine ride
23 Award given by Chris Berman
24 Banged up
25 Semi loads
26 Wedgeshaped weapon tips
27 See 39 Down
28 Number of U.S. presidents born in Texas
29 "___ So Vain"
30 *Everybody Loves Raymond* network
33 "London" has two

35 Figure skater's leap
36 ___ *Misérables*
37 Post-it jotting
39 With 27 Down, star of *The Sopranos*
40 Summon
42 Baby national symbol
43 Didn't pass
44 Arizona necktie
47 Stitched up
48 "Would ___ to you?"
49 Baltimore Colt Hall of Famer Marchetti
50 Radius mate
51 Catty remark
52 Yard event
53 Cap and gown wearer
55 Where the successful go?
56 "You stink!"

HINT: The answer to 21 Across is an anagram of SOLES. See the box next to puzzle 93 for more help.

#57: 26D = ELOPE

100

Commonality   by Nancy Salomon

The title refers to a repeated letter pair shared by the theme answers.

ACROSS
1 1994 Peace Nobelist Yitzhak
6 Pugilist's punches
10 Actress Gilbert of *Roseanne*
14 10% taker
15 Gin flavoring
16 Duffer's sandy hazard
17 Danceable Latin rhythm
19 German auto
20 Lobe locale
21 Once around Indy
22 Belgrade's place
24 Kiddie toy on tracks
28 Samson's seductress
30 *I Love* ___
31 In seventh heaven
32 *Little Women* woman

33 Ask for alms
36 Z4 roadsters
37 Corp. VIP
38 Greek salad cheese
39 "Mayday!" signal
40 Billiard table fabric
42 Crumple, as a wad of paper
44 Big bag
45 Mogadishu residents
46 Certain canine youngster
50 State number 50
51 Witchy woman
52 Govt. Rx watchdog
55 Not "fer"
56 Trendy night spot
60 Organ for breathing
61 Top-notch

62 Bicycle wheel feature
63 Barrels of brew
64 Onion's cousin
65 Bike with a small engine

DOWN
1 Preakness event
2 Turkish title
3 Almond-flavored breakfast pastries
4 Business abbr.
5 Indefinitely large, as numbers go
6 Famed composer of fugues and cantatas
7 First Hebrew letter
8 Long fluffy scarf

9 Begins, as on a journey
10 ___-eyed (head over heels)
11 Island near Curaçao
12 Pie chart dividers
13 Beelike
18 Take ___ off (sit down)
23 Write on metal with acid
25 Web page visits
26 Bullring cheer
27 Butter alternative
28 Society newcomers
29 "Tickle me" doll
32 Lay a wager
33 Dive that creates a big splash
34 Ornamental case
35 Credibility problems

37 Jazz singer Laine
38 Envelope part
40 Convergence points, in math
41 Morally upright
42 "When the ___ breaks..."
43 Concert booster
44 Nasal sounds
45 Sissy on the screen
46 Cue stick application
47 Holland capital, after "The"
48 In debt
49 Self-pitying sound
53 Blue Devils' college
54 In the sack
57 Tiller's tool
58 Distinctive doctrine
59 Navy noncom

HINT: An advisor says defining 36 Across as "Yuppie wheels" would be "so 1980s." See puzzle 75's page for another hint.

#75: 69A = EZIO

101

Easy as Pie — by Mel Rosen

That's what we're shooting for in this collection. The theme answers in this puzzle relate to the title ... that's for sure.

ACROSS

1 Prefix meaning "half"
5 He visits many houses on Christmas Eve
10 Heats in the microwave, slangily
14 Unclose
15 As thin as ___ (2 words)
16 Bryce Canyon's state
17 Satellite TV receiver
18 My Cousin Vinny Oscar winner Marisa ___
19 Truck driver on the radio, in the lingo
20 "Gesundheit!" prompter
22 Cougar or Grand Marquis, in car ads, commonly
23 The People's Court matter
24 Having keen eyes (hyphenated)
27 One who's out for a stroll
30 "Joyful Girl" singer DiFranco
31 Statistic on a pitcher's baseball card (abbr.)
32 Gray wolf
36 MacDowell of Groundhog Day
40 Arithmetical expressions such as ½ and ⅜ (2 words)
44 Forbidden
45 Counterfeit
46 Cooking measure (abbr.)
47 Wheel of Fortune host Sajak
49 Exercise to be studied by a pupil
52 Unadorned (hyphenated)
58 Hog fat
59 Electronic junk mail
60 Bran contribution
64 Prefix with "bat" or "phobia"
65 Patronize, as a restaurant (2 words)
67 Handed-down history
68 Greenish blue
69 Proof of ownership, for a car
70 City NNW of Oklahoma City
71 Ben & Jerry's alternative
72 In a crafty way
73 Proof of ownership, for a house

DOWN

1 Bubbly drink
2 Iliad, for one
3 Interlock, as gears
4 At the pawnshop (2 words)
5 Obeyed "Down in front!"
6 Pleasant scent
7 Parent, upon a child's birth
8 Stadium levels
9 Clueless star Silverstone
10 Green summer squash
11 Facing the pitcher (2 words)
12 Bel ___ cheese
13 Destroy, as sensitive documents
21 Bullfighting cheer
25 ___ Stanley Gardner (author of Perry Mason stories)
26 Itty-bitty biter
27 Direction 90° clockwise from south
28 Opera feature
29 Gentle one
33 Bug spray brand
34 Bikini top
35 Tree with yellow ribbons?
37 Connect-the-___
38 Not ___ many words (2 words)
39 World's Strongest Man channel
41 VH1 stars (2 words)
42 You might get one to purchase a car
43 Lockup room
48 Receivers in entertainment cabinets (2 words)
50 Chips Deluxe baker, in ads
51 Went on a sloop, not a paddleboat
52 Word after "license" or "home"
53 Tied, as sneakers
54 Orderly arrangement
55 "... to fetch ___ of water" (2 words)
56 Sharply dressed
57 "Go ahead, ___ ears" (2 words)
61 Skeleton component
62 Lake the "E" in HOMES stands for
63 ___ Foxx of Sanford and Son
66 Mystery author Josephine ___

HINT: If the answer at 1 Across doesn't immediately jump to mind, start somewhere else. A good place to look is often a fill-in-the-blank such as the one at 63 Down. The box next to puzzle 105 has a free answer for you.

#130: 46D = LEVY

102

Say Again? by Norma Steinberg

In this straightforward puzzle, completing any part of any theme answer will give you a big headstart on the rest of that same answer.

ACROSS
1 Fearless; daring
5 ___ Rica
10 Wild party
14 "... blackbirds baked in ___" (2 words)
15 Zodiac sign before Taurus
16 ___ no good (2 words)
17 Identifies actual culprits (2 words)
19 Plummet
20 Rested overnight
21 Nobel Prize winner ___ Morrison
22 Eat elegantly
23 Elvis ___ Presley
25 Fashions
27 Distribute all over the place
31 Short pencil remainder

32 Snacked
33 Used hand motions
37 Sheriff Taylor's son, in Mayberry
38 "___ Not for Me" (Gershwin standard)
39 Glamorous singing star
40 Becomes useless (2 words)
43 Confused
45 Snakelike fish
46 Cast members
47 Squandered
50 Popular street name
51 Part of the foot
52 Unwanted plant
54 Chicken farm enclosures
59 Clinton's VP

60 Newsboy's cry (2 words)
62 General ___ Bradley
63 Go too fast
64 And others (abbr.)
65 Back of the neck
66 Trunk of the body
67 Alaska city

DOWN
1 Forbids
2 Birthstone for October
3 Green citrus fruit
4 Not shallow
5 "___ we talk?" (Joan Rivers line)
6 Public speaker
7 Simple guy going to a fair
8 Adolescent
9 Lends a hand

10 Very friendly (hyphenated)
11 Showery month
12 Big pebble
13 Aspirations
18 What a star on our flag represents
24 Blushing
26 Egyptian king's nickname
27 Winter precipitation
28 Deal (with)
29 Huge continent
30 "It'll be better" (2 words)
31 Gel
33 Belly
34 Anger
35 At all
36 Their day is in June
38 Clean the tables, in a restaurant

41 Witness
42 Where the pioneers lived (2 words)
43 Cassius Clay's fighting name
44 Fox trot or rumba
46 San Diego baseball team
47 Station ___ (family vehicle)
48 Fragrance
49 Fight
50 Measuring device
53 World's fair, commonly
55 Beasts of burden
56 Director Preminger
57 Baby buggy
58 Merchant's event
61 Uproar

HINT: Sometimes a clue appears to lead to an answer that is singular, not plural. 45 Across in this puzzle is an apt example. The answer is a plural word. See the box next to puzzle 111 for an outright giveaway answer.

103

Traffic Signs — by Roy Leban

Each of the long answers in this puzzle begins with a word or phrase you would see on a traffic sign.

ACROSS

1 Shade of hair
6 Sprint
10 "... rule them with ___ of iron" (Revelation 2:27, *2 words*)
14 Less strict
15 Little sweet sandwich
16 End-of-the-season event
17 Somehow (*4 words*)
20 *The Joy Luck Club* author Amy ___
21 Roves aimlessly
22 Inventor Thomas ___
23 Gun enthusiasts' org. (abbr.)
24 Caustic cleaner
25 Work assignment with no future (*2 words, hyphenated*)
30 Streisand, to her fans
34 Employ vigorously
35 Freezer tray contents
36 Authoritative decree
37 62, in Roman numerals
38 Hiawatha's boat
40 Fail to win
41 Poultry building
42 *Eat Drink Man Woman* director ___ Lee
43 Kind of alarm
44 Big burden
45 Claymation filming technique (*hyphenated*)
48 "Just ___ thought!" (*2 words*)
49 Former nuclear agency (abbr.)
50 *What's My Line?* panelist Francis
54 In ___ (undisturbed)
55 "___, humbug!"
58 Succumb, perhaps (*3 words*)
61 *The Simpsons* teacher ___ Krabappel
62 Leopard's perch
63 Clichéd western film
64 SeaWorld frolicker
65 ___ out (barely achieved)
66 "Untrue!" (*2 words*)

DOWN

1 Smear of ink
2 ___ Lang (Superboy's girlfriend)
3 Plowing team
4 Word often seen in advertisements
5 Harry Morgan series
6 Gizmo
7 Airport landings (abbr.)
8 Ocean
9 Pollen collector
10 Italian wine-producing region
11 "Go, team!" yells
12 Butter stand-in
13 Laura ___ of *Jurassic Park*
18 Weaver's thread
19 Laudatory poem
24 Prefix with "weed" or "motive"
25 Big name in automotive parts
26 Corporation that merged with Mobil in 1999
27 Sequence sometimes ending in "y"
28 Plumbers' targets
29 "By ___!" (emphatic shout)
30 Soundalike of A sharp (*2 words*)
31 Garlic mayonnaise
32 Deep-voiced opera singer
33 Dutch painter Jan ___
38 Film or tape cartridge
39 Prefix meaning "opposed to"
43 Bring into the center of attention (*2 words*)
46 Like matched socks
47 Apportion (out)
48 As well as
50 Affirmative votes
51 Go for a drive
52 Singer Horne
53 Airline that flies to Tel Aviv
54 German admiral who lost the 1914 Battle of the Falkland Islands
55 Joke victim
56 Greek war god
57 Role model
59 Mork's planet
60 ___ Paulo, Brazil

HINT: This puzzle is typical in that it relies on information from a wide variety of sources: world geography and history, television, mythology, the arts, the Bible, and so on. The thing is: Even though you may think you are relatively weak in an area, there is likely to be enough you do know to eventually solve the whole puzzle. For a give-away answer, see the box next to puzzle 118.

#136:
21A = AUMONT

104

Contusions   by Holden Baker

The four long phrases in this puzzle are tied together by the middle word in the center row.

ACROSS

1 Rent-___ (*hyphenated*)
5 Like very much
10 Slopes lift (*hyphenated*)
14 Model's stance
15 Advice to a type-A person
16 Miscellany
17 Epithet for the police (*3 words*)
19 Mountain lion
20 Trapshooting variety
21 Healing ointment from Gilead?
22 Sailboat bottom
23 Hailing shouts from a sailor
25 Came in second
27 Logo's relative
30 Kind of infection, in short
31 Feels poorly
32 "Mamma Mia!" group
35 Military blockade
38 Color TV pioneer (abbr.)
39 Discolored areas, and theme of this puzzle
41 Washday brand
42 Tex-Mex snack
44 Departs
45 Sister and wife of Osiris
46 Actress Carol and "Boop-Boop-A-Doop Girl" Helen
48 Climber's task
50 Cops and sheriffs
52 Port-au-Prince's nation
54 ___ *and the Detectives* (Disney film)
55 Simple rhyme scheme
57 Partner of pains
61 Outside the strike zone
62 1997 Smith and Jones sci-fi comedy (*3 words*)
64 "___ Plenty o' Nuttin'" (Gershwin song, *2 words*)
65 "___ Billie Joe" (1967 Bobbie Gentry hit, *2 words*)
66 Race created by H.G. Wells in *The Time Machine*
67 Female pigs
68 Bowling alley button
69 Half our children, roughly

DOWN

1 N.Y.P.D. broadcasts (abbr.)
2 Make dinner
3 "... so long ___ both shall live?" (*2 words*)
4 Fastens again
5 Prince Valiant's son
6 Pat Boone's daughter
7 Southwestern stews
8 Actor ___ Julia of *Havana*
9 Release from obligation
10 1964 Ustinov/Schell comedy caper film
11 Veined dairy product (*2 words*)
12 Actress Anouk ___ of *La Dolce Vita*
13 *Charlie and the Chocolate Factory* author ___ Dahl
18 ___ *Jury* (Spillane book, *2 words*)
24 Suave actor ___ Sharif
26 Glasgow gal
27 Bring in, as pay
28 Flaky mineral used in some auto finishes
29 Spider with an hourglass on her back (*2 words*)
30 Manuscript enclosure (abbr.)
33 Cartoon bunny
34 One's life, for short
36 Cheshire cat feature
37 Compass point
39 Marrow holder
40 Morales of *La Bamba* and *NYPD Blue*
43 Small villages
45 Foil strips used to decorate Christmas trees
47 Beguile or captivate
49 Run a blade through
50 Clark's exploration partner
51 Friend, to Fernando
52 Underwear brand promoted by Michael Jordan
53 "Take ___ out of crime!" (*2 words*)
56 "Venerable" English saint
58 Saint's aura
59 MBA's major (abbr.)
60 Has fun at Vail
63 "___ if I can help it!"

HINT: The answer to 56 Down is a homophone of the word "bead."
16 Across is also a homophone—of a butter substitute. For a free answer, see puzzle 126.

#107: 57D = ARLO

105 Arrivals   by Victor Fleming

The four long phrases in this puzzle all start with the same word.

ACROSS

1 Spaghetti, for example
6 Rubber ducky's milieu
10 Soccer announcer's shout
14 Not ___ out of place (2 words)
15 Farming unit
16 Patriot Nathan ___
17 "On second thought ..." (5 words)
20 Potato spot
21 "What ___ can I say?"
22 Helpers (abbr.)
23 2001, in Roman numerals
24 Part of CPA (abbr.)
26 Obtain rightful recognition or prosperity (4 words)
34 Doctoral exams
35 Senator ___ Hatch of Utah
36 Keanu Reeves role in The Matrix
37 Silent approving signals
38 Hot dog or taxi place
39 Complaint, slangily
40 One ___ million (2 words)
41 Home of the Minotaur
42 "Iron Mike" ___ of football
43 Have unfavorable consequences (4 words)
46 CIA head Porter ___
47 Witch
48 Whitewater investigator Kenneth ___
51 Hogwash
53 The Naked ___ (Leslie Nielsen film)
56 Gain prominence (4 words)
60 "He's ___ again!" (2 words)
61 Enjoy a book
62 Gets on one's nerves
63 Curtain holders
64 Agts.
65 Baker's need

DOWN

1 Tempo
2 "You, there, on the boat!"
3 Equivalent
4 Even contest
5 Twin sister of Apollo
6 Dugout clubs
7 Need aspirin
8 Prefix meaning "three"
9 Egg layer
10 Pac-Man menaces
11 Schlemiels
12 Arrived, as at O'Hare
13 "___ Fall in Love"
18 Lena of Alias
19 Black of Five Easy Pieces
23 Brooks and Gibson
24 Small, trumpet-like instrument
25 Oklahoma town
26 Shaped like a dunce cap
27 University of Maine city
28 Polite term of address
29 Clan emblems
30 Deliver a keynote speech
31 On a scale of ___ ten (2 words)
32 Year segments
33 Dieter's caution
38 Sellout Broadway shows, for short
39 Life history (abbr.)
41 Musical combination
42 Window covering
44 Small herons with showy plumes
45 "___, I'm Falling in Love Again" (1958 Jimmie Rodgers hit, hyphenated)
48 Frankenstein feature
49 Dog on the Yellow Brick Road
50 In the heart of
51 Ginger cookie
52 Former Ford models
53 ___ monster
54 Maui music makers, commonly
55 Robin's residence
57 Hockey Hall of Famer Bobby ___
58 Itsy-bitsy
59 Sliced dessert

HINT: In a clue such as 23 Down: If two names are joined by the word "and" it means the answer is a pluralized name. The box next to puzzle 135 has a bigger hint for you.

Looking in the Mirror   by Bernice Gordon

We don't expect you to solve the puzzle while looking in the mirror, but doing so would certainly show you what to look for.

ACROSS

1 Door frame upright
5 Complain
9 "When the ___ breaks ..."
14 Soothing lotion ingredient
15 Hodgepodge
16 "Filthy" money
17 City in Arizona
18 Fixes, as fights
19 Book of maps
20 Getting somewhere (*2 words*)
23 Shipped off
24 Flowery necklace
25 Hip (*2 words*)
29 "Do not ___" (hotel door sign)
33 "It's ___ Unusual Day" (*2 words*)
34 Tel ___, Israel
36 "The Pit and the Pendulum" author
37 Hearing some sharp scolding (*3 words*)
41 Extras on *The X-Files* (abbr.)
42 Hankerings
43 1990 Swayze/Moore film
44 Not difficult to pronounce
47 Sounds of contempt
48 ___-Magnon man
49 *Laugh-In* regular ___ Johnson
51 Looking into the future (*2 words*)
57 Made more comfortable
58 Ready for harvest
59 Stunt pilot's maneuver
61 Toss
62 Greek war god
63 Work on a manuscript
64 Sweet, sour, bitter, or salty
65 Rose plots
66 TV's "Warrior Princess"

DOWN

1 Leno who succeeded Johnny Carson
2 The stuff in a styptic pencil
3 Major NYC exhibit hall (abbr.)
4 Bird's bill
5 Trumpet's smaller cousin
6 Straighten up
7 Opposite of "left"
8 Sit for a portrait
9 Knife parts
10 Be smarter than
11 Pac-10 team's monogram
12 Like an overcast sky
13 "For ___ a jolly good ..."
21 Question from Judas (*3 words*)
22 "Sakes ___!"
25 Salary
26 "... ___ man with seven wives..." (*3 words*)
27 Hotsy-___
28 Pres. between FDR and DDE
29 Clamors
30 Under consideration regarding, as an acting role (*2 words*)
31 Awaken rudely
32 Alternatives to suspenders
34 *The African Queen* screenwriter James ___
35 "Brown Eyed Girl" singer ___ Morrison
38 Parachute material
39 Nixon's vice president
40 Greek letter
45 Give emphasis to
46 Pontoon structure
47 Tension
49 Blazing
50 Used a lasso
51 "...season to be jolly, ___ ..." (*2 words*)
52 Phrase on a garage sale sign
53 Seize suddenly
54 Trebek of *Jeopardy!*
55 Enjoyed the roller coaster
56 Slay (*2 words*)
57 Salamander
60 School-support organization (abbr.)

HINT: Before you check the box next to puzzle 145 for a free answer, consider 16 Across: If a clue has a word in quotation marks, it may mean that that word is meant to be taken figuratively, not literally. That's the case this time.

107

Priceless   by Norma Steinberg

In the sense of "at no cost to you."

ACROSS
1 Parts of barns
6 Hot tubs
10 Group of cows
14 Achieve harmony of opinion
15 Tempo
16 At all
17 Actress Dunne
18 Actor/singer Burl
19 Opening at a singles bar
20 Billy ___ Williams
21 Farmers' market handouts (2 *words*)
24 Zodiac sign after Pisces
26 Church services
27 Fingers and toes
29 TV classic *Family* ___
31 Adam's garden

32 Crop, as a snapshot
34 Ruggedly powerful
39 Camera part
40 Apparatus
42 ___ of expertise
43 Sometime in the future
45 As well
46 Raise, as a child
47 Patriot Nathan ___
49 Dignified and serious
51 Moistens, as a turkey
55 Ms. Streep
56 Unfettered (4 *words*)
59 Likely
62 Word on a popular stamp
63 Press out wrinkles

64 Bert's puppet roomie
66 "What he said!"
67 Casino machine
68 Boulders
69 Sunbathes
70 Broadway's equivalent of the Oscar
71 Like Georgia Brown, so the song goes

DOWN
1 Put down
2 Shrek, for example
3 Unspoken-for athlete (2 *words*)
4 Decimal system base
5 Deem appropriate (2 *words*)

6 Some CIA employees
7 Spread macadam
8 High cards
9 "Open ___" (Ali Baba's phrase)
10 Is useful to
11 Bad behaviors
12 Zellweger of film
13 Female attire
22 Takes five
23 Prepare potatoes, in a way
25 Wash out the suds
27 "The Farmer in the ___"
28 Think tank output
29 Duke or count
30 Shock jock Don
33 Factual
35 Before the bell

36 Write on spec
37 Jets or Mets
38 Knitter's purchase
41 Hard question
44 Actress Perlman
48 Lend a hand
50 Calls to customer service
51 Soundalike of A sharp (2 *words*)
52 Fragrance
53 Number of innings in a regulation softball game
54 Adolescence
55 Mentholated
57 Songwriter Guthrie
58 Gift
60 Walleyed fish
61 Exam
65 Argument

HINT: The clue at 1 Across may seem vague. If you write in an answer and it doesn't fit with other answers, don't be afraid to backtrack. This particular hint will work for you often. Don't fixate on what might be an incorrect guess— just back up and try again. For a giveaway, see the box next to puzzle 104.

#144: 44A = OVINE

Thrice upon a Time   by Victor Fleming

A selection of trios in kiddie lit.

ACROSS
1 Fllp, as a coin
5 Kooky
9 March 17 honoree (abbr.)
14 Baseball's Matty or Moises
15 Bradley or Sharif
16 ___ Haute, Indiana
17 Children's poem threesome (*2 words*)
19 ___ Gay (famous warplane)
20 "The Family Circus" cartoonist (*2 words*)
21 Licorice-flavored member of the carrot family
22 Affirmative reply
23 Children's story threesome (*2 words*)
25 ___ Francisco, California
26 Makes mad
27 Gleeful

30 Product identifier (*2 words*)
35 Lotion additive
36 Children's story threesome
37 Jacob's twin
38 Tours within tours (*2 words*)
40 Bygone anesthetic
41 2004 presidential hopeful Howard ___
42 Fed. agency that gave out draft numbers (abbr.)
43 Children's story threesome
47 TV brand
50 New Jersey NHL team
51 Managed forest land (*2 words*)
53 "Likewise" (*3 words*)
54 Children's poem threesome (*4 words*)

55 Figure skater Sonja ___
56 ___ *Brockovich*
57 Yacht's bottom beam
58 Numbers on the back of a baseball card
59 No-win situations
60 Perry Mason creator ___ Stanley Gardner

DOWN
1 Striped cat
2 Fran and Kukla's pal on old television
3 Smudges, as with dirt
4 Like a boat on the bottom of the sea
5 Paid-for Internet name
6 Make ___ (get rich, *2 words*)

7 Aspect, as of a problem
8 Three, in Napoli
9 Soaked in hot water
10 Dividers on Wimbledon courts (*2 words*)
11 Fork tine
12 French city where Van Gogh painted
13 Blue-green
18 Slow down or hold up
21 Flowerless plants
24 They don't tell the truth
25 MPH posting (*2 words*)
27 Owns
28 Boxer Muhammad or his boxing daughter Laila
29 Peas' place
30 Living thing
31 CD store section

32 Fire remnant
33 Actress West of old films
34 Continent with Eng. and It. (abbr.)
36 Goes "Heehaw!"
39 Brit's boob tubes
40 Industrial city NNE of Düsseldorf
42 Beer mugs
43 Harass
44 The Donald's first ex
45 Cheri of *Saturday Night Live* fame
46 Golf's "army" leader
47 Movie previewer
48 Like de Sade
49 Saunter
50 Some Morse Code units (not the dits)
52 Counterfeit
54 Convened

HINT: At 34 Down: For future reference: If the clue contains an abbreviation (except for "e.g." or "etc." in the styles of some editors), the answer is probably an abbreviation as well. There's a bigger hint in the box alongside puzzle 116.

#140: 12D = TORTE

109

Hm, Let's See ...   by Manny Nosowsky

If you don't know the words, just "hm" along. When you decide to tackle puzzle 149, you'll detect a similar thematic approach to this one.

ACROSS
1 Lubricates
5 Run after, as a robber
10 Understands, as a joke
14 Diva's solo
15 Tugs in tug of war
16 Shaped like a racetrack
17 Arranges with effort, as an agreement (2 words)
19 After the bell
20 Take out of the carton, as a new TV set
21 Hesitate while speaking (3 words)
23 Must-have card, to make blackjack
25 "Take a giant ___"
26 Hot tub
29 Witty Bombeck
32 Combo bet at the races

36 Everest's mountain range
39 Kitchen squares
40 Highest point
41 Scarecrow's stuffing
43 "A bit of talcum is always walcum" poet
44 Second call in bridge
46 Like mom made it (hyphenated)
48 Pencil end
50 Spick-and-span
51 ___ Diego
52 Settled, as a bill
54 Never used
56 Mammoth-sized, slangily
61 Blow one's top
65 Some (2 words)
66 Creator of church songs (2 words)

68 Come in last
69 Subject
70 "Oh, for Pete's ___!"
71 Russian ruler until 1917
72 Kicks from office
73 Those folks

DOWN
1 Hawaiian island
2 Iraq neighbor
3 Arm or leg
4 Where Pago Pago is
5 EMT skill (abbr.)
6 "Shh"
7 ___ vera (skin cream ingredient)
8 Run-down areas
9 Subject of a will
10 Yellow color imparter (2 words)

11 "Well, Did You ___?" (Cole Porter song)
12 "Cheerio!" (2 words)
13 Killed, as a dragon
18 Be outstanding
22 One that follows
24 Historic periods
26 Stock unit
27 "The Pied ___ of Hamelin"
28 One-celled animal
30 Traditional story
31 Baseball's Hammerin' Hank
33 Ceramicist's raw materials
34 Inventor Nikola
35 Pasty-looking
37 Germany, Italy, or Japan in WWII (2 words)

38 Identical
42 Get baby off the bottle
45 College administrator
47 Take the helm
49 "Agreed," in London
53 "___ Love Me?" (2 words)
55 Place for a watch
56 Sentry's warning
57 What aliens travel in (abbr.)
58 High, flat area
59 "Ball!" callers, commonly
60 Conniption
62 State with six sides
63 Lap dog, for short
64 Card that barely beats a deuce
67 British bathrooms, for short

HINT: The clue at 71 Across does not refer to a particular person's name, just the title. The box next to puzzle 150 has a free answer for you.

#143: 6D = HAGUE

Join the Club   by Randall J. Hartman

110

You can join clubs with many different focuses. This puzzle highlights four. The dues are minimal, we hope.

ACROSS

1 Profit
5 World Poker Tour stakes
10 Explosive deployed from a plane
14 "Yikes!" (*2 words*)
15 McQueen of *Papillon*
16 Tennis bad boy Nastase
17 Folding seat on deck (*2 words*)
19 Kudrow who played Phoebe on *Friends*
20 On land
21 Wrestling hold
23 Makes one's way
26 Negative vote
27 Yardstick; norm (abbr.)
30 Get copy ready
31 Photo or stamp books
35 Tough trip
37 The night before Christmas, and the night before January 1st
39 Jazz pianist ___ Blake
40 Stir up
41 Dummies
43 Big name in pineapples
44 Trial advocates (abbr.)
46 Kind of list (*hyphenated*)
47 Long-driving golfer John ___
48 Veggie item in some Asian cuisine dishes
50 Giraffe feature
52 ___ Maria (coffee-flavored liqueur)
53 Significant time
54 "To ___ human, to forgive, divine" (*2 words*)
56 She comes into a lot of money
60 Observed Yom Kippur
64 Fusses
65 Organically grown, additive-free nutrition
68 Expanding European alliance (abbr.)
69 Bert's buddy on *Sesame Street*
70 ___ Kournikova of tennis and modeling fame
71 FBI employee (*hyphenated*)
72 Sizes up
73 Optimistic

DOWN

1 "Duchess of Alba" painter
2 Triumphal shouts
3 Ruler measure
4 "Not a chance!"
5 Climbed, as the corporate ladder
6 To the ___ degree
7 4:00 London get-together
8 Wicked
9 Venus Williams's sister
10 Herman Melville book (*2 words*)
11 Mishmash
12 Varied (abbr.)
13 Nose, slangily
18 Oak or pine
22 Big wind
24 Chunk of fairway
25 The first thing to do, in kit instructions (*2 words*)
27 Watchband, for example
28 Very stale from overuse
29 Triangle in the Greek alphabet
32 Sinker of Allied ships (*hyphenated*)
33 ___ Vanilli (discredited pop singing team)
34 "Toodle-oo!" (*2 words*)
36 Important cog in the corporate wheel (*2 words*)
38 Meal with matzoh
42 Greek philosopher who taught Plato
45 Like some losers
49 Stablemate of Comet and Vixen
51 ___ and kin
55 Until now (*2 words*)
56 Put up on a wall, as a painting
57 Dutch cheese
58 Small amount
59 It's repeated after "Que," in a song
61 Ill-advised action (*hyphenated*)
62 Many, many years
63 June 6, 1944 (*hyphenated*)
66 Insect that lives in a hill
67 More than stretch the truth

HINT: At 10 Down: Melville's last story, set on a British ship in the Napoleonic wars, was adapted into two operas and a film ... the latter with Robert Ryan, Peter Ustinov, Melvyn Douglas, and other stars. See the free answer next to puzzle 147 if you need more help.

111 Name Echoes   by Roy Leban

Each theme answer is the possessive form of a name followed by a word that sounds like that possessive.

ACROSS

1 Deficiency
5 Clothing
9 Fiery crime
14 Algerian seaport
15 To ___ (exactly, *2 words*)
16 *The Cider House Rules* costar Michael ___
17 Clearasil target
18 Tear gas alternative
19 Singer ___ Gorme
20 Actress Dunaway's stage? (*2 words*)
23 E-mail screen button
24 Wear down
25 Shows a propensity toward
27 *Cocoon* director Howard
28 Chopping aid
31 Range of the Rockies from Idaho into 6 Down
34 Overhead sports-televising airship

36 Old McDonald's refrain
37 Nigerian-born pop singer
40 Give a personal assurance, as for a friend's word
43 Squabble
44 Bundle of papers or grain
46 Do exploratory work
48 Small stream
51 Affirmative vote
52 EMT's skill (abbr.)
55 ___ Sanford of *The Jeffersons*
57 Sneeze sound
59 Spill the beans
61 Midler's wagers? (*2 words*)
64 Jaguars and Impalas
66 End-of-the-week exclamation (abbr.)

67 Madrid miss (abbr.)
68 Goulashes and others
69 Romance novelist Victoria ___
70 Level at the stadium
71 *Siddhartha* author Hermann
72 Nights before
73 Quite

DOWN

1 Shoe that doesn't need laces
2 Famed jockey Eddie ___
3 Big ravine
4 Fought dirty
5 Not dry yet
6 Salt Lake City's state
7 Like some coffee
8 Playground attraction

9 Highest in a royal flush
10 Romano's salary increase? (*2 words*)
11 Avoid
12 "Come ___, the water's fine!" (*2 words*)
13 Scholarship consideration
21 Airtight closure
22 One of the Gabor sisters
26 Suffix meaning "full of"
29 VII doubled
30 Comedian Philips
32 Cloak-and-dagger org. (abbr.)
33 Right out of the oven
34 Bridges' gift-wrapping decorations? (*2 words*)
35 Young dog

37 Kazakhstan, for example, once (abbr.)
38 Hawaiian tuna
39 Goes astray
41 Wail
42 Work in the garden
45 State with keys (abbr.)
47 Sheep calls
49 Recede, as a tide
50 Grow incisors and molars
52 "My ___ Amour" (Stevie Wonder hit of 1969)
53 Harry ___ of books and films
54 Series of prayers, in Catholicism
56 State's second-in-command (abbr., *2 words*)
58 Where to watch *CSI: Miami*
59 Big party
60 Mandolin cousin
62 Lay a floor, perhaps
63 Young salamanders
65 Wind direction (abbr.)

HINT: At 31 Across: When a clue refers to another part of the puzzle, you are almost always being told to look at the *answer* with that number, not the clue. See the box beside puzzle 131 for a free answer.

#102: 43A = ADDLED

112

Much Ado   by Gail Grabowski

As is typical in many puzzles, the long answers here start with words with something in common. A word in the title is a clue to that commonality.

ACROSS
1 Outburst of days gone by
6 Squeezing snakes
10 Mouse catcher
14 Filmmaker Woody ___
15 It connects the back wheels
16 Time for eggnog
17 Roadster feature
19 "Let's go!"
20 Mexican coin
21 Craving
22 Investigate again, as a police case
24 Require
26 Well-known
27 Protect
30 Materials for formal gowns
31 Get away from

32 More mature
33 Poke fun at
36 Mornings (abbr.)
37 Lawyer's charge
38 Dollar bill
39 Negative responses
40 Cried on stage, maybe
42 Be too dramatic, perhaps
44 Swan Lake, for example
46 Noise
47 Harem keeper
48 "With ___ ring ..."
49 Sound signals
50 Green shade
51 List of performers
55 Hourly pay (2 words)

56 Doodler's sheet (2 words)
59 Bakery appliance
60 Chapters of history
61 Sports complex
62 Permits
63 A few
64 Mommy's mate

DOWN
1 Marshal Wyatt ___
2 Elmer's product
3 Charitable gifts
4 Made a fillet of
5 NBC weekend comedy, briefly
6 Headquartered
7 Some bovines

8 Pie ___ mode (2 words)
9 Nonnegotiable price
10 Wealthy business-person
11 Children's play area (2 words)
12 Plants used in lotions
13 Quaker William ___
18 Looked at
23 Kuwait ruler
25 WSW's opposite
26 Lost color
27 College official
28 Ticklish Muppet
29 Fault-finding person
30 Icy precipitation
32 Frequently

34 "What's gotten ___ you?"
35 Keg contents
40 Choir member
41 Students' sessions
42 Yale student
43 Eyelash enhancer
45 Beings from another planet
46 British bloke
47 Debonair
48 Make fun of
49 Like a truant soldier (abbr.)
50 British baby buggy
52 Mimicked
53 Transmit
54 Cafeteria carrier
57 ___-Magnon man
58 Bachelor's apartment

HINT: When a clue uses a word such as "briefly" or "shortly," as in 5 Down, the idea is to hint at an abbreviation without using a sledge-hammer to get your attention. Puzzle 102's page has an outright giveaway answer for you.

#117: 18D = DRED

113

Hot and Bothered   by Victor Fleming

Although the theme answers don't reflect calm and tranquility, we certainly hope the puzzle itself doesn't leave you hot and bothered.

ACROSS
1 Mel who gave voice to Bugs Bunny
6 Country bumpkin
10 Passion
14 Edmonton NHL player
15 Daredeviltry legend Knievel
16 *Othello* villain
17 Spin doctor's concern
18 Getting miffed (*2 words*)
20 Roundup rope
21 "___ la vista, baby!"
22 Born, in the wedding pages
23 ___ Paulo, Brazil
25 Manhattan or Catalina (abbr.)
27 Miffed (*4 words*)
35 Brings to bear
36 Humorist
37 Ely and Howard

39 Calcutta coin
40 Casino cube
41 Old-time comic actor Arbuckle
42 Weight unit at a pharmacy
43 $5 bill, slangily
44 Covers with hardened steel, as a humvee
45 Getting miffed (*3 words*)
48 Tyrannosaurus ___
49 Gear tooth
50 Shade tree
53 Posed a second time
56 Drying-out period, briefly
61 Miffed (*2 words*)
63 Island off Venezuela
64 Squad
65 "Do ___ others ..."
66 San Francisco gridder, familiarly

67 Landers and Richards
68 Anjou or Bartlett
69 Tries out

DOWN
1 Get really angry
2 Succotash bean
3 "What a shame!"
4 Film images in the darkroom (abbr.)
5 Wood preservative
6 Got another take on film
7 Part of the eye
8 Honey-producing insects
9 Snob
10 Turn sharply
11 Qualify for
12 Pulitzer winner James ___
13 Body of ore

19 Motor company that made the Rambler
24 Vienna's country (abbr.)
26 One-time NFL team (*3 words with abbr.*)
27 Arctic Ocean hazard
28 Community outside the city
29 Katmandu's land
30 Aftershock
31 In debt
32 Old-style cry of disgust
33 *The Chosen* author Chaim ___
34 ___ nous ("just between us ...")
38 The "S" of CBS (abbr.)
40 Uproar
41 Pleasant-smelling

43 Renovated (*2 words*)
44 "Many moons ___ ..."
46 "What ___ you thinking?!"
47 Use one's authority on behalf of (*2 words*)
50 Blues singer ___ James
51 Legal claim
52 Thom ___ shoes
54 Loudness unit
55 Shaving lotion brand
57 Toledo, Ohio's lake
58 Attila's followers
59 Assist in illicit activity
60 Prevents from entering
62 Distance measures in Canada (abbr.)

HINT: The loudness unit at 54 Down is an anagram of "nose," not "note." If you need more help, see the giveaway next to puzzle 140.

#126: 51D = OMNI

114

Ups and Downs   by Holden Baker

An alternate name for this puzzle might have been "Location, Location," but that's the title on #119!

ACROSS
1 "___ it seems" (*2 words*)
5 Read quickly
9 Manly
14 Ukraine's capital
15 Bye-bye (*hyphenated*)
16 Made eyes at
17 Adolescent's woe
18 Straightforward; without tricks or disguise
20 Tube-nosed seabird
22 Skirt length
23 MS-___ (Windows precursor)
24 Angrily
26 Humdinger
28 Firefighters' needs
30 Car from Avis, for example
34 Pre-Columbian Mexican
37 Ticket receipt
39 Issue a challenge to
40 Wealthy
41 Chicks' calls
42 *Desire Under the ___* (O'Neill drama)
43 Prefix meaning "both"
44 Functions
45 Colgate rival
46 University in Waco, Texas
48 Correct, as a computer program
50 Carries laboriously
52 High-rise "patio"
56 Lamb's mother
59 Golfers' gadgets
61 Islands with lagoons
62 Inside the hull, on a ship
65 Vehicles for ETs (abbr.)
66 Russian pancakes
67 Shout "Yay team!"
68 Baseball squad
69 Icy rain
70 Railroad depots (abbr.)
71 Sandra and Ruby

DOWN
1 Giraffe's cousin
2 Kitchen utensil
3 *I ___ Letter to My Love* (Melissa Manchester musical, *2 words*)
4 Past one's prime (*3 words*)
5 Runs out the clock
6 Taxi
7 Physics particle
8 Part of USNA
9 Alabama seaport
10 In the past
11 Not naked
12 Big sandwich
13 Bookie's numbers
19 Prosperous residential areas
21 Workers' discrimination watchdog (abbr.)
25 Affirmative replies
27 Resistance group
29 Knight's charger
31 Cock-and-bull story
32 *A Farewell to ___* (Hemingway novel)
33 For fear that
34 What the "A" in UAE stands for
35 Coors malt-beverage brand
36 Frozen-treat chain that started in Little Rock in 1981
38 Sports surprise
41 Erased
45 Brief and to the point
47 Beat through superior cleverness
49 Animals
51 Soothsayers
53 1966 Michael Caine film remade in 2004 with Jude Law
54 Dolly the sheep, for one
55 Highway curves
56 Recedes
57 What Pussy fell into, in a nursery rhyme
58 Nobelist ___ Wiesel
60 Glasgow resident
63 What 4 x .25 equals
64 RV's turn-in (abbr.)

HINT: The answer to 20 Across is an anagram of the word REPTILE without the I. See puzzle 128's page for a giveaway answer.

#137: 50D = SERE

115 Beastly Behavior   by Diane C. Baldwin

The four long entries use animal names as verbs and, consistently, all in the past tense.

ACROSS

1 Burst of growth
6 Bugler's farewell
10 Piggy bank opening
14 Rags-to-riches author Horatio ___
15 Start of an invention
16 Possess
17 Gobbled greedily (2 words)
19 Divisible by two
20 Engage in espionage
21 Superman's girl
22 Off course
24 Wild plum used to flavor gin
25 Cutting sound heard in a barber shop
26 Built a nest egg (2 words)
32 Satyrs
33 Tousle
34 "What have we here!"
35 Small bills
36 Bottom-of-the-barrel stuff
38 Distort, as statistics
39 Consumed
40 ___ Mawr (Pennsylvania college)
41 Be an embezzler
42 Goofed off (2 words)
46 "No ifs, ___, or buts!"
47 Devoid of emotion
48 Type of tuna
51 Archipelago member
52 Seventh Greek letter
55 Ids' counterparts
56 Behaved boastfully about (2 words)
59 Ultimatum word
60 Ben Franklin flew one
61 Stave off
62 Crystal ball reader
63 Practice boxing
64 Amusing tales

DOWN

1 Lumber mill machinery
2 Plunk down
3 The opposite of "beautiful"
4 Boxing match official
5 Lattice for climbing plants
6 Less cluttered
7 Time-wasting bothers
8 Chapel bench
9 Mental well-being
10 Tibetan mountain guide
11 Volcanic outflow
12 Kitchen hot spot
13 Revival or circus covering
18 Type of mat or bell
23 Shakes off (with "of")
24 Tries for a tan
25 Haul off and belt
26 ___ Domingo
27 Head of a hive
28 Improve, as text
29 Snatched from dreamland
30 In the lead
31 Tomcat's call
32 Ale suds
36 Where ships are repaired (2 words)
37 Some whiskeys
38 Ticket piece
40 Stooped over
41 "___ My Prince Will Come"
43 German equivalent of "emperor"
44 Test fill-in
45 Exercise control
48 Followers in a hive
49 Goggle at
50 Be a busybody
51 Tiniest bit
52 Constantly
53 Slender gull
54 Liberal ___ (college major)
57 Tear
58 Eggs, to a biologist

HINT: The answer at 48 Across is the same as a Spanish word meaning "nice" or "pretty." See puzzle 142's page for a giveaway answer.

#141: 26D = SAUD

116 Tourist Attractions by Sarah Keller

Identified by state only. Even so, you should be very familiar with these tourist attractions.

ACROSS

1 Depart
6 Oregon's capital
11 Amount in classic Brylcreem ads
14 Go over the books
15 Tropical American relative of the raccoon
16 Big block of time
17 Tourist attraction in Arizona (2 words)
19 New Jersey basketball player
20 ___ Like It Hot
21 Singing brothers
22 Editorialize
24 Show surprise or shock
26 Andean beasts
27 Tourist attraction in New Jersey (2 words)
32 Night ___ (Harry Anderson sitcom)
33 Paid killer
37 Mrs. Morgen- stern of Rhoda
38 ___ once (suddenly, 2 words)
40 Phrase that concludes a wedding vow
41 Not likely
44 Set aside as a portion
46 Tourist attraction in New York State (2 words)
49 Hollywood's Hedy
52 Takes a role on stage
53 Open-air entryways
54 Wander
56 Start of Hamlet's soliloquy (2 words)
60 Dot follower, in Internet addresses
61 Tourist attraction in Florida (2 words)
64 Brian of Roxy Music
65 "Candle in the Wind" performer ___ John
66 Start of the U.S. motto (2 words)
67 Neither Rep. nor Ind.
68 Speaks unclearly
69 Like some salsa

DOWN

1 Falls behind
2 New money standard north of the Mediterranean Sea
3 Cain was his son
4 Oil partner
5 Airport schedule abbr.
6 Shrimp dish
7 Super (hyphenated)
8 Potato chip brand
9 Eisenhower's WWII command (abbr.)
10 Nikon competitor
11 Blue jeans material
12 Sports venue
13 Kathy of Misery
18 Broadway players
23 Settles up
25 Word after fire or red
26 Shopper's aid
27 Tums target
28 Fuss
29 Hawaiian festival
30 Type of lily
31 R.E. Lee's side (abbr.)
34 Window frame part
35 Something to worship
36 Negative words
38 Off yonder
39 Type of nut on a car wheel
42 ___ Brith
43 Outbursts
44 Back, at sea
45 "___ in is a rotten egg!" (2 words)
47 Relatives of crows
48 ___-deucy
49 Spiked
50 Observe Yom Kippur, perhaps
51 1983 Keaton/ Garr comedy (2 words)
54 Q-V filler
55 ___about (roughly, 2 words)
57 Associations (abbr.)
58 Take care of extra lipstick
59 Small whirlpool
62 Under the weather
63 The ___ (Broadway musical based on a Baum classic)

HINT: Re 10 Down: If the clue contains a brand name, the answer is almost guaranteed to like- wise be a brand name. There's another hint for you alongside puzzle 139.

#108: 12D = ARLES

117

They're Educational — by Thomas W. Schier

The three long phrases in this puzzle match the theme nicely. They *do not*, however, match each other or form a sequence.

ACROSS
1 Bit of gossip
6 Gemstone defect
10 Miles away
14 Parenthetical comment, as in a play
15 Priest of the East
16 Extensive Asian desert area
17 Junior high, for example (*2 words*)
20 London stroller
21 Frees
22 Cut into two equal parts
23 "... lived happily ___ after"
25 Sounded like a snake
26 Used up carelessly
29 Cause to swell
31 Do tailoring
32 Biblical kingdom north of Edom
33 Untold centuries
36 Institution of higher learning (*3 words*)
40 Twice five
41 Wine and ___
42 Shouts loudly
43 Like old bread
45 Cleans a blackboard
46 National song
49 All-comers tournament
50 Whiskers
51 Actress Garr of *Tootsie*
53 Impending times
57 Highly structured educational institution (*2 words*)
60 Neck-and-neck
61 Read Braille
62 Gain computer access (*2 words*)
63 Teacher's furniture
64 Williams and Turner
65 Trap

DOWN
1 Speak with a rough voice
2 Computer operator
3 Mineral added to paint
4 Dashboard instrument that measures distance traveled
5 Stimpy's TV pal
6 Natural talent
7 Crisco alternative
8 Carter and Irving
9 Isn't now
10 Horror-struck
11 Victims of April 1st jokes
12 Superior to
13 Got all stirred up
18 Scott in an 1857 slavery decision
19 ___ Pet (novelty gift item)
24 Exceedingly
25 Rail rider
26 Float on air
27 Skin lotion ingredient
28 Knock for a loop
29 Carried
30 Put on, as skates
32 Daily delivery
33 Sea shockers
34 Goatish glance
35 "Untouchable" Eliot ___
37 Wax-coated cheese in a ball
38 Ancient stringed instrument
39 Pressured, in a way (*2 words*)
43 Get smaller, as some garments
44 Examination
45 Sweeping story
46 Name of three Ottoman Empire rulers
47 Easily duped
48 Floor or roof squares
49 Face-to-face exams
51 Family diagram
52 Used binoculars
54 "Tom's Diner" singer Suzanne
55 Kuwaiti leader
56 "Auld Lang ___"
58 Fore's counterpart, on a ship
59 Roker and Capone

HINT: The answer at 54 Down is also the name of an old Chevrolet model, and the name of the brightest star in the constellation Lyra. If you need a freebie answer, see the box next to puzzle 112.

#120: 35D = COIF

118

Out in Front   by Norma Steinberg

Out in front of an idealized suburban house, that is. Your results may vary.

ACROSS

1 City transporters
5 "Yes, ___!"
9 Ski resort incline
14 Bassoon's smaller cousin
15 Airport in a Paris suburb
16 Choir part
17 Twangy musical genre
19 ___ Rizzo (Dustin Hoffman's *Midnight Cowboy* role)
20 Casino transaction
21 R2-D2, for instance
22 Hearth leftovers
23 Smooch
24 Cream of the crop
26 Manufacturer's offer

29 Newsman ___ Hume
30 "___ Four" (the Beatles)
33 Fortune teller's clues
34 Sobs
35 Before, in poetry
36 The middle W in WWW
37 Showed displeasure vocally
38 Make booties
39 They sang "Evil Woman"
40 *Polar Express* star Tom ___
41 Stands up to
42 Gridiron judge, for short
43 Formerly
44 By a small margin
45 Gamut
47 Rough up

48 Kitchen appliance
50 Embellish
52 Infantry soldiers (abbr.)
55 Investigator's projects
56 Hillary Clinton's successor (*2 words*)
58 Open-eyed
59 Otherwise
60 Songwriter Guthrie
61 In a bad mood
62 Homeowner's paper
63 Song for two

DOWN

1 ___ salad
2 Competent
3 Boxing match
4 Call, in a hand of poker
5 Sullen

6 Mideast natives
7 As well
8 Unsolved puzzles
9 Gibraltar and others
10 Last, but not ___
11 Unable to decide (*3 words*)
12 Stand for a portrait
13 God of love
18 Dixie breakfast side dish
23 *Citizen* ___ (Welles film)
25 Fibbed
26 Sculling team member
27 Author ___ Zola
28 An easy life (*3 words*)
29 Penniless
31 The Little Mermaid herself

32 Flag-maker ___ Ross
34 Purposely out of sight
37 More ___ for the buck
38 Malden or Marx
40 It's said to be the best policy
41 Flora and ___
44 Kept out
46 Fend off
47 Desktop computer peripheral
48 "Shoo!"
49 Yarn
51 Mrs. Roy Rogers, ___ Evans
52 Spiritual teacher
53 Small land mass
54 Jigger at a bar
57 Naughty

HINT: 1 Down could also have been clued with a reference to the great baseball star Ty, or to the great actor Lee J. If you need more help, look for it alongside puzzle 130.

#103: 29D = JINGO

119 Location, Location   by Ed Early

If you liked puzzle 114, this one should be at least as much fun.

ACROSS
1 Starts
7 Place for a rubber ducky
11 Cut of hog meat
14 Try to intimidate, like a lion (2 words)
15 Zoning unit
16 Parseghian of coaching lore
17 Location for one who's in seventh heaven (5 words)
20 Thermostat component
21 Covered by Prudential, for example
22 Enjoyed
24 Fork prong
25 Up in the air
30 Knight's title
31 Washington lawmaker (abbr.)
32 Trust
34 Shindigs
37 Location for one who's very remote (3 words)
42 Autumn month (abbr.)
43 Walked behind
44 E-mail address ending
47 Take a chance
48 Word that can precede "shirt" or "shop"
49 Change for a five
51 Often-honored actress Streep
53 On-the-scene TV gear
55 Practical
60 Location for the minute hand at half-past (4 words)
63 She survived Lennon
64 Older ski lift (hyphenated)
65 ___ del Fuego
66 Pre-1991 map abbr.
67 Wheel of Fortune's ___ Pictures Studios
68 Prisoner

DOWN
1 Homey in the 'hood
2 Long, long times
3 Slalom course opening
4 Its symbol is Fe
5 Downtimes for toddlers
6 Happy hour seat
7 Cave dweller
8 More sore
9 Prevailing tendency
10 Axes
11 Emmylou or Richard
12 Dahl or Francis
13 Make angry
18 The ___ Kid (1979 Gene Wilder film)
19 Inning statistic
23 Brownish-red pear
25 Furnish with weapons
26 Hawaii garland
27 Like farmer MacDonald, per the song
28 Stereotypical dog name
29 Body powder
33 After taxes
34 U.S. monetary unit (abbr.)
35 Big-eyed birds
36 Exhibition
38 "Pretty soon, maybe" (2 words)
39 Farm female
40 Stephen ___ of Bad Behaviour
41 D.C. summer clock setting (abbr.)
44 Jazz groups
45 Steak smotherers, perhaps
46 Wise counselor
47 Lament
50 "Park your carcass!"
51 Cha-cha's cousin
52 Christine of Chicago Hope
54 Barracks beds
56 Jockey's control strap
57 "There's gold in ___ thar hills!"
58 Bar mitzvah dance
59 Mongol's tent
61 Cook bacon
62 Norma ___ (Sally Field film)

HINT: As you'll see at 11 Down and 12 Down, similarly structured clues can lead either to first names or last names. It's meant to be a puzzle. Oh, and puzzle 144's page removes one of this puzzle's little puzzles.

120

Drink up — by Alan Olschwang

Each theme answer in this puzzle starts with a kind of beverage. And don't let several abbreviations throw you off track.

ACROSS

1 Chicago's downtown area
5 Mideast citizen
9 Claw
14 Madame Bovary
15 Lasso
16 Battery terminal
17 Plantation where pekoe and such is grown (2 words)
19 Scatter, as seed
20 Belong intrinsically
21 Most in need of a good dry-mopping
23 Code-cracking org. that's part of the Department of Defense (abbr.)
24 Sixth sense (abbr.)
26 A Stooge
27 Asian relative of the ox (2 words)

33 Speed-of-sound designator
36 Train stop (abbr.)
37 Made peaceful
38 "Half ___ is better than none" (2 words)
40 Ending for a website address
42 Adored
43 Part of a recipe instruction (2 words)
45 Poisonous snake of Egypt
47 Golf duffers' delights
48 Office workday recesses (2 words)
51 Islam or Christianity (abbr.)
52 NNW's opposite
53 Long-snouted fish

56 Union general Philip or actress Ann
61 Pixy
63 Eagle's nest
64 Breakfast treat (2 words)
66 Sod
67 Writer Wiesel
68 Lulu
69 Balance sheet plus
70 Opposite of "admit"
71 "Don't leave"

DOWN

1 Admit (2 words)
2 Portents
3 Nebraska's largest city
4 Call on a beeper
5 Apprehends
6 Reel partner
7 Mimicked
8 Desensitize
9 Chic; refined

10 Debater's point-of-view
11 Traditional knowledge
12 Keats works
13 Salamander
18 Neighborhood
22 Kind of music
25 Townshend of the Who
27 Pier
28 Detection device
29 Failures
30 Thomas Edison's middle name
31 Ogle
32 Probabilities
33 Neither feminine nor neuter (abbr.)
34 Singing voice lower than soprano
35 Hairdo
39 Most impassioned

41 Takes advantage of
44 Require
46 Janitor's opener of many doors
49 Fingered
50 Retained
53 Titan
54 Sailing (2 words)
55 Make a second attempt
56 Long narrative novel
57 Towel appliqué
58 Important times
59 Greet the judge, in court
60 Cairo's river
62 Australian marsupials, slangily
65 Vietnam Veterans Memorial architect Maya ___

HINT: You might remember a jazz trombonist (first name Jack) whose surname is spelled the same way as the answer at 17 Across. And see puzzle 117's page for a giveaway answer.

#131: 40A = GAUNT

121 Let's Go Bowling   by Randall J. Hartman

This puzzle was evidently written around New Year's Day. If you follow college sports, the theme will show up before you're a quarter through.

ACROSS

1 Cover of darkness
5 Feels sorry for oneself
10 Mystery writer John Dickson ___
14 *On the Waterfront* director ___ Kazan
15 ___ Acrobat (publishing program for PDF files)
16 Bread spread
17 Fruit dessert (*2 words*)
19 Announcement fanfare
20 Reaction in a haunted house
21 Subway stop
23 Show respect, perhaps
26 Self-centeredness
27 Wrestling surface
30 Gen. Robert ___ (*2 words*)
31 Ballroom figure
35 At all times
37 Brother of Cain and Abel
39 "___ at the office" (*2 words*)
40 Mexican mister
42 Dr. ___ of gangsta rap
43 "Just do it" athletic shoes
44 Responded to reveille
45 "___ come back now, hear?"
47 Literary sleuth ___ Wolfe
48 Result of too much pressure
50 Edible mollusk
52 Original Pink Floyd member ___ Barrett
53 "Mamma ___!"
54 Marisa ___ of *My Cousin Vinny*
56 Wash thoroughly
60 Release from prison
64 Listen to
65 Young lady's benefactor, at times (*2 words*)
68 Prefix meaning "opposed to"
69 Wear away, as by wind or water
70 New Mexico art community
71 Sit for a portrait
72 One of the Seven Dwarfs
73 Brontë heroine Jane ___

DOWN

1 Animates, with "up"
2 ___ Baldwin of *Glengarry Glen Ross*
3 Pinocchio, for example
4 Ties up, as shoes
5 Lions and tigers and bears
6 Poem of praise
7 Pork-barreler, for short
8 Subsides
9 Ready for the start of a concert
10 Agricultural machine invented by Eli Whitney (*2 words*)
11 Jai ___
12 Make over
13 Mottled horse
18 Go beyond mere dislike
22 Another time
24 On welfare, presumably
25 Take away
27 Southwestern land formations
28 Prevent
29 Andrea Bocelli or Placido Domingo
32 Angel food and upside-down
33 All possible
34 Put in new grass
36 Sally Rogers portrayer on *The Dick Van Dyke Show*
38 Ring response
41 Varnish ingredient
46 Eel cousin
49 Back-talked
51 Anthropologist Margaret
55 Ticked off
56 London lad
57 Letterman competition
58 Has brunch
59 Continental cash
61 June 6, 1944 (*hyphenated*)
62 Aroma
63 Wall Street inits.
66 Republicans, for short
67 Citrus drink

HINT: Regarding 29 Down: If two items (here, names) are connected by the word "or," the clue directs you to think of a common attribute (or perhaps occupation) the two items share. See puzzle 138 for a giveaway answer.

#146: 28D = LEHI

Hitting the Highway   by Tony Orbach

Sometimes you have to grab a meal where you can. Not that that's always a bad thing.

ACROSS

1 Leg, slangily
4 Unsurpassed
8 Devilfish
14 Whopper
15 Sharif or Epps
16 ___ Rico
17 Winter clock setting for the east coast (abbr.)
18 Doozy
19 St. George, with regard to the dragon
20 In a normal voice
22 Tape machine near the TV (abbr.)
24 When lunch hour ends for many (2 words)
25 Glowing gas used in billboard lights
26 The Lord High Executioner in The Mikado
27 Promissory note of a sort (abbr.)
28 Where to find the 36 Down restaurant (2 words)
31 Ewe's mate
34 Belief in God
37 ___ Tin Tin

38 "___ and Away!" (5th Dimension hit, 2 words)
39 What the restaurant typifies (2 words)
42 ___-bitty
43 Opposite of SSE
44 Maps within maps
45 Org. whose motto is "Be Prepared" (abbr.)
46 Like the restaurant's food (so they say)
48 Despite, briefly
50 Astronaut ___ Shepard
51 Some deli loaves
55 Wheel of Fortune star Pat ___
57 Big name in ATMs and cash registers (abbr.)

58 One begins "The Lord is my shepherd"
59 "Gangsta's Paradise" rapper
61 Sgt. Snorkel's pooch in Beetle Bailey comics
63 ___ de Janeiro
64 Inconsistent
65 Get introduced to
66 Basset hound or golden retriever
67 Word before Storm or Shield
68 Wide receivers
69 Avenue crossers (abbr.)

DOWN

1 Discover bit by bit
2 Way to the altar
3 "Ditto" (2 words)
4 Type of type
5 Ostrich cousin

6 Skirmish exchanges
7 Restaurant's enticement for semi drivers (2 words)
8 Cops in the armed services (abbr.)
9 Cafe ___ (2 words)
10 "Peachy-keen!"
11 Restaurant's suggestion (3 words)
12 "Do you have two fives for ___?" (2 words)
13 In need of a masseuse
21 Not neat
23 Chicago heroine ___ Hart
26 Japanese robe
29 Initials referring to a prince or princess
30 Third largest ocean

32 Your parent's sister
33 EPA ratings on auto stickers (abbr.)
34 Chicago paper, familiarly
35 Red-___ (wieners)
36 Stereotypical sign for a restaurant (3 words)
38 Al and Bobby of Indianapolis racing
40 Deprive of courage
41 Not Dem. or Rep. (abbr.)
46 More corny
47 Weasel-like carnivore
49 Divide in two
52 Three-foot measures
53 Poet who inspired Cats
54 Urban hazes
55 Gulf War missile
56 First-rate (hyphenated)
58 Poker prizes
60 Toronto's province (abbr.)
62 Koppel of Nightline

HINT: 61 Across could also have been clued with a reference to director Preminger. And see puzzle 106 if you need still more help.

#122: 31D = ILA

Temperature's Rising   by Mel Rosen

The key words in these long answers form a progression that the puzzle's title hints at.

ACROSS

1 "___ Silver, away!" (*hyphenated*)
5 Dalmatian's markings
10 Spherical little veggies
14 "If ___ a Hammer" (*2 words*)
15 Russian buckwheat porridge
16 Auto racer Luyendyk
17 Aloof people (*2 words*)
19 Merry-go-round, for example
20 Fast water vessel
21 Spoken for
22 *Blame It on* ___ (Michael Caine comedy)
23 Adam's second son
25 Basinger of *Batman*
28 Welcome reliefs in summer (*2 words*)
34 "We try harder" company

36 Pan Am competitor, commonly
37 Summer month
38 Former Turkish official
40 Jeane Dixon's supposed gift
42 Richly colored violet
43 Like a short play (*hyphenated*)
45 Scaleless fish
47 Property claim
48 Kind
51 Opposite of NNW
52 Actor Sean ___
53 Chorus syllable
55 "So long, señor"
58 Written assurance
64 Extinct bird
65 Perry Como hit of the 1950s (*2 words*)
66 Isolated land
67 Stallone's *Judge* ___

68 Fish-eating predator
69 Have-not's condition
70 Memory failure
71 Study palms

DOWN

1 Breath-holder's utterances, maybe
2 Flapjack chain, commonly
3 University at New Haven, Connecticut
4 Stranger
5 Footwear for someone doing a slalom
6 El ___, Texas
7 Dept. of Labor agency concerned with worker protection (abbr.)
8 What a treater picks up (*2 words*)

9 KLM competitor
10 Lawyer's assistant
11 *Malcolm in the Middle* actor ___ Per Sullivan
12 Subordinate staffer
13 In the public eye
18 Letters in a bank window
21 Prepare to hit a drive (*2 words*)
24 Victoria's Secret purchase
25 Sound effect similar to "Boom!"
26 A former Mrs. Trump
27 Tightwad
29 Have chits outstanding
30 High-tech surgery tool
31 Pueblo people
32 "Mississippi" has four

33 *Gypsy* composer Jule ___
35 Washed one's hair
39 Workout reminders
41 Snoopy, to Charlie Brown
44 Decimal system base
46 Parlay, as a bet (*2 words*)
49 Wool type
50 Move with a mouse
54 Wrath
55 Score when the server leads (*2 words*)
56 Two tablets, maybe
57 At rest
59 Lone Star school, briefly
60 Does the math
61 Grow weary
62 Sicily peak under which Enceladus is buried, in myth
63 Looked at
65 "Good" cholesterol carrier (abbr.)

HINT: If a clue uses a word in a foreign language, as is true in 55 Across this time, the answer should be a word in that same language. For more help, see puzzle 133's page.

Dimension Intentions   by Thomas W. Schier

The key word in the middle entry has contrasting opposites. One has a horizontal implication; the other, vertical.

ACROSS

1 ___ weevil (cotton pest)
5 Dumbfounded
9 Web pages
14 Open space
15 Desperately urgent
16 Render weaponless
17 Have on
18 1970s Olympics gymnast ___ Korbut
19 Goop in the movie *Ghostbusters II*
20 Police force (*5 words*)
23 Europe's highest volcano
24 Popular song
25 Henhouse perches
28 Automobile
30 Hydromassage facilities
34 Clean a blackboard
35 Artist Edouard ___
37 Geologic period
38 Complete (a task) quickly (*4 words*)
41 Consumed
42 Characteristic voice qualities
43 Put forward, as an issue
44 Ballpoint writing instruments
46 Start to fall asleep
47 Large fishing nets
48 "And then ___ row, row, row"
50 Basic stitch in knitting
51 "This assignment will be difficult!" (*4 words*)
59 Sahara stopover
60 Assist in wrongdoing
61 Killer whale
62 Pizza serving
63 Juicy fruit
64 Poet's "soon"
65 Wets but good
66 Small whirlpool
67 "___ you dare!"

DOWN

1 Cry lustily
2 Black-and-white cookie
3 Show partiality
4 Generous bestowal of gifts
5 Beautifies
6 Fred Flintstone's wife
7 Therefore
8 Unhearing
9 Rice-and-seaweed dish
10 Small bays
11 Follow closely
12 Author Bombeck
13 Diving duck
21 Certify
22 Pitched, as a baseball
25 Update an atlas
26 Give a public address
27 "The Old ___ Bucket" (traditional song dating from 1822)
28 Felt concern
29 Annoying little insects
31 Breed of white domestic ducks
32 Got out of bed
33 Depository boxes
35 Stereo's precursor
36 Bullfighter
39 Accord or Passport maker
40 "I've Been Working on the ___"
45 Running gag, slangily
47 Oppressively hot and humid
49 Curvy letters
50 Entreat earnestly
51 Pitch, as a horseshoe
52 Circle over a saint
53 Where most of Turkey is
54 Record for later viewing
55 Out for the night
56 The first James Bond film (*2 words*)
57 Alan Greenspan's concern (abbr.)
58 Fly off the handle

HINT: If you need a free answer, see the box next to puzzle 136. This will help in the meantime: That answer at 61 Across is also the name of the boat in *Jaws*.

#149: 31A = TUTEE

125

Pets in the Movies   by Sarah Keller

What you've got this time is a collection of film titles with something in common.

ACROSS

1 Blessing ender
5 Nickname for Dallas, Texas (*2 words*)
9 Pointed a finger
14 Great review
15 Up to the task
16 Serious stage play
17 On the sheltered side, nautically
18 Classic automobiles
19 Macho dude (*hyphenated*)
20 1990 Mel Gibson/Goldie Hawn thriller (*4 words*)
23 Tiny portion
24 Buzzing sound
25 Baltimore ballplayer
27 Sew up again
31 More crafty
33 Sign in a broadcasting studio (*2 words*)
34 WWII gp. first headed by Oveta Culp Hobby (abbr.)
35 Tough-guy actor ___ Ray
39 1975 Al Pacino crime drama (*3 words*)
42 Being, in Latin
43 "Waiting for the Robert ___" (*2 words*)
44 Order to a blackjack dealer (*2 words*)
45 Littlest ones
47 Lemon-peeling gadget
48 "Sorry, this ___ work for me"
51 Old French coin
52 ___-Locka, Florida
53 1975 French Michèle Morgan/Jean-Pierre Aumont film (*3 words*)
60 Volkswagen model
62 Actor Morales of *La Bamba*
63 Like fine wine
64 Flat circular rubber gasket (*hyphenated*)
65 ___ Lee of bakery fame
66 Stars and stripes
67 "*A votre* ___!" (French toasting phrase)
68 Builder's detail
69 Trig function

DOWN

1 Desert dweller
2 Nation that was formerly known as French Sudan
3 Always
4 Require
5 Bailey's circus partner
6 Letter-shaped construction piece (*2 words*)
7 Shine steadily
8 Lucy's *I Love Lucy* costar
9 Stick
10 Anger
11 Latin dance
12 On-line letters (*hyphenated*)
13 *Divine Comedy* writer
21 Scarlett of Tara
22 Rolls-___
26 Tehran citizens
27 Took a bus
28 Baseball's ___ Slaughter
29 Droops
30 Some down-producing ducks
31 Bank strongboxes
32 After curfew
34 Mickey's creator ___ Disney
36 Trent of Mississippi
37 Capitol's cap
38 Beaut
40 Busybody, slangily
41 Common cold consequence
46 Let loose
47 Signs that include Libra and Pisces
48 Martial arts schools
49 New York Met offering
50 Enjoy leftovers, perhaps (*2 words*)
51 Entrap
54 Dick Tracy's Trueheart
55 "Yesterday!," in business memos
56 Louts
57 Wrinkled citrus
58 Penn of pictures
59 Brink
61 Explosive letters

HINT: The answer at 42 Across is an anagram of SEES. And see puzzle 134 for a giveaway hint.

#147: 27D = LAVES

126 Eat Your Veggies by Manny Nosowsky

These phrases begin with the crucial element.

ACROSS

*1 Papier-___ (material made of pulp paper and glue or paste)
6 Out-of-doors
10 Exhibit shock
14 Having chalky cheeks
15 Infamous Roman emperor
16 Canyon sound
17 Suffix with bed or home
18 Redheaded comic (*2 words*)
20 Rusts
22 Carriers for schoolchildren
23 ___ la la
24 Cotton-on-a-stick brand (*hyphenated*)
26 Racket game area (*2 words*)
31 "___ Believes in Me"
34 Pound fraction
35 Charge ___ (bill for services, *2 words*)
36 At a specified time
37 Sister of Jo, Meg, and Amy in *Little Women*
38 Leave alone (*2 words*)
39 Street
40 Eastern lake, canal, or city
41 Comprehending phrase (*2 words*)
42 Prepare a pumpkin, as for Halloween
43 Bread usually used in a Reuben sandwich
44 Accountant, slangily (*2 words*)
46 Sixty minutes
47 O.R. or E.R. personnel
48 Use crayons
51 "The ___, he's a priest" (Ogden Nash line, *hyphenated phrase*)
56 Russian Orthodox church topper (*2 words*)
59 Polio vaccine developer
60 "Go no further!"
61 Whammy
62 Driver's 180° (*hyphenated*)
63 A lot
64 X-acto knife cut
65 "For ___ sake!"

DOWN

1 Opposite of feminine (abbr.)
2 Concerning (*2 words*)
3 Star of *Mask* and *Moonstruck*
4 Grief, figuratively
5 Sign, as a check's back
6 First word in a fairy tale
7 Little veggies
8 Make a mistake
9 "Neither fish ___ fowl"
10 Arise from bed (*2 words*)
11 *Hamlet* has five
12 Wingtip or moccasin
13 Orchestra that plays light classical music
19 Death notice, for short
21 Lah-di-___
24 Canada's largest province
25 Fruit source
26 On the wagon
27 Ask (about)
28 Loosen, as a knot
29 Gallic Wars chronicler
30 Frequently
31 Brusque
32 "___ ho!"
33 Bitter-___ (die-hard)
36 Convert, as a language
38 In ___ of (replacing)
42 Gets all comfy (*2 words*)
44 "___ in the USA"
45 "___ to Billie Joe"
46 Hula ___ (fad toys introduced in 1958)
48 Amount to pay
49 Lock ___ (track with technology)
50 Simba or Nala, for instance
51 Prefix meaning "all"
52 ___ in line (succeeding)
53 Bump up against
54 Muddy mess
55 Names after Raggedy and Cape
57 CD players on the air (abbr.)
58 Squeak fixer

HINT: 29 Down is probably much more familiar to you as a title of emperors of old Rome. See puzzle 113's page for another hint.

#104: 45A = ISIS

127 Acting Presidential   by Ed Early

The long answers in this puzzle coincidentally begin by spelling the names of three presidents.

ACROSS

1 "Dancing Queen" singers from Sweden
5 Diner handouts
10 Finished
14 Scene of many a werewolf tale
15 "Looks ___ everything"
16 "For goodness ___!"
17 Spotty women's wear (2 words, hyphenated)
20 Normal (abbr.)
21 Little bit
22 Most slippery, in a fishy sort of way
23 Fleshy fruit, such as an apple or pear
24 Gardener's tool
25 "___ Out to the Ball Game" (2 words)
28 Reproaching sounds
29 Clinton's party (abbr.)
32 Two-time loser to Dwight
33 Bide-___ (stereotypical motel name, hyphenated)
34 Optimistic feeling
35 Places for hoops, perhaps (2 words)
38 Early Oscar winner ___ Jannings
39 Holiday occasions
40 Gets emotional
41 Family room
42 Crossword pattern
43 Shabby, or like fondue
44 Exodus author Leon ___
45 Resident of Riyadh
46 American or Delta
49 Floral greeting gift
50 Taboo
53 Forgave, in a way (2 words)
56 Costa ___
57 Single-masted sailboat
58 Take a risk
59 Makes a request
60 Methods (abbr.)
61 Kind of plan offered by Jenny Craig

DOWN

1 Electrical current measures
2 Word before camp or hill
3 Forthright
4 Indiana Jones found it
5 ___ de Pompadour
6 Lose ground, in a way
7 New Jersey hoopster
8 Beneath the ocean's surface
9 Unclothed prankster
10 Ruby Dee's husband, ___ Davis
11 Urn
12 ___ out a living (barely scrapes by)
13 Kind of stop
18 The "A" in AEC
19 The "E" in BPOE
23 Oyster formation
25 Used a VCR
26 Stop on ___ (2 words)
27 Calvin of fashion
28 Woolen fabric
29 The Many Loves of ___ Gillis (1960s sitcom)
30 Olympic swords
31 In disarray
33 After due consideration
34 Mountain identified with Sinai
36 Haunted house feeling
37 "To life!," in ethnic toasts
42 Sandy stuff
43 Moves furtively
44 Forearm bones
45 Dole out
46 Taj Mahal city
47 Colored eye part
48 ___ of lamb
50 ___ B'rith
51 Large homesite
52 Vladimir's veto
54 Comedian Bill, informally
55 Jay Leno's former announcer ___ Hall

HINT: That sitcom at 29 Down lasted about four years. The star was Dwayne Hickman. Gillis's friend Maynard G. Krebs was played by Bob Denver, who later starred in Gilligan's Island. See the box beside puzzle 143 for a gimme.

#150: 40D = OBELISK

128

Put That Down!   by Victor Fleming

The phrases here rely on different forms of the same word. The word is a synonym of the title.

ACROSS

1 Horse feed
5 Big rig
9 Devilfish
14 Raindrop sound
15 New Mexico art colony
16 Miss America, according to the song
17 ___-Seltzer
18 ___ Johnson of *Laugh-In* fame
19 Stuffed grape leaf
20 Adds (an item) to an agenda (*4 words*)
23 Tummies
24 Go fast
25 Lock opener
26 Headmaster's title
27 Sally Field's *Norma* ___

30 Comedian ___ Martin
34 "Ain't ___ Sweet?"
35 Cold, pellet-like precipitation
36 Spiritual blessing ritual (*4 words*)
40 Original garden?
41 ___ *Lobo* (John Wayne film)
42 ___ Lauder (cosmetics brand)
43 Jerry Stiller, to Ben Stiller
44 Cohort
45 Relaxing resort
47 Grown-up boys
48 "Buckle-up" item
53 Spelled out rules in no uncertain terms (*4 words*)
56 Singer ___ Reese

57 Dixieland clarinetist ___ Fountain
58 Donate
59 Flip chart holder
60 Work for
61 Suit to ___ (*2 words*)
62 Angry
63 "Dadgummit!"
64 Mr. Uncool

DOWN

1 October stones
2 ___ once (suddenly, *2 words*)
3 Capital of Japan
4 Involuntary twitch
5 Batter's position
6 Coarse
7 Nocturnal flying insects
8 "Understood" (*2 words*)

9 Where some pilots refuel
10 Pueblo dwelling
11 Entertainer ___ Carter
12 Docile
13 State nicknamed "Heart of Dixie" (abbr.)
21 Like an old bucket of song
22 Swindler
26 HBO rival, in TV listings
27 Angry talk
28 West Wing helper
29 "If all ___ fails ..."
30 Vehicle used in the Iditarod race
31 Vocal fanfare (*hyphenated*)
32 Watched carefully
33 Action star ___ Diesel

34 ___-Caps (Nestlé brand)
35 Isn't out of
37 Baby ___ piano
38 "Texas tea"
39 Shrubby wasteland
44 Bike parts
45 Nissan model
46 Inventor's protection
47 Odometer reading
48 Affirm
49 Kicked off
50 High society
51 Tennis great Rod ___
52 Coarse wool fabric
53 TV producer Norman ___
54 And
55 Newspaper's essay forum (*hyphenated*)
56 Big holiday mo.

HINT: The answer at 33 Down is also a French word meaning "wine." If you want to peek at another answer, see puzzle 119's page.

129 Precinct Personalities　　by Roy Leban

The long phrases in this puzzle all begin with synonyms for the police. Try to maintain order.

ACROSS

1 Colorado ski mecca
6 Utter breathlessly
10 "The Far Side" expletive
14 Book part where the title is displayed
15 Sailing
16 Alan Greenspan's subject (abbr.)
17 Habitual speeder's accessory brand
19 "___ boy!"
20 Itsy-bitsy pasta
21 Institute legal proceedings
22 Soprano's repertoire
23 Genetic initials
24 Artisan working in a certain metal
27 Paid athletes
29 Drop a few pounds
30 Sales pitch
32 In order
34 "O Sole ___"
37 Nursery rhyme character (5 words)
41 Moneymakers for TV stations
42 Give the once-over
43 Singer Pat ___
44 Word following steam or bubble
46 Weakest piece in chess
47 Glenn Frey song (4 words)
52 Old MGM rival
55 Picture puzzle
56 One of the Bobbsey Twins
57 Little-hand indication
58 Part of MIT (abbr.)
59 Teenage girls' fashion items (2 words)
62 Length x width calculation
63 Ending for "stink" or "buck"
64 Joint above the foot
65 Country's Loretta ___
66 Barber's call
67 Farm labor leader ___ Chavez

DOWN

1 With regard to (2 words)
2 Give a cold shoulder to
3 Italian cuisine standards (2 words)
4 Automaker ___ Ferrari
5 Omaha's state (abbr.)
6 Fill the tank (2 words)
7 ___ in the right direction (2 words)
8 Call at poker
9 Goal in golf
10 "Heavens!" (2 words)
11 Middle of some plays (2 words)
12 Skipping, as an event (2 words)
13 Grind, as teeth
18 GI relaxation clubs (abbr.)
22 Mule's sire
24 Drink with a burger and fries
25 Send one's spirits soaring
26 Portnoy's Complaint author Philip ___
28 Period during which most dreaming occurs (abbr.)
30 B&O stop (abbr.)
31 Prof's letters (abbr.)
32 "'Twas the ___ before Christmas ..."
33 Darkroom abbr.
34 Apollo souvenirs (2 words)
35 Charged particle
36 Number of the bowling pin in front
38 "___ chance!" (2 words)
39 Israeli states-man Abba ___
40 Cut the grass
44 Himalayan kingdom
45 Two-time loser to Eisenhower (initials)
46 Youngster's ride
47 Courtroom proceeding
48 Name of eight British kings
49 Buddy of The Beverly Hillbillies
50 Place for new mail and things to do (hyphenated)
51 Wooden shoe
53 ___, Fran and Ollie
54 1987 world figure skating champ Brian ___
57 Sharpen
59 Prohibit
60 It's mined and refined
61 Anatomical pouch

HINT: The answer to 4 Down is an anagram of the word ZONE. There's a free answer for you right next to puzzle 141.

130

What Sentries Say · by Alan Olschwang

There are lots of phrase answers in this one, but don't let that stop you. Just follow orders at the checkpoint.

ACROSS

1 Military chaplain, slangily
6 *CSI* network
9 Adam's lack, theoretically
14 Atheist Madalyn Murray ___
15 "That feels g-o-o-o-d!"
16 Central Florida city
17 "Surrender!" (*4 words*)
20 Extras on *The X-Files*
21 Uses, as a chair (*2 words*)
22 Big Board initials
23 Stretch vehicle, for short
24 Corporate honcho (abbr.)
26 "Halt!" (*4 words*)
32 Shock jock Howard ___
34 Small Hawaiian guitars
35 Actress ___ Peeples
36 Snow pea holders
37 Bowling alley assignments
39 Kissers
40 Significant time period
41 Tex-Mex menu item
42 Tightly packed
43 "Freeze!" (*3 words*)
47 "Bali ___" (*South Pacific* ballad)
48 Lease, as an apartment
49 It's bigger than a pond
52 Arm covering
55 Switch to low beam
58 "Remain right there!" (*4 words*)
61 Earthling's home planet
62 Come to the rescue of
63 Up to the time that
64 Tennis' Monica
65 ___ Plaines, Illinois
66 Part of a best man's duties

DOWN

1 Barbershop symbol
2 At the drop of ___ (*2 words*)
3 Calendar units
4 Get ___ of (eliminate)
5 Farmer's concern
6 Defiant response to a dare (*2 words*)
7 Ocean inlets
8 "Hit the road!"
9 Neither's companion
10 Open ___ worms (*3 words*)
11 Do something different
12 Some shade trees
13 Operate a light beam
18 Weakling
19 Cousins' fathers
23 Items that make up a monogram (abbr.)
25 Chicago trains
26 Auto body type
27 Talk too much (*2 words*)
28 Dwight Eisenhower's nickname
29 How confident puzzle solvers may write (*2 words*)
30 Slashes apart
31 Luxuriation
32 Went quickly
33 Lawn mower choice
37 Extravagant
38 Bandage brand
39 Period after Ash Wednesday
41 Chamomile drink
42 Eat at a restaurant (*2 words*)
44 "___ writing songs of love ..."
45 Registered kinds of dogs, cats, sheep, and so on
46 Establish, as a tax
49 WWII vessels (abbr.)
50 Suit to ___ (*2 words*)
51 Malden or Marx
53 Set the pace
54 Canal that opened in 1825
55 Android on *Star Trek: The Next Generation*
56 Colored eye part
57 Get mushy
59 "Fuzzy Wuzzy ___ a bear ..."
60 Popular card game

HINT: The answer to 14 Across is not spelled the same as the Chicago airport. Puzzle 101's page has another hint.

#118: 15A = ORLY

In the Bag   by Norma Steinberg

131

This puzzle refers to golf. In some more advanced puzzles, the key word in the theme answer isn't always at the front or at the back.

ACROSS
1 Overcook badly
5 Sound of an impact
9 Former
14 The Buckeye State
15 Wander
16 Key ___, Florida
17 Ralph Kramden's job (2 words)
19 Embellish
20 That girl
21 In the open
22 Fork points
23 Clod breakers
24 Being pulled (2 words)
26 "___, young man" (Greeley's advice, 2 words)
29 On bended ___
30 "___ My Party" (Lesley Gore song)

33 Roeper's movie reviewing partner
34 Exonerate
35 Real estate parcel
36 Freshen, as a room's decor
37 Pin's tip
38 Choir voice
39 N.Y. Knicks venue, briefly
40 Too thin
41 Prowl around
42 "Get it?"
43 Hard to find
44 Snuggle
45 Blood pumper
47 Diversify
48 Sudsy beverages
50 Splatter
52 To and ___
55 Prayer enders
56 Tinseltown

58 Mary Poppins star ___ Andrews
59 Dot of land in the sea
60 Rod between wheels
61 Dolts
62 Tree with a partridge, in a yule song
63 Colors

DOWN
1 Comedians Hope and Newhart
2 "I don't think so!" (hyphenated)
3 Ascend
4 ___ off (doze)
5 Hedge shrub
6 Adores
7 Walkie-talkie word
8 Appropriate

9 Serving tray
10 Marconi's invention
11 Adamant (hyphenated)
12 Shrek is one
13 Howard and Reagan, Jr.
18 Chicken's home
23 The good guy
25 Spiffy
26 Bacteria
27 On the plump side, and then some
28 Features of some women's shoes (2 words)
29 Actor Kevin ___
31 ___ Recall
32 Supply fuel to a furnace
34 Romantic pursuit

37 Carson's Tonight Show predecessor
38 Barney's boss, in Mayberry
40 They have to be mowed
41 Ill-humored
44 The person on the phone
46 Top golfer Els
47 Place on the Riviera
48 ___ California (peninsula south of San Diego)
49 Earthbound Aussie birds
51 Pretense
52 Sly
53 Hamlet or Macbeth, for an actor
54 Poetic tributes
57 Clump

HINT: If you need a free answer, see the box beside puzzle 120. In the meantime, it may help you to know that 39 Across is also the common name for an item sometimes added to food in Chinese cuisine.

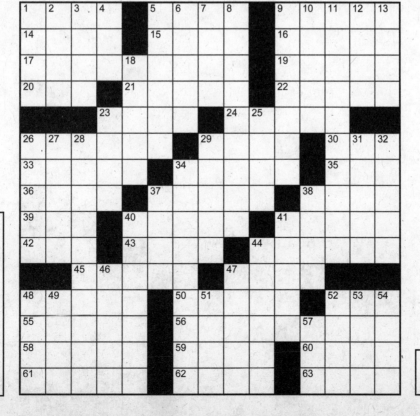

Three Squares

by Randall J. Hartman

In particular, three square meals. That's what to look for in the long theme answers.

ACROSS

1 Jets and Sharks, in *West Side Story*
6 Pet door, typically
10 Redo, as a crossword clue
14 Shakespearean spirit
15 Actress ___ Anderson
16 Completely certain
17 Devilfish
18 *Iliad*, for example
19 "Preach on, brother!"
20 1985 Brat Pack movie, with *The* (*2 words*)
23 ___-day Saints
24 "I get it!"
25 Python cousin, commonly
28 Eisenhower's WWII command (abbr.)
29 Posting on an incoming-flights airport board (abbr.)
32 Some wedding attendants
34 Determine, as a tax
37 Tennis star Monica ___
38 Deals at the diner (*2 words*)
41 Visible mist
42 Marked with a branding iron
43 "Town Without Pity" singer Gene ___
45 U-turn from SSW
46 Charlton Heston presided over it (abbr.)
49 "All-sold-out" Broadway sign
50 Take in calories
52 Organ that helps to filter blood
55 1933 Harlow/Dressler film based on a classic Kaufman/Ferber play (*3 words*)
59 Yacht, for example
61 Former McDonald's head Ray ___
62 Cyberspace message (*hyphenated*)
63 Chip in
64 Perry and Della's creator
65 Petrol measure
66 Abound
67 Surveilled
68 Work with a handlebar (but not a mustache)

DOWN

1 Shoot craps
2 Mount where Noah's Ark landed
3 Fifty-one minutes after the hour, re the next hour (*2 words*)
4 Suggest (*2 words*)
5 Satisfy, as thirst
6 Type of market
7 Hacks off
8 *Gentlemen Prefer Blondes* author Loos
9 Machu ___ (Incan ruins site in Peru)
10 Jacob's twin
11 Ignoramus
12 Wrath
13 Diver's perfect score
21 Newly baked, as bread
22 Collie of TV fame
26 Galena and bauxite
27 Balaam's mount
30 Julia's character in *Ocean's Twelve*
31 Colorado ski resort city
33 Beanball target
34 Right away, poetically
35 Covering for an open window
36 Penn of *Mystic River*
38 Bear's winter home
39 Modern (*hyphenated*)
40 Competitor of Aim toothpaste
41 Titles for Al Gore and Dick Cheney (abbr.)
44 Baseball player in a pinstripe uniform
46 Nullify
47 Put back on the payroll
48 Reindeer feature
51 Fabric used in bathrobes
53 Rinds
54 Boundary
56 Agenda detail
57 Part in a play or film
58 Made a hole in one
59 Dracula's alter ego
60 Score for a free throw

HINT: The answer to 61 Across is an anagram of CORK. You'll find another answer next to puzzle 149.

#148: 27D = SHUL

133

Bouncing along   by Manny Nosowsky

The theme of this puzzle may elude you until you solve 40 Across. That's okay, and it's part of the fun.

ACROSS

1 ___ Curtis of cosmetics
7 Lots of ounces (abbr.)
10 Gets older
14 Good scents
15 Not in
16 Baggage checking tool (hyphenated)
17 It is memorized in arithmetic class (2 words)
19 Make, as an income
20 Found out
21 Elementary swimming stroke (2 words)
23 Thirty-six inches
25 Curvy letter
26 Org. behind the annual Westminster show (abbr.)
29 Funny sayings
31 Tributary of the Missouri River
36 River deposit
38 U-turn from SSW
39 Stabbed
40 Activity whose gear is found at 17-, 21-, 54-, and 64-Across (2 words, hyphenated)
43 State division
44 Relative of the Hopi
45 Doubtless
46 Braying beasts
47 Surprise victory
49 Used a baton
50 Entertainment directors (abbr.)
52 Work for a newspaper
54 Capable (3 words)
59 Miss America's crown
63 Break, as a routine
64 Use your browser (3 words)
66 Idylls of the King lady
67 General on a Chinese menu
68 The optic nerve connects to it
69 Tom, Dick, or Harry
70 Florist's truck
71 "___ choose to run" (Coolidge, 3 words)

DOWN

1 "Hell ___ no fury ..."
2 Ohio's lake
3 ___ Prieta, California (1989 earthquake epicenter)
4 Board for nails
5 Over-the-counter securities acronym
6 Superlative ending
7 Rio ___ (John Wayne film)
8 Sticks out
9 Strides
10 Fired, slangily
11 New alum
12 ___ Warren of the Supreme Court
13 Last word of the year?
18 Part of a scorekeeping task
22 With ___ in My Heart (1952 Jane Froman biopic, 2 words)
24 Like Brie
26 Humane org. (abbr.)
27 Drug bust weights, in headlines
28 Gift bringer Santa
30 Enliven (2 words)
32 Uses a straw
33 Run ___ of the law
34 Literary category
35 Tidied the lawn
37 Daly of Judging Amy
39 Took a cheap shot at, in a way
41 Answer to "Who's there?" (2 words)
42 In and of ___
47 Patriotic chant at the Olympics
48 Paid in support of the church
51 The Amazing Race network (abbr.)
53 Link with (2 words)
54 Kitchen cooker
55 Dog in Peter Pan
56 Take a little off the top
57 His better half was Jekyll
58 Scientologist ___ Hubbard (2 words)
60 Has ___ with (is well-connected, 2 words)
61 Clinton's attorney general
62 Rat-___ (hyphenated)
65 Prefix meaning "three"

HINT: Sometimes, as at 69 Across, a clue might mislead you deliberately. Here, you need to treat the words in the clue a little differently than you might otherwise. See puzzle 110's page for more help if you need it.

SINUS = 31D :321#

134 Heat Wave — by Ed Early

Things are really hot here. You might need to get the garden hose.

ACROSS

1 Raring to go
6 Baba Wawa portrayer ___ Radner
11 End of some e-mail addresses
14 As ___ (ordinarily, *2 words*)
15 Spring Zodiac sign
16 Office PC linkup (abbr.)
17 Acts as a pioneer
19 Genetic code letters
20 Tarnish
21 Exasperates
22 Lard, in essence (*2 words*)
24 Salad greens
26 Purifies, as drinking water
27 Use a Singer
28 Iran-___ Affair
29 Kids around
32 Inlets
33 Cat call
36 Swiss peaks
37 Jogged easily
38 Big sandwich
39 Miss Piggy's pronoun
40 Baseball clout
41 Actress ___ Sarandon
42 Pirate stashes
44 Pocketbook
45 Invites a libel suit
47 Golfer Palmer and historian Toynbee
51 *Star Wars* mentor played by Alec
52 ___ B'rith
53 "___, verily!"
54 Neither relative
55 Comic who lived to be 100 (*2 words*)
58 *A Chorus Line* hit song
59 CATV awards for athletes
60 Radiates
61 Dolphins' stats (abbr.)
62 Blood vessel blockage reliever
63 Cagney's TV partner

DOWN

1 Inscription on a Wonderland cake (*2 words*)
2 Scotland's ___ Island
3 Word after "rear" or "coast"
4 Yale rooter
5 Experiences déjà vu, perhaps
6 Strong winds
7 Some nest eggs, briefly
8 Columnist Smith
9 Intensified
10 Basketball or baseball or hockey statistics
11 Former sweethearts (*2 words*)
12 Charged (*2 words*)
13 No-see-ums
18 Make beer
23 Needle-nosed fish
25 Suffix meaning "believers"
26 Location of some English white cliffs
28 ___ with (meets)
29 Fruity toast topper
30 "Sweet Talkin' Woman" band, commonly
31 British WWII fighter planes
32 Shows up
34 Pitcher's stat
35 Triumphed
37 1951 Marilyn Monroe film (*2 words*)
38 Supreme Court justice ___ Black
40 "Paid" tributes
41 Florida resort island
43 Like sashimi fish
44 Scottish hillside
45 "___ forsake me ..." (*High Noon* tune, *2 words*)
46 U.S. savings certificate
47 Gut-wrenching feeling
48 Song's words
49 Al ___ (pasta order)
50 Fresh-mouthed
52 ___ Mawr College
56 Unlock, poetically
57 Thurman of film

HINT: If you need a free answer, see puzzle 148's page. In the meantime, the answer at 59 Across is very closely tied to the network that does the awarding.

#125: 34A = WAAC

135

Rhymes with Strife   by Randall J. Hartman

The title describes the theme, but we hope this puzzle doesn't cause you much strife.

ACROSS

1 Island to which Napoleon was exiled
5 Ray Bolger's "guts," in *The Wizard of Oz*
10 Grade, as a quiz
14 Silicone solutions
15 ___ Africa
16 Land of the leprechauns
17 Ancient region divided by the Alps
18 Wondrous plant mentioned in Genesis, Proverbs, and Revelation (*3 words*)
20 Villainous scowl
22 Hand out the cards
23 Right-angle shape
24 Chin whiskers
27 Gray freshwater fish
29 Perfect mate, Hollywood-style? (*2 words*)
33 Internet service that alerts you with "You've got mail"
34 Slangy approval
35 Blacksmith's fireplace
39 Use mother-of-pearl to decorate a surface
42 Boxer who won the "Thrilla in Manila"
43 Edgar Bergen dummy Mortimer
44 *Saturday Night Fever* club
45 Horse hair
47 Droop
48 Blade that's used to dress killed game (*2 words*)
52 "In this manner," slangily (*2 words*)
55 Bear and Berra
56 From ___ Z (*2 words*)
57 List ending (*2 words*, abbr.)
60 Second Greek letters
63 Don Knotts role on *The Andy Griffith Show*
67 Walking stick
68 Butter substitute
69 Put up
70 "Orinoco Flow" singer
71 Pitcher Nolan ___
72 Puccini opera that debuted in 1900
73 Part of Orion's "belt"

DOWN

1 Fabergé collectibles
2 Without any extra fat
3 Wood hyacinths
4 Resting overnight
5 JFK arrival, once
6 Rocky peak
7 Felt sorry about
8 To ___ (perfectly, *2 words*)
9 Mystery man's query (*3 words*)
10 Gibson of *What Women Want*
11 Israeli politician ___ Sharon
12 M-1, for one
13 Prepared to pray or propose
19 Arranges a pillow, with "up"
21 British WWII fliers (abbr.)
25 "Hee Haw" banjoist ___ Clark
26 Had a nightmare
28 Explorer Ponce de ___
29 Uttered
30 *Jazz* author ___ Morrison
31 ___ Lama
32 Neigh
36 Fighting change
37 Retired tennis star Steffi ___
38 Advantage
40 Feel sore
41 Beginning of an attempt at explanation (*2 words*)
46 Freudian topic
49 "In a minute or two ..." (*2 words*)
50 Secret agency of the U.S.S.R. (abbr.)
51 Your sibling's daughters
52 Toil
53 European country shaped like a boot
54 Divided Asian peninsula
58 Frizzy hairdo
59 Tells a big fib
61 *Dragonwyck* writer Seton
62 Scorch
64 "Smoking or ___?"
65 Governmental radio station watchdog (abbr.)
66 Airport schedule board posting (abbr.)

HINT: The answer at 11 Down is also the name of Disney's little mermaid, and it's also the name of a character in Shakespeare's *The Tempest*. See puzzle 146 for a bigger hint.

#105: 27D = ORONO

136

They're Edible   by Bernice Gordon

The four three-word phrases in this theme all include things you could eat or drink. All have the same center word.

ACROSS
1 Sidewalk eatery
5 Danes of *My So-Called Life*
11 *JAG* network
14 Country singer ___ Jackson
15 Numbered lines on maps
16 Address that begins with "http"
17 Recipe addition, perhaps (*3 words*)
19 Kung ___ chicken
20 One-___ (baseball variation played in the street, *hyphenated*)
21 *Day for Night* star Jean-Pierre ___
23 Log off (*2 words*)
27 Workers
28 Coves

29 Bakery cooling devices (*2 words*)
32 Polite forms of address
33 Say, "I do"
34 Expression of surprise
35 ___ buco (braised veal shank dish)
36 Yuletide candy shapes
37 At a distance
38 Super ___ (video game console)
39 Trap (*2 words*)
40 Weapon for G.I. Joe
41 Financially efficient
43 Take a second look at
44 Where crops are raised
45 Own
46 Military jeep-truck transport

48 Foot covering
49 "___ live and breathe!" (*2 words*)
50 Rain bit (*3 words*)
56 Costa ___ Sol
57 Gasoline rating
58 Off schedule
59 Noah's ship
60 ___ up (goofed)
61 Comet competitor

DOWN
1 Hat with a visor
2 "The Greatest"
3 Summer cooler
4 Bus. letter abbr.
5 Member of the iris family
6 Dietetic, on packages (*hyphenated*)
7 Vienna, Salzburg, etc. (abbr.)
8 Call ___ day (*2 words*)

9 Story tellers
10 Inlet of the sea
11 Morning eye opener (*3 words*)
12 Cereal ingredient
13 Piggy bank opening
18 Owl's sounds
22 Juilliard degree (abbr.)
23 "I Loves You, Porgy" singer Nina ___
24 Very soon, informally (*3 words*)
25 Where to dunk an Oreo cookie (*3 words*)
26 *Finding* ___ (animated blockbuster)
27 Ambulance alert
29 Financial crisis
30 Eucalyptus leaf eaters

31 Tears into pieces
33 Long skirts
36 Business
37 Broadcasts
39 Lack of excitement
40 Fix an open seam
42 The "n" of "loran" (abbr.)
43 Covered overhead
45 Bell's invention
46 "Mary ___ little lamb ..." (*2 words*)
47 Manipulative person
48 Fashionable resort hotels
51 Bonus NFL periods (abbr.)
52 Menu phrase
53 Agra's ___ Mahal
54 Greek letter
55 Televangelist ___ Humbard

HINT: At 52 Down: If the clue includes the word "phrase," there won't be a "2 words" tag, even in an easy puzzle. Check out the box next to puzzle 103 for a free answer.

137

Stay Optimistic   by Diane C. Baldwin

The three long phrases in this puzzle all pertain to being optimistic. So don't give up.

ACROSS

1 Barn tower
5 Indian royalty
10 Pack to capacity
14 Asian range
15 Give the slip to
16 Like some salad dressings
17 "Do what you can" (*5 words*)
20 Wee hour
21 Angel's instrument
22 God of Islam
23 Sign of poor housekeeping
24 Lacking a sidearm
26 Pixie-like
29 Sled dog
30 Astronaut Armstrong
31 He devised a code that now bears his name
32 Healthful getaway
35 "Heed that inner longing" (*3 words*)
39 Be obliged
40 Grape or tomato plants
41 "Do ___ others ..."
42 Time lag
43 Jaclyn, Will, and Kate
45 Insists
48 "Bigger ___ a breadbox"
49 Was skittish
50 Long-piled carpet
51 Mine extraction
54 "Never give up" (*4 words*)
58 Roof line
59 Hair-raising
60 Hoofed it
61 Birdhouse resident
62 Beauticians, often
63 ___ in (surrounds)

DOWN

1 Sport for large athletes
2 Where shahs once ruled
3 Ontario, for instance
4 Spaniard's cheer
5 Go back over
6 Tip off
7 Capture, in the game of checkers
8 Fuss and bother
9 Cock and bull
10 In a nonchalant manner
11 Engage in ransacking
12 Pseudonym
13 Traditional stories
18 Therefore
19 Hit bottom, slangily
23 Pickling spice
24 Spiritual teachers
25 World power, once (abbr.)
26 Data
27 Remark by a Persian or Siamese
28 Stack up
29 "Hogwash!"
31 Birds that can mimic human speech
32 Enraptured
33 Orbit, for one
34 Old Testament prophet
36 Work too hard
37 Droop
38 Bring to a downfall
42 Intensify
43 Physiques
44 Christmas visitors
45 Out of kilter
46 Get wool from a sheep
47 Strainer
48 *A League of ___ Own*
50 Withered
51 Fairytale baddie
52 Leeway
53 Nips in the bud
55 Actor Beatty
56 Piano ivory
57 High degree

#145: 33D = CURIO

138

What You Pay For?   by Victor Fleming

The title may make you think twice after you start solving, but you'll catch on once you see the first word of each theme answer.

ACROSS
1 No longer in style
6 ___ d'oeuvres
10 Prankster's pre-Halloween buy
14 Mountaineer's tool (2 words)
15 Baldwin of *The Shadow*
16 Insignificant
17 Energy (*hyphenated*)
19 ___-Tass (Russian news org.)
20 Train components
21 Be after the appointed time (2 words)
23 State education leader
26 Aloe ___
27 Be victorious
28 Exercised too much (2 words)
30 Sawyer of TV news

32 Complied with
33 Org. frequently in Tom Clancy novels
34 Bank (on)
35 Side view
38 ___ seed (rye bread bit)
41 Number dialed before two ones, in an emergency
42 Pea sheller's discard
43 Supermarket chain that began in Poughkeepsie, NY in 1926 (abbr.)
44 Steel plow maker
46 Cab driver's fare calculator
49 Dorothy's auntie and namesakes
50 Quarry
52 Endorsed for money, as a check

53 Military plane
55 Andy in the funnies
56 Race in *The Time Machine*
57 Look at (*4 words*)
62 Peeples and Vardalos
63 "Like, no way!" (*2 words*)
64 Join
65 Ellipsis
66 Curtain fabric
67 One of the senses

DOWN
1 Sty squealer
2 Top card
3 Prepared
4 Cup companion
5 Become larger
6 ___ Christian Andersen
7 Aged
8 Rue
9 Scrub hard

10 ___ *and the Detectives* (1964 Disney film)
11 Escape punishment for (*3 words*)
12 Potatoes au ___
13 Peaceful
18 Lead ___ (main story)
22 Ralph who campaigned in 2000 and 2004
23 Easy victory
24 "...happily ___ after"
25 Make pretty angry (*3 words*)
26 By way of
29 Go out, as a flame
31 Dockworkers' org. (abbr.)
34 Extreme
36 Christmas tree
37 Klutzy

38 ___-2 inhibitor (Vioxx, for example)
39 Tommie ___ of the Miracle Mets
40 36 inches
42 Salary
44 Represent someone who's been sued
45 Actor Estevez
46 Nobelist Mother ___ of Calcutta
47 Plan, as a tour (2 words)
48 Madrid's country, in Madrid
51 Befitting a king
54 Rude fan's noise
55 Lunch site
58 ___-tac-toe
59 Speak ill of, in slang
60 Mel of the Polo Grounds
61 Service charge

HINT: Sometimes, as in the clue at 49 Across, you'll see the phrase "and namesakes." That tells you to pluralize an answer name even though the clue only has one hint as to what that name is. See puzzle 122's page for a free answer.

#121: 51D = MEAD

139 All-Inclusive by Earl W. Reed

In this puzzle the last words of the first three long answers form a common phrase that the fourth long answer defines.

ACROSS

1 Jazz singer ___ Fitzgerald
5 Wood strip
9 Not confident
14 Work hard
15 Parlor piece
16 *Home* ___ (Macaulay Culkin film)
17 Security system on a briefcase (*2 words*)
20 Retain
21 Spring month (abbr.)
22 ___ kwon do
23 Chess piece that starts next to a knight
26 Let out ___ (sound shocked, *2 words*)
29 Hanoi holiday
31 Cheap but speculative investment choice (*2 words*)
35 Oil, slangily (*2 words*)
37 Steeple top
38 Eminem's genre
39 Chilled ale or lager, familiarly (*2 words*)
42 ___ Flanders (*The Simpsons* character)
43 One-celled creature
45 Does an impression of
47 Wasteful legislation (*2 words*)
50 Psychic initials
51 Hand out
52 Within arm's reach
54 $$$ dispenser (abbr.)
56 "She's So High" performer ___ Bachman
58 Move the cradle
61 Everything (or, the theme suggested by the last words of this puzzle's other long answers, *3 words*)
67 Sal of *Exodus*
68 In ___ of (rather than)
69 "Gotcha" equivalent (*2 words*)
70 Cosmetician ___ Lauder
71 Late-night exhale
72 Jazz trumpeter ___ Baker

DOWN

1 And so on, briefly
2 "Check this out!"
3 Citrus wedge often added to a Corona
4 Saskatchewan neighbor
5 Taxpayer's ID (abbr.)
6 Hawaii's Mauna ___
7 Skin Bracer rival
8 1966 Clavell best seller
9 Sunbather's shade
10 Ailing
11 Superfluous debate topics (*2 words*)
12 Ancient Peruvian
13 Fake out, in sports lingo
18 Debut on Wall Street (abbr.)
19 Wild party
24 Prefix meaning "vision"
25 Tip, like a sailboat
27 Balance sheet item
28 Popular fuel additive (abbr.)
29 "I love you," in Madrid (*2 words*)
30 Test
32 Lowest point
33 Scuzzball
34 Sneakers brand
35 Snare
36 Strikebreakers
40 Red sky at night, so they say
41 World's longest river
44 Library volumes (abbr.)
46 Type of workout
48 Garage occupant
49 "You don't say!"
53 Exist
54 "Stop looking ___!" (annoyed sibling's cry, *2 words*)
55 "Now hear ___!"
57 Carrie's role in *Star Wars*
59 Turn in, as chips
60 Patella's place
62 Itsy-bitsy
63 Gardener's tool
64 Clinch a title, with "up"
65 Attila, notably
66 Obtain

HINT: At 8 Down: The answer, when uncapitalized, is a word meaning a successful foreign businessman operating in Hong Kong or China. See puzzle 123's page for a free answer.

#116: 15A = COATI

Behind the Door   by Gail Grabowski

140

What connects these thematic phrases together? Their first parts can all be, well, behind a door. Or, at least, the word "door."

ACROSS
1 Winter forecasts
6 Makes a mistake
10 Performs on stage
14 Bite on, puppy-style (2 words)
15 Bearded farm animal
16 Go to the mall
17 Central Florida city
18 1978 Village People hit
19 Rabbit relative
20 Garden plant (2 words)
22 Quote, as a reference source
23 Parking place
24 Tilted
26 Take place
30 Salad ingredients
32 Currency that replaced the Italian lira
33 Shipping container
34 Soda can opener
37 "Take ___ from me!" (2 words)
38 Pesky kids
39 The Wizard of Oz dog
40 Egg carton amount (abbr.)
41 Not tight
42 Military force
43 Arm joints
45 Grade school break
47 Most secure
49 Golfer's goal
50 Opera solo
51 Visa or American Express (2 words)
58 Fixes, as a sporting event
59 Prefix for dynamic
60 Birch-bark boat
61 Tennis champ Arthur
62 Not spicy
63 Book's name
64 Butterfly catchers
65 Golf instructors
66 Scornful smile

DOWN
1 Snooty person
2 Pleasant
3 October birthstone
4 Place for a mural
5 Paper fastener
6 King Tut's homeland
7 Frolic
8 Indy 500, for example
9 Hollywood hopefuls
10 Garbage container
11 National retail outlet (2 words)
12 Rich dessert
13 Drive too fast
21 Long period of time
25 Wide shoe width
26 Brain's place
27 Sedan or coupe
28 Professional boxing match (2 words)
29 Bust a balloon
30 Hula skirt material
31 Hourly amount
33 Cornfield bird
35 24-hour bankers (abbr.)
36 Young males
38 Military training site (2 words)
39 Tic-___-toe
41 Ton fractions (abbr.)
44 Apartment contracts
45 Worn-out garment
46 Puts up
47 Popular food wrap name
48 Get out of bed
49 Eggs on
52 Will beneficiary
53 Folksinger ___ Guthrie
54 Son of Adam and Eve
55 Poker "payment"
56 Part in a play
57 Bambi, for instance

HINT: 20 Across is a common salad ingredient. See the box next to puzzle 108 for a giveaway.

It's Obvious   by Thomas W. Schier

141

The theme is in the clues, as you will see soon enough. We hope the answers are also pretty obvious.

ACROSS

1 Prepare grapes for wine
6 Yellowish-brown
11 Workout center
14 Taken-back autos
15 Not firmly attached
16 Pro's opposite
17 Obvious (*3 words*)
19 Dull routine
20 Chief executive officer (abbr.)
21 Go into hysterics
22 Taper off
24 Will's contents
26 Confidence game
27 Obvious
33 Force out
36 Harvester inventor ___ McCormick
37 Negligent
38 Racetrack assignment
39 Jittery from coffee, say
40 Dracula portrayer ___ Lugosi
41 Bathing suit top
42 Definitive Rudolph Valentino role
43 ___ and Gomorrah
44 Obvious (*4 words*)
47 Partnership
48 Girlfriends, in Spain
52 Desert caravan animal
54 Teri in *Young Frankenstein*
57 Koran chapter
58 Lumberjack's tool
59 Obvious (*hyphenated*)
62 Chihuahua of cartoons
63 Supply more weapons to
64 Kate's sitcom pal
65 Three-ingredient sandwich (abbr.)
66 Sore throat cause
67 Computer memory units

DOWN

1 Thin, delicate pancake
2 Brings up, as a child
3 Turn topsy-turvy
4 Chow mein topper (*2 words*)
5 He was between FDR and DDE (monogram)
6 Microscopic pond organism
7 Forenoon
8 Dock docker
9 Curvy letter
10 Fills the suitcases again
11 Like some eggs or messages
12 Be sullen
13 Poker pot starter
18 City west of the Provo River
23 Lamb's call
25 Dynamite letters
26 Ibn ___ (1940s Arabian king)
28 More like the Arctic
29 Damascus is its capital
30 Tiring trips
31 *Mission: Impossible* theme composer ___ Schifrin
32 Final or midterm test
33 Isle of Napoleon's exile
34 Jelly containers
35 Law
39 Noisy strike
40 In a youthful manner
42 Driveway basecoats
43 ___ Houston of Texas history
45 Rocker Tommy ___
46 Blowgun ammo
49 Burden of the conscience-stricken
50 Golfer Palmer, to his "army"
51 Wise people
52 Energy provider, for short
53 *Beverly Hills Cop* character ___ Foley
54 Reverse or neutral
55 Farm unit
56 Expressway access
60 So far
61 Taxi

HINT: The answer to 57 Across is an anagram of URSA. If you need an outright freebie, see the box alongside puzzle 115.

#129:
44D = BHUTAN

142 It's a Guy Thing   by Holden Baker

The four long phrases in this puzzle happen to pertain to the same gender. Compare to the next puzzle.

ACROSS
1 Got in under the tag, perhaps
5 Billiard bounce
10 Overly fussy sort
14 Electricity carrier
15 Bridge bid, informally (*2 words*)
16 Charged particles
17 Riyadh native
18 It's in a bag on the mound
19 Paul who sang "Diana" in 1957
20 Frequent night-club attender (*3 words*)
23 Weapon for Patton
24 Landed proprietors, in Scotland
28 Football's Bob or Brian
31 List of terms and definitions

33 Unburden
34 Top banana's foil, in comedy (*2 words*)
36 Take ___ view of (*2 words*)
38 Federal emissions-watching group (abbr.)
39 Kind of tropical palm
40 Native American shaman (*2 words*)
45 Rumsfeld's org. (abbr.)
46 Cell occupant
47 Family cars
49 Breathing ailment
50 Exxon, formerly
51 Intellectual author (*3 words*)
57 March Madness org.
60 Popular sitcom of the 1990s

61 Journey
62 Those in favor
63 Inclined, poetically
64 "What ___ can I say?"
65 Ness or Lomond
66 Hindu disciplines
67 Owner's document

DOWN
1 Enjoyed the pool
2 Italian monetary unit replaced by the euro
3 Tehran's country
4 Oratorical contest
5 Small crown
6 Aimée of *La Dolce Vita*
7 Take five
8 "Don't count ___!" (*2 words*)
9 Soliloquy
10 They tickle the ivories

11 *Apollo 13* director ___ Howard
12 Fountain pen filler
13 Federal property and records management org. (abbr.)
21 Woofer output
22 Laundry
25 ___ Inn (hotel chain)
26 Fire-breather of myth
27 Church councils
28 Pop's pop
29 Add-ons to congressional bills
30 Shout of accomplishment (*3 words*)
31 One staring in wonderment
32 *Schindler's List* star ___ Neeson

35 Russo of *Ransom*
37 Hodgepodge
41 Robin Cook novel made into a Michael Douglas film
42 In a senseless way
43 Says "yes"
44 Bird's home
48 Sign on the ___ line
50 "Maria ___" (1941 Dorsey hit)
52 Butter substitute
53 Banner
54 ___ Gardner of mystery
55 Stand up
56 Risked a ticket
57 Gridiron organization (abbr.)
58 Dove noise
59 Circle section

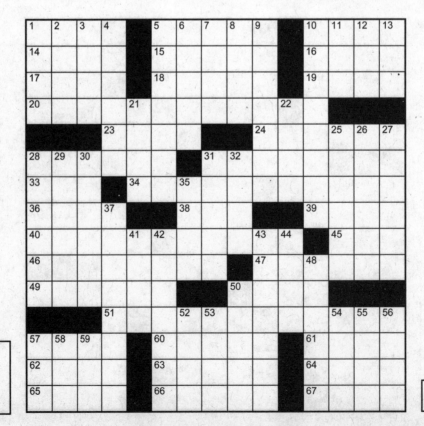

HINT: 62 Across is not PROS. See the box next to puzzle 129 for more.

#115: 32A = FAUNS

It's a Gal Thing   by Mel Rosen

Offering a natural counterpoint to the previous puzzle. We don't play favorites.

ACROSS

1 Amorphous lump
5 Daily work hours
10 Minor argument
14 Bad fellow in *Othello*
15 Capital of Vietnam
16 Part of the ear
17 She goes down the aisle at a wedding (*2 words*)
19 Warning sign
20 Disappears gradually (*2 words*)
21 Touched lightly
23 Be litigious
24 Avant-garde prefix
25 Was jealous of
29 Form of address for a married couple (*3 words* with abbrs.)
34 Bank transactions
35 TV journalist Sawyer
36 "Oh, wow!"
37 Dairy bar staple
38 Main artery

39 Cabernet Sauvignon, for example
40 New American's course (abbr.)
41 Choreographer ___ de Mille
42 Felt concern
43 Went back to the cutting room
45 Beermaker's grain
46 Basic unit of Japanese currency
47 Old mattress's problem
48 ___ *Thesaurus* (standard reference book for synonyms)
51 Snooze in the afternoon (*3 words*)
56 Bone dry
57 Broadway musical cast member (*2 words*)

59 *Pretty Woman* star Richard ___
60 Ear-related
61 Peruvian of olden times
62 Auctioneer's final word
63 High-IQ organization
64 Inquisitive

DOWN

1 Letterman stage manager ___ Henderson
2 In ___ land (spacy, *hyphenated*)
3 Start of a hymn
4 Boxer Riddick ___
5 ___ of Turin
6 The ___, Netherlands
7 Monogram letter (abbr.)
8 Not against

9 Pinball foul
10 Like ski runs
11 Cheerleader (*2 words*)
12 Busy as ___ (*2 words*)
13 Watch over
18 Troublesome letters for Sylvester
22 Author Rice, who writes about vampires
25 Fudd of the cartoons
26 Form of urban pollution
27 Teener from San Fernando area (*2 words*)
28 Cartoonist's supply
29 Bogged
30 Charlie Brown's expletive
31 Former *Saturday Night Live* player Gasteyer

32 Actress Zellweger
33 Somewhat disreputable
35 Finished
38 FBI employee (abbr.)
39 Big battle
41 "It ___ Necessarily So"
42 Homes for hamsters
44 Conveyed a title
45 Scott of *Enterprise*
47 Lee and Teasdale
48 Cleaning cloths
49 Cookie sandwich
50 Insurance fraud, for instance
51 Ripped
52 "Are you fer or ___?"
53 El ___ (weather phenomenon)
54 Pinball paths
55 Broadway offering
58 Shade of color

HINT: See the box next to puzzle 9 if you need a give-away answer. In the meantime, it may help you to know that the name in the clue at 145 Down is a first name, not a last name.

#127: 10D = OSSIE

144 Looking/Sounding Good   by Victor Fleming

Any dapper musician could have been part of the answer at 20 Across. The fun is getting your mind around the cute wordplay.

ACROSS
1 Railroad stop (abbr.)
4 Bouncy tunes
9 Houston ballplayer
14 Break, as a balloon
15 State known for its taters
16 Believer in the essential worth of all religions
17 Mischievous pixie
18 ___ *Buddies* (1980s sitcom that starred Peter Scolari and Tom Hanks)
19 *The Woman* ___ (Gene Wilder film, *2 words*)
20 Clue for 41 and 61 Across (*2 words*)
23 Triangular traffic sign
24 Prophet
25 Barracks no-show (abbr.)
28 Long fluffy scarf
30 Hi-___ graphics
32 Hawaiian tuna
33 Baseball legend ___ Ruth
36 Swiss peaks

39 "___ a dark and stormy night ..." (*2 words*)
41 Followed by 61 Across, solution for 20 Across (*4 words*)
44 Pertaining to sheep
45 Playthings
46 Deli loaves
47 Robbins or Allen
48 Stomach muscles, informally
50 Dove's soft call
52 Furthermore
54 Misfortunes
57 2000 presidential contender Ralph ___
61 See 41 Across (*4 words*)
64 Floats used to mark channels
66 Native of Muscat

67 Newspaper department heads (abbr.)
68 Heche and Bancroft
69 Extravagant sales pitch
70 Casual Friday castoff
71 "Whither thou ___ ..."
72 Singer ___ Gorme
73 Cooperstown's Mel ___

DOWN
1 Like Cajun food
2 Oscar winner Marisa
3 "An ___ a day ..."
4 Instinctual energy studied by Freud
5 Wedding vows (*2 words*)
6 Goes on and on

7 "___ Were the Days"
8 1993 film starring Richard Gere and Jodie Foster
9 "This won't hurt ___!" (*2 words*)
10 Mr. Claus
11 Toss out, as trash (*2 words*)
12 *Norma* ___
13 Suffix with "fact" or "planet"
21 Popular catalogue company based in Freeport, Maine (phrase with abbr.)
22 Mine find
26 Chicago airport
27 Talks like Sylvester the Cat
29 Satisfied sigh
31 Bro's sib
33 Regional flora and fauna

34 Ibuprofen brand
35 Biblical name for sulfur
37 Frees (*2 words*)
38 Paid athlete
40 Neck part that may contain a frog
42 Lipton product
43 PC key label
49 Storage container
51 Recorded (*2 words*)
53 "Most definitely!" (*2 words*)
55 Like some mashed potatoes
56 Dignified and proper
58 Because of (*2 words*)
59 Break up, informally (*2 words*)
60 Clear the tripmeter
62 Aide (abbr.)
63 "The ___ Love Belongs to Somebody Else" (*2 words*)
64 Word after punching or sleeping
65 First *numero*

HINT: The snippet at 39 Across is the start of an 1830 novel by Edward George Bulwer-Lytton. Snoopy's writing efforts never seemed to get very far past it. Puzzle 107's page has a free answer for you.

#119: 59D = YURT

145

Cynical Observation by Alan Olschwang

Puzzles with quotations are tougher because so many letters are initially unclued. Even so, we think you'll enjoy this comment on role models.

ACROSS

1 Turkey stuffing herb
5 Country that controlled Lebanon for many years
10 End of a dry spell
14 Recipient of a deceptive gift horse
15 Serves the tea
16 Suffix with "kitchen" or "luncheon"
17 Right-hand person
18 Charge (2 words)
19 Three-piece suit piece
20 Mark Twain quote, part 1 (3 words)
23 Trying to escape
24 Dublin or Shannon natives
28 Plane grounded in 2000 (abbr.)
29 Quote, part 2 (2 words)
32 Sings jazz like Ella Fitzgerald
35 Calf in a range herd
36 Finish first
37 Centers of activity, as some airports
38 Quote, part 3 (2 words)
39 Fork part
40 Path of a tossed horseshoe
41 Southern Pacific island group
42 Impressions
43 Quote, part 4 (2 words)
45 ___ Andreas fault
46 "I ___ Parade" (2 words)
47 Beginnings
51 Quote, part 5 (3 words)
55 "It Must Be Him" singer Vikki ___
58 Foremost battle line
59 Canal completed in 1825
60 College credit hour
61 Great Green Bay quarterback Brett ___
62 Approach
63 Do artistic work with acid
64 Winter hazard
65 Della's character on Touched By an Angel

DOWN

1 17 Across and other helpers, collectively
2 Disney's mermaid
3 "In ___ Trust" (2 words)
4 Optometrist's exams (2 words)
5 Burst of speed
6 Not old
7 Ladder step
8 Some savings plans, for short
9 Dog in The Thin Man
10 Adore
11 Devoured
12 Some tag players
13 Trapeze artist's "insurance"
21 Make like a snake
22 Merry-go-round or roller coaster
25 Golfer Hale ___
26 Period of time spent at a particular job
27 Sharpens
29 ___ the trail of (chasing closely, 2 words)
30 Mexicali thirst quencher
31 Shred
32 Shoulder warmer
33 Novelty object
34 Desperate Housewives network, in ads
35 Russian legislature
38 Cry of disgust
39 Crowded dwelling
41 Males-only affair
42 Comedian ___ Carvey
44 Fireplace floor
45 Group of six
47 Literary or music category
48 Binge
49 Sewing machine inventor ___ Howe
50 Tarot readers
52 Light switch positions
53 Like some vaccines
54 Bird of peace
55 Hint
56 Picnic pest
57 Pop musician Ocasek

#145: 39D = AGNEW

146

Go Fish   by Manny Nosowsky

We'll turn up the difficulty a little for the next five puzzles by eliminating most of those "2 word" tags and by using some less straightforward clues.

ACROSS

1 Music for two
5 Rosemary or thyme
9 Hang over furniture, say
14 Air France destination
15 Opera highlight
16 Be champ again
17 1960s sitcom with castaways
20 More dangerous, as some winter roads
21 Lose control on a slick street
22 Baby blues
23 1995 Sandra Bullock thriller
25 Prolonged unconscious state
27 Students in *The Paper Chase*
30 Slice for a sandwich
34 Figure with three unequal sides
39 Kayak paddle
40 Natives of Bangkok
41 Class rank stat.
42 Where social graces are taught
47 Battery terminal
48 Hawaii's Garden Island
49 Twelve months
52 Off course
56 Hawk or peddle
59 The Hawkeye State
62 Actress Davis of the "Matrix" movies
63 Specially contracted men's wear
66 Egg-shaped
67 Blueprint
68 Sour tasting
69 There are five in a shilling
70 "The ___ the limit!"
71 Grandson of Eve

DOWN

1 Exert less than full effort
2 *Spenser: For Hire* star Robert
3 Jock's wife, in *Dallas*
4 Bayer competitor
5 Female ogre
6 Big Band and others
7 Hockey arena
8 Fundamental
9 A.M.A. members
10 Acquire skills again
11 Not at home
12 Tree with needles
13 Some football linemen
18 Greek goddess of peace
19 "Who wants ice cream?" reply
24 Extra inning
26 Postgraduate deg.
28 Where Samson defeated the Philistines
29 Smelled awful
31 Breakfast waffle brand name
32 Purina competitor
33 "Have I got a ___ for you!"
34 Dagwood's nap site
35 Abel's brother
36 *The New Yorker* cartoonist Peter
37 Latvian capital
38 Political topic
43 Charmingly simple, in a rural sort of way
44 "Get it?"
45 Gives a darn
46 Opposite of bald
50 Balloon filler
51 Easy wins
53 From China or Japan, for example
54 Explosive liquid
55 Exams
56 "Cut that out!"
57 Gutter for a roof
58 Big cat
60 Take a stroll
61 Every 24 hours
64 Tribute from Keats
65 Rank of a USNA grad.

HINT: An answer is waiting for you in the box next to puzzle 121. In the meantime, the crucial elements of this theme (which relates to the title, of course) are what I call "accidents of spelling." That is, the first several letters of each long answer just happen to spell something fishy.

147

Homophone Trio   by Diane C. Baldwin

This puzzle's theme is in the clues, not in the grid! That's why some clues are in capital letters.

ACROSS

1 What the "A" in UAE stands for
5 Rock to and fro
9 Caught forty winks
14 ___ Scotia
15 Spaceflight org.
16 Lollygag
17 Christmas song
18 Watchful one
19 Lawn tool
20 GNU
23 Presidential nickname of the 1950s
24 Praiseful poem
25 Song (the music part, that is)
29 Criminals break them
31 Matched, as a poker bet
34 Mindful
35 Big book
36 Gillette razor brand
37 NEW
40 Enrages
41 Tennis do-overs
42 "Some people can't take ___!"
43 Donkey's ancestor
44 Male children
45 FBI employees
46 From ___ Z
47 Rapper Dr. ___
48 KNEW
57 Ritual table
58 Part of the leg
59 Himalayas continent
60 Alaska, after 1959
61 It's south of Kans.
62 Benevolent
63 Sharpened
64 House in a tree
65 Single-named New Age singer

DOWN

1 "I" in The King and I
2 Place for shingles
3 Profess as true
4 Indonesian island
5 Underhanded
6 True Grit star
7 Between ports
8 Spinner's product
9 Cavalry chargers
10 Soup server's utensil
11 "Cogito, ___ sum": Descartes
12 Make ready, briefly
13 Ancient Phoenician seaport
21 Apple drink
22 Pisa landmark
25 Frenzy
26 Washstand pitchers
27 Washes up
28 Smelter fodder
29 Hay storage places
30 Maker of "Famous" cookies
31 Oktoberfest mug
32 "___ you the clever one!"
33 Lacks
35 Typical MTV watcher
36 1975 Wimbledon winner Arthur
38 Burst into flower
39 Raring to go
44 Rudely watched
45 Former PLO leader Yasir
46 ___ worse than death
47 Some pickles
48 It's north of Oreg.
49 Saxophone size
50 "The Man" Musial
51 Something to click on
52 Placid or Tahoe
53 Boat trail
54 "The proof of the pudding ___ the eating"
55 Smaller than small
56 "Mary ___ little lamb"

HINT: At 11 Down: René Descartes was a mathematician and philosopher of the first half of the 17th century. The quotation in this clue and answer was the focus of his philosophy. Translated, it means, "I think, therefore I am." Puzzle 125's page has a gimme.

#110: 51D = KITH

148

Have a Bellyful   by Bonnie L. Gentry

An original quip commenting humorously on progress through life is the feature here.

ACROSS

1 ___ Jessica Parker
6 Former leader of Iran
10 Rush-hour subway rarity
14 Sports facility
15 Concluding musical section
16 "Don't Throw Bouquets ___"
17 Quip, part 1 (*4 words*)
20 Not challenging
21 AMA members
22 Under the surface, like some talent
23 Round dessert
24 Macmillan and Robbins
25 Navy's goat or the San Diego Chicken
29 Karate move
30 Find repulsive
31 "For ___ jolly good fellow"
32 Just ___ (not much)
36 Quip, part 2 (*3 words*)
39 Auctioneer's final word
40 Airport alternative to Charles de Gaulle
41 Front steps
42 Smallest bills
43 Cause a snafu
44 States confidently
48 Bill's partner in an "excellent adventure"
49 One who's getting the water out of the boat
50 "I knew it!"
51 Restful resorts
55 Quip, part 3 (*4 words*)
58 Big fusses
59 They're used to count to 20
60 New Age keyboardist
61 Triangle ratio
62 Deficit
63 Harpoon cousin

DOWN

1 Equivalent
2 Oratorio part
3 Checkers selection, often
4 Capp of comics
5 *Shallow* ___ (Gwyneth Paltrow/Jack Black film)
6 Frighten
7 Harleys, in bikers' slang
8 Citrus drink
9 Cry "Taxi!"
10 Took care of
11 Lucy Ricardo's landlady
12 Rephrase
13 Camp shelters
18 Cut (a movie)
19 Cutty ___ (Scotch whisky brand)
23 Meat that's not kosher
24 ___ fit (tantrum)
25 "Say Hey" Willie
26 Ending for "peek" or "bug"
27 Synagogue
28 Twine
29 Yachts' stabilizers
31 "___ Johnny!"
32 Behaves
33 Ring ref's decisions
34 Moises of baseball
35 Johnny of Disney's *Pirates of the Caribbean* film series
37 Falsehood
38 Not new
42 Sweet sandwich
43 Menu choice
44 Palestinian president Mahmoud ___
45 ___ Arabia
46 Squelch
47 Alex P. Keaton's mom on *Family Ties*
48 "___ Foolish Things"
50 Adam's second son
51 Exchange one thing for another
52 Cornmeal bread
53 Kournikova of tennis
54 Use a swizzle stick
56 Pal of Pooh
57 Cobb and Hardin

HINT: The airport at 40 Across (an anagram of ROLY) was the world's 5th busiest outside the United States in 1993 in terms of passengers. By 2002 it had fallen out of the top 10. See the box next to puzzle 132 for a free answer.

#134: 2D = ARRAN

149

Be Verrry, Verrry Quiet! by Ed Early

If you ever took music lessons you may recall that "very softly" is signaled by the letters PPP, meaning "double pianissimo." That's the theme.

ACROSS
1 Saguaro and prickly pear
6 Cunard liner, commonly
10 On ___ with (equal to)
14 Crazy as ___
15 Forearm bone
16 City in California or New Jersey
17 Li'l Abner's dad
19 Oil cartel
20 Ask too many questions
21 Consumed
22 More than sufficient
23 Golfer Irwin
24 Put off
26 Fuse rating unit
29 Impostors
30 Glances from Groucho
31 One-on-one student
32 Clairvoyance, e.g.
35 They call balls and strikes
36 Rationed, with "out"
37 Prefix with "vision" or "photo"
38 Pail's partner
39 Room boundaries
40 Try to buy at auction
41 The ___ Brothers ("Wake Up Little Susie" duo)
43 Hilltops
44 Brake sound
46 Lacking rain
47 Added liquor
48 Desert havens
50 ___-Magnon
53 ___ about (around)
54 "Punch and Judy" venue
56 Exhausted, with "out"
57 "It's all clear now"
58 Car contract
59 E-mail command
60 Shore bird
61 Ran out

DOWN
1 Creator of 17 Across
2 Banned orchard spray
3 Make a forgery
4 Summit
5 For a long time (*2 words*)
6 Current stock price
7 Actress Sommer
8 Floods
9 ___ *Not Spock* (Leonard Nimoy book)
10 Sandy or Roberto of baseball
11 Bagel toppers, sometimes
12 Fred's vaudeville partner
13 Prepared some potatoes
18 Ivy League member
22 Sheltered, at sea
23 Word embroidered on a towel
25 ___ out a living (just got by)
26 Styptic pencil ingredient
27 Office missive
28 Spice mill item
29 Entirely
31 Kind of cookie
33 Vending machine opening
34 Corrals
36 Ste. Jeanne ___
37 Even-steven
39 Tend the garden
40 Brush part
42 Went off course
43 Manitoba native
44 Applies some brake power
45 Sacajawea's transport
46 Colorado comedy festival city
49 Mimic
50 Neighbor of Sudan
51 Jack's *Titanic* love
52 Had markers out
54 Place for an orchestra
55 One of a D.C. hundred

HINT: At 38 Across: This kind of clue tells you to think of a word often paired with the word in the clue, typically in a phrase such as "A and B," where the answer word could be either A or B in the pairing. In this case, the answer word is the A part of the pairing, at least in my head. See puzzle 124's page for another hint.

#132: 9D = PICCHU

150 Unthemed   by Charles E. Gersch

There are lots of long answers here, but the vocabulary and clues should be okay.

ACROSS

1 *The Jazz Singer* star
9 Dug up, as a farm field
15 David Duchovny's actress-wife
16 Put bubbles in the fish tank
17 Drive too close to the car in front
18 Red gemstone
19 Morales of *La Bamba* and *NYPD Blue*
20 Stuffed the clothes in the suitcase
22 Gun enthusiasts' org.
23 Frasier Crane's brother
25 Use a spyglass
26 "The ___ Love" (Gershwin standard)
27 Type of evidence gathered in *C.S.I.: Crime Scene Investigation*
28 Much too big for one's britches
30 Secret group
31 Action figure dubbed "a real American hero"
33 Classic model trains
35 Jillian and Landers
37 Male deer
38 Near
41 Babbling stream
44 Part of a mechanic's bill
45 ___ *in Toyland* (Victor Herbert operetta)
48 Beatty of Superman films
50 Pizzeria cooker
51 Fabricated
52 Lawn neatener
54 ___ Paese (cheese)
55 Space station segment
57 Make a backup
58 Kind of shower or veil
60 More fetching to look at
62 Make certain
63 Connects with
64 Changes a lock
65 Five cards in sequence, in poker

DOWN

1 Go to, as a concert
2 Living in a rental apartment
3 Game played with a pelota and a cesta
4 Stan's partner in slapstick films
5 Stocking stuffer?
6 Something to wash up with
7 Recorded and ready to play back
8 Daughters of siblings
9 Beeper
10 Superman's protection against kryptonite
11 Hockey Hall of Famer Bobby
12 Aspirant, slangily
13 Never-ending
14 The fine print, so to speak
21 Boat backbones
24 Not later
26 Tropical fruit
29 Curved
30 Like sandpaper
32 *Seinfeld* actor Alexander
34 "Let ___" (Beatles hit)
36 "When It Hurts ___" (Lauryn Hill song)
38 Defeat decisively
39 Shirley's sitcom roomie
40 Tall, tapering, four-sided monument
42 Continuing without interruption
43 "Behold, he that ___ Israel shall neither slumber nor sleep" (Psalms 121:4)
46 Grownups
47 Southern Wisconsin college
49 Timber fungus
51 Double agents
53 652, in Roman numerals
55 *Frankenstein* author ___ Shelley
56 Perpetually
59 Scheduled to arrive
61 Maestro ___-Pekka Salonen

HINT: The answer at 61 Down is an anagram of the word SEA. See puzzle 127's page for another hint.

#109: 11D = EVAH

151

Words of Encouragement   by Mel Rosen

If you follow the instruction at 62 Across, you should find this puzzle to be quite 38 Across. In other words, 17 Across!

ACROSS

1 Little white lies
5 Individual grass leaves
11 San Diego animal attraction
14 Opera song
15 ___ *Fables* (collection of tales with morals)
16 Bit of work
17 "This is easy!" (*3 words*)
19 Kilmer of *Tombstone*
20 Golf legend Sam ___
21 "The ___ from Ipanema"
22 Mechanical memorization
23 Gridiron officials, commonly
25 Got ready for business
27 Juan Carlos's *nación*
30 Gymnast Korbut and namesakes

32 ___ Maria (liqueur)
33 Financial option, for short
35 Hindu melody
38 "Easy!"
42 Rocker Clapton
43 Paris subway
44 Baby's "piggy"
45 Risk taker
47 The capital of Greece
49 Bassett of *Malcolm X*
52 Ballet dancer's knee bend
53 The ___ of Avon (Shakespeare)
54 Windmill feature
57 Approaches
61 "A mind ___ terrible thing to waste" (*2 words*)
62 "This is easy!" (*3 words*)
64 George W., to Jenna and Barbara

65 Pickup truck capacity (*2 words*)
66 John-Rice-Disney retelling of a Verdi opera
67 Chicago trains
68 General aviation plane manufacturer
69 Cry

DOWN

1 Summer air movers
2 Element whose symbol is Fe
3 Mosquito attack
4 Arid African expanse
5 Arrid competitor
6 Hosiery brand
7 ___ Spumante
8 Room access
9 Literary wrap-up
10 Retired fast flier (abbr.)

11 "Werewolves of London" composer Warren ___
12 Deliver a keynote speech
13 Made goo-goo eyes at
18 Like the cousins on *The Patty Duke Show*
22 Correct one's carpentry, perhaps
24 Snake's tooth
26 Saying what's just been said
27 Extras on *The X-Files* (abbr.)
28 Locale
29 Henry VIII's last wife Catherine ___
30 Abalone-eating mammal
31 Departed

34 "Alas!" (*2 words*)
36 Slalom course opening
37 Elvis Presley's middle name
39 Helped
40 Like some vaccines
41 ___ Plaines, Illinois
46 Gully
48 Donkey's bray
49 Stay a while
50 Twangy
51 Homecoming figures, commonly
52 *Evita* subject
55 Some city roads (abbr.)
56 Bottom lines
58 Play to ___ (draw; *2 words*)
59 Ferris wheel, for example
60 Brittle cookie
62 Elmer, to Bugs Bunny
63 One ___ million (*2 words*)

HINT: You don't always have to start at 1 Across. Look for fill-in-the-blank clues like 61 Across or 63 Down. For more help, see the box to the right of puzzle 157.

#193: 40D = RUHR

Letter Perfect   by Nancy Salomon

You should find this as easy as ... (nope, not "pie").

ACROSS

1 "Champagne Music" accordionist Lawrence ___
5 Gal's guy
10 Facial arch
14 Pizzeria cooker
15 Run ___ of (come into conflict with)
16 Architect ___ Saarinen
17 "Heigh ho, heigh ho, it's off to work ___" (2 words)
18 Liquid-Plumr competitor
19 Close at hand
20 First half of a sequence
23 High-speed modem connection (abbr.)
25 Get ready to fire a rifle
26 Meyers of *Kate & Allie*
27 Atlantic and Pacific
29 Arnaz who loved Lucy
31 CIA's Soviet counterpart
34 Bring up
35 Oak or elm
37 Church topper
39 The sequence in this puzzle (2 words)
42 Honeydew, for one
43 *Born Free* lioness
44 Help in a heist
45 British verb ending
46 Campus group, for short
48 Spiff (up)
50 Witness
51 Happy ___ clam (2 words)
52 Prefix meaning "three"
53 Second half of a sequence
59 Felipe, Matty, or Jesus of baseball
60 Maker of digital pianos
61 "___ upon a time ..."
64 Nintendo rival
65 Of a forearm bone
66 "Holy cow!"
67 Owl's call
68 African antelope
69 "All right already!" (2 words)

DOWN

1 "Unbelievable!"
2 Garden of Eden woman
3 Lawyer, slangily (2 words)
4 Door opener
5 Trend followers
6 ___ Zimbalist, Jr. of *The F.B.I.*
7 Bread buy
8 Breath-taking organ
9 Greetings from Hawaii
10 1974 film about a stray dog
11 Stink to high heaven
12 Spoken
13 Wriggler on a fishing hook
21 Container in a six-pack
22 From Kilkenny or Dublin
23 Song from *The Sound of Music* (hyphenated)
24 Parts of plays
28 Singer Guthrie
29 Handed out cards
30 Snakelike swimmers
31 Israeli commune member
32 Country whose capital is Athens
33 On the mend
36 Perlman of *Cheers*
38 Former *Tonight Show* host Jack ___
40 Deduce
41 Computer security safeguard
47 Come to the aid of
49 ___ Romana
50 Short and stubby
51 Birdlike
53 Mathematician/ focus of *A Beautiful Mind*
54 Butter stand-in
55 ___ stick (children's toy)
56 Like most basketball stars
57 Annapolis initials
58 Toy on a string
62 USCG rank
63 Surprised shriek

HINT: You may also know the company at 60 Across for its calculators and watches. For a bigger hint, see puzzle 164.

#186: 58A = ERSE

153

A Simple Ditty   by Tony Orbach

This seems like an obvious follow-up to the previous puzzle. Follow 20-, 23-, 38-, and 54 Across. Join in!

ACROSS

1 Eden man
5 Brewer's ingredient
9 Brand of sink unclogger
14 Soprano superstar
15 Salve additive
16 Encored on TV
17 Get ___ a good thing (2 words)
18 School club
19 Bowlers' term
20 Start of the end of a lyric (4 words)
23 More of the lyric
24 Bugs Bunny's are big
25 "What Kind of Fool ___?" (2 words)
27 Packing a wallop
30 Actor who played Jackson Pollock in Pollock (2 words)
35 Fruit-juice drinks
36 A state of rapture or ecstasy
37 Roadie's responsibility
38 More of lyric (4 words)
42 Airport listing, for short
43 Dress up
44 What the little hand indicates
45 Daddy ___ (big cousin of a spider)
47 Blacks out
49 "Heart of Dixie" state (abbr.)
50 Roseanne star Roseanne
51 What the whole lyric covers (3 words)
54 End of the lyric (3 words)
60 Disney's animated mermaid
62 Shiny wrap
63 Former Chief Justice ___ Warren
64 Test, in a manner of speaking (2 words)
65 Classify
66 K-6 school designation (abbr.)
67 Kind of tea
68 "___ the Lonely" (Roy Orbison hit)
69 Silent assents

DOWN

1 Tennis score after deuce, often (2 words)
2 Serpico producer De Laurentiis
3 Declare bluntly
4 Easily understood; evident
5 Refrigerator attachment
6 Ration
7 MGM cofounder Marcus ___
8 Abound
9 Medical providers (abbr.)
10 Fix
11 Riyadh resident
12 DEA agent
13 Some binary digits
21 Slugger ___ Griffey Jr.
22 Internet search engine
26 Jazz flutist Herbie ___
27 Committee
28 "___ Billie Joe" (2 words)
29 Dallas native
30 Wide-spouted pitchers
31 Pillow filler
32 Fabric once known as "artificial silk"
33 Tossing-in-one's-cards comment (2 words)
34 Cowboy boot attachments
36 Dirty air
39 Like a hard-to-believe tale
40 Brainstorms
41 Baker's dozen count
46 Freestanding shady structure
47 Britcom ___ Towers
48 Former Bush spokesman ___ Fleischer
50 '30s nightclub employee, slangily (hyphenated)
51 Organization for 50-and-older folks (abbr.)
52 Flip-a-coin test answer
53 Comment from a pig
55 "Presuming that to be true ..." (2 words)
56 Lunch time, for many
57 Christmas play prop, perhaps
58 TV equine (2 words)
59 Shade trees
61 Caustic cleaner

HINT: The answer at 22 Down is also a shout meaning "Yippee!" For an even bigger hint, turn to puzzle 171's page.

#179: 34A = FINIS

Timberland   by Ed Early

The growth may be really thick here.

ACROSS

1 Enjoy, as gum
5 Singer ___ Page
10 Burlap material
14 Topnotch (*hyphenated*)
15 Pop singer Neville
16 Military branch (abbr.)
17 Its target is tartar
19 1994 Jodie Foster film
20 Photo ___ (campaign activities)
21 Nile cobra
22 Wine punch
24 Temper tantrum
25 Fights (*2 words*)
26 Eva or Zsa Zsa
29 Craving
30 Building beam (*hyphenated*)
31 Charged particle
32 Hard chewy candy
36 Green citric refresher
38 Request to hold, as a library book

39 Tennis star Andre ___
40 Word before "blood" or "news"
41 Baby beef
42 Petty (*hyphenated*)
44 Parts of hammer heads
45 Without feelings of disgrace
48 Goof
49 Natalie Wood and Rita Moreno in *West Side Story*
50 He was quoted in the *Little Red Book*
51 Sticky stuff
54 Furnace fodder
55 Top golfer (*2 words*)
58 Czech runner ___ Zátopek
59 Perfect
60 Go on the fritz

61 Purges
62 Pennies
63 ___ time (never; *2 words*)

DOWN

1 Roman statesman and moralist
2 Basketball target
3 Slaughter at Cooperstown
4 Dripping
5 Miller beer rival
6 Organization for seniors (abbr.)
7 One-man Broadway show about Capote
8 Horseshoe throws
9 Occupied as a residence
10 1991 Spike Lee film (*2 words*)

11 Employers
12 *Rocky* actress ___ Shire
13 Note that's the same as D sharp
18 Nudity-on-stage musical
23 Belonging to a certain Roman emperor
24 Former United States Open site (*2 words*)
25 Animated TV chihuahua
26 ___ monster (large southwestern U.S. lizard)
27 "Speak softly and carry ___ stick" (Teddy Roosevelt; *2 words*)
28 "The Crimson Tide"
29 Anonymous Jane

31 Related to a particular style or group
33 Unencumbered
34 *Mrs. Bridge* author ___ Connell
35 Long swimmers
37 Nile dam site
38 Participant in a lab experiment
40 Auction action
43 Next to
44 Ship's front
45 Stomach ailment
46 Model ___ Campbell
47 Dignified
48 English nobles
50 Wiener schnitzel, for example
51 Billy or nanny follower
52 Supreme creator, in Norse mythology
53 Capital on a fjord
56 Senior military leader (abbr.)
57 Two ___ kind (*2 words*)

HINT: The clue at 49 Across refers to ethnicity, not role or gang names. Since the clue has two names separated by "and," the answer is plural. See puzzle 178 for more help.

155

Meow! by Bernice Gordon

You won't need nine lives to solve this one.

ACROSS

1 Ladies' pro "roundball" league (abbr.)
5 Stage or film performer
10 TV advice giver Dr. ___
14 Debtor's promises (abbr.)
15 Strongarm
16 Prepare for "The Star Spangled Banner"
17 Moves warily
19 Lawyer-author ___ Stanley Gardner
20 Trapped
21 Christian springtime holiday
23 Big battle
24 *Today* cohost ___ Lauer
25 In a docile way

29 Adjective with computer or property
33 Label on some sale items (*2 words*)
34 Make an outline of
35 Gold, in Mexico
36 1964 Ann-Margret adventure/comedy movie (*4 words*)
40 Dine
41 Drizzling
42 Hospital staffer
43 Tutor
45 Took a breather
47 Boring way to learn
48 Precious stone
49 African adventure
52 Friendly at parties
57 Like diehard fans

58 Sneak thief (*2 words*)
60 Wander
61 "Are you calling me ___?" (*2 words*)
62 Puerto ___
63 Filled with wonder
64 Cooks with pork fat
65 *Planet of the* ___

DOWN

1 Rub dry
2 Person, place, or thing
3 Smooch
4 Organization (abbr.)
5 Noisy quarrel
6 One who murmurs amorously
7 Walked the boards
8 Calendar abbr.

9 Work done in a lab, perhaps
10 Magician's exclamation
11 "Java" trumpeter Al ___
12 Cruise stopover
13 Groucho's smirk
18 Two-masted sailing boat
22 Baffled (*2 words*)
24 Substantial
25 George ___ (Sulu on *Star Trek*)
26 From Mongolia or Japan
27 Catchers' gloves
28 Winter clock setting for New York (abbr.)
29 Word processor command
30 Like seven of Nolan Ryan's baseball games (*hyphenated*)

31 Take for ___ (cheat; *2 words*)
32 Ran easily
34 On two occasions
37 Gaffe
38 Of the sea
39 Third word in many limericks
44 Swapped
45 Happens again
46 VIP in Kuwait
48 Spoil (*2 words*)
49 Detective novelist ___ Paretsky
50 Swear
51 Quitting time for many
52 Recipe direction
53 Taj Mahal city
54 Radar screen signal
55 Boot binding
56 Greek god of love
59 Pie ___ mode (*2 words*)

HINT: The answer at 12 Down is not PORT. There's a free answer for you in the box next to puzzle 185.

#165: 22D = ADELA

156

D-Day   by Thomas W. Schier

Every theme answer has four of a certain letter.

ACROSS

1 Fergie's first name
6 Prayer endings
11 Road club service
14 Kind of acid in protein
15 "I ___ Know What Time It Was"
16 Former Supreme Court Justice Fortas
17 Scornful comment (*hyphenated*)
19 Heavy shipping weight
20 McMahon and Asner
21 Biblical garden
22 Sized up
24 Enter (*2 words*)
25 Lubricate again
27 Unpaid stock benefit (*2 words*)
33 Not ___ (only mediocre; *2 words*)
34 Breezed through, as a test
35 High craggy hill
36 "___ your pardon!" (*2 words*)
37 After-school group (abbr.)
38 Bus ride tab
39 Rainbow shape
40 Slush beverage brand
42 City west of Montgomery, Alabama
43 1948 Norman Mailer novel (with "The"; *4 words*)
47 Thick slices of cheese
48 Mythical predatory birds of great size
49 Try to steal personal information on the Internet
51 Inner tube's surrounding
52 Letters on a promissory note
55 Saturn model
56 Miscellaneous assortment of things (*3 words*)
60 Nitroglycerine cousin (abbr.)
61 *Let's Make* ___ (*2 words*)
62 J.R. Ewing's mother
63 "Many moons ___..."
64 Comes closer
65 Actresses Meg and Peggy

DOWN

1 Umpire's call
2 In the heart of
3 Eliminates
4 Furthermore
5 Sink a putt (*2 words*)
6 Number next to a plus sign
7 Bearing
8 Byrnes of *77 Sunset Strip*
9 Opposite of SSW
10 Banned sports-performance enhancer
11 Informer
12 Reed instrument
13 Travel
18 *The Sopranos* actress Falco
23 Come to the rescue of
24 Rum drink
25 Costa ___
26 Woman in 21 Across
27 From Tibet or China
28 Hooded snake
29 Registers, as at a hotel (*2 words*)
30 Out of style
31 ___ Jean Baker (Marilyn Monroe)
32 Fear greatly
37 Autograph-signing implements
38 Interest rate setters, for short
40 Resident of Boise or Pocatello
41 Metered vehicle
42 South Carolina in 1860, for example
44 Noisy public transportation
45 Court cases
46 Trumpet
49 Gyro bread
50 ___ Kong
51 Deposed Russian ruler
52 On the West Coast, maybe (*2 words*)
53 Norse god
54 Applications
57 1950s presidential monogram
58 Government narcotics watchdog (abbr.)
59 Ron ___ (1960s Tarzan actor)

#158: 69A = SERE

157

Countdown by Alan Olschwang

Working toward the lower end of the ordinal number series.

ACROSS

1 Where lambs live (also, a pigeon coop)
5 Raisin rum cake
9 Manhattan Project physicist Enrico ___
14 Graduate, in common lingo
15 "This must weigh ___!" (*2 words*)
16 Egg-shaped
17 Lo-cal, in ads
18 Small city
19 Conserve, in a way
20 Just out of the medals (*2 words*)
23 Ocean
24 Leg, slangily
25 Evening meals
27 Play together
32 Actress ___ Dawn Chong
33 Spy organization called "The Company" (abbr.)
34 TV drama set in New York City (*2 words*)
39 Immigrants' island
42 Card game
43 Evening wrap
44 Not quite tops (*hyphenated*)
47 Fish with long, narrow jaws
48 None at all
49 Romantic ballad
52 Is so minded (*2 words*)
56 "Lord, is ___?" (question in Matthew 26:22; *2 words*)
57 Dallas NBAer, in headlines
58 George and Martha, originally (*2 words*)
64 In the slightest (*2 words*)
66 Airline to Israel (*2 words*)
67 Highlands hillside
68 Use different Clairol
69 Bad habit
70 Actress Turner
71 Fruit-bearing plants
72 Altar exchanges (*2 words*)
73 Make ___ meet

DOWN

1 Baby bull
2 Potpourri
3 Ballerina's skirt
4 Come out
5 A place to step when you're wet (*2 words*)
6 At the summit
7 Go for the ping
8 Pavlova and Freud
9 Animal's leg portions
10 Holiday forerunner
11 Waken
12 Scrooge
13 Conceptions
21 Road cover
22 Milk component
26 Type of moss
27 Chills the chardonnay
28 Cairo's river
29 After-bath powder
30 Freshwater fish
31 Fork parts
35 The Kennedy matriarch
36 Forum wear
37 Attired
38 Roll call response
40 Charged particles
41 Evidence of a cold
45 552, in old Rome
46 Little things
50 Greek vowel
51 Agile
52 Intelligent
53 "Peter, Peter, pumpkin ___ ..."
54 Go around
55 Rome's ___ Fountain
59 Rode the banister
60 Tex-Mex menu item
61 Middle East country
62 Come down
63 Affirmative votes
65 Soap ingredient

HINT: At 57 Across: that shortened NBA team nickname differs by one letter from the similarly shortened Cleveland team nickname. See puzzle 199 for more.

#151: 52A = PLIE

158

Yoo-hoo, Where Are You?   by Diane C. Baldwin

This puzzle features places you could be. Not exactly expert-level hide-and-seek, but fun nonetheless.

ACROSS

1 Time-wasting bothers
5 Made yarn
9 Yo-Yo Ma's instrument
14 Churlish chap
15 Voice inflection
16 Shaped like an egg
17 Division word
18 Ill-mannered
19 Earthen dike
20 Revolved, like the moon around the Earth
22 Woman's apparel
23 Used an ATM
25 Some whiskeys
27 Docs' organization (abbr.)
28 Small inroad
30 Long-haired cat
35 Ship's cargo area
37 Cheerleader's shout
38 Hide preparer
39 Israel's ___ Sharon
41 Vitality
43 Page or LuPone
44 Warm-blooded vertebrate
46 One flew in *Flubber*
48 That's partner
49 White deer or buffalo, say
50 Some folding money
52 Before, to a bard
53 Ballet skirt
55 Social bloopers
57 Colonel's insignia
61 Give the right to
63 Committee head
64 Basic bit
65 Burden of proof
68 Macho types
69 Parched or withered
70 "North forty" piece
71 Signs of what's to come
72 ___ *Brockovich* (Julia Roberts film)
73 Circus big top

DOWN

1 "The Greatest" boxer
2 Put on (clothing)
3 Cornered, perhaps (*4 words*)
4 Bird on a birth announcement
5 Determined pedestrian
6 Look peeved
7 Secretly bought or sold (*hyphenated*)
8 Poverty-stricken
9 Sudden chilly weather (*2 words*)
10 In any way
11 Valentine sentiment
12 Tells it like it isn't
13 Praiseful poetry
21 Word after trundle or twin
23 ___ Islands (Caribbean destination)
24 Without scruples
26 Chow down
29 Siesta activity
31 Tiny flier
32 Undecided (*3 words*)
33 Decide to take the pension
34 Springs up
36 Actress Moore
40 Portable lights
42 Barrie's *Peter* ___
45 Comic ___ Costello
47 Dietary plan
51 Kicked back
54 Try to get one's goat
56 Parade sight
57 Canyon sound
58 "Pardon me"
59 Hunter's prey
60 Mortgage security
62 Aaron Spelling's daughter
66 Footed vase
67 Part of a tennis match

HINT: If you need it, puzzle 156's page has a free answer for you. In the meantime, note the clue at 43 Across: When "or" divides two names you'll need to think of a first name or last name they have in common.

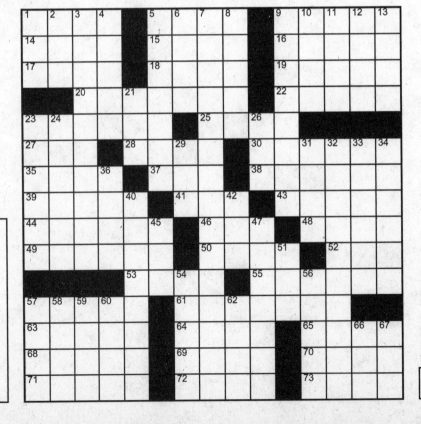

#194: 15A = ETUDE

159

It's Really Dark — by Mel Kenworthy

So dark, in fact, that there's no light at all. But that doesn't mean it's dismal.

ACROSS

1 Model airplane wood
6 Pigpens
11 Letters designating a full theater
14 Margarines
15 *Lara ___: Tomb Raider*
16 Roofer's gunk
17 Classic children's literature story about a horse (*2 words*)
19 *Brokeback Mountain* director ___ Lee
20 Enthusiastic Spanish agreement (*2 words*)
21 Itinerary stopovers
22 Nations
24 South American mountain chain
26 Worthy of being put in the trash
27 Took without paying
30 Unsurpassed
31 Boat paddle
32 Divisions of Hindu cultural life
36 Muslim holy man
40 Rich chocolate, cream-filled, decorated dessert
43 Auction off
44 Comedian, presumably
45 Pistol, in old detective movies
46 Suffix with "kitchen" or "cigar"
48 Haywire
50 Distress signal
52 Molten rock
55 Port-au-Prince's land
56 Dog in *Peter Pan*
57 "... believe ___ the whole thing!" (*2 words*)
61 Physicians' group (abbr.)
62 Voted against an applicant
65 *On ___ Majesty's Secret Service*
66 Flip chart holder
67 Take another shot at
68 Classifieds
69 Sleuth played by Bogart
70 Fields' yields

DOWN

1 Barker and Feller
2 "___ want for Christmas ..." (*2 words*)
3 Pastoral expanses
4 Enjoying the company of others; gregarious
5 Set, as a price
6 Public outburst
7 The T of TWA
8 Debtor's written promises
9 Small salamander
10 Phonograph record needle
11 Smelled terrible
12 Country music star Travis
13 Associations (abbr.)
18 Compete on eBay
23 Horseplay
25 Race decider, perhaps
26 Former Senator Helms
27 Weeps loudly
28 Word after "tall" or "fairy"
29 Spoken
30 Spelling competitions
33 ___ worse than death (*2 words*)
34 "You've got ___ nerve!"
35 Robert Morse's show about Capote
37 They followed the Star of Bethlehem
38 Aliases, for short
39 Shea Stadium's baseball team
41 Sport shoe attachment
42 Public conveyance
47 Native American groups
49 *The Naked and the Dead* author Norman ___
50 Celebrated
51 Perjurers
52 Sprayed rioters, perhaps
53 Sock part
54 Chew the fat
55 "Now, *that's* funny!" (*2 words*)
56 Agency that put a man on the moon (abbr.)
58 Saxophone type
59 Maryland athlete, informally
60 Big name in ice cream
63 It disappears when you stand up
64 Parenthesis shape

HINT: The title of the show at 35 Down was based on Capote's first name. For more help, see puzzle 163's page

#187: 17A = OMANI

160 Get a Move On!   by Gail Grabowski

The important word starts the long phrases here.

ACROSS

1 Tennis champ Arthur ___
5 Put to shame
10 Author ___ Stanley Gardner
14 NASA's 1969 landing site
15 Phone answerer's word
16 Totally trash
17 Insect control device (*2 words*)
19 Italian wine region
20 Winnie-the-Pooh's creator
21 Garden tools
22 Storage structure
23 Sweetheart
24 Went faster (*2 words*)
26 Gather, as crops
29 Colorful Mexican shawl
32 Took the train
35 Grasslands
38 Jaunty cap
39 Words before "carte" or "king," on a menu
40 Services with cups, saucers, and so on
42 Mom's compassion, briefly
43 Sauce made with basil
45 Practice like a boxer
46 Legendary story
47 Tourist's souvenir (*hyphenated*)
49 "The Gift of the ___"
51 Kennel club categories
54 Misfortunes
57 Stallion stopper
59 Evening, in adspeak
61 Behave after a stimulus
63 Street
64 Pub game participant (*2 words*)
66 Memo phrase (*2 words*)
67 Internet memo
68 Hackman of Hollywood
69 Kennedy and Koppel
70 Held another meeting
71 Art Deco illustrator

DOWN

1 Two-band radio
2 Not liquid or gas
3 According to ___ (by the rules)
4 Catch in a trap
5 "I thought so!"
6 Amy, Jo, and Meg's sister
7 Some choir members
8 Sheep counter's desire
9 Racetrack runners
10 Sign of a correction
11 Annual sorority event (*2 words*)
12 Dietetic, in ads
13 Oklahoma city
18 "Wish you ___ here"
25 Young socialites
27 Pub brew
28 Vegetable soup ingredients
30 Animal skin
31 Engrave with acid
32 Spellbound
33 Bullring shouts
34 Auto's instrument panel
36 Nile snake
37 Stitched line
40 Pulled apart
41 Singing syllable
44 Ranting speeches
46 Odometer's measure
48 "Love Me ___" (Presley song)
50 Young lady
52 Sawyer or Keaton
53 Longtime senator ___ Thurmond
55 Type of cake
56 Fragrance
57 Court order
58 Sharpen
60 Suffix with "major"
62 Genealogy diagram
65 Teacher's favorite

HINT: The answer at 67 Across is not E-MAIL, but it's a related word. See puzzle 170's page for another, bigger hint.

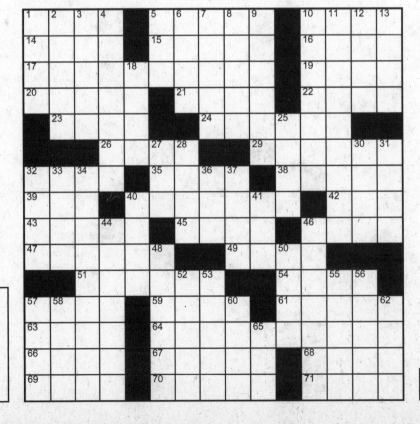

161

Big Winners   by Ed Early

Prizes are awarded in the spring. For what, you may ask? Here are three answers, as well as the answer to "What prize?"

ACROSS

1 Country singer ___ Jackson
5 Polite hat-tipper's word
9 Shaft between wheels
13 Fabric fluff
14 The Lone Ranger's sidekick
15 Sacred bird of the Egyptians
16 Big winner in 1954 (3 words)
19 Rhubarb
20 Film's ___ Redgrave
21 Classic Jaguar model
22 Move to the music
24 Proofreading notations meaning "keep this in"
26 Saudi citizen
29 Cry from the crow's-nest (2 words)
33 "___ corny as Kansas in August" (2 words)
36 Out of harm's way

39 Not express
40 Big winner of 1939 (4 words)
43 Immature egg, to a zoologist
44 Beach makeup
45 Russian jets
46 Hang on to
48 "It's the end of the world ___ know it!" (2 words)
50 Very angry
53 On a scale of ___ ten (2 words)
57 Hoggery
60 One with aspirations
63 Medical people (abbr.)
64 Big winner in 1965 (4 words)
67 Hawkeye State
68 Solidly built
69 Actress Catherine ___-Jones
70 Oxidation

71 Use a whetstone
72 Robert ___ of The Sopranos

DOWN

1 "Sit down and take ___ off" (2 words)
2 ___ Blair of The Exorcist
3 Russian author ___ Chekhov
4 Ultimate degree
5 Sound in a haunted house
6 Puts chips in the poker pot
7 Mushroom cloud experiment (hyphenated)
8 Food tidbit
9 Televise
10 Microsoft video game system introduced in 2001
11 Chain piece

12 Villa d'___
14 Airline once controlled by Howard Hughes
17 At any time
18 Femme follower
23 Attorney-to-be's course (2 words)
25 Winter yard decorations, of a sort
27 "___ live and breathe!" (2 words)
28 Belfry inhabitants
30 602, to Nero
31 Be suspended
32 Delta 88, for one
33 "The Firebird" composer Stravinsky
34 Go from here to there
35 "Sometimes you feel like ___ ..." (2 words)

37 Government loan guarantor (abbr.)
38 Highest volcano in Europe
41 Bizarre sort
42 Department leaders (abbr.)
47 Phrase that means the opposite of "ASAP"
49 Creeping critter
51 11:50, vis-à-vis midnight (2 words)
52 Wore (2 words)
54 Collectible Ford flop
55 Unimaginative
56 Obie's cousin, and hint to this puzzle's theme
57 Commotion
58 First word of many commandments
59 Evergreen shrubs
61 Pouty expression
62 Little salamander
65 Made a lap
66 Israeli submachine gun

HINT: It may help you to know that the opposite of the answer at 24 Across is DELES. See puzzle 177 for a giveaway answer.

#173: 22D = OMSK

Punctuated   by Alan Olschwang

The title reflects how each of the long phrase answers begins.

ACROSS

1 "I Walk the Line" singer Johnny
5 Actor Baldwin
9 Christmas carols
14 Kind of rug
15 Move, in Realtor-speak
16 "Live Free ___" (New Hampshire's motto; *2 words*)
17 Aunts, in Alhambra
18 Confiscate
20 Room in *la casa*
21 Good things to have on the books
22 1" pencil, maybe
23 ___ about (roam)
25 Creative people
27 One way to populate a region
32 Beer's cousin
33 Caboose's place
34 Geronimo or Cochise
38 Former James Bond portrayer Connery
40 Duffer's pursuit
42 Stretched tight
43 Piano note that's the same as F natural
46 Note
49 Pro hoopster's league (abbr.)
50 Gum doctor
53 Related to a region of Spain
56 The Crystals' "Da ___ Ron Ron"
57 ___ Locka, Florida
58 Counsel
61 Stag or gander
65 Instrument places, inside cars
67 "Woe is me!"
68 Swing clarinetist Shaw
69 "Let's ___" (Cole Porter tune; *2 words*)
70 Decimal system units
71 Like pennies minted in 1943
72 Covetous feeling
73 Popular cookie

DOWN

1 Lions and tigers
2 Opera song
3 Make airtight
4 Tries (*3 words*)
5 Pastoral region of Greece
6 Tolstoy and Durocher
7 Shade trees
8 Attack (*2 words*)
9 Flight that makes no intermediate landings
10 Former fort near Monterey, California
11 Ideal places
12 Police rank below captain (abbr.)
13 Some former Yugoslavians
19 Open courtyards
24 Picnic pest
26 "Tune ___ eleven" (*2 words*)
27 Lawyer's undertaking
28 Shouts in the bull ring
29 Jacob's first wife in Genesis
30 Energy; verve
31 San Antonio mission
35 "What ___ do?" (*2 words*)
36 Central parts of wheels
37 Coup d'___ (revolt)
39 California wine valley
41 Crimson
44 Put on a new tag
45 Madrid museum
47 Lack of pretentiousness; simplicity
48 Yoko ___
51 Enter with hostile intent
52 Marinara ingredient
53 Musical endings
54 Separated
55 Have a bite of
59 Kind of golf club
60 404, to Nero
62 New York Yankee or Baltimore Oriole, briefly
63 Narrow street
64 Tiger-in-your-tank brand
66 Go in haste

HINT: 1 Across and 38 Across have similar clues in that you're given either a first name or a last name without the helpful underscore to help you decide which name is missing. That's like the clues in harder puzzles. See puzzle 184's page for a bigger hint.

163 Making Your Mark   by Mel Rosen

The four longest answers end with the same word.

ACROSS

1 Barrel-shaped wine vessels
6 Garage band's tape
10 Garbage barge
14 "... to fetch ___ of water" (2 words)
15 "Terrible" tsar
16 Alligator ___ (avocado)
17 Net profit or loss (2 words)
19 "My Way" composer Paul ___
20 Risky business, briefly
21 "That's ___ ask!" (2 words)
22 Bohemian
23 They sway when you dance the rumba
25 À la ___ (menu option)
27 Cavalry swords
30 Money paid by some commuters
33 Alda and Arkin
34 Wine bottle plugs
35 Once around the track
36 "Darn!"
37 Tennis player Monica ___
38 Use a book as authority
39 Quantity (abbr.)
40 Ushers know where they are
41 Muscle or tendon
42 Term used when referring to the Pope
44 Police car warnings
45 Answering machine button
46 Bath powder
47 Mint ___ (Kentucky Derby drink)
49 Beer bubbles
51 Previously owned
55 "Come ___, the water's fine!" (2 words)
56 What the winner is first to cross (2 words)
58 Fork prong
59 Exam that's answered aloud
60 Brother of Moses
61 French holy women (abbr.)
62 Corrals
63 Woman's garment, usually

DOWN

1 Taxis
2 Each (2 words)
3 Stuff to the gills
4 Chefs' workplaces
5 ___-Pitch softball
6 Some pickles
7 Very bad
8 Salon services
9 Hydrogen's atomic number
10 Ancient Greek city
11 Stripe that divides a two-lane road
12 Sturdy trees
13 Fay ___ (star of the 1933 film King Kong)
18 Vacation-planning aids
22 Barks, in the comics
24 1040 auditing agency (abbr.)
26 Inquires
27 Buffy portrayer ___ Michelle Gellar
28 Mission to remember
29 Divider between warring armies (2 words)
30 Lightning strikes
31 Gobbled up
32 Ejects, volcano-style
34 Truce (hyphenated)
37 Observes
38 Round in shape
40 Lead-pipe cinch
41 The "S" of RSVP
43 Actresses Worth and Papas
44 ___ Club (Costco competitor)
46 Coin toss outcome
47 Writes quickly
48 College credit hour
50 Putting ___ act (2 words)
52 Father a foal
53 Hall of Famer Slaughter
54 Bears' lairs
56 Dandyish dude
57 "I've been ___!"

#159: 36A = IMAM

164 Snookums   by Victor Fleming

Or, terms of endearment. At least, that's what the long answers start with.

ACROSS

1 Camper's shelter
5 Tom's dad's job, in a nursery rhyme
10 Main idea
14 The Beehive State
15 Do penance
16 One way to learn
17 Instruments with 88 keys (*3 words*)
20 Chicago trains
21 Someone on your side
22 Term of employment
23 Beseech
24 Ill will
26 Ill will
29 Yearns deeply
30 Guzzler
31 Beer ingredient
32 Sock part
35 Boxer who won titles in five divisions (*3 words*)
39 Electrical switch positions
40 Bed-and-breakfasts
41 Kind of checking account (*hyphenated*)
42 2004 Jude Law film
44 City or county near Dallas
45 List of typos
47 Office assistant
48 Bergen dummy Mortimer
49 Unexpected obstacle
50 "Ta-ta!"
53 First few days of a new job (or a new marriage; *2 words*)
57 Word of regret
58 Colleague of Kukla, on old TV
59 Gumbo ingredient
60 Sentry's shout
61 More peculiar
62 Consider

DOWN

1 Toothpaste container
2 List-shortening abbr.
3 Puts the collar on
4 "___ will be done ..."
5 Let ride, at the track
6 Boot-shaped nation
7 Small horse
8 Finale
9 Iron-pumper's unit
10 Free
11 Greek column type
12 Boulder
13 Exam
18 Stocking keeper-upper
19 ___ of Capri
23 Galileo's home
24 Pepper grinders
25 Chip in
26 Former name at the gas station
27 Subject, usually, in grammar class
28 Hot chocolate containers
29 Late great golfer Stewart
31 Craze
32 President before Wilson
33 Sandwich cookie
34 Tempting spot
36 Fissure
37 Tense (*2 words*)
38 Not any
42 Run in
43 Godiva's title
44 Infant's wear
45 ___ *Gay* (historic plane)
46 Kidney-related
47 Ward of Daddy Warbucks
48 Former Iranian leader
49 Real-estate sign
50 Kid's transport
51 Time long past
52 Dutch cheese
54 Bovine cry
55 Antiquated
56 Angler's pole

HINT: That film at 42 Across was a remake of a 1966 film for which Michael Caine was nominated for a Best Actor Oscar. See puzzle 198 for a giveaway answer.

#152: 68A = ELAND

Fore and Aft   by Sarah Keller

You'll quickly find a similarity in the structure of these long answers.

ACROSS

1 Two of a kind
5 Out-of-favor refrigerant gas
10 "___ a Lady" (Tom Jones hit)
14 "What ___ is new?"
15 2 to 1, for example
16 Not slack
17 Type of carpeting (*hyphenated*)
19 "Concerning," as phrased on a legalese memo
20 Facial expressions that go along with jeers
21 Status of a top Broadway player
23 Big name in insurance
26 Revise, as a manuscript
27 Like dishwater
30 Concert necessity
32 ___ *Gay* (WWII bomber)
35 Cosmetic additive
36 Chef who shouts "Bam!" on TV
38 Cheese partner in a sandwich
39 Family card game
40 Female Russian noble
41 Folk singer DiFranco
42 Roof sealant
43 Eye part
44 Pantyhose woe
45 ___ Lauder of cosmetic fame
47 Statistic for stature (abbr.)
48 Television and the press
49 Bunyan's Babe and others
51 Country singer K.T. ___
53 Oscar ___ (*The Odd Couple* role)
56 One whose work is hung in a museum
60 Environmental science (abbr.)
61 Type of confrontation (*hyphenated*)
64 Oxford or loafer
65 All by oneself
66 ___ Sharif of *Funny Girl*
67 Towel inscription
68 Slender candle
69 Rajah's wife

DOWN

1 Church benches
2 Astronaut Shepard
3 "'Twas on the ___ of Capri ..."
4 Let go of
5 Winter windshield obstruction
6 Like sashimi
7 Airport posting (abbr.)
8 Squelches the squeaks
9 Actor Nick ___
10 Recipe instruction, for example, when preparing cake batter (*2 words*)
11 Type of combat (*hyphenated*)
12 Recently adopted money standard
13 Thorny rose supporter
18 Deuce beater
22 Journalist ___ Rogers St. Johns
24 Quarterback nicknamed "Broadway Joe"
25 Italian explorer ___ Vespucci
27 Pan-fry
28 Forearm bones
29 Type of salesman (*hyphenated*)
31 Writes in block letters
33 Veranda
34 Girlfriend, in Mexico
36 Language suffix
37 ___ coo (ooon; *2 words*)
40 Joyce Kilmer poem
44 Summoned (*2 words*)
46 Banishes
48 Spanish surrealist Joan ___
50 What Jack Sprat could eat (*2 words*)
52 "See ya!"
53 Interlock
54 Tylenol target
55 Simba's mate in *The Lion King*
57 "___ Rock" (Simon and Garfunkel hit; *3 words*)
58 Do a supermarket checker's task
59 Hatcher of *Desperate Housewives*
62 One of New York's finest
63 Opposite of WSW

HINT: At 8 Down: Puzzle composers sometimes like to write a clue with several words using the same starting letter. Alliteration won't make a clue harder, per se, but it will probably make you think a little more. Puzzle 155's page has more assistance.

166

What to Wear   by Mel Rosen

Wardrobe choices, ranging from white tie and tails to denims.

ACROSS

1 She played Darlene on *Roseanne*
5 Tennis star and husband of 8 Down
11 Thompson of *Back to the Future*
14 Part of USA (abbr.)
15 Trounce (2 words)
16 Breakfast buffet item
17 Tuxedo or evening gown (2 words)
19 "You stink!" (heckler's shout)
20 Poker player's declaration (2 words)
21 Rock singer ___ Apple
23 Unser outings
24 Receptacle for valuables
26 Native of ancient Peru
29 The "E" of B.P.O.E.
30 Eighteen-wheeler
31 When lunch ends, for some (phrase with abbr.)
32 Independent auditors (abbr.)
33 Hamburger condiment
34 Slacks and shirt, for example (2 words)
38 Vice president in 2006
39 Entertains like Eminem
40 Seance phenomena
41 Pet bird's enclosure
42 Verified datum
46 Another name for Cupid
47 Santa's sackful
48 Not virtues
49 A case of the ___ (boredom)
51 Camp Swampy private ___ Bailey
52 It follows Thurs.
54 Once-faddish polyester garb (2 words)
57 *Grey's Anatomy* network
58 Sergeant's command (2 words)
59 Gets the sun
60 Greek letters
61 Opposite of wide
62 Protected, on ship

DOWN

1 Political columnist William ___
2 Indifferent to right and wrong
3 Start over, in pool
4 Multitudes
5 Up to the task
6 H.S. proficiency test (abbr.)
7 Swiss river
8 ___ Graf, tennis star and wife of 5 Across
9 "Wake Up, Little ___"
10 ___ facto
11 From Beirut
12 Freudian topic
13 In the past
18 Bonehead
22 Next-to-last bowling frame
24 Navy commando
25 "Get lost!," in Pig Latin
27 Computer "brains" (abbr.)
28 Fuse rating unit
30 Neuter, as a female dog
31 Horse-feed bits
32 Poolroom sticks
33 Come to terms (with)
34 Buddy
35 Physical fitness program
36 Mimic a mad dog
37 Dawdles
38 Former aviation-regulating agcy.
41 More snuggly
42 Saint's day celebration, in Latin America
43 Real
44 Singer ___ Dion
45 African fly
47 Greek letter
48 Neckline shape
50 Actor ___ Alda
51 Make tea
52 Send via phone
53 Statistic in baseball's triple crown (abbr.)
55 Patriotic organization for men (abbr.)
56 Donut-and-dance org. of WWII (abbr.)

HINT: That river at 7 Down can have a final E in its name. The name of its major city (Berne) is also spelled with or without a final E. The rule seems to be that if the city is "Berne," the river's name has no final E, and vice versa. There's another hint beside puzzle 162.

Quite Suitable — by Alan Olschwang

This puzzle was constructed according to Hoyle.

ACROSS

1 Actor Sean ___
5 Organization that protests fur coats (abbr.)
9 "Sir," in colonial India
14 On an ocean liner
15 ___ for All Seasons (2 words)
16 City on the Mohawk River
17 Preparation
19 Texas hold'em game
20 Damascus denizen
21 Pajamas for kids
23 WWI flying heroes
25 Corn serving
26 America's Uncle ___
29 Objects of the greatest affection
35 Spray no longer used on apple orchards
37 Take to court
38 Improve, slangily (2 words)
39 Prom transports
41 Sitter's creation
43 ___ Haute, Indiana
44 Monastery superiors
46 Beat walker
48 "___ here" (ditto)
49 Oahu attraction (2 words)
52 Possessed
53 Recline
54 Math course
56 Retired but holding an honorary title
61 Metal receptacle for trash (or, a depth charge, slangily)
65 Powered bicycle
66 Golf course building
68 Utopian
69 Nobleman
70 Revue component
71 Suspicious
72 "Auld Lang ___"
73 Afternoon entertainments

DOWN

1 Quarterback option
2 Catch sight of
3 Close at hand
4 First name in gymnastics
5 Members of a native Nebraska people
6 Post-punk music genre with lots of expression
7 Puts gunk on a roof
8 Short sock
9 Really spicy
10 At the crest of
11 Do some backpacking
12 Champagne bucket
13 Taverns
18 Per unit
22 Consumes
24 King of Israel
26 Dieter's choice
27 Defense component
28 Venomous arboreal snake
30 Extend
31 Has second thoughts about
32 First name in talk shows
33 Country now called Myanmar
34 Risk a ticket
36 Board partner
40 In an impassive manner
42 Bard
45 State of irritation
47 Simple story that has a lesson
50 They may be wild
51 Part of a table setting
55 Spirit
56 Early Oscar winner ___ Jannings
57 Method
58 Fencer's sword
59 Raise
60 Dispatch, as the dragon
62 Pickle gourd, briefly
63 Nepal's continent
64 Takes home
67 Coffee server

HINT: The answer to 6 Down is also the first name of an eccentric stand-up comedian. See puzzle 169 for more assistance.

#181: 49A = AMAHL

168 Choices by Diane C. Baldwin

Whichever choice you make ... doesn't matter to me.

ACROSS

1 911 responders (abbr.)
5 Pottery imperfection
9 Gives a heads-up to
14 *Gone With the Wind* plantation
15 Theater section
16 "It's all in ___ work" (*2 words*)
17 *The Clan of the Cave Bear* author Jean ___
18 Member of the woodwind section
19 All-night dance parties
20 "I'm doing this regardless of your feelings" (*5 words*)
23 Cries of delight
24 Crackpot
25 "Ain't That ___" (oldies hit; *2 words*)
29 Lingerie item
31 Egyptian snake
34 Use a ladder (but not to elope)
35 Bed end
36 Amorous glance
37 "This is my final offer" (*5 words*)
40 Kitchen hot spot
41 English noble
42 Cyclist Armstrong
43 Garnet's color
44 Unique
45 Pause uncertainly
46 Junk mail, mostly
47 Seuss's ___-I-Am
48 "Surprising as this is ..." (*4 words*)
56 Former NY governor ___ Cuomo
57 Polly, to Tom Sawyer
58 Roof edge
59 Farewell, in France
60 Forest sight
61 Zenith
62 Soon-to-be adults
63 Planted, as grass
64 Saucy

DOWN

1 And others (abbr.)
2 Hawaii's neighbor
3 Difficult journey
4 Yard or garage event
5 Furnish garments
6 Tramps
7 Helicopter pioneer ___ Sikorsky
8 Strip off
9 Preliminary exercise (*hyphenated*)
10 Modify for use
11 Norah Jones's father ___ Shankar
12 Russian refusal
13 Former draft organization (abbr.)
21 Poetic feet
22 Band together
25 Performing artist
26 Work laboriously
27 Went on a 3 Down, maybe
28 Last word in Bibles
29 "I beg your pardon!"
30 Hang laxly
31 Talent broker
32 Serving of bread
33 Pumpkin-eater of rhyme
35 Young horse
36 Nearly round
38 On edge
39 Shrine to remember
44 Abominable
45 Plump out
46 Extraterrestrial
47 Tendon
48 Instructed or ordered
49 One of the Great Lakes
50 Tub-like containers
51 Continental currency
52 Harvest the grain
53 Scruff of the neck
54 Walkie-talkie word
55 School book
56 Tumbling cushion

HINT: If a clue looks like a snippet of conversation and it is inside quotation marks, as is the case at 29 Down, the answer is also a remark or bit of conversation. If you'd like another hint, see puzzle 176.

#174: 45D = DULLEA

169

Body Weather by Thomas W. Schier

The puzzle's author has found some phrases for you that combine, well, just what the title says.

ACROSS

1 Thrill to pieces
6 Dinner dish
11 Pat on
14 Whiskey-sour flavoring
15 Spoke at length (*2 words*)
16 At-bat statistic (abbr.)
17 Of light color (*hyphenated*)
19 Chew the fat
20 Not naughty
21 Java concoction
23 Put back in a box
27 Grew choppers
29 Fascination
30 Yellowstone Park attraction
31 Feudal lord
32 Hudson Bay natives
33 "Liquid gold"
36 School organizations that get mothers and fathers involved (abbr.)

37 Drift
38 Silent screen star Theda ___
39 The Beatles' "And I Love ___"
40 Fields of expertise
41 Hall's singing partner
42 Stately dance in ¾ time
44 *Murder on the ___ Express*
45 Sent out
47 Puts into cipher
48 Hawaiian island
49 Print indelibly
50 Massachusetts cape
51 Showing affection (*hyphenated*)
58 Fury
59 Famous Texas mission

60 Common cosmetic
61 "We ___ it!"
62 Actresses Hayworth and Tushingham
63 Exorcism battler

DOWN

1 Santa's toy-making assistant
2 Shepherd's workplace
3 "What ___, a mind reader?" (*2 words*)
4 Rocky outcropping
5 Trap
6 Cost
7 Narrow street
8 Massachusetts cape
9 Hammer in obliquely
10 Infinite

11 Nearly unable to speak (*hyphenated*)
12 Fall off
13 Used the velodrome
18 Toy Charlie Brown can never fly correctly
22 Munched on
23 Essayist ___ Waldo Emerson
24 On the A-list
25 Thinking rationally (*hyphenated*)
26 Carpets
27 Typical takers of driving tests
28 Used binoculars
30 "Swell!"
32 Words to live by
34 *Me, Myself & ___* (Jim Carrey flick)

35 Shoe inserts
37 Quiz choice
38 Scott ___ of *Charles in Charge*
40 Opposed to military combat
41 Grove of fruit trees
43 "Give ___ rest!" (*2 words*)
44 Not repeated
45 Traditional Spanish hero (*2 words*)
46 New Zealand tribesman
47 Community character
49 Actress Samms
52 "The Greatest"
53 Deserter
54 Salmon-to-be
55 Stomach, to a tot
56 Psyche component
57 Animal's lair

HINT: The answer at 2 Down is just another word for "pasture." See puzzle 183's page for another hint.

170

Car Parts · by Gail Grabowski

That's what the long phrases share as endings.

ACROSS

1 Fizzy drink
5 Side dish with dressing
10 Defrost
14 Cain's brother
15 "All kidding ___ ..."
16 Judge's garment
17 Unwanted person (*2 words*)
19 Creator of Perry and Della
20 Regard highly
21 Officially withdrew
23 Pay increase
26 Spud
27 Overhead trains
30 "Not guilty," for one
31 "To ___ is human ..."
32 Bert of *The Wizard of Oz* fame
34 Italian money replaced by the Euro
36 Goose ___ (skin reaction)
40 Thread holder
42 Gun lobby org.
43 Prying person
44 Sun-dried brick
45 Dublin's land
47 Cabbagelike plant
48 Little rascal
50 *A Doll's House* heroine
52 "This minute!"
53 Male operatic voice
55 Pesky insects
57 Trawler's gear
59 Butter units
63 Dog in "Beetle Bailey"
64 Vehicle used to extinguish blazes (*2 words*)
67 Butter alternative
68 Church platform
69 Ponytail material
70 Homeowner's document
71 Borscht vegetables
72 Little kiddies

DOWN

1 Sidewalk eatery
2 Osaka sashes
3 Out in ___ field (wrong)
4 Shorten, as slacks
5 Site for cutting logs
6 Shade of blonde
7 False statement
8 Citrus drinks
9 Erase
10 Elm's main stem
11 Large crowd
12 More adept
13 Garden nuisance
18 Jalopy
22 No-nos in some diets
24 River through Paris
25 Lobe adornment
27 *Born Free* lioness
28 Sgt. Friday's employer (abbr.)
29 "Scat!"
33 Sherwood Forest hero
35 Home run king Hank
37 Cry of pain
38 Equestrian sport
39 Eject, as lava
41 Lousy car
46 They remove mistakes
49 Ready-built residence
51 Business letter abbr.
53 Book's name
54 Lauder of cosmetics
56 A ___ for sore eyes
57 Any edible item
58 Piece of bathroom flooring
60 "Later!," in Rome
61 Create with yarn
62 Church speeches (abbr.)
65 Map highway (abbr.)
66 Have breakfast or dinner

HINT: Solvers at any expertise level have different frames of reference from the puzzle editor and from the puzzle writers. If you encounter new information, as you may with 50 Across here, that's not a bad thing. Maybe it will inspire you to learn more about a subject and, we hope, you'll remember the item the next time it appears in a puzzle. See puzzle 190's page for more help if you need it.

#160: 71A = ERTE

171 Heat Wave   by Ed Early

These four theme entries will keep you warm by the hearth.

ACROSS
1 Radio antennas
6 Blemishes
11 Have debts
14 ___ Sketch (drawing toy; *2 words*)
15 ___ Gay (WWII B-29 bomber)
16 Bagel topping
17 Is a pioneer
19 Roman 551
20 Theory of relativity scientist
21 Grain threshing leftovers
23 Being a snitch
24 Hollywood hopeful
25 Showed the way
26 Early auto inventor Charles, or film actor Dan
27 Runner-up in a match race
30 Keyboard errors
31 Cut the grass
34 Austrian range
35 Tablecloth fabric
36 "___ we go again ..."
37 Architect I. M ___
38 Baseball clout
39 Checked out, crook-style
40 Pirate stashes
42 Neighbor of Syria and Israel (abbr.)
43 Invites a libel suit
45 Ask for, as donations
49 *Star Wars* mentor played by Alec
50 Tweak (*hyphenated*)
51 Neither's partner
52 Comic who lived to be 100 (*2 words*)
54 Half of two
55 German ironworks center
56 Kindled again
57 NFL scores (abbr.)
58 Certain earrings
59 Road curves

DOWN
1 Coin collector near a parking space
2 Courtyards within buildings
3 Meager
4 Prickly plants
5 Tasting more like a pretzel
6 Baseball commissioner Bud ___
7 Putting ___ act (*2 words*)
8 Peri Gilpin's *Frasier* role
9 Atomic orbiter
10 Walks nonchalantly
11 One-time significant others (*2 words*)
12 Rex Stout's detective Nero ___
13 Have real being
18 Turn in the road
22 "We ___ the World"
24 Building manager, commonly
26 Force units
27 It disappears when you stand up
28 "¡Go, matador!"
29 British WWII fighter planes
30 Multiplication word
32 Metal-bearing mineral
33 United in holy matrimony
35 Place for a rendezvous (*2 words*)
36 The usual crowd
38 "Paid" tributes
39 Cause ___ (controversial issue)
41 Uncooked
42 Unaccompanied
43 "___ Forsake Me, Oh My Darlin'" (*High Noon* tune; *2 words*)
44 U.S. savings certificate (*hyphenated*)
45 Billboards
46 Ringlets
47 Bellybutton variety
48 Tries out
50 Dancer ___ Astaire
53 School based in Columbus (abbr.)

HINT: Instead of using a foreign word to signal a foreign word in the answer, the clue at 28 Down uses a punctuation mark to achieve the same goal. See puzzle 197's page for more help.

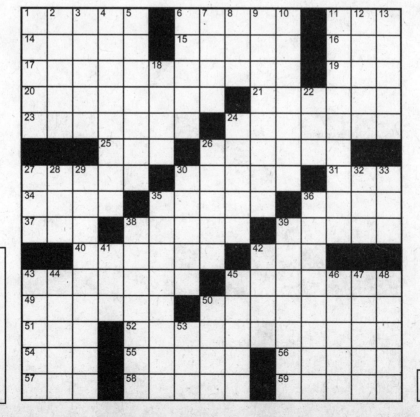

#153: 50D = B-GIRL

Say When   by Diane C. Baldwin

These long phrases form an interesting progression.

ACROSS

1 In the thick of
5 Big party
9 One begins "The Lord is my shepherd"
14 Bombay garb
15 Victim in Genesis
16 Come after; follow
17 Dr. Frankenstein's helper
18 Frog's cousin
19 Jeweled headband
20 "Not a chance!," slangily (3 words)
23 Mine extraction
24 Keg quaff
25 Restitution
29 Low coral islands
31 Bar bill
34 Fable's lesson
35 Auctioneer's cry
36 "Smooth Operator" singer
37 Occasionally (4 words)
40 Shaving cut
41 Lyric verse
42 Romanced
43 Salon offering
44 Rocket skyward
45 Escapades
46 Makes the stakes higher
47 Miss the mark
48 Forever and ever (5 words)
57 Angle less than 90°
58 ___ stick (bouncing toy)
59 Improve a manuscript
60 One in desperate straits
61 Lendl of tennis
62 Forenoon, to a bard
63 Kind of drum
64 Elevator units
65 Something to cop

DOWN

1 Laos's locale
2 Biblical wise men
3 Mineral supplement
4 Malicious gossip
5 Croc's Everglades cousins
6 "... to fetch her poor dog ___" (2 words)
7 Hamburger grade
8 The Four Seasons director Alan ___
9 Floral leaves
10 Shoot at from an ambush
11 "Right away!" (abbr.)
12 Item in a tackle box
13 Not at all nice
21 Pious
22 Austrian composer Franz Josef ___
25 Last words in prayers
26 Drive-in show
27 Vertical
28 London stoolie
29 Cringe in submission
30 "What a pity!"
31 California-Nevada border lake
32 "Doe, ___ ..." (song lyric)
33 Folds up
35 Vending machine offering
36 Standstill
38 Lariat knot
39 Dopey or Sneezy
44 Bailiwick
45 Sings like Bing Crosby
46 Say out loud
47 ___ Allan Poe
48 Puts a label on
49 Graphics image
50 Soviet moon-probe rocket
51 Larger-than-life
52 ___ Scotia
53 Interim office worker
54 Fan mail recipient
55 Bog down
56 Sicilian spouter

HINT: At 50 Down: If you don't recall the Soviet space program cited in the clue, you may know the answer as a large green moth or as the Roman goddess of the moon. If you still need some help, see puzzle 154's page.

173

The Attraction of Opposites — by Ed Early

The four long entries in this puzzle are paired off against each other.

ACROSS

1 Homer and Marge Simpson's boy
5 Musical finale
9 Prefix with red or structure
14 Lotion additive
15 Left in a hurry
16 Actors' parts
17 Close (a door) with anger
18 Jazz singer Fitzgerald
19 Be in store for
20 Nursery rhyme character who met a pieman (2 words)
23 Legend near "6" on a phone
24 Bug
25 "The Shadow of Your ___"
27 Surrealist Salvador ___
30 NFL team displaced from the Superdome
33 "___ first you don't succeed ..." (2 words)
37 Practical experience (2 words)
39 Yogi of notable quotes
41 Eisenhower, popularly
42 Nose, slangily
43 Condition of financial security (2 words)
46 Hissing radiator sound
47 Isle of Capri attraction
48 Reason to call a plumber
50 Parts of speech including cat and mouse
52 NFL Hall of Fame quarterback Joe ___
57 All Quiet on the Western Front conflict (abbr.)
59 Adamant one (2 words)
62 Theater walkway
64 "Not guilty," for instance
65 Dinner tab
66 Chip maker
67 Rotate
68 Thing in a list
69 Snappish
70 Visualizes
71 Young men

DOWN

1 Low opera voices
2 Exhausted (2 words)
3 Wanders aimlessly
4 Arizona city that hosts the Fiesta Bowl
5 Fast cat
6 Artist's choice
7 It may be kosher
8 "Dilbert" cartoonist Scott ___
9 Tehran natives
10 "Immediately!"
11 Vibrant dances from Spain
12 Jockey's strap
13 Concerning (2 words)
21 Certain watch readout (abbr.)
22 Siberia's second largest city
26 Kingly beasts
28 Den
29 Ruffled one's feathers
31 Ring decisions (abbr.)
32 Retired airplanes (abbr.)
33 "___ your pardon!" (2 words)
34 Emotion conquered by daredevils
35 Fire setters
36 "___ Remember" (Fantasticks song)
38 Crossing sign silhouette
40 With keen perception
44 ___ avail (2 words)
45 Destroyers, in naval slang
49 Kung ___ chicken
51 Building bosses (abbr.)
53 Company that merged with Exxon
54 Muscular Japanese dog
55 Created a mosaic
56 Captains' spots
57 Be on standby
58 Zinfandel, for example
60 Collage-making material
61 "Wish you were ___"
63 "___ Freedom Ring"

HINT: Words that came from Italian (which itself arose from Latin) may have kept their original plural forms as well as taken on English-style forms. That's the case at 1 Down. See puzzle 161 for another hint.

#189: 49D = ADELE

174

Made in the Shade   by Alan Olschwang

We think you've got this one covered. (Hint: The theme is in the clues, not the grid.)

ACROSS
1 Little devil
6 Mausoleum
10 Kitchen boss
14 Parcel out
15 Qatar citizen
16 Bush's alma mater
17 UMBRELLAS (*2 words*)
20 Scheduled to arrive
21 Golfer's goof
22 Takes a risk
23 Heidi's nationality
25 Junior
26 Small acting role (*hyphenated*)
29 Main character in *A Christmas Carol*
33 Once more
34 Song by Verdi
36 "Aren't ___ pair?" (line from "Send in the Clowns"; *2 words*)
37 UMBRELLAS (*2 words*)
41 Early nighttime, in poetry

42 "That's ___ to me!"
43 Pastry filler
44 Goes back over text
47 Seesaws' neighbors
48 Shoshonean language
49 Financial crisis
51 MPs go after them (abbr.)
54 Baylor University's city
55 Suffix meaning "somewhat"
58 UMBRELLAS (*2 words*)
62 Auto racer ___ Luyendyk
63 A colleague of Goldie on *Laugh-In*
64 Bowie's last stand
65 Warrior princess of TV
66 Accomplishment

67 Go back to the audio engineering board

DOWN
1 Drain
2 Knucklehead
3 Moises or Felipe of baseball
4 Blister-protection padding
5 Organization for school supporters (abbr.)
6 Tex-Mex snacks
7 Stackable cookies
8 Superhero's secret identity preserver
9 Ammo for some air rifles
10 ___ de Bergerac

11 Rogaine-user's hope
12 "Waiting for the Robert ___" (*2 words*)
13 Parker who played Daniel Boone on TV
18 Goatee's place
19 Stink bomb's output
24 Expert, slangily
25 Read a bar code
26 One in shallow water
27 See eye to eye
28 "Rawhide" singer Frankie ___
29 Titles for Guinness and Hopkins
30 Possessed
31 "Come and ___, coppers!" (crook's challenge; *2 words*)
32 Relaxes

34 Curbside-stand drinks
35 Word on a ticket
38 Put chips in the pot
39 1151, in old Rome
40 One of the Monty Python gang (*2 words*)
45 *2001: A Space Odyssey* star Keir ___
46 ___-bitsy
47 Stuck-up sort
49 Kindergarten adhesive
50 Was sore
51 Comet competitor
52 "Wish you ___ here"
53 Lena ___ of *Alias*
54 Hidden microphone
56 *The King and I* country
57 Type of engine
59 Fleeting fame
60 Paddle
61 Word after "White" or "bobby"

HINT: The clue at 35 Down does not refer to a traffic citation. See puzzle 168's page for more help.

175

Who's What?   by Sarah Keller

This puzzle's theme is in the clues, not the answers. It shouldn't slow you down too much.

ACROSS
1 Have on
5 Be in a bee at school
10 Party for men only
14 Not working
15 Place for a barbecue
16 Golfer's transport
17 Hair-styling aids
18 Actress Susan
19 Besides
20 STEEL (2 words)
23 Pub purchase
24 Vegetable soup item
25 Tease unmercifully
27 M*A*S*H extra
29 Distinctive atmosphere
32 "Put a ___ on it!"
33 Electric shaver manufacturer
36 Pouches
37 WOOD (2 words)
39 China's continent
41 Telly of Kojak
42 "___ the ramparts ..."
43 Military center
44 Intended
48 "Bad, Bad ___ Brown"
50 School organization (abbr.)
52 Barely passing grade
53 STONE (2 words)
58 Drum partner in a parade
59 Knight's protection
60 Makes an offer at an auction
61 Move, in broker language
62 Property claims

63 Dot of land in the sea
64 Ticks off
65 Country once known as Zaire
66 Fortune-teller

DOWN
1 Native American dwelling
2 First woman to swim the English Channel, Gertrude ___
3 Joined by a common cause
4 Catch a breath
5 "___ the rod and spoil ..."
6 Black-and-white bamboo eater
7 Singer ___ James
8 Bert Lahr's role in The Wizard of Oz
9 Sitcom actress ___ Anderson
10 La ___ Opera House
11 Old-time actress Bankhead
12 ___ and Old Lace
13 Classic Pontiac (abbr.)
21 Center in Orlando
22 Airport posting (abbr.)
26 NFL scores (abbr.)
28 South American Indian
29 Advil alternative
30 The Bruins of the NCAA, commonly
31 Muddy up
34 Civil rights activist Parks

35 Baseball stats for pitchers (abbr.)
36 Business letter enclosure (abbr.)
37 BB gun
38 Malcolm-___ Warner of The Cosby Show
39 "You've got mail" Internet provider
40 More run-down
43 "See ya!"
45 Give counsel to
46 Haystack find?
47 More concise
49 Sandwich cookies
50 Fork part
51 Main body part
54 Math course, for short
55 The Kingston ___
56 Warning sign
57 Storklike creature
58 Part of TGIF (abbr.)

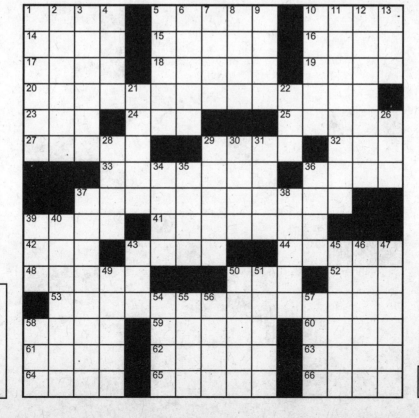

HINT: If there is a brand name in a clue (see 29 Down), the answer often is one as well. There's a bigger hint for you at puzzle 200.

#200: 51D = AILEY

176

Parental Guidance   by Victor Fleming

The key to understanding this puzzle's theme is the answer at 43 Across.

ACROSS

1 1915–19 boxing champ ___ Willard
5 Triangular appetizer-turnover, in Indian cuisine
11 *Boston Legal* network
14 1997 title role for Peter Fonda
15 Bleach brand
16 Long fluffy scarf
17 Unpretentious (*hyphenated*)
19 Take a curtain call
20 Hardly hazy
21 Have ___ to pick (*2 words*)
23 "Beware the ___ of March"
24 Gave, as to charity
26 Airport sights
29 Mr. ___ (victim in the game of *Clue*)
30 Spot for an icicle
31 Like a fair playing field
32 Area 51 sighting, some say (abbr.)
35 Bread maker in a children's tale (*4 words*)
39 Misjudge
40 More polite
41 Vehicle
42 Late Senator ___ Thurmond
43 Word that can precede the last word of 17-, 35-, & 55 Across
45 North Carolina resident
48 Scoop holder
49 More dangerous, as some winter roads
50 Brain region controlling higher functions
54 Furious
55 Protected migratory fowl (*2 words*)
58 Before, in poetry
59 Puts one's two cents in
60 Prophet's reading
61 Hi-___ graphics
62 Kilowatt counters
63 Classic sneakers brand

DOWN

1 Ashley or Naomi
2 Aristocratic race in *The Time Machine*
3 Makes hems, for example
4 Lookout
5 Tea biscuits
6 Baldwin and Waugh
7 Castle protection
8 Retired hockey star Bobby ___
9 Inebriate
10 Part of a lumberman's tool (*2 words*)
11 Monastery leader
12 "Ain't That a Shame" singer Pat ___
13 Imitated a crow
18 Ocean motion
22 Cuba's ___ of Pigs
24 Delaware capital
25 Frankfurt's river
26 Townshend of The Who
27 Bert who played a lion
28 Confidently declare
29 Brazilian seaport
31 Rank above major (abbr; *2 words*)
32 "Nah!" (*hyphenated*)
33 Merry celebration
34 ___ about (roughly; *2 words*)
36 Room-to-room talking device
37 It may be spare or flat
38 Appointment management aid
42 That woman
43 Swampy area
44 Blood type, for short (*2 words*)
45 Race official
46 Without ___ in the world (*2 words*)
47 Amusement park magnets
48 One who yields
50 Candy or sugar follower
51 *Gladiator* city
52 Like Goodwill goods
53 ___ wear department
56 Monkey's cousin
57 Minor quibble

HINT: 45 Across does not refer to a specific person, but a nickname for someone from that state. There's more help for you near puzzle 182.

177 All Together Now   by Levi Denham

There are bunches of gatherings for you this time.

ACROSS

1 Actress ___ Blanchett
5 Wound covers
10 Hole punchers
14 "___ your pardon!" (*2 words*)
15 Meditates on
16 PGA star ___ Mickelson
17 Crime-fighter
19 Sympathetic sorrow
20 Diminish in intensity
21 Cigarette ingredient
22 Shake by sudden impact
23 Rear-end someone, say (*2 words*)
25 Muslim teacher
28 Mass hysteria (*2 words*)
31 Polished gem surfaces
34 Capital of West Germany
35 Republicans, collectively (abbr.)
36 On ___ (even; *2 words*)
37 Poisonous snake of the Nile
38 Motion picture prefix
39 *Funeral in Berlin* author ___ Deighton
40 Helper
42 Oft-repeated statements
44 Theme park provision for swarms of people (*2 words*)
47 Fish hawk
48 Keep in office
52 Some MIT grads (abbr.)
53 Water-testing organization (abbr.)
55 Pacific island nation
56 Tolstoy's ___ *Karenina*
58 Tendency to agree with others
60 Stink up the place
61 Wine taster's concern
62 Sheltered, at sea
63 The Red Planet
64 Expression of disbelief or impatience
65 Loch ___

DOWN

1 Stogie
2 Addis ___, Ethiopia
3 Office break time, briefly
4 Hourglass, perhaps (*2 words*)
5 Dallas campus monogram
6 Manner
7 Dog in *The Thin Man*
8 Brewski
9 Pre-1991 map abbr.
10 Fill with dismay
11 Spinning toy
12 Afire
13 On the ___ (secretly)
18 John Gunther's *Death ___ Proud* (*2 words*)
22 Spain's King ___ Carlos
24 Atlanta-based cable channel (abbr.)
25 Matterhorn, for example (abbr.)
26 Do penance
27 Excessively promotes
29 Barnaby Jones portrayer Buddy ___
30 M-Q filler
31 Edie of *The Sopranos*
32 Mimics
33 Countertop appliance (*2 words*)
37 Fuss
38 Surname of "Dirty Harry"
40 Citrus quenchers
41 Like perilous winter roads
42 "What ___ you up to?"
43 Biblical verb
45 Brings about, as havoc
46 Painful shock
49 French novelist ___ Zola
50 Volcanic peaks
51 Makes off with
53 Goes astray
54 Piglet's pal
56 Escort's offering
57 Teachers' group (abbr.)
58 The Cumberland ___
59 Hillbilly's dad

HINT: For 43 Down: There are more than 40 occurrences of this verb in the KJV. The earliest is in Genesis 4:7. See puzzle 189 for a blatant giveaway.

#161: 61D = MOUE

178

Is Chuck Here?   by Mel Kenworthy

The theme is in the clues. The fun is in the solving.

ACROSS

1 Harmful gaseous element
6 Rights advocacy organization (abbr.)
10 Yields to gravity
14 "Sakes ___!"
15 It was Persia in the past
16 Harness race pace
17 CHARLIE (escape-artist horse in a Marguerite Henry story; *2 words*)
19 "Tickle me" doll
20 Cheek glistener
21 Colorado ski resort
22 Swerve
23 Egypt and Syria, once (abbr.)
25 Pen name of a prolific author of short stories with ironic twists (*2 words*)
27 CHARLIE (as related to Herman; *2 words*)
33 Host at a roast
34 Think out loud
35 "Honest" presidential nickname

38 Workout places
39 Shatner's ___ *War*
40 "Wanna make ___?" (*2 words*)
41 Pretty ___ picture (*2 words*)
42 Painter's garment
44 Express contempt
45 CHARLIE (character in seafood ads; *2 words*)
47 One who dies for a religious cause
50 Citrus drink
51 Antiquing device
52 Nile dam site
56 ___ Erie (Cleveland's waterfront)
60 "It's ___ of your business!"
61 CHARLIE (Berlin landmark)

63 Change for a five
64 Invisible emanation
65 Chef protector
66 Deli loaves
67 Apricot pit, for example
68 Jai alai basket

DOWN

1 Means of travel for Huck Finn
2 What Washington couldn't tell (*2 words*)
3 Opera star
4 Says (an expression) way too many times
5 Keanu Reeves role in *The Matrix*
6 Feels under the weather
7 Farmer's yield
8 Boot binding

9 Obscure; not familiar
10 Seagal or Spielberg
11 "Over the Rainbow" composer Harold ___
12 ___ Pyle from Mayberry
13 Mezzanine, for one
18 Feel concern
24 Had dinner
26 Go quickly
27 Butte's cousin
28 Basketball : refs :: baseball : ___
29 "March Madness" hoops group (abbr.)
30 Chopper blade
31 Small spot
32 Rikki-___-Tavi (mongoose in *The Jungle Book*)

35 "___ Ben Adhem" (Leigh Hunt poem)
36 Swiss capital
37 Sundance Kid's girlfriend ___ Place
40 Gazelle, for example
42 Farm enclosure
43 Salsa band percussion
44 Benchmark (abbr.)
45 Place emphasis on
46 Went under
47 Country estate
48 Intense suffering
49 *Bridget Jones's Diary* star ___ Zellweger
53 Elisabeth of *Leaving Las Vegas*
54 "___ Off to See the Wizard"
55 Learning institute (abbr.)
57 Runs on TV
58 Shoelace problem
59 Highest volcano in Europe
62 Candidate's fund-raiser (abbr.)

HINT: 27 Across refers to a sitcom of the 1960s. And at 17 Across: The same nickname was given to an inept pilot in a *M*A*S*H* episode. There's another hint for you alongside puzzle 196.

Related Endings
by Thomas W. Schier

Not synonyms this time, but eight letters the same. In case you care: The common root word is Latin, meaning "to lead."

ACROSS
1 Rail line
6 After-shower wear
10 More than half
14 Actress ___ Hunt of *Twister*
15 Off-base G.I. (abbr.)
16 Stay in neutral
17 Ludicrous
18 KISS rocker ___ Simmons
19 Parent, as a child
20 Subjects of EPA studies (*2 words*)
23 Country to the north of Mexico (abbr.)
24 Weird
25 Judicial enactments
28 Bar bill
31 Liquor from Jamaica

32 Bid fond ___ (say goodbye)
34 Conclusion
36 DX divided by V
39 Assembly-line manufacturing processes (*2 words*)
42 Unit of electrical current
43 Divulged
44 Confused condition
45 Side of a triangle
46 ___ Moines, Iowa
48 Unappetizing food
49 Hoarse
53 Telepathy, commonly
55 Meetings of long-lost acquaintances
61 Overhanging lower edge of a roof

62 Yemen port city
63 Musical instrument with a pedalboard
64 At any time
65 Real estate document
66 Hurricane that hit South Florida in 2005
67 Tennis units
68 Tickle Me ___ doll
69 Brew in a teapot

DOWN
1 Rarefied, as air
2 Nevada city on the Truckee River
3 Jai ___ (court game)
4 Population enumerations
5 Joints for bending
6 Widespread fad

7 Was indebted to
8 Employee's monetary reward
9 Thrilling; intense
10 Folk singer Makeba
11 Gray's "___ the Spring" (*2 words*)
12 Nonstandard talk
13 To the point
21 Double-crosser
22 Has confidence in
25 Dalai ___
26 Eve's mate
27 Trace of smoke
29 Get an ___ effort (*2 words*)
30 ___ one's time (waited for an opportunity)
33 Optimistic
35 Fully exposed
36 Brat's stocking stuffer

37 Straight dope
38 "The jig ___!" (*2 words*)
40 The fashion industry, so-called (*2 words*)
41 Attending, if not physically (*2 words*)
45 Solitary individuals
47 Word on a Champagne label
49 Forest plants
50 Rise and fall rhythmically
51 Beam fastener
52 Sing in the Alps
54 Puts away for future use
56 Judge
57 Reverse
58 Get a lustful eyeful
59 Identifier on a family crest
60 Ginger cookie

HINT: The actress answering the clue at 14 Across also starred in the sitcom *Mad About You*. If you need another hint, see puzzle 153.

#197: 30D = NATATORIUM

180 Perseverance Pays by Earl W. Reed

The advice suggested by the title is presented three times here. Stick to it!

ACROSS

1 Sag noticeably
6 "The Blue Ribbon Beer"
11 Cargo weight unit
14 Cheaper art version, briefly
15 Muse of poetry
16 Lance ___ (judge for the O.J. Simpson trial)
17 Reinventing the ___ (wasting one's effort)
18 Meaty morsel
19 Thanksgiving's day of the week (abbr.)
20 "Persevere!" (3 words)
22 NFL Hall of Fame quarterback Dawson
23 Archaic, in the dictionary (abbr.)
24 The "way" of Lao-Tzu
25 Those who slalom
27 Knock over
28 Piano note that's identical to D flat
30 The "A" of NEA
33 Feng ___ (Chinese décor placement principles)
34 Bern's river
37 "Persevere!" (4 words)
40 Climber's challenge
41 Bailiff's call
42 Credit report entries
43 Civil War fort near Charleston
45 Golf's Ernie ___
46 Aphrodite's love
48 Plopped down
49 High-school graduates-to-be (abbr.)
52 Stiller of Zoolander
53 "Persevere!" (3 words)
57 Former Press Secretary ___ Fleischer
58 Sea World's famous whale
59 Sporty Mazda
60 Square root of 100
61 Out ___ (1997 Lemmon-Matthau film)
62 Film swashbuckler ___ Flynn
63 Heart chart, briefly
64 Microphone holder
65 Manufacturer of green and gold tractors

DOWN

1 Popular British sci-fi TV show
2 Hard work after surgery, informally
3 Cracks, like a poptop
4 Neighbor of Idaho (abbr.)
5 Seasoned campaigner
6 Basil and pine nut sauce
7 The Gateway ___ (St. Louis landmark)
8 Stark naked
9 "We Built This City" rock group
10 Atchison, ___, and Santa Fe Railroad
11 Where name, author, and publisher appear in a book (2 words)
12 Fill-in-the-blank option on a form
13 Some parts of speech
21 Power ___ (refreshing sleep)
26 They fought the Iraqis in the late 1970s
27 Cruise-Preston film with Migs
28 Tide rival in the laundry
29 Canal to the Red Sea
30 Organization promoting purebred dogs (abbr.)
31 Sunday oration (abbr.)
32 Cumin or oregano
33 ___ terrier (Scottish breed)
35 Dianetics author L. ___ Hubbard
36 LTJG's inferior
38 "Fair to middling" (3 words)
39 Inopportune
44 Centers
45 Word found on many parfum bottles
46 Lessen in intensity
47 Baseball star ___ Jeter
48 Bomb ___ (defusers)
49 Bass drum's counterpart
50 Helicopter assembly
51 Swampy spot
54 Mars Lander org.
55 Extras in The Untouchables (hyphenated)
56 Goodyear product

#190: 52D = URSA

181

Twelve Icons by Ed Early

Remarkably, all twelve icons of the cycle identified at 40 Across are contained in this grid.

ACROSS

1 Egg layer
4 Sends a message via the Internet (*hyphenated*)
10 Close with force and noise
14 Lacto-___-vegetarian
15 * Long-tailed primate
16 * Rooster
17 * Mouse's larger cousin
18 Military school students
19 Owl's sound
20 * Cobra, for example
22 Artist's model's sessions
24 Holds in high regard
27 Kid's ball material
28 Journalist ___ Rogers St. Johns
30 Desert traveler's illusion
34 Off-road wheels (abbr.)
37 Pebble Beach pastime
39 Airplane "driver"
40 Time display and theme of this puzzle (*2 words*)

44 "The Wolf in Sheep's Clothing" writer
45 Achy
46 Devoured
47 ___ *Madness* (1936 anti-marijuana film)
49 ___ *and the Night Visitors* (opera written for television)
52 Enlarge, as a hole
54 Show contempt for (*2 words*)
58 Type of alternative medicine
62 *Jurassic Park III* star Téa ___
63 *Beverly Hills Cop* character ___ Foley
64 Cyberspace stock transaction site (*hyphenated*)

67 * Porky or Petunia of cartoons
68 "Come on, get ___!"
69 * Mythical winged reptile
70 Opposite of WNW
71 Concludes
72 Puts a new price label on
73 Sunday speech (abbr.)

DOWN

1 * Seabiscuit, for example
2 Cowgirl Dale ___
3 ___ home (out; *2 words*)
4 Was host at a roast
5 Extinct bird of New Zealand
6 &
7 Eisenhower and Turner

8 Grant entry to (*2 words*)
9 "You can't beat the ___"
10 Composer Lalo ___ of *Mission: Impossible* and *Dirty Harry* themes
11 "Laughing" bird
12 Slip ___ (make an error; *2 words*)
13 Places to buy things (abbr.)
21 Mauna ___ (Hawaii's highest point)
23 "Rubbish!"
25 Actresses Tilly and Ryan
26 Wild plums
29 Big name in siding
31 *M*A*S*H* lead Alan ___
32 * U.S. Navy's mascot

33 Raison d'___ (justification for existence)
34 Rent-___ (*hyphenated*)
35 Quaker's pronoun
36 Workshop grip
38 Crop-growing places
41 Without extras (*2 words*)
42 Olympic swords
43 Skinny
48 Film designation (especially for violence or language; *2 words*)
50 Actresses Hunt and Hayes
51 Brenda who sang "I'm Sorry"
53 Anglican bishop's headdress
55 Boxing ring boundaries
56 Herb of the carrot family
57 * Clemson's mascot
58 * Loser to the tortoise, in a fable
59 * Plowing team
60 Pencil carbon
61 Ending for "Dixie" or "auto"
65 Turkish title
66 * Pooch

HINT: The answer phrase at 33 Down comes from French, to be sure, but the dictionaries now consider it suitably assimilated into English. There's another hint accompanying puzzle 167.

182

At Arm's Length

by Diane C. Baldwin

Featuring one part of the body.

ACROSS

1 Cry loudly
5 Beast of a man
10 Lendl of tennis fame
14 The Buckeye State
15 Site for a boutonniere
16 Chess or checkers
17 Refuses to help (*4 words*)
20 Drain-cleaning substance
21 Bismarck or Preminger
22 Pitcher's place
23 Told-you-so exclamations
24 Sadden
26 Fourth of July event
29 Drive-in offering
30 Muslim leader
31 Carryalls
32 Caboodle's partner
35 Doesn't applaud (*4 words*)
39 Billboards
40 Propelled a boat with oars
41 Soda pop
42 Actor Glover
43 Hard to swallow
45 Disproves
48 Some raincoats, for short
49 Isolated
50 In the altogether
51 Diary of sorts
54 Signals rejection (*3 words*)
58 Threshold
59 Hair-raising
60 Geometry calculation
61 Something to sow
62 Goofed up
63 The tops

DOWN

1 ___ over (stun)
2 Crow's-nest shout
3 Dark red color
4 Land parcel
5 Cheerily carefree
6 Swim floats
7 As far as (*2 words*)
8 Kind of pot or bag
9 Santa's helper
10 Pay no attention to
11 Ambiguous
12 Affirmations in tent meetings
13 Geeky people
18 Burden
19 Pixie-like
23 Pork products
24 Lavished affection
25 Holiday precursors
26 Leaning Tower locale
27 In the thick of
28 "Gosh darn!"
29 Legal tender
31 Urban settings
32 Sheet bend or clove hitch
33 Put in neutral
34 Despot of the past
36 Mounts the soapbox
37 Zilch
38 Pretenses
42 Demanded payment
43 Like most fishhooks
44 Chills Champagne
45 Has status
46 Steer clear of
47 Write a fake signature on a document
48 Ike's first lady
50 Perry Mason portrayer Raymond ___
51 Folk wisdom
52 Has obligations
53 Tiny flier
55 Links starting place
56 That woman
57 Pat daintily

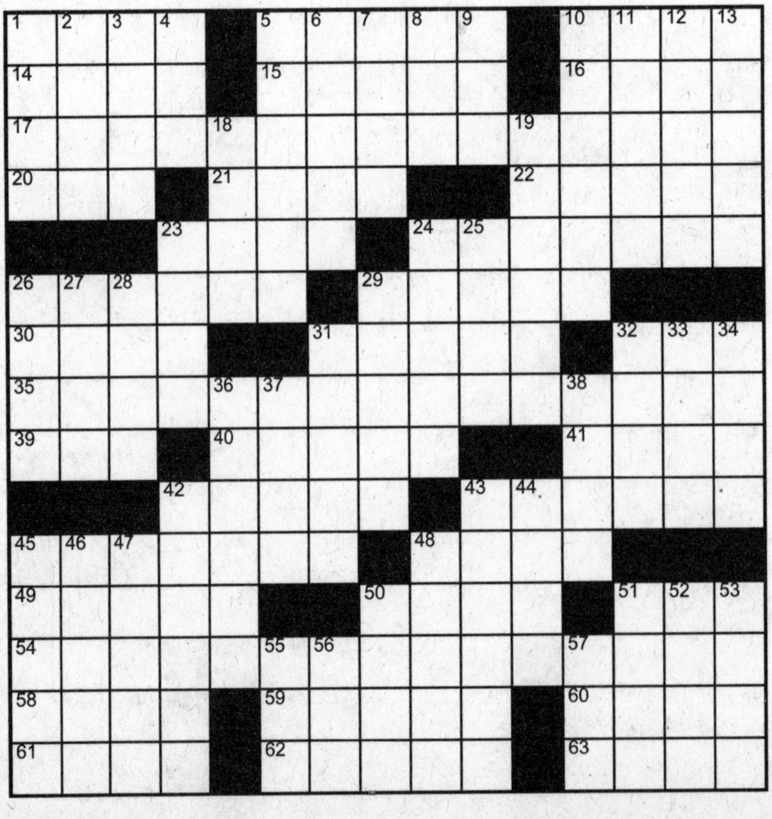

HINT: When you see "kind of" or "sort of" in a clue, treat it as a fill-in-the-blank. Look at 8 Down, for example. And take a look at puzzle 174's page for more help.

#176: 29A = BODDY

183

Unreal World — by Thomas W. Schier

The three long answers in this puzzle begin with appropriate adjectives.

ACROSS

1 21st U.S. president Chester ___ Arthur
5 Clobbered (*2 words*)
11 Mineral spring
14 Get up from bed
15 Western Texas city (*2 words*)
16 Ad ___ (improvise)
17 Send out
18 Soccer shot not taken with the feet
19 In the least
20 Unreal painters (*2 words*)
23 Alfred ___ (husband of Lynn Fontanne)
24 Community character
25 Computer-telephone link
28 Bones between the lumbar and tail vertebrae

31 ___ tree (cornered; *2 words*)
32 Small tavern
35 Superman's protection against kryptonite
39 Unreal trip (*2 words*)
42 Went up in the air
43 Perceived
44 Race in a marathon
45 In the midst of
47 ___ Glover of *Saw* and the *Lethal Weapon* films
49 Reddish orange hair coloring
52 Sorority gal
54 Unreal associate (*2 words*)
61 Director ___ Burton of *Corpse Bride*
62 Supervise

63 Sturdy wagon
64 Drink on draft
65 Maroon
66 Presidential assistant
67 Massachusetts Senator Kennedy
68 Spiff up
69 Watery expanses

DOWN

1 Length × width, for a rectangle
2 Tree branch
3 Condition of sale (*2 words*)
4 Annoy or provoke
5 Irish author Brendan ___
6 Vote into office
7 Give ___ on the back (*2 words*)
8 Vocal fanfare (*hyphenated*)
9 On-line patron
10 Baggage carrier

11 Lower, as prices
12 Kidney bean variety
13 Immeasurable space
21 Rhythmical Cuban dance
22 Milan's country
25 Drop the ball
26 Fiery gemstone
27 Resident of Copenhagen
28 Singer Gordon Sumner on stage
29 Circumference segments
30 Shoreline indentation
33 "That ___ unfair!" (*2 words*)
34 Light submachine gun
36 Bring in, as pay
37 "Son of ___!" (*2 words*)

38 Declare untrue
40 Nasal vocal quality
41 More peculiar
46 Young unmarried woman
48 Gymwear name
49 Strike out against (*2 words*)
50 *J'Accuse* author ___ Zola
51 Designated
52 Washing machine phase
53 Frequently
55 Number of Supreme Court justices
56 Diva's musical piece
57 Sit for a bit
58 One of the Great Lakes
59 Nothing, in Spanish
60 Prepares Easter eggs

HINT: The answer at 28 Across is plural but not a normal English plural structure. See puzzle 181's page for a giveaway answer.

184 An Average Puzzle — by Thomas W. Schier

The four long phrases in this puzzle are all clued the same way: AVERAGE.

ACROSS

1 "Oops!" (*hyphenated*)
5 Piano note that's the same as F sharp (*2 words*)
10 Dance music group
14 ___ Anderson of *WKRP in Cincinnati* fame
15 Singer ___ Lenya
16 Hawaiian feast
17 Put ___ in (make some real progress; *2 words*)
18 Swashbuckler ___ Flynn
19 Bone dry
20 AVERAGE (*2 words*)
23 Alphabetic sequence
24 Hoosegow
25 AVERAGE (*3 words*)
31 Boo-boo
32 Sit for a picture
33 Word before "You're it!"
36 Starting from the beginning
37 Illusion-producing paintings (*2 words*)
39 Serve, as tea
40 Fireplace fodder
41 Play, as a trumpet
42 Quiz answer
43 AVERAGE (*2 words*)
47 ___ *Miz*
48 Cheers for matadors
49 AVERAGE (*hyphenated*)
56 Perform in a choir
57 Wear away
58 Melodramatic outburst
59 Rural way
60 Pinker inside, like steak
61 Jedi master in *Star Wars*
62 Working hard (*2 words*)
63 Vehicles for snowy slopes
64 Remain

DOWN

1 ___ Bator, Mongolia
2 Freight train stowaway
3 "Put a lid ___!" (*2 words*)
4 Snooty type
5 1970 Oscar winner ___ Jackson (for *Women in Love*)
6 Lose track of
7 Personal correspondence (abbr.)
8 On the summit of
9 Show on TV
10 Magician David ___
11 Intangible atmosphere
12 Toe growth
13 Failure
21 Cake decorator
22 Bar of soap
25 Country singer ___ McCoy
26 "Are you coming, yes ___?" (*2 words*)
27 Shorthand inventor John ___
28 Give rise to
29 Opposite of vertical (abbr.)
30 Took without paying
34 Vienna's country (abbr.)
35 Jennlfer of *Dirty Dancing*
37 Elderly persons
38 Mystery-story pioneer Edgar Allan ___
39 Colorful patterns
41 ___ Rabbit
42 One of the Flintstones
44 Hit the runway
45 Invalidated
46 Birch-family trees
49 Royal decree
50 Opposed
51 Spoken
52 Additional amount
53 "___ Rhythm" (Gershwin tune; *2 words*)
54 Zippo
55 Aussie's "hello"
56 Health resort

HINT: The magician at 10 Down once spent 44 days in a clear box hanging above the Thames River in London. See puzzle 188 for more help.

#162: 29D = LEAH

185

What a Gem!   by Roy Leban

The top and bottom phrases feature words used to describe one of the words in the middle phrase.

ACROSS

1 "Cheerio!" (*hyphenated*)
5 Where high school graduates continue studies (abbr.)
9 Swedish singing group
13 Retired for the night
14 Of birds
16 "Phooey!"
17 Propellerhead
18 Blend with traffic
19 Lose control, in a way
20 Music genre exemplified by KISS, Alice Cooper, and David Bowie (*2 words*)
23 Words from an 11 Down
24 Portrait artist's medium
25 Behaviorist B.F. ___
27 Make a mistake
30 Said "Not guilty" in court, maybe
32 Glitch
33 Use a pager
35 ___-de-la-Cité (Notre Dame locale)
36 One pill and a teaspoon, for example
39 Sports field (*2 words*)
43 Salesman's delivery
44 Male cat
45 Concept
46 Ticket end
48 Second-year student, for short
50 Pose, as a question
51 Blondie Bumstead, for one
54 Lion's cry
56 Group that recommends sugarless gum (abbr.)
57 Get something going (*3 words*)
62 One hole on a course?
64 Strong string
65 Modem speed unit
66 Nutso
67 Wading bird
68 Matured, like cheese
69 Lost
70 It needs repaying
71 Optimistic

DOWN

1 Tart taste
2 Adam's second son
3 Actress ___ Garr of *Mr. Mom*
4 Enhance (*2 words*)
5 Showy roselike flower
6 Try too hard to market
7 Commuter line from NYC (abbr.)
8 Former capital of Nigeria
9 Commercial spots
10 Well-known neutralizer (*2 words*)
11 One with a veil
12 Words often separated by a slash
15 Giraffes' features
21 Waitperson's reward
22 In a way, slangily
26 Wynonna's mom
27 Recedes
28 Bring in
29 Freedom fighters (with "the")
31 Shoulder muscles, briefly
34 Pro golfer Calvin ___
37 Chemical endings
38 State north of Nebr. (abbr.)
40 Promo paragraph
41 Entryway handle
42 Helpless
47 Space for a ship at anchor
49 "Fat chance!"
51 Type of lily
52 "Goodbye," in Spain
53 Got married again
55 Concrete reinforcement rod
58 Suffix with "billion" or "concession"
59 Villain in the play *Othello*
60 Pool sticks
61 Swirling water
63 Big name in RV grounds

186

Seeing Double   by Alan Olschwang

Once you see how any one theme answer is constructed you'll solve this in a twice ... er, trice.

ACROSS

1 Wild guess
5 Dressed like a choral singer
10 Hard to come by
14 Holds title to
15 Say lines so the balcony can hear
16 Jet black, in poetry
17 Last exam before graduation? (*2 words*)
19 Sulk
20 "Four score and seven years ___ ..."
21 Parking lot sight
22 Drench in liquid
23 Like some apples
25 Roller ___

27 Get five nickels for a quarter? (*2 words*)
31 Actress Lenya
32 Shoe ties
33 "Mayday!" call
36 Pub drinks
37 Thin wood strips
38 Black fly
39 Get married
40 Fraction of a pound
41 Fry lightly
42 Rather restrained putdown? (*2 words*)
44 Party giver
47 Piquancy
48 Declares
49 Shakespeare's river
51 Joseph Smith followers (abbr.)

54 Actress Russo
55 The practice of law? (*2 words*)
58 Scottish Gaelic
59 Diameter halves
60 Queen ___ Boleyn
61 Perch on a front stoop
62 Change, as a law
63 Mild expletive

DOWN

1 Family room furniture
2 Small branch
3 Made some critical comments
4 "Be Prepared" group (abbr.)
5 Prove wrong by evidence

6 Exclude
7 U2 lead
8 Greek vowel
9 First state (abbr.)
10 Recline
11 Concerning
12 Awaken
13 Go in
18 Shirt size
22 Droops
24 Picnic problem
25 Seal on a letter
26 Billfold fillers
27 Eagle's weapon
28 Target on a golf course
29 Metallic sounds
30 Opening in a ship's deck
33 Cuddling
34 Inauguration highlight
35 Proofreader's "save"

37 Baseball Hall of Famer ___ Aparicio
38 Halfback's goal
40 Corrida shouts
41 Angle
42 Actress Meryl
43 Impassive
44 Jackrabbits, for example
45 Not concealed
46 Perceive
49 Senate page, for instance
50 Conceited
52 Actor ___ Andrews
53 Luge
55 La la forerunner
56 St. Louis pro footballer
57 *Norma* ___ (Sally Field film)

HINT: The answer at 16 Across may be more familiar to you with a letter "y" on the end. If you need another hint, see puzzle 152's page.

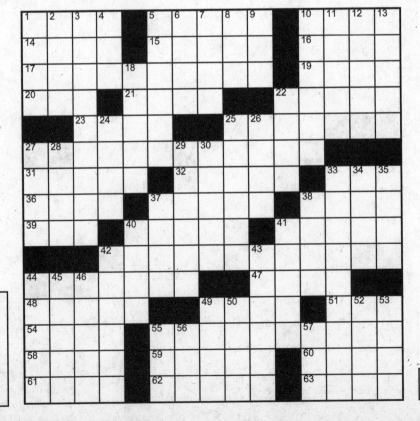

#198: 36A = WICCA

187

This Will Stop Traffic!   by Alan Olschwang

The thematic answers this time reflect something you see while driving.

ACROSS

1 Big, thick book
5 Circle over a saint's head, in old art
9 ___ fide
13 Sham
14 Falter
15 Turn over ___ leaf (*2 words*)
16 Controversial poet ___ Pound
17 Native of Muscat
18 Surgery reminder
19 International aid organization (*3 words*)
22 Polished up, as prose
23 Signals that astute poker players notice
24 Sister's sibling, slangily
26 Comprehend
27 Mel of baseball fame
30 Foot cover
34 Lode load
36 Religious leader
38 Oz thoroughfare (*3 words*)
42 Lowest point
43 Important time
44 Inconsequential
45 Begley and Begley Jr.
46 Give ___ try (*2 words*)
49 Retirees' provider (abbr.)
51 Tart candies
53 Originate
58 Wisconsin NFL team
62 Strauss who made denim clothing
63 Made a goof
64 Eye part
65 Barbara of *I Dream of Jeannie*
66 Good employee's reward
67 Egypt's river
68 Less than a few
69 "Immediately!" in medical dramas
70 Salon substances

DOWN

1 Not here
2 Seeped
3 ___ Gras
4 Precise
5 Easter entrées
6 Mariner's "Halt!"
7 Glasses parts
8 Bird associated with Baltimore
9 Foundation
10 First word in many fairy tales
11 Without ice, at a bar
12 Askew
14 President Wilson
20 One of Jeff Davis's soldiers
21 Office worker
25 Sovereignty symbol
27 Double reed instrument
28 Ski lift
29 Neap, for example
30 "Auld Lang ___"
31 Run
32 Auto pioneer
33 New Haven student
35 Before, in poetry
37 Provide weaponry
39 Hunter in the sky
40 Tax collector (abbr.)
41 Waterfall
47 Potatoes, for instance
48 Mountain where Noah's ark landed
50 Circle part
51 Fishing net
52 Home of the Golan Heights
54 Supplementing the hard way
55 High home
56 Warble
57 Highway curves
58 Campbell of "By the Time I Get to Phoenix" fame
59 Make over
60 Tied
61 Pain in the neck, so to speak

HINT: Just as a clue signals a foreign language with a foreign word, it may also signal that it is not to be taken literally. "So to speak" in 61 Down is one example of how that is done. See puzzle 159 for another hint.

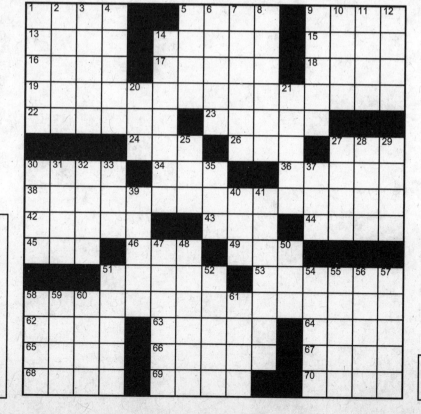

Take a Hike   by Ed Early

A common type of crossword theme involves incidentally spelling related words at the start of phrases. Here is an example.

ACROSS

1 Drive the getaway car for, perhaps
5 "What am ___?" (auction query; 2 words)
9 Fasteners
14 Spouse
15 Imogene ___ of Your Show of Shows
16 Swing Era bandleader ___ Shaw
17 Cardiac regulator
19 Feudal lord
20 NFL Hall of Famer ___ Marino
21 Planet of ___ (2 words)
23 The Wild Bunch director Peckinpah
26 "Hey, there!"
29 Popular place
30 Gymnast's gear
33 Brian ___ of rock-music promotion
34 ___ Grows in Brooklyn (classic Kazan film; 2 words)
35 Gold (Spanish)

36 Hiroshima, ___ Amour
38 Travel ___ (tour in an auto; 2 words)
39 "What ___ that?!"
40 Egyptian leader ___ el-Sadat
43 NFL intermissions (abbr.)
44 Former name of Tokyo
45 Pope between Clement VIII and Paul V
46 Yes, in Montreal
48 Some exercise equipment
50 Has on hand for sale
53 Fashionable resort hotels
54 Served a meal to
55 One of the Netherlands Antilles

57 Stephen ___ of The Crying Game
59 Newspaper pages devoted to commentaries (2 words)
60 Where King John signed the Magna Carta, many believe
66 Gets up
67 Author ___ Rice, who writes about vampires
68 Flintstone dad
69 Malicious
70 Acorn, for one
71 Repair

DOWN

1 Electric measure, commonly
2 Sound heard by Bo Peep
3 More of the same (abbr.)

4 Miffed, with "off"
5 Defiant schoolyard retort (3 words)
6 ___ choy
7 Hockey rink surface
8 Missile found in pubs
9 Guitarist Eddie Van ___
10 Operatic solos
11 Hesse novel (or, "Born to be Wild" rockers)
12 Urban bird
13 Takes care of (2 words)
18 Cartography experts
22 Go quickly
23 Run a blade through
24 With pretentious display
25 Certain nobleman's wife
27 Not as fast
28 Rantings

31 Vegan's no-no
32 "Forget about it!" (2 words)
36 Sweet wine now produced mainly in Madeira
37 "The ___ Love Belongs to Somebody Else" (2 words)
41 Wheel holder
42 Institute in Providence (abbr.)
46 The World of Suzie Wong playwright Paul ___
47 Heaven on earth
48 Company that developed Dungeons & Dragons (abbr.)
49 Mended argyles
51 West Pointer
52 Affectionate, in slang
56 Historic periods
58 Radio switch
61 Half of deux
62 SSW's opposite
63 Before, in verse
64 Cub Scout subgroup
65 Byrnes or Hall

HINT: 25 Down is a word you probably don't know, but it is related to the theme of the puzzle. If you keep plugging away, however, you can figure it out. Check out puzzle 166 for a free answer.

189

Out in Front   by Ed Early

The first and third long phrases start with the important words. The middle phrase ends with one.

ACROSS
1 Shakespearean king
5 Lined up
10 Rum cake
14 Compulsion
15 Cut in two
16 River to the Caspian
17 Italian coin replaced by the euro
18 Frequently
19 Hard or soft follower
20 Induce purposeless pursuit (4 words)
23 ___ Lee cakes
24 "Blowin' in the Wind" singer Bob ___
25 Boxing matches
29 Posed
31 Battling (2 words)
32 Author/adventurer ___ Heyerdahl
34 Play sections
38 1988 Oliver Reed horror film (4 words)

41 Upper house legislators (abbr.)
42 Chess piece that may become a queen
43 It's strengthened by aerobic exercise
44 The stuff we breathe
45 Singer ___ Twain
46 Plotting clique
50 Rights-advocacy organization (abbr.)
52 "Run!" (4 words)
59 Small land mass
60 Bridge player's decision, sometimes
61 Destroy
62 Playwright ___ Coward
63 Go out with ___ (2 words)
64 ___ mater

65 Place for an altar
66 Potato pancake
67 Bog

DOWN
1 Calm interval
2 Canal to the Hudson River
3 Taj Mahal locale
4 Interpret
5 Supreme Court justice Clarence ___
6 1960 Olympic decathlon winner Johnson
7 Extreme
8 "Thanks ___ so much"
9 Repudiate
10 Like a squirrel's tail
11 "It's been ___ pleasure!" (2 words)
12 Model airplane wood

13 Film maker Woody ___
21 Houston athlete
22 Summer clock setting in Chicago (abbr.)
25 "Blueberry Hill" singer ___ Domino
26 ___ Jury (Spillane classic; 2 words)
27 Pop singer ___ Stefani
28 Mocking laughs
29 Anon
30 Kennel sound
32 Pre-1917 Russian ruler
33 Fell with an axe
34 Taking a cruise, perhaps
35 Jackie ___ of action films
36 ___ Garr of Young Frankenstein

37 Miss, in Madrid (abbr.)
39 Wire service inits.
40 "I hear you!" (hyphenated)
44 Sitcom visitor from Melmac
45 Heavy hammer
46 Cups and saucers
47 Legendary Greek fable writer
48 Cotton units
49 Designer Simpson
50 Facing the pitcher (2 words)
51 Armor defect
53 Reverend ___ Roberts
54 "What If It's You" singer ___ McEntire
55 Baghdad's country
56 Remarkable person or idea
57 Largest city in Peru
58 Nylon woe

HINT: The answer to 57 Down is probably the only city most people know in Peru. There's another hint for you on the page with puzzle 173.

#177: 45D = WREAKS

Wall Street Words   by Gail Grabowski

190

Even if you pay little attention to the financial pages you should find the time here well-invested.

ACROSS
1 *Moby Dick* pursuer
5 Payment method
9 Lumps of dirt
14 Monopoly, for one
15 Choir voice
16 Citrus fruits
17 Very much (2 words)
18 Feeling sad
19 Happening
20 Money used for who-knows-what (2 words)
22 Air ducts
23 Annually (2 words)
24 Filmmaker Craven
25 "___ You Lonesome Tonight?"
26 Tavern totals (2 words)

30 Breakfast item
34 In favor of
35 Orchestra woodwind
36 Fictitious name
37 Sheep's call
38 Aroma
39 Actress ___ Anderson
40 Coupe or convertible
41 Foot joints
42 Eyes suggestively (2 words)
44 Aunt, in Acapulco
45 Tree liquid
46 Stalemate
51 Japanese fish dish
54 Agent 007 (2 words)
56 Court case
57 Angered

58 Busy as ___ (2 words)
59 Houston baseballer
60 Old Italian money
61 New driver, often
62 More despicable
63 At the end
64 Makes a mistake

DOWN
1 Shocked
2 Oscar winner ___ Berry
3 Love, to Pierre
4 Seamstress Ross
5 Money for a taxi (2 words)
6 Fascination
7 Astound
8 Weeded the garden

9 Keen-witted
10 Farm animals
11 Sign of the future
12 Fender-bender result
13 Retired airplanes (abbr.)
21 Gets better
24 Kid's card game
26 Feathery wrap
27 Brother of Cain
28 Skeleton segment
29 Broadway backgrounds
30 Place for a picture
31 Hand-cream ingredient
32 Speeder's penalty

33 Equally distributed amount (2 words)
34 Distant
37 Baseball club
38 Ginger cookies
40 Ballplayer's hat
41 Pointed, as a weapon (2 words)
43 Popeye, for example
44 Oven control devices
47 Lessen
48 Not tipsy
49 Scornful smile
50 Perfect places
51 Wild guess
52 Constellation bear
53 Uses a sofa
54 Nursery rhyme tumbler
55 Diva's solo

HINT: At 26 Across: If a clue carefully avoids using an obvious word, there is usually a good reason. See puzzle 180's page for a free answer.

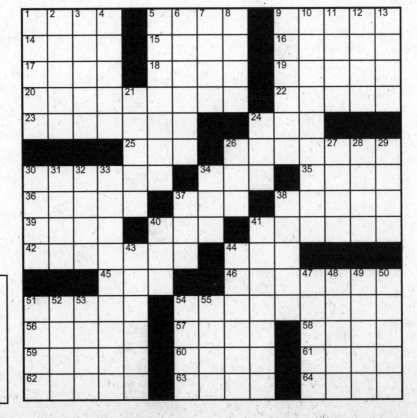

#170: 2D = OBIS

191 Headwear — by Thomas W. Schier

The long phrases all end with related words.

ACROSS

1 Observed
5 Family auto
10 Toothpaste holder
14 Sticky strip
15 *House of Frankenstein* actress Verdugo
16 Romantically linked duo
17 Guesstimate words
18 Capital of France
19 Landlocked African republic
20 "How was ___ know?" (*2 words*)
21 Dr. Seuss classic, with *The* (*4 words*)
23 Considered as similar
25 Actor ___ Brynner of *The King and I*
26 Reduces in value
28 Blot lightly (*2 words*)
32 Birthday party urging (*2 words*)
34 Water barrier
36 Binding substance
37 ___ favor ("please," to Pedro)
38 "___ blu, dipinto di blu" ("Volare" lyrics)
40 Golfing standard
42 Vase for flowers
43 "___ or not ..." (*Hamlet* soliloquy starter; *2 words*)
45 Movie set big shot (abbr.)
47 Peruse again
49 In a crafty way
51 Three-wheeled cousin of a rickshaw used in Southeast Asia
53 Poetic night
55 Some state or federal legislators
58 Sea mass in the Arctic Ocean (*3 words*)
62 Tennis court divider
63 Pakistan neighbor
64 Propelled a raft
65 Exclusively
66 *Finding ___* (animated blockbuster film)
67 *Kate & ___* (1980s sitcom)
68 Recover, medically speaking
69 Fly like an eagle
70 Examinations
71 Eyelid sore

DOWN

1 Expressionless
2 Keep an ___ the ground (*2 words*)
3 English horse race dating from 1779
4 Keanu Reeves in *The Matrix*
5 Kept apart
6 Makes very happy
7 Laughed at contemptuously
8 Has ___ with (possesses pull; *2 words*)
9 Beyond unkind
10 Interim period between stimulus and response
11 Bountiful's state
12 Dracula portrayer ___ Lugosi
13 Send out, as light rays
21 Cruise ship accommodation
22 1963 Paul Newman movie
24 Confident puzzle solver's tool
27 Extraction from a maple tree
29 State flower of Texas
30 Atmosphere
31 Watch, as the flock
32 Goes for
33 Fast Eddie's game
35 Liquid mixtures used in steeping foods
39 Mouth part
41 Newscast summary
44 Rigby of a Beatles song
46 Deals in used cars
48 Maze animal
50 "___ dern tootin'!"
52 Guile
54 Try to bite, like a puppy (*2 words*)
56 Team racing event
57 Prevailing fashion
58 Bowler's targets
59 Nabisco treat
60 Tibetan monk
61 Singer Nat "King" ___
65 Sounds of surprise

#163: 56D = FOP

192 Seasonality by Alan Olschwang

Noting quarterly changes.

ACROSS

1 Black card
6 Highly skilled
11 ___ de deux (ballet dance for two performers)
14 Home run king Hank ___
15 *West Side Story* heroine
16 Furrow
17 Certain theatrical production (*2 words*)
19 Historical period
20 ___ gin fizz
21 Greek vowels
22 Student writing assignment
24 Halfback's statistic
26 Canonized French women (abbr.)
27 Asters, for example (*2 words*)
32 Written to be sung by a group
36 Deposit, as an egg
37 Mount Rushmore's state (abbr.)
38 Stereotypical dog's name
39 Have a meal
40 Roger who played James Bond in seven films
41 Type of tennis or golf tournament
42 Shoulder-hand connector
43 Chased for payment
44 February crowd pleaser (*2 words*)
47 Nemesis
48 At the very back of the boat
53 Trade association
55 Cleveland's state
57 Woman's singing range
58 Busy month for the IRS (abbr.)
59 Party time for some (*2 words*)
62 Peas' place
63 Computer operators
64 Revere
65 Printer's measures
66 Debra of *The Ten Commandments*
67 Out of bed

DOWN

1 Pert
2 *American Idol* judge Abdul
3 Knight's mail
4 Like some stadiums
5 Compass heading (abbr.)
6 Lager-style beer from Holland
7 Computer input
8 Cupid, to Greeks
9 Movie, in *Variety* headlines
10 Like instinctively (*2 words*)
11 Pushed forward urgently (*2 words*)
12 Invisible emanation
13 Judge's order
18 Imperial
23 Applies, as patches (*2 words*)
25 At a great distance
26 Like a fox
28 Camel cousin in the Andes
29 Liposuction target
30 Seldom seen
31 Bus station handout, for short
32 Brag
33 Pueblo people
34 North American warblers
35 Hertz or Avis offering
39 Unit of work
40 Essential
42 Exist
43 Clear, as a car window
45 Comes to rest (*2 words*)
46 Name of a common principal thoroughfare, for short (*2 words*)
49 ___ Gras
50 Bread spreads
51 Prolonged gaze
52 It lets you through a turnstile
53 Yawn
54 Second word in many fairy tales
55 Neighbor of Calif.
56 Add to the payroll
60 Message from MADD, for example (abbr.)
61 Prohibit

HINT: The clue at 60 Down refers to a type of advertising on behalf of a non-profit or charitable organization. The box next to puzzle 194 has another hint.

#156: 49A = PHISH

Body Language   by Victor Fleming

In which the long phrases end with related words.

ACROSS

1 Captain's superior officer (abbr.)
4 "My stars!"
9 Traditional truism
14 Prefix with dermis
15 "You think you're so ___!"
16 Reef component
17 Mineo of film
18 Ward off, as a tackler (hyphenated)
20 "We can't ___ heroes, because somebody has to sit on the curb and clap ..." (Will Rogers; 2 words)
22 Sporty VW model
23 Peters out, as the tide
24 Tommy ___ (1960s teen idol who married Nancy Sinatra)
27 Corporation money managers (abbr.)
29 Good way to start off (4 words)
34 Indian royal
35 Former SSR (abbr.)
36 City or child preceder
38 ___-Magnon
39 New England college
42 Summer, in France
43 Type of committee (2 words)
45 Razor-billed ___
46 Relative of an English horn
47 "As for counter-arguments ..." (4 words)
51 "Now ___ this!"
52 Bridle controls
53 Singer ___ Lane
56 Nutritional abbr.
58 ___ 180 (reverses; 2 words)
61 Deceive playfully (3 words)
65 Spicy
66 Follow stealthily
67 Do right by, with "for"
68 Courtroom affirmation (2 words)
69 Group's character
70 Acclaims
71 This Is Spinal ___ (mockumentary)

DOWN

1 Flat-topped hill
2 "Be ___!" ("Help me out!"; 2 words)
3 Sean Connery costar in Diamonds Are Forever (3 words)
4 Dead Sea Scrolls writer
5 Clock setting in London (abbr.)
6 River flowing into the Rhine
7 Pull laboriously
8 Hilarious person
9 "___ du lieber!"
10 Pampers, as a grandchild (2 words)
11 Native of Oman or Egypt
12 Style of dress
13 Shade trees
19 Endowment
21 "Who Let the Dogs Out" group, the ___ Men
25 Bongo or conga
26 Punjabi believer
28 "Think nothing ___" (2 words)
29 Quint's boat in Jaws
30 Elaine ___ (Taxi role)
31 "Super!"
32 Single, at Yankee Stadium (hyphenated phrase)
33 Grand ___ (Wyoming peak)
37 Clarinet mouthpiece insert
39 Feel sympathy (for)
40 German industrial area
41 ___-Ball (arcade game)
44 Desdemona's husband
46 Cry made with a head-slap (2 words)
48 Rake in
49 Trial by fire
50 Some chip features
53 Recessed area of a church
54 Ram (into)
55 Totally unexciting
57 The Thin Man dog
59 Schweppes product
60 Capping
62 Gives the go-ahead
63 Gehrig of baseball
64 "Bitter" part

HINT: 4 Down does not refer to any one specific person, but generically to one of the monastic people of Palestine from the 2nd century B.C. to the 2nd century A.D. who, it is believed, wrote the Dead Sea Scrolls. Puzzle 151's page has another hint, even if you don't need it.

194

Saluting 57 Across   by Ed Early

The puzzle pays homage to a movie star of the 1920s–'60's (and the star of the TV series *The Big Valley*).

ACROSS
1 Collapses
5 Bother persistently (*2 words*)
10 Gratuities
14 Cover girl Macpherson
15 Piano piece
16 Square yardage
17 "I cannot tell ___" (*2 words*)
18 In the boonies
19 Canine sound
20 1943 movie starring 57 Across (*3 words*)
23 Move stealthily
24 Napoleon, for one (abbr.)
25 Ambassadorial fashion accessory
29 Break out, as from prison
34 Company whose slogan was "His Master's Voice"
37 Milne bear
39 Lubricated
40 1944 movie starring 57 Across (*2 words*)
43 Totally confused (*2 words*)
44 Nullified tennis serves
45 Boom box buys (abbr.)
46 Reply to a drill instructor, perhaps (*2 words*)
48 Designer ___ St. Laurent
50 Back muscle, briefly
52 Book of maps
57 Star honored by this puzzle (*2 words*)
64 Half a Jim Carrey film title
65 Cyberspace message (*hyphenated*)
66 "Dedicated to the ___ Love" (*2 words*)
67 Rim
68 Backbone
69 Tennis score called after deuce, often (*2 words*)
70 Gardener's bane
71 Stories
72 No-___-land

DOWN
1 They're sold at Christmas
2 Detective ___ Pinkerton
3 Fly like a parasailer
4 "Ta-ta!" (*2 words*)
5 Toy ball brand
6 "... three men in ___" (*2 words*)
7 Expert
8 On ___ (for the thrill; *2 words*)
9 "___ Why" (1966 Elvis Presley song; *2 words*)
10 Manila folder extensions
11 Baghdad locale
12 Andes nation
13 Rice wine
21 Gives the nod
22 Kind of bath salts
26 Mimic
27 Erosion loss
28 Baklava ingredient
30 President's title, re the armed forces (abbr.)
31 "Put ___ on it!" (*2 words*)
32 Vet's visitors
33 Big name in ice cream
34 Mechanical learning procedure
35 Use a four-letter word
36 Lincoln and Fortas
38 60" plasma set, e.g. (abbr.)
40 Dawn to dusk
41 Muhammad Ali's boxing daughter
42 Wind direction (abbr.)
47 Most extraordinary
49 ___ Andreas Fault
51 Home of the NFL's Buccaneers
53 Wee hour (*2 words*)
54 ___ Carter (Wonder Woman portrayer)
55 ___ the hole (*2 words*)
56 Shirts' foes, in pickup games
57 Played, as a bugle
58 Assistant
59 Fit of anger
60 Raised, as racehorses
61 Spinnaker or jib
62 Pitchfork prong
63 Pub orders

HINT: If a clue uses the adverb "most," as 47 Down does in this puzzle, it's a good bet the answer ends in EST. See puzzle 158 for more.

#192: 34D = OVENBIRDS

195 Linen Store   by Mel Rosen

Offering some specific items you might find around the house.

ACROSS

1 Financial transaction
5 Chats
10 After-bath soother
14 *Born Free* lioness
15 Sheep's call
16 Beekeeper played by Peter Fonda
17 Kitchen cleanup linens
19 International treaty
20 Prefix meaning "egg"
21 Garden of Eden reptile
22 Use inefficiently, as time
23 ___ leaf (statue adornment)
24 "The Star-Spangled Banner" lyricist
25 One who provides venture capital
26 It's sometimes full of venom
28 More foxy
31 Former Notre Dame coach Parseghian
32 ___ West (W.C. Fields costar)
35 Liv ___ (frequent star in Ingmar Bergman films)
37 Dining room linens
39 Singer nicknamed "Old Blue Eyes"
40 *Horton Hears a ___* (Dr. Seuss story)
41 Wind direction (abbr.)
42 Lift a glass to
44 Two-master
48 Wretchedly bad
50 FedEx alternative
53 Halloween shout
54 Trophy or medal
55 Jazz pianist Count ___
57 Surgery sites, briefly
58 Humane organization (abbr.)
59 Boudoir linens
61 Mouse-spotters' shrieks
62 ___ *of Two Cities* (2 words)
63 It's decorated at Christmastime
64 Sprinted race
65 Domesticates
66 Computes a total

DOWN

1 Started (2 words)
2 Singer ___ Newton-John
3 Give, as homework
4 Slangy turndown
5 Steakhouse offering (hyphenated)
6 Without exception
7 Onion's kin
8 Cauliflower's cousin
9 Avenue crossers (abbr.)
10 Rapper Shakur
11 Anchorage citizens
12 Speaker's stand
13 Et ___
18 "For shame!" sound
22 Creature comfort
25 Underneath
27 FBI employee
29 *Star Wars* director George
30 Feeling under the weather
33 Let up
34 Rocker ___ John
36 "Hi!" on the high seas
37 Some ornamental pins
38 Age of Aquarius, for one
39 Veggie with an edible pod
41 Took out
43 Scuffle
45 On ship
46 Phrased
47 Red ink figures
49 Garbage
51 Plumber's concerns
52 Reverend's remarks (abbr.)
55 Type of blocker
56 Sandler of *Little Nicky*
59 Flying mammal
60 Airport schedule information (abbr.)

HINT: The answer at 47 Down is not DEBITS, but it's a word that implies the same thing. Also, see puzzle 165's page.

#185: 51D = CALLA

196

Not Against   by Victor Fleming

In this one, the theme clues provide one word (the same word each time) and you must complete the phrases. Expect more demanding clues hereafter.

ACROSS
1 Victor, as of a tourney
6 "Ten ___ a-leaping"
11 Used to own
14 Boring tool
15 Letter-shaped girder
16 Suffix with Siam or Japan
17 "For ___!" ("If my existence depended on it!"; 4 words)
19 "Eureka!"
20 Govt. securities
21 Make merry
23 Holler
26 ___-Magnon man
27 Agree
28 Set free
30 Not outside
32 Borders on
33 Apple seeds' site
34 ___ Minor
37 Social customs
38 GP's org.

39 Orgs.
40 "Say no more!"
41 Stretch over
42 Ride without pedaling
43 Deteriorate
45 Monopoly designee
46 Gun on a Civil War battlefield
48 Voluminous info source (abbr.)
49 DDE's WWII command
50 ___ food cake
51 Self-___ (pride)
54 Express disapproval
55 "For ___!" ("under any circumstances!"; 3 words)
60 Wedding ceremony reply

61 "Goodnight ___" (1950 hit)
62 Having no point
63 Actor Beatty or composer Rorem
64 "Nonsense!"
65 Explorer Sebastian

DOWN
1 Garfield or Sylvester
2 "Say what?"
3 "Act your ___!"
4 Defrost
5 Daughter of royalty
6 Purposely misinform
7 Clarinet's kin
8 Foul-callers
9 Beavers' construction
10 Soviet anti-spy org. in James Bond stories

11 "For ___!" ("That's a big surprise!"; 2 words)
12 Colorless
13 Handed out the cards
18 Carter's predecessor
22 Retired quarterback "Boomer" ___
23 Money, slangily
24 Futuristic slave
25 "For ___!" (for personal safety; 3 words)
27 Consumed completely, with "up"
29 First instruction of a procedure
30 Helen Reddy, tunefully
31 Turkmenistan neighbor
33 Part of Batman's garb

35 Hawaii's spot in an atlas, often
36 The Jetsons' dog
39 Learned individual
41 Taxpayer's ID (abbr.)
44 What the tide will do
45 Brewski
46 Log home
47 Cell terminal
48 Siouan people from Nebraska
51 "Have You ___ Seen a Dream Walking?"
52 FedExed or faxed
53 First name in the Louvre
56 Prospector's prize
57 Slap the cuffs on
58 Rock musician Brian
59 As of now

HINT: Several of these clues employ abbreviations to show you that their answers are also abbreviations. Also, see puzzle 172.

197

ASAP! Please?   by Mel Kenworthy

Presenting a clever contradiction in terms.

ACROSS

1 St. Louis landmark
5 Internal combustion engine
10 Monogram letter, in brief
14 Bridges of Hollywood
15 Clear sky color
16 Close
17 Actress Blanchett
18 Start of a prayer (*3 words*)
20 Therapeutic spot
21 Neighbor of Wisc.
22 "Rome wasn't built ___"
23 Cost
25 Melancholy
26 Black-and-blue spot
28 Prayer, part 2

33 Fuses metal
34 More conniving
35 ___ Parseghian of football coaching fame
36 ___ and crafts
37 Football Hall of Famer Bart ___
38 For men only
39 Scottish dissent
40 Big, usually white, birds
41 Title for Macbeth
42 Prayer, part 3 (*3 words*)
44 Electric mixer attachment
45 Quick swim
46 Guiding principle
47 They're twirled in parades
50 Algerian seaport
51 Eminem's genre
54 End of prayer (*3 words*)
56 ___ monster

57 Class reunion attendee, briefly
58 "The Hunter" constellation
59 Auto import
60 Start of a Belafonte lyric
61 Hanky-___
62 FBI agent

DOWN

1 *Sesame Street* skills
2 Gather from the fields
3 Launched from a medieval contraption
4 Tint
5 Animosity
6 Layer about 20 miles above the Earth
7 Execute an about-face
8 Fort ___ (old California military base)

9 Sign up, as for a class
10 Enter forcefully
11 "___ I say more?"
12 ___ *Fugitive from a Chain Gang* (1932 Paul Muni film)
13 Card that beats a deuce
19 "... the bombs bursting ___ ..."
21 Overlook
24 Disencumbers
26 ___ *Devil* (first color 3-D feature film)
27 Encored on TV
28 Any tree, shrub, or vine
29 Ventilates
30 Indoor swimming pool
31 Whooping bird
32 Raring to go

34 Oliver's partner in slapstick films
37 Relative of a consignment store
38 Herring's cousin
40 Playground item
41 Adolescent
43 1966 Mary Martin and Robert Preston musical
44 Muscular
46 Criminal
47 Nickname for Dallas
48 Gillette razor brand
49 Busboy's load
50 Getting ___ years (aging)
52 *M*A*S*H* star Alan
53 Twinge
55 Chorus syllable
56 Prankster's plan

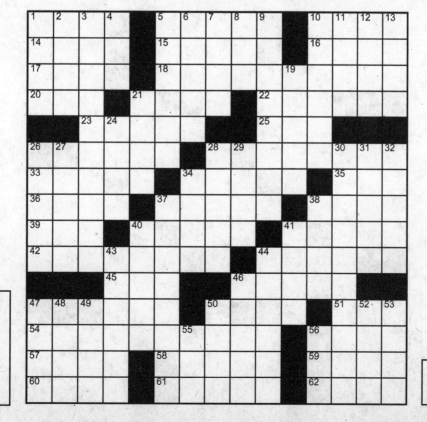

HINT: An alternative clue for 8 Down involves luggage bound for Chicago's O'Hare Airport. See puzzle 179's page for more help.

198

Zero-G   by Levi Denham

There's not a single G in this grid, including where you might expect to see them in the long answers!

ACROSS

1 Sultan's palace area
6 Follow a scent
11 CIA forerunner
14 "Be careful what you ___ me"
15 Artist Matisse
16 F. Lee Bailey's field
17 Stairway to heaven?
19 Color
20 "That's all ___!"
21 Tricky billiard shot
23 Brainy one
26 Commuter's pickup point
28 "Minute Waltz" composer
29 California's state motto
30 "___ ever occurred to you ..."
31 Have a life
32 Fed. eavesdropping org.
35 Big name in copiers
36 Neopagan religious movement
37 Air freshener target
38 Sphere
39 Performed in a satisfactory way
40 Noise at a street protest
41 Annual PGA event
43 Striped equines
44 *Dances with Wolves* star
46 Free of all moisture
47 "Maids a-milking" group
48 First extra inning
49 That woman
50 Mouse with a discerning palate?
56 "It's freezing!"
57 Metal fastener
58 Turn aside
59 Ouija board answer
60 Many months
61 Car contract

DOWN

1 President between FDR and DDE
2 Satisfied sigh
3 Deli bread choice
4 Country situated in the Horn of Africa
5 Like romantic evenings
6 Less outgoing
7 Straight A student, maybe
8 One ___ million
9 End of the work week, for short
10 Director's milieu
11 Any still-popular song of the 1940s?
12 Last word
13 Use a broom
18 Skinny
22 Pop a question
23 Doofus
24 Place to sit
25 Police who crash parties?
26 Century or Skylark
27 ___ Minor (constellation with the North Star)
29 Parolee, maybe
31 Duck valued for its down
33 Sub detector
34 Bohemian
36 Rub clean
37 Austin Powers catchphrase
39 Consoling words to a weeping tot
40 Smack dab in the middle
42 Fr. holy woman
43 *The Twilight ___*
44 Comic Bill who created Fat Albert
45 Earthy hue
46 Outperforms
48 One who's preparing to drive a golf ball
51 Hasten
52 *Green Acres* star Gabor
53 Lipton beverage
54 Hosp. trauma centers
55 AAA suggestion

HINT: Regarding 48 Down: The answer to a clue that starts with "one who" probably ends in R or ER. See puzzle 186 for an outright giveaway.

199

Political Definition   by Ed Early

This puzzle features an excerpt from *Bonfire of the Vanities*. Quotation puzzles are harder to solve, but this should be okay.

ACROSS
1 Dallas inst.
4 Sound reflection
8 They're doing their best
14 Moisten
15 Coward of the theater
16 Citizen Kane portrayer
17 With 23-, 38-, and 46 Across, quote by 58 Across
19 Come about
20 1601, classically
21 Cal Ripken, Jr., for his whole career
23 See 17 Across
29 Trapeze artist's "insurance"
30 City that now includes Jaffa
31 Cowboy, often
35 Expressions of understanding
36 Amusement park attraction
37 Admits the truth
38 See 17 Across
39 Take the tiller
40 Ready to eat
41 It's used for battering
42 Rodeo accessories
43 Make more exorbitant
45 Smallish batteries
46 See 17 Across
52 It may be stored in a blood bank
53 Opera setting for *Aida*
54 Sagacious
58 See 17 Across
60 Noise
61 Solo from *Aida*
62 Brought about
63 Verb on a jukebox
64 Some bakery loaves
65 Junior nav. officer

DOWN
1 Mystic
2 Pinochle declarations
3 New York city
4 Suffix with ethyl or methyl
5 *CSI* officer
6 Real-life model for Citizen Kane
7 Colonel North, to friends
8 Casino "boxcars"
9 Expose
10 Workers' gp. that received the 1969 Nobel Peace Prize
11 Bent pipe
12 Gun the engine
13 Harrisburg-Baltimore dir.
18 Big name in ballpoints
22 Big name in lawn care producto
24 Binary digits
25 Bakery offering
26 Climbing vines
27 Word with terminal or jockey
28 Civil rights figure Medgar
31 Like winters in Buffalo
32 Madonna role
33 See 42 Across
34 Nerd
35 Unit of resistance
38 "___ bet?"
39 Enclosure with a ms.
41 Send back to office
42 *The Man from ___* (1955 Jimmy Stewart film)
44 Related to digestion
45 Storage site for weapons
47 "When You Wish Upon ___"
48 ___-Cone (cold treat)
49 Squiggle over "n" in some Spanish words
50 Mischievous
51 Monopoly player's papers
54 Pack animal
55 Sault ___ Marie
56 He beat Botvinnik for the chess title in 1960
57 Multipurpose truck, commonly
59 "Fuzzy Wuzzy ___ a bear ..."

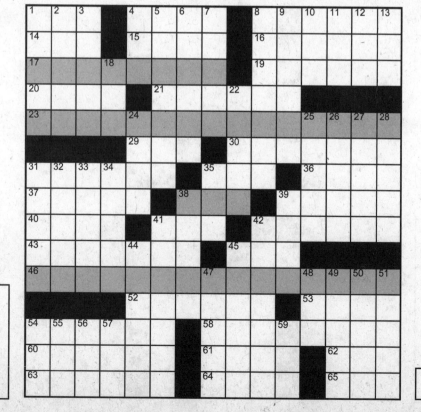

#157: 1A = COTE

200

Texas Transplants · by Monica Brenner

How to refer to famous people if they moved to the Lone Star State. We hope you enjoyed this collection of *Casual Crosswords*.

ACROSS

1 Hired fill-in
5 Ritchie Valens hit "La ___"
10 .45 maker
14 *The African Queen* screenwriter
15 German autos imported by GM
16 CB sign-off
17 Gun sound
18 Extraordinarily smart people
19 Bowling area
20 If Eisenhower's Secretary of State moved to Texas, you could describe him as ... (*3 words*)
23 Television Tarzan Ron ___
24 My daughter, to my brother
25 Professional basketball activity
29 Stink
33 Behave humanly?
34 "Drat!"
37 Rich dessert, to a dieter
38 If actress Anjelica moved to Texas, you could describe her as ... (*3 words*)
42 *Ripley's Believe ___ Not*
43 Commerce on the Internet
44 Suffix with Jacob or meteor
45 Lady of Spain
48 Gathered, as grain
50 Albacore and bluefin
53 Enclosure
54 If author Jane moved to Texas you could describe her as ... (*3 words*)
60 E-J fillers
61 Firebox transmittal
62 Grandson of Adam and Eve
64 See 12 Down
65 Advantage
66 Home of the NCAA Bruins
67 PED ___ (traffic warning sign)
68 Methods (abbr.)
69 Tropical tree

DOWN

1 Place for a file folder label
2 "Good gravy!"
3 Hash house handout
4 Long John Silver's prosthesis
5 Hobgoblins
6 King Kong and Mighty Joe Young
7 ___ *Black* (1997 sci-fi flick)
8 Russian pancakes
9 Stage whispers
10 Limerick lasses
11 440-yard path
12 With 64 Across, actress in *Havana* and *Chocolat*
13 Three, in Mexico
21 South American plain
22 Step into character
25 Radar O'Reilly's sodas on *M*A*S*H*
26 Savage
27 Firebug's crime
28 Pennsylvania port city
30 Out
31 Bill worth 10 sawbucks
32 Gave an edge to
35 It's dynamite!
36 Deep pile rug
39 Running easily
40 Lubrication devices under auto hoods
41 ___ *Gold* (Peter Fonda flick)
46 Regard with regret
47 Archives
49 Join the pot
51 Choreographer Alvin
52 Latches onto
54 Crazy like ___
55 Type of tangelo
56 Front of the lower leg
57 In ___ (bored)
58 Peruvian of yore
59 Four-time Super Bowl coach Chuck
63 Waterston of *Law & Order*

HINT: Clues such as 33 Across, that end in a question mark, often signal a mild pun or other misleading idea. If you think about the clue long enough, the intention should become clear. See puzzle 175's page for another hint.

#175: 38D = JAMAL

Answers

1   Starting Off

2 $4.00

3   Starting Positions

4   Come By Any Time!

5 Some of the Hard Stuff

```
CUFFS  CHUG  LAMP
AGLET  AONE  EDIE
PLANE  MOONSTONE
 IGNITED  REARER
 SEGAL  JET  ERS
OUTLET  LASTS
RHO  REGIS  OOHED
GONE  REMOW  BALI
SHELL  SONAR  ISA
 FORTS  SABLES
REA  DUE  ANDES
AGREES  ARTISTS
BRIMSTONE  ATOLL
BEAM  LANA  NONOS
ITSY  EKES  TWEET
```

6 A Tense Situation

```
BUSES  AWED  TORN
EPOXY  LIMO  OHIO
ATHINGOFTHEPAST
ROOT  ONE  AIRER
  VINE  EGGCASE
PAVING  URALS
EXIST  INURE  WAS
CLEARANDPRESENT
KEW  ALEUT  YALTA
 SNORE  FELLER
HIFISET  SIDE
OMANI  STE  SATS
BACKTOTHEFUTURE
ODIE  POOR  SARAN
SEER  TOWN  EXACT
```

7 Bleached!

```
NUMBS  PIKER  WON
AGREE  OLIVE  HUE
WHITECOLLAR  ITS
 TSAR  ONO  TET
ISWEAR  SUPERS
NTH  WATTS  TEK
TAI  FERN  ERNST
ETTA  EMAIL  MILE
LEEZA  PIPE  GIT
 PUN  ELENA  HMO
SPORTY  GLUTEN
PAT  IAM  ATTN
ATA  WHITEHAIRED
SIT  AOLER  ROUES
MOO  RODEO  SNERT
```

8 In Living Color

```
SLABS  ACTI  MELT
TANYA  NARC  ODOR
ARIEL  GREENMILE
RAT  MOLE  CASTLE
IMAGINE  TRY
 UNO  RESERVE
ELSIE  ASIA  REEK
YELLOWSUBMARINE
EGAD  EIRE  LANDS
DOGSLED  OPT
 IKE  ENHANCE
UNREAD  BREA  IRA
REDDRAGON  BOXES
IRAN  YURI  ELOPE
SOSA  SYNE  TENTS
```

9 Somewhat Racy

```
CALF  VIAL  WHO
OBOE  INLET  BOOP
BLUECOLLAR  LOWE
BED  ALAS  ABUSED
 BREW  CLUE
WALLET  GRANDEUR
ABOUT  COOL  ALTO
VICE  SOUSA  NOTA
EDAM  TAGS  DUPED
RELOCATE  SABERS
 NUNS  MANE
TRADED  JEST  ELK
HULA  BLUEHEAVEN
EMMY  YENTA  BITE
EPA  NOSY  ELSE
```

10 In the Dairy Section

```
STAT  LING  GARTH
ARIA  OBOE  IDAHO
MILKTEETH  REPOS
EPEEIST  RILESUP
 EDITS  DINS
 THEBIGCHEESE
HUR  ERRS  HYBRID
AHEM  ASH  BOLD
GOBACK  EELS  SKY
SHAVINGCREAM
 NEAT  TROTS
BADNEWS  SIGNALS
AXIOM  BUTTERNUT
JETTA  ARAB  OKRA
ADZES  GIBE  ESPY
```

11 The Secret's Out

```
B E A M   A T L A S   S P R Y
A X L E   G E E S E   T R U E
S P I L L E D T H E B E A N S
H O T   E N D S     R E T I E
    L A C Y   M A I D E N S
S N O O P Y   B A L D S
L O O N   L O Y A L   S P A
U N Z I P P E D O N E S L I P
G E E   E L D E R   H A T E
    S N U G S   C L I M A X
E C L I P S E   C L A P
A R E N A   B R I M   F I T
S A N G L I K E A C A N A R Y
E V I L   D I T C H   A M O K
D E N Y   S T A K E   G E N E
```

12 Shawls and Such

```
F L A K E   A C T   R A V E L
R A V E N   P R O   O L I V E
O V E R T   T A G   S L A I N
G A S C A P   M A N T I L L A
    H I R E S   O R E
M A R I L Y N   S M U D G E D
A L O E S   S T E A M   R A E
R O O F   L U N A R   B A T E
E N S   B E E T S   R A T E D
S E T T E E S   O P E N E R S
    A R C   K N E A D
B A B U S H K A   P L A C I D
E L A T E   E Y E   I N O N E
S O B E R   G A L   S N O R E
S T A R K   S K I   M A K E R
```

13 Quite "Suit"-able

```
P E N N   P A P A   S W E A R
A S E A   A D E S   K I D D O
S P A D E W O R K   I N T E L
S Y R I A N   T O P L E V E L
    A C E S   U R L
S A M   H E A R T O F G O L D
A L A R   S U E   T U R N E R
L I M O S   L A P   L A I N E
A B B O T S   C O P   D O T S
D I A M O N D H E A D   N O S
    L I E   T R I G
E M E R I T U S   A S H C A N
M O P E D   C L U B H O U S E
I D E A L   E A R L   S K I T
L E E R Y   S Y N E   T E A S
```

14 Just Say the Word

```
C L U B   B A S I S   E B B S
L A T E   E R A S E   F L I P
A N T E   S E L M A   F E T A
I K E   S T A T E F L O W E R
M A R R I E S   A I R
    C O L D   S T R E T C H Y
A C H O O   C A R E D   H U E
B O A T   T R U E R   H A L L
E L O   K E A T S   T O T A L
L A S T N A M E   M I N T
    H E M   W O R K E R S
E X P R E S S L I N E   R E P
P E R U   T A U N T   O L E O
E N O S   E R I C H   L E S T
E A S T   R I S E S   D Y E S
```

15 High and Low

```
B L O N D   P I N T   C A P S
R E V U E   A S E A   O P E N
O N E N D   N E A T   V E R A
W A R   U N D E R T H E R U G
    A L C O A   E A R
D E N I E D   B U R N T U P
A D D E D   R A K E D   P R O
B I O S   E A S E D   S T O W
S T U   H Y P E S   P H O N E
    S T R E E T S   L E A N E D
    O F T   F O R G O
D O W N T O E A R T H   G U M
I D E A   O R N O   A M O C O
S I L L   T I N S   P O O L S
H E L D   H E A T   S O D A S
```

16 Scary Stuff

```
W I S P   M A M I E   F L E D
E D N A   A L O N E   R E L Y
A L A R M C L O C K   I V A N
K E G   A R E N A   A G I L E
    P L O Y   S C H
    S C A T S   S T A R T L E R
S C A N S   S T A G E N A M E
H A R I   F L U B S   I R A N
E L E C T I O N S   A G G I E
S A W B O N E S   E T H E L
    U R N   T R O T
C R A T E   D R O O L   A A A
L A S T   D R E A D L O C K S
O R E O   A N I S E   W H I P
D E A N   D O N T S   L E N S
```

17 On Hand

```
JABS . BARD . SWELL
ELEE . ABEE . EERIE
FLEA . DEBS . NERVE
FINGERLAKES . OER
. . OVAL . QUARRY
STREEP . USUAL .
THORNS . NAILGUNS
EEL . AFT . NIL
PALMTREE . GEMINI
. BOARD . RRATED
SOMALI . SINS .
ERA . KNUCKLEHEAD
ENNUI . HAIL . ISLE
MOIRE . OGLE . NAVE
STAIN . HELD . GUAM
```

18 Fundamental Elements

```
SWARM . TARA . WEST
OHBOY . RTES . AMMO
ROBOT . OLES . TIED
EARTHQUAKE . ELLA
. . SUNS . SPRYLY
LEAF . ICE . SIC .
ALLI . TESS . TORSO
SMARTER . PAYLOAD
HOSEA . SCOT . OVID
. ELS . HOP . REDS
CHANCE . ANAT .
RANG . AIRFREIGHT
ANTI . LOGE . ADIEU
MOON . ATEE . CELEB
PINE . BARD . HALLS
```

19 Another Tense Situation

```
SCAR . IMOFF . WRAP
URGE . MOVES . HULL
TEED . ADULT . ONLY
RANSOMELIOLDS .
AMTOO . EXPO . CBS
. XMAN . STALE
ASH . PLASMA . IRON
THESHIPPINGNEWS
BAMA . TAYLOR . DYE
AMANA . KNEE .
YEN . APSO . EXTRA
. DEALINFUTURES
HAHA . ALIAS . LENS
OMAR . ZOOMS . TATA
PAWS . ASNER . STAY
```

20 On Two Wheels

```
BTU . FOAM . SCARAB
URN . EASE . LATINO
RICKSHAW . INTONE
SPLITUP . SCOOTER
TEEN . BAKER .
. KAPLAN . NIGH
AGO . MEIN . WEENIE
TENSPEEDBICYCLE
UNMASK . BATH . HAD
BEET . MORTON .
. INDEX . ARAB
CHARIOT . PAPRIKA
RESIGN . PUSHCART
ARISEN . BRIE . TOT
MOSTLY . SLAW . ANY
```

21 It's a Guy Thing

```
BEGAN . SHAD . SELA
ELOPE . HERO . CLOP
SMITS . ARID . AURA
SON . TAKEAGANDER
. GOLLY . EXTENT
GOSPEL . CARLY .
ANTE . SPOUSE . TDS
SCANS . OAT . SHOOT
PEG . CARLOS . EMMA
. PANES . HARBOR
ESCORT . TORSO .
BULLSESSION . SHE
SEAL . NEED . ELLIS
EDIE . NAME . SEEPS
NERD . AMIS . SAYSO
```

22 Ways To Go

```
DEMO . SWAMI . BAGS
OVAL . CABIN . ALIT
FILE . ARENT . SIZE
FLIGHTPATH . SEMI
. ITEM . IRONON
CLERKED . DNA .
HOLIER . HIGHROAD
ELMO . EON . ONCE
FASTLANE . INSURE
. ORE . DRESSER
INLAWS . ARKS .
MEAL . EASYSTREET
PESO . NITRO . AXLE
EDEN . IDIOM . PISA
LYRE . CARTE . STEM
```

23   Un-Cover Story

S	M	I	L	E		O	R	B	S		A	T	N	O
H	A	M	E	L		L	I	E	U		C	R	O	P
E	X	P	O	S	E	D	N	E	G	A	T	I	V	E
A	I	L		A	M	B		S	A	L		B	I	N
R	N	A		B	O	S		R	E	D	U	C	E	
S	E	N		B	A	Y	E	R		G	A	T	E	S
		T	E	A	R		N	E	W		V	E	S	T
		N	A	K	E	D	C	I	T	Y				
C	A	R	D		S	P	F		N	E	S	T		
O	D	E	O	N		A	O	R	T	A		A	S	P
H	U	F	F	E	D		R	U	E		G	N	U	
A	L	E		O	R	A		S	R	S		L	E	T
B	A	R	E	N	E	C	E	S	S	I	T	I	E	S
I	T	E	M		A	N	D	I		P	O	N	Z	I
T	E	E	S		M	E	S	A		S	T	E	E	N

24   Terms of Endearment

T	M	A	N		S	H	A	P	E		S	H	A	D
E	A	S	E		P	O	L	L	Y		T	O	N	Y
S	W	E	E	T	I	E	P	I	E		A	N	T	E
T	R	A	D	E	R		S	E	L	F	L	E	S	S
			L	A	I	N		S	E	A	L	Y		
	C	H	E	S	T	E	R		T	O	O	B	A	D
P	O	E		E	S	P	I	E	S			N	U	D	E
S	C	A	D	S		A	L	I		L	E	N	I	N
S	O	R	E		S	L	E	D	G	E		C	O	Y
T	A	T	T	L	E		S	E	R	A	P	H	S	
			T	R	A	M	S		R	I	G	A		
I	N	H	A	B	I	T	S		L	U	N	G	E	S
N	A	R	C		T	U	R	T	L	E	D	O	V	E
K	N	O	T		E	N	T	R	E		A	R	E	A
S	U	B	S			S	T	A	I	D		S	E	N	T

25   A Time for...

S	A	L	E	M		S	W	A	B		A	Q	U	A
A	L	I	B	I		T	H	U	R		T	U	R	N
A	D	M	A	N		A	I	D	E		S	A	N	D
B	A	B	Y	C	A	R	R	I	A	G	E			
			E	R	R		D	R	A	T	S			
A	R	R	E	S	T		S	A	T	E		H	O	O
S	H	E	L		Y	O	U	T	H	G	R	O	U	P
S	O	F	A	S		F	A	R		S	E	R	R	A
A	D	U	L	T	M	O	V	I	E		N	A	C	L
Y	E	S		O	O	Z	E		X	B	O	X	E	S
	S	E	I	K	O			C	A	R				
		S	E	N	I	O	R	M	O	M	E	N	T	
J	U	J	U		L	O	N	E		N	E	V	E	R
A	T	O	Z		I	T	E	M		C	R	E	T	E
M	E	N	U		T	A	L	E		S	E	N	S	E

26   End-to-End Entertainment

S	C	A	B		T	R	A	M		H	E	D	D	A
P	O	R	E		R	O	D	E		O	R	I	O	N
A	B	L	E		O	M	A	R		B	R	O	W	N
	B	O	N	D	J	A	M	E	S	B	O	N	D	
			R	A	N			C	E	L				
N	O	R	T	O	N		M	A	R	S		B	I	B
O	N	I	O	N		M	E	N	U		S	U	M	O
B	E	T	T	E	R	A	N	D	B	E	T	T	E	R
L	I	E	S		U	G	L	Y		L	A	T	T	E
E	N	S		C	L	I	O		S	I	N	E	A	D
			T	H	E			L	O	T				
	N	E	V	E	R	S	A	Y	N	E	V	E	R	
T	E	N	S	E		T	U	R	N		A	B	U	T
O	R	D	E	R		E	R	I	E		S	A	M	E
P	O	S	T	S		P	A	C	T		T	Y	P	E

27   House-Raising

E	P	I	C	S		A	L	D	A		T	O	T	E
A	L	G	A	E		P	E	R	M		A	V	O	N
R	O	O	F	G	A	R	D	E	N		D	E	N	Y
S	T	R	E	A	M		A	V	E	M	A	R	I	A
			L	U	V		I	S	O					
L	O	P	E		C	E	I	L	I	N	G	F	A	N
A	M	E	X		K	I	M		A	E	R	O	B	E
L	E	A	C	H		L	A	D		T	A	L	E	S
A	G	R	E	E	S		G	U	S		P	I	T	T
W	A	L	L	S	T	R	E	E	T		H	O	S	S
			S	R	I		S	A	T					
E	G	G	H	E	A	D	S		R	E	G	I	M	E
Z	O	N	E		F	L	O	O	R	M	O	D	E	L
R	O	A	M		E	E	L	S		P	R	E	S	S
A	N	T	S		D	Y	E	S		T	E	A	S	E

28   Rhyme Time

A	I	D	E		S	I	T	S		G	L	O	W
C	O	R	D		C	O	R	E		B	R	I	B	E
T	W	O	S	E	A	T	E	R		R	I	G	I	D
S	A	P		X	R	A	Y	S		A	S	H	E	S
			A	C	E	S			M	I	S	T		
P	A	R	R	E	D		E	C	O	N	O	M	I	C
A	T	O	M	S		O	P	A	L		M	E	R	E
S	L	O		S	T	P	E	T	E	R		T	E	N
T	A	M	S		O	R	E	S		E	V	E	N	T
A	S	H	T	R	A	Y	S		S	M	O	R	E	S
			E	Y	E	D		B	O	O	N			
S	C	A	L	E		D	O	U	B	T		E	S	P
N	O	T	I	F		E	G	G	B	E	A	T	E	R
O	M	E	N	S		E	R	L	E		A	C	M	E
B	O	R	G		R	E	E	D		S	H	I	P	

29 Attack!

```
IMPEL  STEM  RACK
NOOSE  PORE  ASHE
CRUST  UNIT  SHAY
ANN  STRIKEAPOSE
  DOGIN   OUSTED
DACRON  EARN
EGAD  GALL  TAPER
PEKE  EXILE  LULU
PEERS  LAID  ISLE
   ICES  DISHES
SLUDGE  PINTO
CUTANDDRIED  VET
ONIT  RAIL  OPERA
RACE  IDOL  ORRIN
ERAS  CATS  ROSES
```

30 Good Advice

```
SHED  MISS  STUBS
EURO  ANAT  COCOA
CLIP  IDLE  ATLAS
TAKEADEFPBREATH
   REX   LED
LAGOON  CLAD  REV
ALARM  SHIN  DIRE
SITBACKANDRELAX
EKES  RIOT  OBESE
RED  LENS  BASSES
   SAD   OLD
STOPYOURFUSSING
CANOE  SATE  NOEL
ACTOR  EVES  OTTO
TOOLS  SENT  WASP
```

31 Four-H Club

```
SARA  DRATS  HALL
ALOU  NACHO  ALOE
HEADMASTER  NANA
INDIE  STEADIER
BESTMAN  ARTS
   OMITS  ODETS
PATH  ANO  AMORAL
OBOE  SANER  WINO
LEGALS  TAI  NEST
STALE  GORED
   TIER  PLUMAGE
MANHATER  CAROM
AMOS  HEARTTHROB
LISP  ENTER  ROSE
IDEA  READY  EWER
```

32 Count on It!

```
KIEV  GAMES  ETAS
ESAI  ABASH  TWIN
NASA  SINAI  COSA
ONEGOODTURN  ILK
   RULER  TOFFEE
SAFARI  ABSORB
ABO  NOSE  SAYSO
ABUTTED  EVENSUP
BARER  ESTA  ERA
   BREAST  RAFAEL
TRAINS  ELITE
HOG  THREEAMIGOS
EDGE  CARON  NOME
FEEL  AGENT  TREE
TORY  NUDES  SEND
```

33 Auto Focus

```
RIDE  SLAP  FIT
EMUS  HAIRS  TODO
BUMPERCROP  IRON
ASP  VIES  RARELY
   HAND  TIME
CAPONE  CONTESSA
OLIOS  YANG  ACID
MEND  DOPEY  SAND
BREW  IDES  MINCE
STRIPPER  BOLTED
   NELL  LADY
TALKTO  SORE  DIP
EDIE  MOTORMOUTH
LAND  AROSE  OPED
LYE   OWED  HEMS
```

34 Lights, Please!

```
LAWN  ANOUK  LYRE
AGEE  GENRE  HEEP
MOVIEHOUSE  ANNO
AGENDA  SALESTAX
   SST  ORALLY
MAMMOTHCAVE
ACORN  ERTE  CALF
SHUE  FLOOR  BLUR
HEED  IMON  JELLO
  PLANETARIUM
UPBEAT  DRY
HARDSELL  ANGELA
ABIG  ROOTCELLAR
ULEE  ENSUE  OBIT
LORD  DITTY  WARS
```

35 Phrases on Location

```
BARB _ ARITH _ ALDA
OHIO _ RATIO _ NOON
TOPOFTHEMORNING
HYENA _ METHANE _
_ SCAD _ SEER _
SIP _ ICED _ RABBIS
ALE _ ANTES _ OLDE
MIDDLEOFTHEROAD
BARE _ XEROX _ AHA
ADOPTS _ REAP _ TON
_ AYES _ WRIT _
_ TERRACE _ RAGES
BOTTOMOFTHEHEAP
ERNE _ ENTER _ ONTO
DEAD _ NESTS _ EAST
```

36 Neutral Corners

```
EBBS _ BEAD _ PRO
GARP _ RACED _ BLIP
GRAYMATTER _ LACE
SET _ ACES _ OKAYED
_ WHEN _ SPEC _
MASHES _ TWINKLES
ASTIR _ THAN _ DORE
RIOT _ SHINS _ EDIE
LANE _ WONK _ PAGED
ANYWHERE _ HERESY
_ IMAN _ HAND _
BMINOR _ BOND _ NUT
LOVE _ BROWNSTONE
ALAS _ YENTA _ ANTE
HEN _ POOH _ BOOS
```

37 We Deliver

```
MISSM _ SMOG _ DIVA
OVINE _ TODO _ EDEN
DEMON _ ROOF _ BERG
_ OBSTETRICIANS
PIN _ AVA _ GOTSET
ASST _ SKIRUNS _
CLANG _ TERM _ SPA
KEYNOTESPEAKERS
STS _ TRAM _ NOTIT
_ ACUTELY _ DUDE
APACHE _ AAH _ PER
POSTALWORKERS _
ISSO _ OHMS _ MAHRE
LEAR _ VINE _ ATONE
EDYS _ ERIN _ NEPAL
```

38 What a Spread!

```
SADA _ GAPED _ AFAR
OPUS _ ALEVE _ TORO
ASTI _ SLAIN _ TRIO
ROYALJELLY _ ITEM
_ EELS _ DRYLY
RANLATE _ SHOES _
EGOS _ TEAM _ EMU
NATUREPRESERVES
ERA _ BUOY _ DEAD
_ CHIRP _ SAVANNA
ACHES _ HIFI _
CLAD _ TRAFFICJAM
TING _ HASTO _ HALO
ONCE _ OTTER _ OVER
REED _ READD _ PACE
```

39 Jam Session

```
MELT _ ACTED _ APSE
CREE _ SHOER _ LEER
GRAM _ PAULA _ EDNA
RASPBERRYBERET
ATE _ ANT _ TOSIR
WASPS _ SPURS _ TNN
_ LIT _ AAA _ NAES
_ BLUEBERRYHILL
SRAS _ ALI _ SAT
TOY _ TRYST _ REMAP
SWEAR _ ETD _ AWL
_ STRAWBERRYWINE
BETS _ ERASE _ ELIA
OREO _ DIVES _ RENT
ASSN _ SEERS _ ERGS
```

40 Fun with A-E-I-O-U Sounds

```
ROAM _ COAL _ AMISH
ACNE _ OBIE _ MENLO
MAILROOMS _ BACON
ARMOIRE _ SMELL _
DIANAS _ HEARTIER
ANTS _ BANS _ INNO
NAE _ APES _ COMEDY
_ MILESTONE _
PAROLE _ LOTS _ TAB
ONEL _ NYET _ CELL
INDEBTED _ PHOEBE
_ SHAYS _ ALUMNUS
EATIN _ MULETEAMS
STALK _ ASIA _ AGEE
EARLS _ NEED _ TEND
```

41 Whenever...

```
A D A M   S H A M   B O N E D
N O R A   L I M O   U P O N A
T W E N T Y F O U R S E V E N
S N A I L   I S S U E R
      A C T     S E S A M E S
S T A S   E S T E S   T E S T
A R M   A R I A   L O T T O
F I V E M I N U T E B R E A K
I T E M S   P O L S   R T E
R O T A   T R E E S   O S E S
E N S N A R E   E A R
    A B U S E S   S I D E A
F O R T Y E I G H T H O U R S
E R I E S   D O O R   L A R K
W E N D S   E S P Y   E L S A
```

42 On Broadway

```
A O L   A I D   U S A   M M I
P R I O R T O   P H I   R U N
R E N T C O N T R O L   M U D
I G E T A   S N O W   M A M E
C A M E R A   T O M M Y G U N
O N E R O U S   T E A R O U T
T O N   D I N   C R O S S
    H A I R B R U S H
E L D E R   C U P   C I R
G O E S B A D   M A C R A M E
G Y P S Y C A B   T H O R P E
H A R E   C R O P   A M M A N
E L I   G R E A S E P A I N T
A T V   R U T   S K I N N E R
D Y E   R E O   T E N   E L Y
```

43 The Sounds of Music

```
F A R M   S U E S   A S G O D
A L E E   I N R E   S W E D E
R O A R   E D I E   P I N O N
C H R I S R O C K   E N T R Y
E A S T E R   S A N G
    W A S P   I S S U E S
B L A B S   W O R D   E R L E
A I D A   M A R I E   T I L E
G R A B   O P E D   E S S E N
S A Y Y E S   D E N T
    B L T S   O N T I M E
D E L L A   P O P W A R N E R
A T E U P   E V A N   I D E A
L A N E S   N E R O   B I T S
I L O S E   D R E W   E A S E
```

44 Guy Flicks

```
M O S S   S O L I D   D O R M
O H I O   T H O S E   E L I A
P A T C H A D A M S   J E T S
U R I   A G E D   O S A G E S
P A N A C E A   E L E V
    J E R R Y M A G U I R E
S A J A K   A U T O   B O A
A L E X   P O S S E   O I L S
I T A   T E R I   O D D L Y
D O N N I E B R A S C O
    A R K S   M E E R K A T
R E D S E A   U S N A   E P A
E X E S   B A R T O N F I N K
N I N A   O R S E R   A T E E
E T T U   O C A L A   T H A N
```

45 Nothing Could be Finer

```
A D A P T   E N O S   S O L O
H I R E E   P O L E   A P O P
O C E A N L I N E R   T E A R
Y E A   P O L O   B U N N Y
    S I N O   S E A R S
A L L N I G H T D I N E R
A L O E S   I A G O   S A Y
P O N D   J E T T Y   F A Z E
O N E   C A L M   L I M O S
G R I Z Z L E D M I N E R
    A M A Z E   O A K S
B O N E R   A N N E   O W E
O L G A   F O R T Y N I N E R
L E E S   O R E G   E R U P T
T O R Y   P E S O   W A S T E
```

46 Sounds Like...

```
A L M A   C P A S   W O W E D
D O E S   U C L A   A K I T A
D O L L A R S A N D C E N T S
S T E E L   S K I   Y E A H
  S E E O F F   A M I D
    P E R L E   S M O R E S
S P A   A A R P   A K I R A
P O T P O U R R I S C E N T S
U N T I L   E O N S   G E E
D E N Z E L   R U N G S
    Z O O T   P S A L M S
A S T A   L O B   B E A U S
S T O P M A K I N G S E N S E
S A R I S   E T A L   V E A L
T R E E S   N E M O   E T N A
```

47 Skin-Deep Folks

```
F I A T . K A P P A . S P O T
A G R A . E L I O T . A R I A
S O M E P E O P L E . F E N D
T R Y . E P E E S . T A S K S
. . . D R U . . P A R S . . .
A R E S U P E R F I C I A L .
N E X T . V I R E O . G E L .
T H E . W A I V E R S . E N F
S A U . A C T E D . U N T O .
. B U T T H A T S J U S T O N
. T R E E . . . A S A . . . .
C R I E R . O S A G E . H I D
L A V A . T H E S U R F A C E
A C E D . O M A H A . I R O N
M E S S . A S N E R . T E N T
```

48 Formerly Known As...

```
T W A . D R U B . . E L S E
H A S . T I E T O . E X I L E
E X P O U N D E R . S T E E L
S E C U R E . . A S C E N D S
E R A S E . S E X T O N . . .
. . . T E L E X . A R D E N T
A G O . N E A P S . T E N O R
M I K E . S T O P S . R O V E
P R E X Y . O S I E R . S A Y
S L O P E S . E N T E R . . .
. . O L E A R Y . V A P I D .
S N A R L E R . E U G E N E .
N O L T E . E X P R E S S E R
A N G E R . N E A R S . O R B
P E A R . A D D S . . S T Y .
```

49 Grammatical Pauses

```
I C E D . O L G A . O P A L S
N O L I . B A R T . V E N O M
C O L O N I Z E R . A G O G O
A L E R O . E N I D . A D O G
. . . A R M . A U R A S . . .
. C O M M A N D M O D U L E .
O R C A . S E A . P E S E T A
B O O . P H D . N O N . N U B
J U M P O N . A B U . A D D S
. P E R I O D I C T A B L E .
. . . A S T I R . S H A . . .
D A W N . E A T A . A L G A E
A L I C E . D A S H B O A R D
M O P E D . E X P O . N I L E
P E E R S . M I S T . E T O N
```

50 Critical Review

```
T I S . R A S P E D . A C T
U S N A . E X H A L E . I O U
T H E C O V E R S O F . R O B
O T E R I . L E T I T B E . .
R A R E L Y . D O S . O D O R
S R S . P I G . R E G N A N T
. . . C A P O N . R E L E E .
. T H I S B O O K A R E . . .
C L E A N . T R E Y S . . . .
H A M S T E R . B E A . A B A
A B E T . N E B . P R E L I M
. R E A C T E D . E S T E S .
P O I . T O O F A R A P A R T
B A T . A R R I V E . N I C E
S T Y . N E T T E D . R E L .
```

51 Self-Description

```
W A R . G R O A N S . M E R E
A L A . O O M P A H . A C E S
S E V E N T E E N A C R O S S
P R E T E E N . M A C N E E .
S O S A . . . L E T . O W S .
. . . A L P H A . A R M . . .
A B C . S A R A N . P O I S E
C R O S S W O R D P U Z Z L E
S A N K A . A P A I L . E Y E
. . . S A S . M O U N T . . .
E R E . S I S . . . S A S H .
B E R L I N . M A A N D P A .
S E V E N T Y S I X C L U E S
E V E N . R E E L I N . L A T
N E S T . O R E L S E . T R Y
```

52 Applause! Applause!

```
H O R A . D R U I D . A L G A
A M E N . Y A H O O . S E A L
H A N D M E D O W N . S N I T
S N O R E R . H A N D E D T O
. . . . E L S A . E A T S . .
P A S T S . U T E . T S A R S
A B U T . S T E V I E . H E E
T E R I . A H E A D . T A T E
I T E . B L O N D S . E N I D
O S H E A . R Y E . C E D E S
. . . A L A N . S C A N . . .
H A N D L E R S . R I A T A S
O L D E . H A N D I N G O U T
U S E R . R I O D E . E T T A
R O D S . U N W E D . R O O T
```

53 — No Theme

```
OMAR  EDICT  SPUD
LATE  MACHO  ALSO
DUTCHTREAT  PAST
EVITA  EDNA  LYRE
RECITE  CLAIM
  FELINE  SNORE
COPY  BOO  MIGNON
AKA  DOUBLES  ELI
NARROW  LED  DYED
TYKES  PETITE
  PLEBE  CAVIAR
ELLA  ANTS  LINDA
COAX  SPACECADET
RICE  EATAT  TELE
USED  SLAMS  EXES
```

54 — Little Poems

```
GAMA  CASH  ASTRO
UPON  UNTO  UNION
LAVA  RTES  DANTE
PRIMETIME  RITES
STEERS  DUEL
  RYAN  SYMBOL
ARABS  SALE  AIDE
WILL  SAVES  IDOS
ALMA  OPEN  ALERT
YESMEN  LOSS
  ERGO  TICKED
OMEGA  FAIRSHARE
LAMAS  FIRE  OTIS
GRIME  EDIE  PICK
ACTED  RASP  SEAS
```

55 — Relatively Speaking

```
BOCA  SHEDS  FAR
ADOS  TUNIC  WACO
MOTHERLODE  ETNA
ARSENALS  PEAHEN
  TIS  STARE
  ASSET  MARTYRED
PRIOR  HIVES  TAE
ASSN  BARES  RISE
LOT  SALES  GAMER
ONESIDED  DOMED
  READY  SAO
ASHAME  MESSIAHS
LOOM  BROTHERRAT
PLOY  TORTE  ACHE
ODD  SENOR  SHAW
```

56 — A Sense of Direction

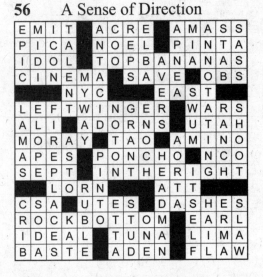

```
EMIT  ACRE  AMASS
PICA  NOEL  PINTA
IDOL  TOPBANANAS
CINEMA  SAVE  OBS
  NYC  EAST
LEFTWINGER  WARS
ALI  ADORNS  UTAH
MORAY  TAO  AMINO
APES  PONCHO  NCO
SEPT  INTHERIGHT
  LORN  ATT
CSA  UTES  DASHES
ROCKBOTTOM  EARL
IDEAL  TUNA  LIMA
BASTE  ADEN  FLAW
```

57 — Tootsy Talk

```
BEST  COMB  BUNTS
ODOR  OVER  INERT
WIFE  LIMA  AIMED
STAYSONONESTOES
  IRE  VEE
METALS  PLOD  FLO
ALAMO  TREK  ARIA
COMESTOONESFEET
OPEN  WOWS  LAUGH
NED  PALL  HORDES
  ALI  MAT
DIGSINONESHEELS
ORATE  NODS  CLUE
NIGER  TOIL  HALT
TSARS  ONCE  ONUS
```

58 — B-Hive

```
ALBUM  AHAS  LETS
SOUSA  PART  EXIT
ALGER  PLAY  NINA
PAS  BILLBRADLEY
  BILGE  OBSESS
LAUREL  SANE
USNA  OPAL  TABBY
SENT  ORLON  GORE
HAYES  OLEO  ABEL
  EASY  TRIBAL
ABSORB  ARENA
BEAUBRIDGES  RCA
ARTS  ODOR  TAKEN
SLIT  ALLI  EVENT
HENS  DEEP  DARTS
```

59 Crib Notes

```
G A B S   S M A R T   A B U T
A S I A   M A C H O   V A S E
B A B Y S I T T E R   I B E X
E P I S T L E   A N A L Y S T
        E E R   A R A B
E L B O W S   S A D E   O T C
R E A R S   S O L O S   O H O
V I R E   C A N E S   O M E N
I C Y   C U I N G   M E E S E
N A G   A L L Y   C A R R E Y
    R C M P   T A R
H E A R S A Y   R E D T I D E
A N N E   B A B Y S I S T E R
R O D S   L L A M A   P E L L
P S S T   E L M E R   S M E E
```

60 Now Playing

```
R I C A   I D O L   M A R I E
O M A N   N O P E   O D O R S
A B U T   F L E A   T O T E S
M U S I C A L C H A I R S
S E E   R N S   R O E
      L U C   B R A N D N E W
C O M E D Y C L U B   O L E
A B I T E   A A S   C A R L A
S O S   M Y S T E R Y M A N
T E S T I E S T   N E E
      E N L   I R A   A B S
    W E S T E R N O M E L E T
B L A M E   T U T U   T O G A
B E R E T   A B E T   C H A N
S E N D S   L Y L E   H A N D
```

61 A Visit to the Clothing Store

```
I C O N   C H O W   S E N O R
N O P E   H A S H   E V O K E
C H A R   I S L E   T E A R S
H O L D O N T O Y O U R H A T
      D O E   O P T
W I E L D S   B U M S   S I T
A N V I L   R A S P   G A L E
K E E P Y O U R S H I R T O N
E R R S   P I E R   C E A S E
S T Y   W I N D   S I G N E T
      S A N   F O E
T I G H T E N Y O U R B E L T
A D O R E   E A R N   L U A U
N E W E R   C L A D   I R I S
S A N D Y   K E Y S   P O R K
```

62 Have a Bawl

```
B E L L   R E S T   A W A R D
O D I E   E C H O   R O G E R
L I M E   B O A R   T R A D E
T E A R S O N M Y P I L L O W
      P R O   R E D
R A I S I N   P I E R   L E S
A D L E R   T O D O   B A L E
W I L L O W W E E P F O R M E
L O A F   H A M S   E A G E R
S S T   M I S S   A L T E R S
      E A R   A D O
B I G G I R L S D O N T C R Y
A D O R N   A L A N   O L E O
R E B E L   M A G I   T I E R
N A S T Y   A P E S   S O L E
```

63 Thoroughfares

```
S P I C   A T E U P   I F F Y
A I D A   P E R S E   R I L E
M A I N S T R E E T   A F E W
    A P E R S   U N I T A S
  S T R E S S   K N I S H
A N O I N T   C H I L E A N S
R O B E D   L A M A S   V A N
E R A S   L I N E S   L E G O
N E C   F E V E R   M A N G O
A R C H I V E S   M I N U E T
    O A R E D   L U N G E D
M O R S E L   E E R I E
E R O S   L O V E R S L A N E
R E A L   E L I Z A   L I E N
C O D E   D E L A Y   A R O D
```

64 "Now Hear This!"

```
A L A S   P E T S   A C T O R
B E L T   A C H E   P R I M E
Y A L E   S H O T   A I L E D
S P E A K S O U T   T E E N S
S T Y M I E   O O H S
      C R A G   B Y W A Y S
W H I S K   P A L E   O B O E
A I D A   R E L A Y   L U K E
G R E Y   A X E S   A F T E R
S E A S O N   S T E W
      U R G E   M O T I V E
M A N N A   B A B B L E S O N
E R E C T   O L E O   R A I D
S C A L E   N E T S   R A C E
S H R E D   Y E A S   A C E D
```

65 — A Bit of S&M?

S	C	A	B			E	L	O	P	E			S	S	T	S
E	L	M	O			L	O	V	E	S			A	C	H	E
T	O	M	B			E	L	E	C	T			W	H	O	A
S	T	O	C	K	M	A	R	K	E	T			O	R	R	
			A	R	E				S	E	A	S	O	N	S	
H	A	S	T	I	N	G	S					N	H	L		
A	R	C			S	T	A	T	U	E			A	M	O	S
W	E	A	R			A	P	A	R	T			D	A	R	T
K	A	L	E			L	E	S	S	E	E			R	C	A
			E	N	S				H	A	R	R	I	M	A	N
T	I	M	E	O	F	F					N	I	T			
E	G	O			S	L	O	T	M	A	C	H	I	N	E
A	L	D	A			E	R	R	O	L			A	C	E	D
C	O	E	D			S	T	O	O	L			C	O	R	E
H	O	L	D			H	E	N	R	Y			A	N	O	N

66 — F Troupe

S	O	M	E			J	E	S	T			C	I	G	A	R
U	P	O	N			A	L	O	E			A	D	O	R	E
R	A	N	I			I	C	O	N			R	I	O	T	S
F	R	E	D	F	L	I	N	T	S	T	O	N	E			
S	T	Y			R	E	D			P	O	T				
		O	P	E	D			S	C	A	N			T	D	S
A	G	R	E	E			S	T	A	R			E	A	R	N
F	E	D	E	R	I	C	O	F	E	L	L	I	N	I	
R	E	E	K			R	A	R	E			A	L	L	O	T
O	R	R			J	E	R	K			E	T	A	L		
		E	O	N			A	L	I			I	R	A		
		F	A	T	H	E	R	F	L	A	N	A	G	A	N
A	L	O	H	A			A	L	A	I			C	H	I	T
L	I	N	E	N			F	E	R	N			E	T	T	E
S	T	E	R	N			T	A	M	E			S	S	T	S

67 — July Celebration

A	P	E	R			I	B	I	S			P	S	H	A	W
R	O	U	E			D	U	N	K			E	T	U	D	E
C	O	R	D			I	N	D	Y			R	A	G	E	S
S	L	O	W	P	O	K	E			F	O	R	E	S	T	
			H	E	T	U	P			A	N	S				
S	A	D	I	E			M	E	A	L			A	P	A	R
H	U	R	T	L	E			N	Y	C			N	O	T	E
E	D	I	E			V	I	D	E	O			D	I	E	M
D	I	V	A			E	R	E			N	A	S	S	A	U
S	E	E	N			R	A	N	G			S	T	E	M	S
			D	O	T			C	O	L	O	R				
R	U	M	B	A	S			E	V	E	N	I	N	G	S	
O	R	A	L	S			I	D	E	A			P	E	A	T
I	S	S	U	E			T	A	R	S			E	A	V	E
L	A	K	E	S			S	Y	N	E			S	P	E	W

68 — Flag Day

S	P	A	T			F	L	A	R	E			A	R	F	S
E	A	V	E			R	E	M	U	S			L	O	D	E
E	M	I	R			E	V	E	N	T			T	A	R	T
R	E	D	R	I	D	I	N	G	H	O	O	D				
E	L	L	E	N				S	E	W			S	T	Y	
D	A	Y			E	A	S	T			R	E	T	I	R	E
			A	P	P	E	A	R				E	G	O	S	
		W	H	I	T	E	E	L	E	P	H	A	N	T		
G	O	A	D			D	O	P	I	E	R					
A	R	R	E	S	T			N	O	G	S			T	R	A
B	E	D			T	E	N				S	O	R	E	R	
		B	L	U	E	I	N	T	H	E	F	A	C	E		
A	L	A	I			O	C	O	M	E			A	D	E	N
M	I	L	K			F	E	V	E	R			L	E	N	A
P	E	L	E			F	R	A	N	S			L	S	T	S

69 — Every Day in Every Way...

H	A	R	S	H			C	A	S	T			B	L	T	S
O	M	A	H	A			A	L	T	O			R	A	I	L
H	U	M	I	D			S	L	O	P			A	I	D	E
U	S	E	R			F	A	I	R	H	A	I	R	E	D	
M	E	N	T	O	R			M	A	N	N					
			F	E	E	S			T	O	W	E	R	S		
G	O	O	D	F	E	L	L	A	S			A	L	O	E	
O	M	A	R			S	O	N				S	I	L	L	
G	E	R	E			B	E	T	T	E	R	H	A	L	F	
O	N	S	A	L	E			H	I	V	E					
			M	O	N	A			E	X	C	E	P	T		
B	E	S	T	S	E	L	L	E	R			H	A	L	O	
E	L	I	E			F	O	U	R			C	O	V	E	R
A	L	M	A			I	N	T	O			A	R	E	A	S
M	A	I	M			T	E	E	S			P	E	S	T	O

70 — Three Places

B	A	S	I	L			A	B	C	D			P	A	P	A
A	T	O	N	E			P	E	L	E			I	R	O	N
S	A	N	A	N	D	R	E	A	S	F	A	U	L	T		
E	N	G	I	N	E			T	R	I	O			B	E	E
			R	O	T	S			A	R	R	E	A	R	S	
C	A	N			N	E	W	T			E	G	G			
O	P	A	L			C	O	I	L			E	R	E	C	T
S	A	N	A	N	T	O	N	I	O	T	E	X	A	S		
T	R	A	D	E			P	E	N	D			T	I	N	A
			L	A	P			S	T	I	R			T	A	R
L	A	T	E	R	A	L			S	O	A	P				
A	V	A			E	N	O	S			U	N	R	O	B	E
S	A	N	F	R	A	N	C	I	S	C	O	B	A	Y		
T	I	G	E			M	E	A	N			O	V	I	N	E
S	L	O	W			A	R	T	S			R	E	E	K	S

71 Moving Right Along

```
P E N N   . .   P A D S . .   T W O S
E R I E   . . F O L I O . .   R A G A
P A C E S E T T E R . . . .   A L L I
U S E R I D . . A T T A C K E D . .
P E R . . S O A R . . I N T O . .
. . . . D I R T . . L E I S U R E
V E T O . . A T T E S T . . T A D
F A R N S . . I A N . . A L O N G
E R E . . C A R R O T . . A N D Y
P L A C A T E . . R E A P . .
. . . . D O N T . . T E E N . . B I B
C A M P S I T E . . T A C O M A
A R I A . . M A R C H T O W A R
R E L Y . . E L S I E . . S I G N
P A L S . . S E E D . . . . T E E S
```

72 Doubling Up

```
S W I S S . . F L A P . . C U T S
O R D I E . . L O B E . . E P I C
W A L L A W A L L A . . . N O R A
S P E E . . A X L E . . A S N E R
. . . . N O D . . . . S Q U A D S
C I R C U S C I R C U S . .
U S H E R . . O M A H A . . L E D
B A E R . . V A T . . P O L O
A K A . . S I E G E . . L A S S O
. . . . S I S T E R S I S T E R
J O S T L E . . . . P E T . .
A R E A L . . M A G I . . R E B A
C A R Y . . . B A D E N B A D E N
O T T O . . O M A R . . A M I N D
B E A N . . G A M E . . R I T Z Y
```

73 The Cat's Meow

```
A V E R . . C O B B . . L O B E S
G I V E . . O L I O . . E R O D E
A X E D . . M I N G . . A B B I E
P E R S I A N G U L F . . B E D
E N T E R . . . . S A L S A . .
. . . . A M P L E . . W E I R D O
S O P . . A L E X . . S T A K E D
A L O T . . A D I E U . . M E A D
G A L O O T . . T R I M . . R N S
A V E N U E . . S A T I N . .
. . . . V I T A E . . M E C C A
P E A . . P U S S Y W I L L O W
U S U A L . . T H A I . . S A R A
M A L T A . . E A R L . . O R E S
P U T T Y . . E D D Y . . N A S H
```

74 A Race to the Finish

```
B R A T . . L A R K . . A M E N D
A O N E . . A L O E . . M O R A Y
R A T E . . P O M P . . P O I S E
B R I N G S U P T H E R E A R . .
. . . . R E D . . . . E R E . .
S L A T E D . . I S L E . . C U B
C A N O E . . A N T E . . U L N A
R U N S N E C K A N D N E C K . .
E G O S . . W H E Y . . R I F L E
W H Y . . W E E D . . B A T T E R
. . . . E R R . . . S A P . .
L E A V E S I N T H E D U S T . .
A T S E A . . T A R A . . I N C A
S A I N T . . E D A M . . A T O M
S L A S H . . M A Y A . . L O T S
```

75 Getting a Round

```
C A T . . A L P O . . B A R H O P
U N O . . G O O N . . I N D O O R
R O W H O U S E . . S T A N Z A
A S E A . . T E M P T . . K E Y
D E L L A . . . P E R S E . .
. . . . F R O N T R O W S E A T
M E N . . B U O Y S . . E P P I E
A T E D I R T . . O P E N E R S
A T B A T . . R A N A T . . E S T
M U R D E R E R S R O W . .
. . . . A R O A R . . N O T C H
I F I . . B L A B S . . M O L E
D A N C E R . . Y O U R B O A T
E L T O R O . . E Z I O . . T R U
A L L D A Y . . D O T E . . H E P
```

76 Countdown

```
C O S A . . B A S H . . F E R M I
A L U M . . A S I A . . O V O I D
L I L T . . T A L L . . R E U S E
F O U R T H P L A C E . . S E A
. . . . A I M . . . S U P P E R S
J A C K P A A R . . R A E . .
E R R . . T H I R D W A T C H
T T O P S . . A D O . . S T O L E
S E C O N D B E S T . . G A R
. . . . S I X . . S E R E N A D E
B E N E F I T . . . U R I . .
U M A . . F I R S T F A M I L Y
R I V A L . . O L A F . . B R A E
P L A T E . . T I L L . . L A N A
S E L E S . . S M E E . . E N D S
```

77 — Hold It!

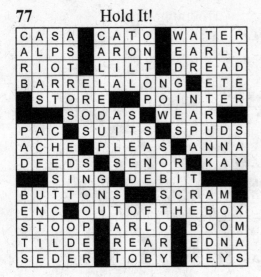

```
CASA  CATO  WATER
ALPS  ARON  EARLY
RIOT  LILT  DREAD
BARRELALONG   ETE
 STORE   POINTER
  SODAS  WEAR
PAC SUITS  SPUDS
ACHE PLEAS  ANNA
DEEDS SENOR  KAY
  SING DEBIT
BUTTONS  SCRAM
ENC OUTOFTHEBOX
STOOP ARLO BOOM
TILDE REAR EDNA
SEDER TOBY KEYS
```

78 — It's Play Time!

```
ALPO  SPCA  CRAMS
TEAL  POOL  HANOI
BASEBALLDIAMOND
ACTOR OARS  XKE
THE ADIN SEA
 SMILE   ROTS
FOOTBALL  MAMIE
ENROLLS ANIMATE
STARE  GRIDIRON
SOLE   RANDS
 DAB ELAL  PST
EWE LEAN ENLAI
BASKETBALLCOURT
BLAIR EDIE UTAH
STUNT LEDS NONE
```

79 — State Sights

```
ORAL  GERMS  ASTO
NOLA  EAUDE  DEAN
CALIFORNIAPOPPY
EDITOR  VORTEX
 YEGG  METE
CAP SIR ERA ORA
ALAI AIDA SAXON
WISCONSINCHEESE
EATEN HADA RYES
DRE ETA EMS EST
 SCAM  REPO
ABSCAM  RESALT
COLORADOROCKIES
INAN LOTTO ARNO
DOME ESSEN REOS
```

80 — Chockablock

```
METS  RITA  SCADS
ALEE  URIS  TAROT
TIMECLOCK  ERASE
TAP LINK  BALLET
  JAN   KOKO
 LAUGHINGSTOCK
CREWS OBEY  ZEN
RINSE ASA SPADE
ALI AGED PUREE
BENJAMINSPOCK
 ALOE   ARK
SWARMS ROUT TAO
CARGO POPPYCOCK
ADIOS OBIE AURA
MEANT DEER PREY
```

81 — Nice Talk

```
SAFER LIMA  BABE
OLIVE IDES  ELEV
LANES MOOS  TORE
ONE COOLWEATHER
 POURS  TREATY
KERNEL  VISA
IRIS OMEN BASED
NINE NIECE GURU
GETTY SPAR APIE
 ARTS  REPENT
ATTIRE BOXER
GRANDFINALE SIP
LACE ODES METOO
ODOR REST PRANK
WEST MATE TERSE
```

82 — Let's Get Together

```
ATALL LIMO  IBET
TOSCA ETAL  MERE
HANDTOHAND BLOT
ODE ERRS  PAILS
SYRINGE ARABY
 HEARTTOHEART
UNMOWN OTS  CUE
SOAPS SPY TEHEE
MAD SOI MILERS
CHEEKTOCHEEK
 SLOAN EASEOFF
WEEPS SYNC  TRU
ZINC HEADTOHEAD
ASST EMMA RERIG
GEES SUEY EXILE
```

83 Warning Sign

```
L A S T _ G A S P S _ S E A N
O N L Y _ O C A L A _ H A L O
S T O P M O T I O N _ O G L E
E S P I E D _ D D T _ E L A L
_ _ S L I M _ S A C H E T S _
A L I T _ D E B _ S O O _ _ _
L O G _ _ E R I C _ C R E S T
L O O K B A C K I N A N G E R
S P R E E _ Y E T I _ _ G E E
_ _ E L S _ D E E _ H Y P E _
C H A N T E D _ D L I I _ _ _
E A R N _ A R A _ S A G G E D
C U R E _ L I S T E N H E R E
I T I S _ E V I A N _ U R L S
L E D S _ D E A N S _ P E E K
```

84 Do I Hear an Echo?

```
M A T E R _ H A R P _ C L O G
E L O P E _ A L E E _ R U D E
M E N I N B L A C K _ A L O T
O R T _ O U T S _ O C C U R _
S T O R I E S _ P E A K _ _ _
_ _ U R N _ C A S S E T T E _
P L A N _ A J A R _ T R E A T
A E T N A _ A C K _ E J E C T
L A T I N _ P T A S _ A S T A
S H A N G H A I _ T L C _ _ _
_ _ G L E N _ C O O K S U P _
_ B E B O P _ E O N S _ N N E
L A V A _ C A D D Y S H A C K
A L E C _ A G E E _ E M I L E
P E R K _ T O N S _ S O L E S
```

85 Group Therapy

```
R A S H _ A L A S _ A C R E S
O G L E _ T O R Y _ B L O A T
B O Y S C H O I R _ S A L S A
E R E _ H E M S _ B E S E E N
D A R W I N _ E V A N S _ _ _
_ _ E L S A _ A S T A I R E _
M A R D I _ G A L E _ C R U D
A P O D _ G H O U L _ T A N G
S E M I _ H A L E _ S I S S Y
T R A N C E S _ D E M O _ _ _
_ _ G E N T S _ V A N D A L _
S T A B A T _ L A O S _ A T E
L A N A S _ P A C K H O R S E
A T O N E _ I S L E _ D E E R
B E N D S _ T H U D _ D D A Y
```

86 Which Came First?

```
S W A B _ A T E A T _ S A I D
H A V E _ E R R O R _ P I N E
A H E N I S O N L Y _ R E A P
N I M _ D O T S _ B A L S A _
A N A _ L P S _ B U T L E R _
N E R V E S _ E W E S _ O C T
A S I A _ S O L E S _ _ _ _ _
_ _ A N E G G S W A Y O F _ _
_ _ E L A T E _ P A C S _ _ _
E L S _ A N O X _ R O S I L Y
M A K I N G _ L A B _ R I N _
A B I N D _ D E S I _ D N A _
I R I S _ A N O T H E R E G G
L E N T _ H I N G E _ N A T O
S A G S _ A L T O S _ S L O G
```

87 Four in a Row

```
R A G S _ B R E W S _ G O A L
O L A V _ R E R A N _ O G L E
M O R E _ A N N I E _ O R A N
P U B L I C D E F E N D E R S
_ _ T O E _ R O N _ _ _ _ _ _
A S N E W _ S P A _ D E B A R
L E O _ A N K A R A _ S E L A
F I L M N O I R C L A S S I C
A N T E _ R E S E A L _ E V E
S E E R S _ R E D _ O U T E R
_ _ C I A _ T N N _ _ _ _ _ _
P E T E R S T U Y V E S A N T
A R I D _ P A V E S _ A R E A
N I N E _ I R E N E _ F I S T
G E T S _ C O A S T _ E A S E
```

88 At Arm's Length?

```
B A W L _ B R U T E _ I V A N
O H I O _ L A P E L _ G A M E
W O N T L I F T A F I N G E R
L Y E _ O T T O _ M O U N D _
_ _ H A H S _ D E P R E S S _
P A R A D E _ M O V I E _ _ _
I M A M _ T O T E S _ K I T _
S I T S O N O N E S H A N D S
A D S _ R O W E D _ C O L A _
_ _ D A N N Y _ B I T T E R _
R E F U T E S _ M A C S _ _ _
A L O N E _ B A R E _ L O G _
T U R N S T H U M B S D O W N
E D G E _ E E R I E _ A R E A
S E E D _ E R R E D _ B E S T
```

89 — Going to the Front

L	E	A	R	■	C	R	O	A	T	■	C	A	M	S
U	R	G	E	■	R	I	N	S	E	■	A	L	O	E
L	I	R	A	■	E	V	I	T	A	■	B	I	R	D
L	E	A	D	T	O	A	N	I	M	P	A	S	S	E
■	■	■	■	E	L	L	E	■	A	L	T	E	R	■
W	A	S	H	M	E	■	■	S	A	T	■	■	■	■
A	S	T	O	P	■	T	H	O	R	■	A	T	M	E
T	H	E	H	O	U	S	E	O	F	U	S	H	E	R
T	Y	P	O	■	P	A	W	N	■	R	I	A	L	S
■	■	■	A	I	R	■	■	F	I	N	I	T	E	■
C	H	E	A	T	■	■	A	S	E	A	■	■	■	■
H	E	A	D	F	O	R	T	H	E	H	I	L	L	S
A	L	T	O	■	K	E	B	A	B	■	N	O	A	H
O	L	E	S	■	I	F	A	L	L	■	O	N	C	E
S	O	R	E	■	E	S	T	E	E	■	N	E	E	D

90 — Name That Celebrity

B	A	L	D	■	P	E	K	O	E	■	A	J	A	R
A	L	E	E	■	A	R	E	N	A	■	T	O	T	E
L	A	N	A	T	U	R	N	E	R	■	T	H	I	N
L	I	O	N	E	L	■	S	A	L	M	I	N	E	O
■	■	■	C	A	S	H	■	■	S	E	L	L	■	■
O	S	C	A	R	■	A	M	P	■	G	A	E	L	S
M	A	L	I	■	G	R	O	A	N	S	■	N	E	A
E	L	A	N	■	A	L	I	C	E	■	A	N	O	N
G	E	R	■	A	D	O	R	E	D	■	B	O	N	E
A	S	K	E	R	■	W	A	R	■	A	B	N	E	R
■	■	G	R	I	P	■	■	S	O	L	E	■	■	■
A	L	A	N	L	A	D	D	■	R	E	L	I	E	D
C	U	B	E	■	G	R	E	T	A	G	A	R	B	O
E	L	L	S	■	E	A	S	E	L	■	N	E	A	R
D	U	E	T	■	S	T	I	E	S	■	E	D	N	A

91 — Gear Shifting

H	U	S	H	■	T	I	A	R	A	■	I	W	A	S
E	T	T	E	■	A	N	I	O	N	■	L	E	I	S
A	U	R	A	■	B	U	N	T	S	■	S	L	R	S
D	R	I	V	E	U	P	T	H	E	W	A	L	L	■
U	N	P	E	G	■	■	I	S	L	E	■	D	I	D
P	S	S	■	R	O	O	■	■	■	T	B	O	N	E
■	■	L	E	T	P	A	S	S	■	O	N	E	L	■
■	N	E	U	T	R	A	L	C	O	R	N	E	R	■
M	A	N	S	■	A	L	B	U	M	E	N	■	■	■
S	T	A	T	E	■	■	D	E	A	■	N	E	C	■
G	U	M	■	K	W	A	N	■	■	L	L	A	M	A
■	R	E	V	E	R	S	E	O	S	M	O	S	I	S
Y	A	L	E	■	A	C	A	R	E	■	U	C	L	A
O	L	E	G	■	P	A	T	E	R	■	S	A	I	L
U	S	D	A	■	S	P	O	O	F	■	E	R	O	S

92 — By the Numbers

B	I	A	S	■	T	O	M	S	■	M	A	S	T	S
Y	O	G	I	■	H	O	O	T	■	I	W	E	R	E
T	W	E	N	T	Y	O	N	E	■	L	E	V	E	L
E	A	S	I	E	R	■	K	E	E	L	■	E	E	L
■	■	■	S	R	O	S	■	D	E	I	O	N	■	■
A	L	T	E	R	I	N	G	■	K	E	A	T	O	N
B	A	H	■	A	D	O	R	E	S	■	H	Y	P	E
A	S	I	A	N	■	W	A	L	■	S	U	S	I	E
S	S	R	S	■	A	S	S	I	S	T	■	I	N	D
H	O	T	T	E	R	■	P	O	L	E	A	X	E	S
■	■	Y	O	U	T	H	■	T	E	A	R	■	■	■
M	O	N	■	R	Y	E	S	■	E	D	A	M	E	S
A	M	I	G	O	■	F	O	R	T	Y	F	I	V	E
R	A	N	U	P	■	T	U	B	E	■	A	N	E	W
C	R	E	T	E	■	S	L	I	D	■	T	E	N	S

93 — "Duh!"

T	H	O	U	■	U	K	E	S	■	D	I	A	N	A
R	O	U	T	■	N	A	P	E	■	E	L	L	I	S
I	N	T	O	■	D	R	E	W	A	B	L	A	N	K
P	E	E	P	H	O	L	E	■	F	U	S	S	E	S
S	Y	R	I	A	■	■	P	A	T	■	■	■	■	■
■	■	A	L	L	S	T	A	R	■	S	T	I	R	■
U	P	S	■	V	I	P	E	R	■	A	I	S	L	E
R	A	C	K	E	D	O	N	E	S	B	R	A	I	N
G	L	U	E	S	■	K	O	R	E	A	■	R	E	D
E	M	M	Y	■	T	E	R	S	E	S	T	■	■	■
■	■	F	U	N	■	■	■	E	R	R	E	D	■	■
S	H	A	K	E	N	■	S	O	Y	S	A	U	C	E
H	A	D	N	T	A	C	L	U	E	■	C	R	O	W
O	L	D	I	E	■	A	U	R	A	■	K	A	L	E
P	O	S	T	S	■	L	E	S	S	■	S	L	E	D

94 — Way to Go...Not!

C	A	S	E	■	H	A	R	P	O	■	H	E	A	L
H	U	L	L	■	O	R	I	O	N	■	E	T	T	A
I	R	I	S	■	H	I	P	P	E	T	Y	H	O	P
C	A	P	■	B	O	D	E	■	E	D	E	N	S	■
■	■	S	T	A	H	L	■	S	A	R	A	L	E	E
P	L	A	Y	B	O	Y	B	U	N	N	Y	■	■	■
R	O	C	K	Y	■	■	L	E	T	S	■	F	A	R
O	B	O	E	■	S	U	E	D	E	■	R	U	L	E
B	E	G	■	F	A	M	E	■	M	A	L	T	A	■
■	■	C	L	I	P	P	E	T	Y	C	L	O	P	■
S	C	H	O	O	L	S	■	G	A	M	E	S	■	■
P	R	I	M	O	■	U	G	L	Y	■	C	A	W	■
R	I	V	E	R	H	O	R	S	E	■	J	A	V	A
A	M	E	R	■	U	N	I	O	N	■	A	L	O	T
T	E	S	S	■	H	A	S	N	T	■	W	E	N	T

95 — Troubled

```
S H E M ■ R A T E S ■ A G E D
T A X I ■ U B O A T ■ N O D E
A T A D I S A D V A N T A G E
R E M I S S ■ D E T A I L E R
■ ■ S L I T ■ S I R ■ ■ ■
S P A ■ E A R L ■ C R A V A T
L E T S ■ N A I L ■ O V I N E
A T A L O S S F O R W O R D S
K A R A T ■ H E R E ■ W A R T
E L I T E S ■ R E F S ■ L E S
■ ■ L I C ■ N E W S ■ ■ ■
P A R O L E E S ■ R A T T L E
A T C R O S S P U R P O S E S
C R A G ■ T A U P E ■ L A I T
E A S Y ■ A R R I D ■ E R S E
```

96 — Mixed Priorities

```
D E A N ■ P R A M ■ O S C A R
R A C E ■ R A J A ■ C H O K E
E C H O ■ I V A N ■ C O L I N
W H E N E V E R Y O U W A N T
■ ■ R E D ■ P L Y ■ ■ ■
S P R O U T ■ S L I T ■ C O B
T R O O P ■ T H O U ■ S O U L
R I G H T T H I S M I N U T E
I D E S ■ H I N T ■ L A R G E
P E R ■ G O N E ■ T I P T O P
■ ■ T A R ■ B A A ■ ■ ■
E V E R Y N O W A N D T H E N
E E R I E ■ W A L K ■ R O U E
L I L T S ■ E L S E ■ E R R S
S L E E T ■ D E A R ■ K N O T
```

97 — Chronometry 101

```
A S H E ■ C L A S S ■ A L D A
B O O K ■ O A S I S ■ W A A C
C L U E ■ W R I S T W A T C H
S E R ■ T A R A ■ R I C H E
■ ■ G L O R Y ■ C L O T H E D
I S L A N D ■ T H E N ■ ■
T H A T S ■ O R A N G U T A N
O U S T ■ E V E N S ■ N I T E
R E S E T T I N G ■ A D M I T
■ ■ R A N T ■ S L E E P S
D I S P U T E ■ S H A R P ■
A S T I N ■ S T A N ■ I R E
C L O C K M A K E R ■ B E E N
H A N K ■ A L I V E ■ A C E D
A M Y S ■ C I T E D ■ R E F S
```

98 — Making Progress

```
I C E T ■ D R U M S ■ W A S H
N A T O ■ E E R I E ■ O S L O
C R A W L S P A C E ■ R E E L
A S L E E P ■ L E S ■ L A D D
■ ■ L O O M ■ T A D ■ ■
A H S ■ S T E P F O R W A R D
L O A D ■ A L E ■ L A V E R
L O G A N ■ G A S ■ O R I B I
O H A R E ■ E T S ■ I L I E
W A L K T H R O U G H ■ A D D
■ ■ E S E ■ P L U G ■ ■
S E A N ■ A L S ■ A M U S E D
A N T I ■ R U N I N P L A C E
A V O N ■ S C A L D ■ L U R E
B Y N G ■ T Y P E S ■ S L U R
```

99 — Spoonerisms

```
A D L A I ■ T A T A ■ A W L S
B E A U S ■ U S E D ■ C H A T
L A C K O F P I E S ■ T A R A
E R E ■ L O E S S ■ P I C K Y
■ ■ E A R L ■ H O O K ■ ■
■ H A S T E O F T U N N E Y
C A R P E ■ A W R Y ■ D O E
B U R Y ■ A L L O T ■ N O U N
S L O ■ E X E C ■ S O U R S
■ S W E D E S O F B E T T E
■ H A I L ■ A O N E ■ ■
S I E G E ■ G U I L D ■ M S G
E L A L ■ F I L L O F B E A R
W I D E ■ A N N E ■ O O O L A
N E S T ■ R O A D ■ R O W E D
```

100 — Commonality

```
R A B I N ■ J A B S ■ S A R A
A G E N T ■ S L O E ■ T R A P
C H A C H A B E A T ■ A U D I
E A R ■ L A P ■ S E R B I A
■ C H O O C H O O T R A I N
D E L I L A H ■ L U C Y ■ ■
E L A T E D ■ B E T H ■ B E G
B M W S ■ C E O ■ F E T A
S O S ■ F E L T ■ B A L L U P
■ T O T E ■ S O M A L I S
C H O W C H O W P U P P Y ■
H A W A I I ■ H A G ■ F D A
A G I N ■ C H I C H I C L U B
L U N G ■ A O N E ■ S P O K E
K E G S ■ L E E K ■ M O P E D
```

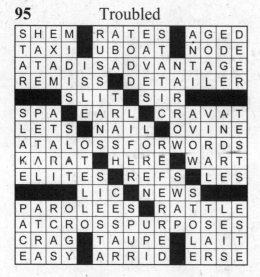

101 — Easy As Pie

```
SEMI  SANTA  ZAPS
OPEN  ARAIL  UTAH
DISH  TOMEI  CBER
ACHOO  MERC  CASE
   CLEARSIGHTED
WALKER    ANI
ERA  LOBO  ANDIE
SIMPLEFRACTIONS
TABOO  FAKE  TSP
   PAT  LESSON
PLAINVANILLA
LARD  SPAM  FIBER
ACRO  EATAT  LORE
TEAL  TITLE  ENID
EDYS  SLYLY  DEED
```

102 — Say Again?

```
BOLD  COSTA  BASH
APIE  ARIES  UPTO
NAMESNAMES  DROP
SLEPT  TONI  DINE
    ARON  STYLES
SCATTER  STUB
NOSHED  GESTURED
OPIE  BUT  DIVA
WEARSOUT  ADDLED
   EELS  PLAYERS
WASTED  MAIN
ARCH  WEED  COOPS
GORE  EXTRAEXTRA
OMAR  SPEED  ETAL
NAPE  TORSO  NOME
```

103 — Traffic Signs

```
BLOND  DASH  AROD
LAXER  OREO  SALE
ONEWAYORANOTHER
TAN  GADS  EDISON
   NRA  LYE
DEADENDJOB  BABS
EXERT  ICE  FIAT
LXII  CANOE  LOSE
COOP  ANG  FALSE
ONUS  STOPMOTION
   ASI  AEC
ARLENE  SITU  BAH
YIELDTOPRESSURE
EDNA  TREE  OATER
SEAL  EKED  NOTSO
```

104 — Contusions

```
ACAR  ADORE  TBAR
POSE  RELAX  OLIO
BOYSINBLUE  PUMA
SKEET  BALM  KEEL
   AHOYS  PLACED
EMBLEM  STAPH
AILS  ABBA  SIEGE
RCA  BRUISES  ERA
NACHO  GOES  ISIS
   KANES  ASCENT
LAWMEN  HAITI
EMIL  ABAB  ACHES
WIDE  MENINBLACK
IGOT  ODETO  ELOI
SOWS  RESET  SONS
```

105 — Arrivals

```
PASTA  BATH  GOAL
AHAIR  ACRE  HALE
COMETOTHINKOFIT
EYE  ELSE  ASSTS
   MMI  CERT
COMEINTOONESOWN
ORALS  ORRIN  NEO
NODS  STAND  BEEF
INA  CRETE  DITKA
COMEHOMETOROOST
   GOSS  HAG
STARR  SLOP  GUN
COMEDOWNTHEPIKE
ATIT  READ  RILES
RODS  REPS  YEAST
```

106 — Looking In the Mirror

```
JAMB  CARP  BOUGH
ALOE  OLIO  LUCRE
YUMA  RIGS  ATLAS
 MAKINGHEADWAY
    SENT  LEI
WITHIT  DISTURB
AMOST  AVIV  POE
GETTINGANEARFUL
ETS  YENS  GHOST
SAYABLE  SNORTS
   CRO  ARTE
 FACINGFORWARD
EASED  RIPE  LOOP
FLING  ARES  EDIT
TASTE  BEDS  XENA
```

107 — Priceless

```
L O F T S . S P A S . H E R D
A G R E E . P A C E . E V E R
I R E N E . I V E S . L I N E
D E E . F R E E S A M P L E S
. A R I E S . M A S S E S . .
D I G I T S . T I E S . . . .
E D E N . T R I M . H E F T Y
L E N S . S E T U P . A R E A
L A T E R . A L S O . R E A R
. . . H A L E . S O L E M N .
B A S T E S . . M E R Y L . .
F R E E A S A B I R D . A P T
L O V E . I R O N . E R N I E
A M E N . S L O T . R O C K S
T A N S . T O N Y . S W E E T
```

108 — Thrice Upon a Time

```
T O S S . D A F T . S T P A T
A L O U . O M A R . T E R R E
B L I N D M I C E . E N O L A
B I L K E A N E . F E N N E L
Y E S . L I T T L E P I G S .
. . S A N . I R E S . . . . .
H A P P Y . B R A N D N A M E
A L O E . B E A R S . E S A U
S I D E T R I P S . E T H E R
. . D E A N . S S S . . . . .
. B I L L Y G O A T S . R C A
D E V I L S . T R E E F A R M
A S A M I . M E N I N A T U B
H E N I E . E R I N . K E E L
S T A T S . T I E S . E R L E
```

109 — Hm, Let's See ...

```
O I L S . C H A S E . G E T S
A R I A . P U L L S . O V A L
H A M M E R S O U T . L A T E
U N B O X . H E M A N D H A W
. . A C E . . S T E P . . . .
S P A . E R M A . E X A C T A
H I M A L A Y A S . T I L E S
A P E X . S T R A W . N A S H
R E B I D . H O M E S T Y L E
E R A S E R . N E A T . S A N
. . P A I D . . N E W . . . .
H U M O N G O U S . E R U P T
A F E W . H Y M N W R I T E R
L O S E . T O P I C . S A K E
T S A R . O U S T S . T H E Y
```

110 — Join the Club

```
G A I N . A N T E S . B O M B
O H N O . S T E V E . I L I E
Y A C H T C H A I R . L I S A
A S H O R E . L E G L O C K .
. . W E N D S . N A Y . . . .
S T D . E D I T . A L B U M S
T R E K . E V E S . E U B I E
R I L E . D O P E S . D O L E
A T T Y S . T O D O . D A L Y
P E A P O D . N E C K . T I A
. . E R A . E R R I S . . . .
H E I R E S S . A T O N E D .
A D O S . H E A L T H F O O D
N A T O . E R N I E . A N N A
G M A N . R A T E S . R O S Y
```

111 — Name Echoes

```
L A C K . D U D S . A R S O N
O R A N . A T E E . C A I N E
A C N E . M A C E . E Y D I E
F A Y E S P H A S E . S E N D
E R O D E . F A V O R S . . .
R O N . A X E . W A S A T C H
. . B L I M P . E I E I O . .
S A D E . V O U C H . S P A T
S H E A F . P R O B E . . . .
R I V U L E T . Y E A . C P R
. . I S A B E L . A C H O O .
B L A B . B E T T E S B E T S
A U T O S . T G I F . S R T A
S T E W S . H O L T . T I E R
H E S S E . E V E S . V E R Y
```

112 — Much Ado

```
E G A D S . B O A S . T R A P
A L L E N . A X L E . Y U L E
R U M B L E S E A T . C M O N
P E S O . Y E N . R E O P E N
. . N E E D . F A M O U S . .
D E F E N D . S A T I N S . .
E L U D E . O L D E R . R I B
A M S . F E E . . . . O N E .
N O S . A C T E D . E M O T E
. . B A L L E T . C L A M O R
. S U L T A N . T H I S . . .
A U D I O S . P E A . C A S T
W A G E . S C R A P P A P E R
O V E N . E R A S . A R E N A
L E T S . S O M E . D A D D Y
```

113 — Hot and Bothered

```
B L A N C   R U B E   Z E A L
O I L E R   E V E L   I A G O
I M A G E   S E E I N G R E D
L A S S O   H A S T A   N E E
      S A O     I S L
B E N T O U T O F S H A P E
E X E R T S   W I T   R O N S
R U P E E   D I E   F A T T Y
G R A M   F I N   A R M O R S
  B L O W I N G A G A S K E T
    R E X     C O G
E L M   R E S A T   R E H A B
T I C K E D O F F   A R U B A
T E A M   U N T O   N I N E R
A N N S   P E A R   T E S T S
```

114 — Ups and Downs

```
O R S O   S C A N   M A C H O
K I E V   T A T A   O G L E D
A C N E   A B O V E B O A R D
P E T R E L   M A X I   D O S
I R A T E L Y   L U L U
      H O S E S   R E N T A L
A Z T E C   S T U B   D A R E
R I C H   P E E P S   E L M S
A M B I   U S E S   C R E S T
B A Y L O R   D E B U G
      L U G S   T E R R A C E
E W E   T E E S   A T O L L S
B E L O W D E C K S   U F O S
B L I N I   R O O T   N I N E
S L E E T   S T A S   D E E S
```

115 — Beastly Behavior

```
S P U R T   T A P S   S L O T
A L G E R   I D E A   H A V E
W O L F E D D O W N   E V E N
S P Y   L O I S   E R R A N T
      S L O E   S N I P
  S Q U I R R E L E D A W A Y
F A U N S   M U S S   O H O
O N E S   D R E G S   S K E W
A T E   B R Y N   S T E A L
M O N K E Y E D A R O U N D
    A N D S   N U M B
B O N I T O   I S L E   E T A
E G O S   C R O W E D O V E R
E L S E   K I T E   A V E R T
S E E R   S P A R   Y A R N S
```

116 — Tourist Attractions

```
L E A V E   S A L E M   D A B
A U D I T   C O A T I   E R A
G R A N D C A N Y O N   N E T
S O M E   A M E S   O P I N E
      G A S P   L L A M A S
A T L A N T I C C I T Y
C O U R T   A S S A S S I N
I D A   A L L A T   I D O
D O U B T F U L   A L L O T
      N I A G A R A F A L L S
L A M A R R   A C T S
A T R I A   R O V E   T O B E
C O M   D I S N E Y W O R L D
E N O   E L T O N   I N G O D
D E M   S L U R S   Z E S T Y
```

117 — They're Educational

```
R U M O R   F L A W   A F A R
A S I D E   L A M A   G O B I
S E C O N D A R Y S C H O O L
P R A M   R I D S   H A L V E
      E V E R   H I S S E D
W A S T E D   B L O A T
A L T E R   M O A B   E O N
F O U R Y E A R C O L L E G E
T E N   D I N E   Y E L L S
      S T A L E   E R A S E S
A N T H E M   O P E N
H A I R S   T E R I   E V E S
M I L I T A R Y A C A D E M Y
E V E N   F E E L   L O G I N
D E S K   T E D S   S N A R E
```

118 — Out In Front

```
C A B S   M A A M   S L O P E
O B O E   O R L Y   T E N O R
B L U E G R A S S   R A T S O
B E T   R O B O T   A S H E S
    K I S S   E L I T E
R E B A T E   B R I T   F A B
O M E N S   C R I E S   E R E
W I D E   B O O E D   K N I T
E L O   H A N K S   F A C E S
R E F   O N C E   B A R E L Y
    R A N G E   M A U L
S T O V E   A D O R N   G I S
C A S E S   L A U R A B U S H
A L E R T   E L S E   A R L O
T E S T Y   D E E D   D U E T
```

119 Location, Location

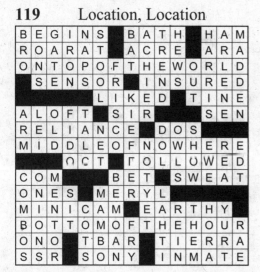

```
B E G I N S ■ B A T H ■ H A M
R O A R A T ■ A C R E ■ A R A
O N T O P O F T H E W O R L D
■ S E N S O R ■ I N S U R E D
■ ■ ■ L I K E D ■ T I N E ■ ■
A L O F T ■ S I R ■ ■ S E N
R E L I A N C E ■ D O S ■ ■
M I D D L E O F N O W H E R E
■ ■ O C T ■ F O L L O W E D
C O M ■ ■ B E T ■ S W E A T
O N E S ■ M E R Y L ■ ■ ■
M I N I C A M ■ E A R T H Y
B O T T O M O F T H E H O U R
O N O ■ T B A R ■ T I E R R A
S S R ■ S O N Y ■ I N M A T E
```

120 Drink Up

```
L O O P ■ A R A B ■ T A L O N
E M M A ■ R O P E ■ A N O D E
T E A G A R D E N ■ S T R E W
I N H E R E ■ D U S T I E S T
N S A ■ E S P ■ M O E ■ ■ ■
■ ■ W A T E R B U F F A L O
M A C H ■ S T A ■ L U L L E D
A L O A F ■ E D U ■ L O V E D
S T I R I N ■ A S P ■ P A R S
C O F F E E B R E A K S ■ ■
■ ■ ■ R E L ■ S S E ■ G A R
S H E R I D A N ■ S P R I T E
A E R I E ■ M I L K T O A S T
G R A S S ■ E L I E ■ O N E R
A S S E T ■ D E N Y ■ S T A Y
```

121 Let's Go Bowling

```
P A L L ■ M O P E S ■ C A R R
E L I A ■ A D O B E ■ O L E O
P E A C H M E L B A ■ T A D A
S C R E A M ■ S T A T I O N
■ ■ S T A N D ■ E G O ■ ■ ■
M A T ■ E L E E ■ D A N C E R
E V E R ■ S E T H ■ I G A V E
S E N O R ■ D R E ■ N I K E S
A R O S E ■ Y A L L ■ N E R O
S T R E S S ■ C L A M ■ S Y D
■ ■ M I A ■ T O M E I ■ ■
C L E A N S E ■ ■ P A R D O N
H E A R ■ S U G A R D A D D Y
A N T I ■ E R O D E ■ T A O S
P O S E ■ D O P E Y ■ E Y R E
```

122 Hitting the Highway

```
G A M ■ B E S T ■ M A N T A S
L I E ■ O M A R ■ P U E R T O
E S T ■ L U L U ■ S L A Y E R
A L O U D ■ V C R ■ A T O N E
N E O N ■ K O K O ■ I O U ■ ■
■ ■ T H I S E X I T ■ R A M
T H E I S M ■ R I N ■ U P U P
R O A D H O U S E D I N I N G
I T T Y ■ N N W ■ I N S E T S
B S A ■ H O M E M A D E ■ ■
■ ■ T H O ■ A L A N ■ R Y E S
S A J A K ■ N C R ■ P S A L M
C O O L I O ■ O T T O ■ R I O
U N E V E N ■ M E E T ■ D O G
D E S E R T ■ E N D S ■ S T S
```

123 Temperature's Rising

```
H I Y O ■ S P O T S ■ P E A S
I H A D ■ K A S H A ■ A R I E
C O L D F I S H E S ■ R I D E
S P E E D B O A T ■ T A K E N
■ ■ ■ R I O ■ A B E L ■ ■ ■
K I M ■ C O O L B R E E Z E S
A V I S ■ T W A ■ A U G U S T
P A S H A ■ E S P ■ P A N S Y
O N E A C T ■ E E L ■ L I E N
W A R M H E A R T E D ■ S S E
■ ■ ■ P E N N ■ ■ T R A ■ ■
A D I O S ■ G U A R A N T E E
D O D O ■ H O T D I G G I T Y
I S L E ■ D R E D D ■ E R N E
N E E D ■ L A P S E ■ R E A D
```

124 Dimension Intentions

```
B O L L ■ A W E D ■ S I T E S
A R E A ■ D I R E ■ U N A R M
W E A R ■ O L G A ■ S L I M E
L O N G A R M O F T H E L A W
■ ■ ■ E T N A ■ ■ H I T ■ ■
R O O S T S ■ C A R ■ S P A S
E R A S E ■ M A N E T ■ E R A
M A K E S H O R T W O R K O F
A T E ■ T O N E S ■ R A I S E
P E N S ■ N O D ■ S E I N E S
■ ■ ■ H E D ■ ■ P U R L ■ ■
T H A T S A T A L L O R D E R
O A S I S ■ A B E T ■ O R C A
S L I C E ■ P E A R ■ A N O N
S O A K S ■ E D D Y ■ D O N T
```

125 Pets In the Movies

A	M	E	N	■	B	I	G	D	■	A	I	M	E	D
R	A	V	E	■	A	B	L	E	■	D	R	A	M	A
A	L	E	E	■	R	E	O	S	■	H	E	M	A	N
B	I	R	D	O	N	A	W	I	R	E	■	B	I	T
■	■	■	H	U	M	■	■	O	R	I	O	L	E	■
R	E	S	E	A	M	■	S	L	Y	E	R	■	■	■
O	N	A	I	R	■	W	A	A	C	■	A	L	D	O
D	O	G	D	A	Y	A	F	T	E	R	N	O	O	N
E	S	S	E	■	E	L	E	E	■	H	I	T	M	E
■	■	R	U	N	T	S	■	Z	E	S	T	E	R	■
D	O	E	S	N	T	■	■	S	O	U	■	■	■	■
O	P	A	■	C	A	T	A	N	D	M	O	U	S	E
J	E	T	T	A	■	E	S	A	I	■	A	G	E	D
O	R	I	N	G	■	S	A	R	A	■	F	L	A	G
S	A	N	T	E	■	S	P	E	C	■	S	I	N	E

126 Eat Your Veggies

M	A	C	H	E	■	O	P	E	N	■	G	A	S	P
A	S	H	E	N	■	N	E	R	O	■	E	C	H	O
S	T	E	A	D	■	C	A	R	R	O	T	T	O	P
C	O	R	R	O	D	E	S	■	■	B	U	S	E	S
■	■	■	T	R	A	■	■	Q	T	I	P	■	■	■
S	Q	U	A	S	H	C	O	U	R	T	■	S	H	E
O	U	N	C	E	■	A	F	E	E	■	T	H	E	N
B	E	T	H	■	L	E	T	B	E	■	R	O	A	D
E	R	I	E	■	I	S	E	E	■	C	A	R	V	E
R	Y	E	■	B	E	A	N	C	O	U	N	T	E	R
■	■	■	H	O	U	R	■	■	D	R	S	■	■	■
C	O	L	O	R	■	■	O	N	E	L	L	A	M	A
O	N	I	O	N	D	O	M	E	■	S	A	B	I	N
S	T	O	P	■	J	I	N	X	■	U	T	U	R	N
T	O	N	S	■	S	L	I	T	■	P	E	T	E	S

127 Acting Presidential

A	B	B	A	■	M	E	N	U	S	■	O	V	E	R
M	O	O	R	■	A	R	E	N	T	■	S	A	K	E
P	O	L	K	A	D	O	T	D	R	E	S	S	E	S
S	T	D	■	T	A	D	■	E	E	L	I	E	S	T
■	■	■	P	O	M	E	■	R	A	K	E	■	■	■
T	A	K	E	M	E	■	T	S	K	S	■	D	E	M
A	D	L	A	I	■	A	W	E	E	■	H	O	P	E
P	I	E	R	C	E	D	E	A	R	L	O	B	E	S
E	M	I	L	■	E	V	E	S	■	C	R	I	E	S
D	E	N	■	G	R	I	D	■	C	H	E	E	S	Y
■	■	■	U	R	I	S	■	A	R	A	B	■	■	■
A	I	R	L	I	N	E	■	L	E	I	■	B	A	N
G	R	A	N	T	E	D	C	L	E	M	E	N	C	Y
R	I	C	A	■	S	L	O	O	P	■	D	A	R	E
A	S	K	S	■	S	Y	S	T	S	■	D	I	E	T

128 Put That Down!

O	A	T	S	■	S	E	M	I	■	M	A	N	T	A
P	L	O	P	■	T	A	O	S	■	I	D	E	A	L
A	L	K	A	■	A	R	T	E	■	D	O	L	M	A
L	A	Y	S	O	N	T	H	E	T	A	B	L	E	■
S	T	O	M	A	C	H	S	■	H	I	E	■	■	■
■	■	■	K	E	Y	■	S	I	R	■	R	A	E	■
S	T	E	V	E	■	■	S	H	E	■	H	A	I	L
L	A	Y	I	N	G	O	N	O	F	H	A	N	D	S
E	D	E	N	■	R	I	O	■	E	S	T	E	E	■
D	A	D	■	P	A	L	■	S	P	A	■	■	■	■
■	■	■	M	E	N	■	S	E	A	T	B	E	L	T
■	L	A	I	D	D	O	W	N	T	H	E	L	A	W
D	E	L	L	A	■	P	E	T	E	■	G	I	V	E
E	A	S	E	L	■	E	A	R	N	■	A	T	E	E
C	R	O	S	S	■	D	R	A	T	■	N	E	R	D

129 Precinct Personalities

A	S	P	E	N	■	G	A	S	P	■	D	A	N	G
S	P	I	N	E	■	A	S	E	A	■	E	C	O	N
F	U	Z	Z	B	U	S	T	E	R	■	A	T	T	A
O	R	Z	O	■	S	U	E	■	A	R	I	A	S	■
R	N	A	■	C	O	P	P	E	R	S	M	I	T	H
■	■	■	P	R	O	S	■	L	O	S	E	■	■	■
S	P	I	E	L	■	N	E	A	T	■	M	I	O	■
T	H	E	M	A	N	I	N	T	H	E	M	O	O	N
A	D	S	■	O	G	L	E	■	B	O	O	N	E	■
■	■	■	B	A	T	H	■	P	A	W	N	■	■	■
T	H	E	H	E	A	T	I	S	O	N	■	R	K	O
R	E	B	U	S	■	N	A	N	■	H	O	U	R	■
I	N	S	T	■	B	O	B	B	Y	S	O	C	K	S
A	R	E	A	■	A	R	O	O	■	A	N	K	L	E
L	Y	N	N	■	N	E	X	T	■	C	E	S	A	R

130 What Sentries Say

P	A	D	R	E	■	C	B	S	■	N	A	V	E	L
O	H	A	I	R	■	A	A	H	■	O	C	A	L	A
L	A	Y	D	O	W	N	Y	O	U	R	A	R	M	S
E	T	S	■	S	I	T	S	O	N	■	N	Y	S	E
■	■	■	L	I	M	O	■	C	E	O	■	■	■	■
■	S	T	O	P	O	R	I	L	L	F	I	R	E	■
S	T	E	R	N	■	U	K	E	S	■	N	I	A	■
P	O	D	S	■	L	A	N	E	S	■	L	I	P	S
E	R	A	■	T	A	C	O	■	D	E	N	S	E	■
D	O	N	T	E	V	E	N	B	L	I	N	K	■	■
■	■	■	H	A	I	■	R	E	N	T	■	■	■	■
L	A	K	E	■	S	L	E	E	V	E	■	D	I	M
S	T	A	Y	W	H	E	R	E	Y	O	U	A	R	E
T	E	R	R	A	■	A	I	D	■	U	N	T	I	L
S	E	L	E	S	■	D	E	S	■	T	O	A	S	T

131 — In the Bag

```
B U R N . P L O P . P R I O R
O H I O . R O V E . L A R G O
B U S D R I V E R . A D O R N
S H E . O V E R T . T I N E S
. . . H O E S . I N T O W . .
G O W E S T . K N E E . I T S
E B E R T . C L E A R . L O T
R E D O . P O I N T . A L T O
M S G . G A U N T . S N E A K
S E E . R A R E . C U D D L E
. . H E A R T . V A R Y . . .
B E E R S . S P I L L . F R O
A M E N S . H O L L Y W O O D
J U L I E . I S L E . A X L E
A S S E S . P E A R . D Y E S
```

132 — Three Squares

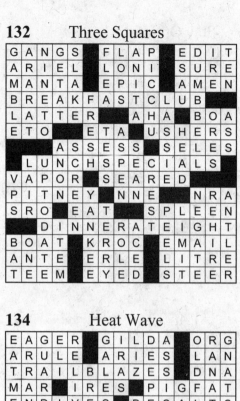

```
G A N G S . F L A P . E D I T
A R I E L . L O N I . S U R E
M A N T A . E P I C . A M E N
B R E A K F A S T C L U B . .
L A T T E R . A H A . B O A .
E T O . E T A . U S H E R S .
. . A S S E S S . S E L E S .
. L U N C H S P E C I A L S .
V A P O R . S E A R E D . . .
P I T N E Y . N N E . N R A .
S R O . E A T . S P L E E N .
. D I N N E R A T E I G H T .
B O A T . K R O C . E M A I L
A N T E . E R L E . L I T R E
T E E M . E Y E D . S T E E R
```

133 — Bouncing Along

```
H E L E N E . L B S . A G E S
A R O M A S . O U T . X R A Y
T I M E S T A B L E . E A R N
H E A R D . D O G P A D D L E
. . . Y A R D . E S S . . . .
A K C . Q U I P S . O S A G E
S I L T . N N E . K N I F E D
P L A Y I N G P I N G P O N G
C O U N T Y . U T E . S U R E
A S S E S . U P S E T . L E D
. . . M C S . E D I T . . . .
O N T H E B A L L . T I A R A
V A R Y . S U R F T H E N E T
E N I D . T S O . R E T I N A
N A M E . V A N . I D O N O T
```

134 — Heat Wave

```
E A G E R . G I L D A . O R G
A R U L E . A R I E S . L A N
T R A I L B L A Z E S . D N A
M A R . I R E S . P I G F A T
E N D I V E S . D E S A L T S
. . . S E W . C O N T R A . .
J E S T S . C O V E S . M E W
A L P S . L O P E D . H E R O
M O I . H O M E R . S U S A N
. . T R O V E S . B A G . . .
D E F A M E S . A R N O L D S
O B I W A N . B N A I . Y E A
N O R . G E O R G E B U R N S
O N E . E S P Y S . E M I T S
T D S . S T E N T . L A C E Y
```

135 — Rhymes With Strife

```
E L B A . S T R A W . M A R K
G E L S . S O U T H . E R I N
G A U L . T R E E O F L I F E
S N E E R . D E A L . E L L .
. . B E A R D . M U L L E T .
S T E P F O R D W I F E . . .
A O L . Y E A H . F O R G E .
I N L A Y . A L I . S N E R D
D I S C O . M A N E . S A G .
. . H U N T I N G K N I F E .
L I K E S O . Y O G I S . . .
A T O . E T A L . B E T A S .
B A R N E Y F I F E . C A N E
O L E O . E R E C T . E N Y A
R Y A N . T O S C A . S T A R
```

136 — They're Edible

```
C A F E . C L A I R E . C B S
A L A N . R O U T E S . U R L
P I N C H O F S A L T . P A O
. . . O C A T . A U M O N T .
S I G N O U T . S T A F F . .
I N L E T S . P I E R A C K S
M A A M S . M A R R Y . O O H
O S S O . C A N E S . A F A R
N E S . B O X I N . R I F L E
E C O N O M I C . R E R E A D
. . F A R M S . P O S S E S S
H U M V E E . S H O E . . . .
A S I . D R O P O F W A T E R
D E L . O C T A N E . L A T E
A R K . M E S S E D . A J A X
```

137 Stay Optimistic

S	I	L	O		R	A	J	A	H		C	R	A	M
U	R	A	L		E	L	U	D	E		O	I	L	Y
M	A	K	E	T	H	E	M	O	S	T	O	F	I	T
O	N	E		H	A	R	P			A	L	L	A	H
		D	U	S	T		G	U	N	L	E	S	S	
I	M	P	I	S	H		H	U	S	K	Y			
N	E	I	L		M	O	R	S	E		S	P	A	
F	O	L	L	O	W	Y	O	U	R	D	R	E	A	M
O	W	E		V	I	N	E	S			U	N	T	O
	D	E	L	A	Y		S	M	I	T	H	S		
A	S	S	E	R	T	S		T	H	A	N			
S	H	I	E	D		S	H	A	G		O	R	E	
K	E	E	P	O	N	K	E	E	P	I	N	G	O	N
E	A	V	E		E	E	R	I	E		T	R	O	D
W	R	E	N		D	Y	E	R	S		H	E	M	S

138 What You Pay For?

P	A	S	S	E		H	O	R	S		E	G	G	S
I	C	E	A	X		A	L	E	C		M	E	R	E
G	E	T	U	P	A	N	D	G	O		I	T	A	R
		C	A	R	S		R	U	N	L	A	T	E	
R	E	G	E	N	T		V	E	R	A		W	I	N
O	V	E	R	D	I	D	I	T		D	I	A	N	E
M	E	T		C	I	A		R	E	L	Y			
P	R	O	F	I	L	E		C	A	R	A	W	A	Y
		N	I	N	E		P	O	D		I	G	A	
D	E	E	R	E		T	A	X	I	M	E	T	E	R
E	M	S		P	R	E	Y		C	A	S	H	E	D
F	I	G	H	T	E	R		C	A	P	P			
E	L	O	I		G	E	T	A	L	O	A	D	O	F
N	I	A	S		A	S	I	F		U	N	I	T	E
D	O	T	S		L	A	C	E		T	A	S	T	E

139 All-Inclusive

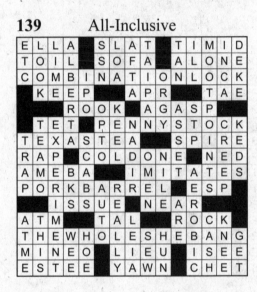

E	L	L	A		S	L	A	T		T	I	M	I	D
T	O	I	L		S	O	F	A		A	L	O	N	E
C	O	M	B	I	N	A	T	I	O	N	L	O	C	K
	K	E	E	P		A	P	R		T	A	E		
		R	O	O	K		A	G	A	S	P			
	T	E	T		P	E	N	N	Y	S	T	O	C	K
T	E	X	A	S	T	E	A		S	P	I	R	E	
R	A	P		C	O	L	D	O	N	E		N	E	D
A	M	E	B	A		I	M	I	T	A	T	E	S	
P	O	R	K	B	A	R	R	E	L		E	S	P	
		I	S	S	U	E		N	E	A	R			
A	T	M		T	A	L		R	O	C	K			
T	H	E	W	H	O	L	E	S	H	E	B	A	N	G
M	I	N	E	O		L	I	E	U		I	S	E	E
E	S	T	E	E		Y	A	W	N		C	H	E	T

140 Behind the Door

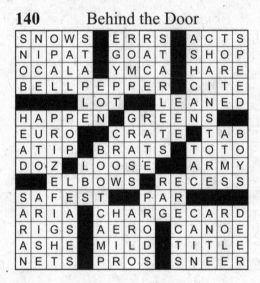

S	N	O	W	S		E	R	R	S		A	C	T	S
N	I	P	A	T		G	O	A	T		S	H	O	P
O	C	A	L	A		Y	M	C	A		H	A	R	E
B	E	L	L	P	E	P	P	E	R		C	I	T	E
			L	O	T			L	E	A	N	E	D	
H	A	P	P	E	N		G	R	E	E	N	S		
E	U	R	O		C	R	A	T	E		T	A	B	
A	T	I	P		B	R	A	T	S		T	O	T	O
D	O	Z		L	O	O	S	E		A	R	M	Y	
	E	L	B	O	W	S		R	E	C	E	S	S	
S	A	F	E	S	T		P	A	R					
A	R	I	A		C	H	A	R	G	E	C	A	R	D
R	I	G	S		A	E	R	O		C	A	N	O	E
A	S	H	E		M	I	L	D		T	I	T	L	E
N	E	T	S		P	R	O	S		S	N	E	E	R

141 It's Obvious

C	R	U	S	H		A	M	B	E	R		S	P	A
R	E	P	O	S		L	O	O	S	E		C	O	N
E	A	S	Y	T	O	G	R	A	S	P		R	U	T
P	R	E	S		R	A	N	T		A	B	A	T	E
E	S	T	A	T	E		S	C	A	M				
		U	N	M	I	S	T	A	K	A	B	L	E	
E	J	E	C	T		C	Y	R	U	S		L	A	X
L	A	N	E		W	I	R	E	D		B	E	L	A
B	R	A		S	H	E	I	K		S	O	D	O	M
A	S	C	L	E	A	R	A	S	D	A	Y			
	T	E	A	M			A	M	I	G	A	S		
C	A	M	E	L		G	A	R	R		S	U	R	A
A	X	E		E	Y	E	C	A	T	C	H	I	N	G
R	E	N		R	E	A	R	M		A	L	L	I	E
B	L	T		S	T	R	E	P		B	Y	T	E	S

142 It's a Guy Thing

S	L	I	D		C	A	R	O	M		P	R	I	G
W	I	R	E		O	N	E	N	O		I	O	N	S
A	R	A	B		R	O	S	I	N		A	N	K	A
M	A	N	A	B	O	U	T	T	O	W	N			
		T	A	N	K			L	A	I	R	D	S	
G	R	I	E	S	E		G	L	O	S	S	A	R	Y
R	I	D		S	T	R	A	I	G	H	T	M	A	N
A	D	I	M		E	P	A			S	A	G	O	
M	E	D	I	C	I	N	E	M	A	N		D	O	D
P	R	I	S	O	N	E	R		S	E	D	A	N	S
A	S	T	H	M	A			E	S	S	O			
	M	A	N	O	F	L	E	T	T	E	R	S		
N	C	A	A		E	L	L	E	N		T	R	I	P
F	O	R	S		L	E	A	N	T		E	L	S	E
L	O	C	H		Y	O	G	A	S		D	E	E	D

143 It's a Gal Thing

B	L	O	B		S	H	I	F	T		S	P	A	T
I	A	G	O		H	A	N	O	I		L	O	B	E
F	L	O	W	E	R	G	I	R	L		O	M	E	N
F	A	D	E	S	O	U	T		T	A	P	P	E	D
			S	U	E			N	E	O				
E	N	V	I	E	D		M	R	A	N	D	M	R	S
L	O	A	N	S		D	I	A	N	E		G	E	E
M	I	L	K		A	O	R	T	A		W	I	N	E
E	3	L		A	G	N	E	S		C	A	R	E	D
R	E	E	D	I	T	E	D		B	A	R	L	E	Y
		Y	E	N				S	A	G				
R	O	G	E	T	S		T	A	K	E	A	N	A	P
A	R	I	D		C	H	O	R	U	S	G	I	R	L
G	E	R	E		A	U	R	A	L		I	N	C	A
S	O	L	D		M	E	N	S	A		N	O	S	Y

144 Looking/Sounding Good

S	T	A		L	I	L	T	S		A	S	T	R	O
P	O	P		I	D	A	H	O		B	A	H	A	I
I	M	P		B	O	S	O	M		I	N	R	E	D
C	E	L	L	I	S	T	S	M	O	T	T	O		
Y	I	E	L	D		S	E	E	R		A	W	O	L
		B	O	A			R	E	S		A	H	I	
B	A	B	E		A	I	P	S		I	T	W	A	S
I	D	R	A	T	H	E	R	B	E	S	H	A	R	P
O	V	I	N	E		T	O	Y	S		R	Y	E	S
T	I	M		A	B	S		C	O	O				
A	L	S	O		I	L	L	S		N	A	D	E	R
		T	H	A	N	O	U	T	O	F	T	U	N	E
B	U	O	Y	S		O	M	A	N	I		E	D	S
A	N	N	E	S		S	P	I	E	L		T	I	E
G	O	E	S	T		E	Y	D	I	E		O	T	T

145 Cynical Observation

S	A	G	E		S	Y	R	I	A		R	A	I	N
T	R	O	Y		P	O	U	R	S		E	T	T	E
A	I	D	E		R	U	N	A	T		V	E	S	T
F	E	W	T	H	I	N	G	S	A	R	E			
F	L	E	E	I	N	G				I	R	I	S	H
			S	S	T		H	A	R	D	E	R	T	O
S	C	A	T	S		D	O	G	I	E		W	I	N
H	U	B	S		P	U	T	U	P		T	I	N	E
A	R	C		S	A	M	O	A		D	E	N	T	S
W	I	T	H	T	H	A	N		S	A	N			
L	O	V	E	A			G	E	N	E	S	E	S	
		A	G	O	O	D	E	X	A	M	P	L	E	
C	A	R	R		F	R	O	N	T		E	R	I	E
U	N	I	T		F	A	V	R	E		N	E	A	R
E	T	C	H		S	L	E	E	T		T	E	S	S

146 Go Fish

D	U	E	T		H	E	R	B		D	R	A	P	E
O	R	L	Y		A	R	I	A		R	E	W	I	N
G	I	L	L	I	G	A	N	S	I	S	L	A	N	D
I	C	I	E	R		S	K	I	D		E	Y	E	S
T	H	E	N	E	T		C	O	M	A				
			O	N	E	L	S		B	R	E	A	D	
S	C	A	L	E	N	E	T	R	I	A	N	G	L	E
O	A	R		T	H	A	I	S			G	P	A	
F	I	N	I	S	H	I	N	G	S	C	H	O	O	L
A	N	O	D	E		K	A	U	A	I				
		Y	E	A	R			E	R	R	A	N	T	
S	E	L	L		I	O	W	A		E	S	S	I	E
T	A	I	L	O	R	M	A	D	E	S	U	I	T	S
O	V	O	I	D		P	L	A	N		T	A	R	T
P	E	N	C	E		S	K	Y	S		E	N	O	S

147 Homophone Trio

A	R	A	B		S	W	A	Y		S	L	E	P	T
N	O	V	A		N	A	S	A		T	A	R	R	Y
N	O	E	L		E	Y	E	R		E	D	G	E	R
A	F	R	I	C	A	N	A	N	T	E	L	O	P	E
			I	K	E			O	D	E				
M	E	L	O	D	Y		L	A	W	S		S	A	W
A	W	A	R	E		T	O	M	E		A	T	R	A
N	E	V	E	R	B	E	F	O	R	E	S	E	E	N
I	R	E	S		L	E	T	S		A	H	I	N	T
A	S	S		S	O	N	S		A	G	E	N	T	S
			A	T	O		D	R	E					
W	A	S	F	A	M	I	L	I	A	R	W	I	T	H
A	L	T	A	R		C	A	L	F		A	S	I	A
S	T	A	T	E		O	K	L	A		K	I	N	D
H	O	N	E	D		N	E	S	T		E	N	Y	A

148 Have a Bellyful

S	A	R	A	H		S	H	A	H		S	E	A	T
A	R	E	N	A		C	O	D	A		A	T	M	E
M	I	D	D	L	E	A	G	E	I	S	W	H	E	N
E	A	S	Y		D	R	S		L	A	T	E	N	T
				P	I	E		H	A	R	O	L	D	S
M	A	S	C	O	T		K	I	C	K				
A	B	H	O	R		H	E	S	A		A	T	A	D
Y	O	U	R	K	N	E	E	S	B	U	C	K	L	E
S	O	L	D		O	R	L	Y		S	T	O	O	P
			O	N	E	S		M	E	S	S	U	P	
A	S	S	E	R	T	S		T	E	D				
B	A	I	L	E	R		A	H	A		S	P	A	S
B	U	T	Y	O	U	R	B	E	L	T	W	O	N	T
A	D	O	S		T	O	E	S		Y	A	N	N	I
S	I	N	E		H	O	L	E		S	P	E	A	R

149 — Be Verrry, Verrry Quiet!

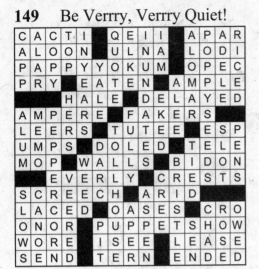

```
C A C T I   Q E I I   A P A R
A L O O N   U L N A   L O D I
P A P P Y Y O K U M   O P E C
P R Y   E A T E N   A M P L E
    H A L E   D E L A Y E D
A M P E R E   F A K E R S
L E E R S   T U T E E   E S P
U M P S   D O L E D   T E L E
M O P   W A L L S   B I D O N
    E V E R L Y   C R E S T S
S C R E E C H   A R I D
L A C E D   O A S E S   C R O
O N O R   P U P P E T S H O W
W O R E   I S E E   L E A S E
S E N D   T E R N   E N D E D
```

150 — Unthemed

```
A L J O L S O N   P L O W E D
T E A L E O N I   A E R A T E
T A I L G A T E   G A R N E T
E S A I   P A C K E D   N R A
N I L E S   P E E R   M A N I
D N A   O B E S E   C A B A L
  G I J O E   L I O N E L S
    A N N S   S T A G
C L O S E T O   B R O O K
L A B O R   B A B E S   N E D
O V E N   M A D E   E D G E R
B E L   M O D U L E   C O P Y
B R I D A L   L O V E L I E R
E N S U R E   T I E S I N T O
R E K E Y S   S T R A I G H T
```

151 — Words of Encouragement

```
F I B S   B L A D E S   Z O O
A R I A   A E S O P S   E R G
N O T H I N G T O I T   V A L
S N E A D   G I R L   R O T E
    R E F S   O P E N E D
E S P A N A   O L G A S
T I A   T N O T E   R A G A
S T R A I G H T F O R W A R D
  E R I C   M E T R O   T O E
    D A R E R   A T H E N S
A N G E L A   P L I E
B A R D   V A N E   N E A R S
I S A   D I V E R I G H T I N
D A D   O N E T O N   A I D A
E L S   C E S S N A   W E E P
```

152 — Letter Perfect

```
W E L K   F E L L A   B R O W
O V E N   A F O U L   E E R O
W E G O   D R A N O   N E A R
  A B C D E F G H I J K L M
D S L   A I M   A R I
O C E A N S   D E S I   K G B
R E A R   T R E E   S P I R E
E N G L I S H A L P H A B E T
M E L O N   E L S A   A B E T
I S E   F R A T   S P R U C E
    S E E   A S A   T E R
N O P Q R S T U V W X Y Z
A L O U   C A S I O   O N C E
S E G A   U L N A R   Y I P E
H O O T   E L A N D   O K O K
```

153 — A Simple Ditty

```
A D A M   M A L T   D R A N O
D I V A   A L O E   R E R A N
I N O N   G L E E   S P A R E
N O W I K N O W M Y   A B C S
    F E E T   A M Í
P O T E N T   E D H A R R I S
A D E S   S W O O N   A M P
N E X T T I M E W O N T Y O U
E T A   A D O R N   H O U R
L O N G L E G S   F A I N T S
    A L A   B A R R
A T O Z   S I N G W I T H M E
A R I E L   F O I L   E A R L
R U N B Y   S O R T   E L E M
P E K O E   O N L Y   N O D S
```

154 — Timberland

```
C H E W   P A T T I   J U T E
A O N E   A A R O N   U S A F
T O O T H B R U S H   N E L L
O P S   A S P   S A N G R I A
    F I T   R E B E L S A T
G A B O R   D E S I R E
I B A R   I O N   T O F F E E
L I M E A D E   R E S E R V E
A G A S S I   B A D   V E A L
  T W O B I T   P E E N S
U N S H A M E D   E R R
L A T I N A S   M A O   G O O
C O A L   T I G E R W O O D S
E M I L   I D E A L   F A I L
R I D S   C E N T S   A T N O
```

155 Meow!

W	N	B	A	■	A	C	T	O	R	■	P	H	I	L
I	O	U	S	■	F	O	R	C	E	■	R	I	S	E
P	U	S	S	Y	F	O	O	T	S	■	E	R	L	E
E	N	S	N	A	R	E	D	■	E	A	S	T	E	R
■	■	■	W	A	R	■	M	A	T	T	■	■	■	■
T	A	M	E	L	Y	■	P	E	R	S	O	N	A	L
A	S	I	S	■	■	T	R	A	C	E	■	O	R	O
K	I	T	T	E	N	W	I	T	H	A	W	H	I	P
E	A	T	■	R	A	I	N	Y	■	■	A	I	D	E
I	N	S	T	R	U	C	T	■	R	E	S	T	E	D
■	■	■	R	O	T	E	■	G	E	M	■	■	■	■
S	A	F	A	R	I	■	S	O	C	I	A	B	L	E
A	V	I	D	■	■	C	A	T	B	U	R	G	L	A	R
R	O	V	E	■	A	L	I	A	R	■	R	I	C	O
A	W	E	D	■	L	A	R	D	S	■	A	P	E	S

156 D-Day

S	A	R	A	H	■	A	M	E	N	S	■	T	O	W
A	M	I	N	O	■	D	I	D	N	T	■	A	B	E
F	I	D	D	L	E	D	E	D	E	E	■	T	O	N
E	D	S	■	E	D	E	N	■	R	A	T	E	D	■
■	■	■	G	O	I	N	■	R	E	O	I	L	■	■
A	C	C	R	U	E	D	D	I	V	I	D	E	N	D
S	O	H	O	T	■	A	C	E	D	■	T	O	R	■
I	B	E	G	■	P	T	A	■	■	F	A	R	E	■
A	R	C	■	I	C	E	E	■	S	E	L	M	A	■
N	A	K	E	D	A	N	D	T	H	E	D	E	A	D
■	■	S	L	A	B	S	■	R	O	C	S	■	■	■
P	H	I	S	H	■	■	T	I	R	E	■	I	O	U
I	O	N	■	O	D	D	S	A	N	D	E	N	D	S
T	N	T	■	A	D	E	A	L	■	E	L	L	I	E
A	G	O	■	N	E	A	R	S	■	R	Y	A	N	S

157 Countdown

C	O	T	E	■	B	A	B	A	■	F	E	R	M	I
A	L	U	M	■	A	T	O	N	■	O	V	O	I	D
L	I	T	E	■	T	O	W	N	■	R	E	U	S	E
F	O	U	R	T	H	P	L	A	C	E	■	S	E	A
■	■	■	G	A	M	■	S	U	P	P	E	R	S	■
I	N	T	E	R	A	C	T	■	R	A	E	■	■	■
C	I	A	■	■	T	H	I	R	D	W	A	T	C	H
E	L	L	I	S	■	U	N	O	■	S	T	O	L	E
S	E	C	O	N	D	B	E	S	T	■	G	A	R	■
■	■	■	N	I	L	■	S	E	R	E	N	A	D	E
S	E	E	S	F	I	T	■	I	T	I	■	■	■	■
M	A	V	■	F	I	R	S	T	F	A	M	I	L	Y
A	T	A	L	L	■	E	L	A	L	■	B	R	A	E
R	E	D	Y	E	■	V	I	C	E	■	L	A	N	A
T	R	E	E	S	■	I	D	O	S	■	E	N	D	S

158 Yoo-hoo, Where Are You?

A	D	O	S	■	S	P	U	N	■	C	E	L	L	O
L	O	U	T	■	T	O	N	E	■	O	V	O	I	D
I	N	T	O	■	R	U	D	E	■	L	E	V	E	E
■	O	R	B	I	T	E	D	■	D	R	E	S	S	■
B	A	N	K	E	D	■	R	Y	E	S	■	■	■	■
A	M	A	■	D	E	N	T	■	A	N	G	O	R	A
H	O	L	D	■	R	A	H	■	T	A	N	N	E	R
A	R	I	E	L	■	P	E	P	■	P	A	T	T	I
M	A	M	M	A	L	■	C	A	R	■	T	H	I	S
A	L	B	I	N	O	■	O	N	E	S	■	E	R	E
■	■	■	T	U	T	U	■	G	A	F	F	E	S	■
E	A	G	L	E	■	E	N	T	I	T	L	E	■	■
C	H	A	I	R	■	A	T	O	M	■	O	N	U	S
H	E	M	E	N	■	S	E	R	E	■	A	C	R	E
O	M	E	N	S	■	E	R	I	N	■	T	E	N	T

159 It's Really Dark

B	A	L	S	A	■	S	T	I	E	S	■	S	R	O
O	L	E	O	S	■	C	R	O	F	T	■	T	A	R
B	L	A	C	K	B	E	A	U	T	Y	■	A	N	G
S	I	S	I	■	I	N	N	S	■	L	A	N	D	S
■	■	■	A	N	D	E	S	■	J	U	N	K	Y	■
S	T	O	L	E	■	■	B	E	S	T	■	■	■	■
O	A	R	■	C	A	S	T	E	S	■	I	M	A	M
B	L	A	C	K	F	O	R	E	S	T	C	A	K	E
S	E	L	L	■	A	M	U	S	E	R	■	G	A	T
■	■	■	E	T	T	E	■	A	M	I	S	S	■	■
■	F	L	A	R	E	■	M	A	G	M	A	■	■	■
H	A	I	T	I	■	N	A	N	A	■	I	A	T	E
A	M	A	■	B	L	A	C	K	B	A	L	L	E	D
H	E	R	■	E	A	S	E	L	■	R	E	T	R	Y
A	D	S	■	S	P	A	D	E	■	C	R	O	P	S

160 Get A Move On!

A	S	H	E	■	A	B	A	S	H	■	E	R	L	E
M	O	O	N	■	H	E	L	L	O	■	R	U	I	N
F	L	Y	S	W	A	T	T	E	R	■	A	S	T	I
M	I	L	N	E	■	H	O	E	S	■	S	H	E	D
■	D	E	A	R	■	S	P	E	D	U	P	■	■	■
■	■	■	R	E	A	P	■	S	E	R	A	P	E	■
R	O	D	E	■	L	E	A	S	■	B	E	R	E	T
A	L	A	■	T	E	A	S	E	T	S	■	T	L	C
P	E	S	T	O	■	S	P	A	R	■	M	Y	T	H
T	S	H	I	R	T	■	M	A	G	I	■	■	■	■
■	■	■	B	R	E	E	D	S	■	I	L	L	S	■
W	H	O	A	■	N	I	T	E	■	R	E	A	C	T
R	O	A	D	■	D	A	R	T	P	L	A	Y	E	R
I	N	R	E	■	E	N	O	T	E	■	G	E	N	E
T	E	D	S	■	R	E	M	E	T	■	E	R	T	E

161 — Big Winners

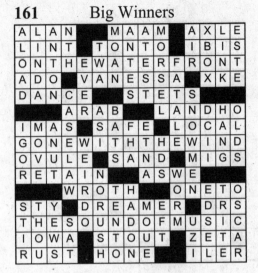

```
ALAN  .MAAM.AXLE
LINT  .TONTO.IBIS
ONTHEWATERFRONT
ADO.VANESSA.XKE
DANCE.STETS.
.ARAB.LANDHO
IMAS.SAFE.LOCAL
GONEWITHTHEWIND
OVULE.SAND.MIGS
RETAIN.ASWE.
.WROTH.ONETO
STY.DREAMER.DRS
THESOUNDOFMUSIC
IOWA.STOUT.ZETA
RUST.HONE.ILER
```

162 — Punctuated

```
CASH.ALEC.NOELS
AREA.RELO.ORDIE
TIAS.COMMANDEER
SALA.ASSETS.NUB
.GAD.ARTISTS
COLONIZATION.
ALE.TAIL.APACHE
SEAN.PAR.TAUT
ESHARP.MEMO.NBA
.PERIODONTIST
CATALAN.DOO.
OPA.ADVICE.MALE
DASHBOARDS.ALAS
ARTIE.DOIT.TENS
STEEL.ENVY.OREO
```

163 — Making Your Mark

```
CASKS.DEMO.SCOW
APAIL.IVAN.PEAR
BOTTOMLINE.ANKA
SPEC.ALLI.ARTSY
.HIPS.CARTE.
SABERS.BUSFARES
ALANS.CORKS.LAP
RATS.SELES.CITE
AMT.SEATS.SINEW
HOLINESS.SIRENS
.ERASE.TALC.
JULEP.FOAM.USED
ONIN.FINISHLINE
TINE.ORAL.AARON
STES.PENS.DRESS
```

164 — Snookums

```
TENT.PIPER.GIST
UTAH.ATONE.ROTE
BABYGRANDPIANOS
ELS.ALLY.STINT
.PRAY.MALICE.
ENMITY.PINES.
SOUSE.MALT.TOE
SUGARRAYLEONARD
ONS.INNS.NOFEE
.ALFIE.DENTON
.ERRATA.AIDE.
SNERD.SNAG.BYE
HONEYMOONPERIOD
ALAS.OLLIE.OKRA
HALT.ODDER.DEEM
```

165 — Fore and Aft

```
PAIR.FREON.SHES
ELSE.RATIO.TAUT
WALLTOWALL.INRE
SNEERS.STARDOM
.AETNA.EDIT.
SUDSY.AMP.ENOLA
ALOE.EMERIL.HAM
UNO.TSARINA.ANI
TAR.RETINA.SNAG
ESTEE.HGT.MEDIA
.OXEN.OSLIN.
MADISON.ARTIST
ECOL.FACETOFACE
SHOE.ALONE.OMAR
HERS.TAPER.RANI
```

166 — What to Wear

```
SARA.AGASSI.LEA
AMER.BEATUP.EGG
FORMALDRESS.BOO
IRAISE.FIONA.
RACES.SAFE.INCA
ELKS.SEMI.ONEPM
.CPAS.CATSUP
CASUALCLOTHES.
CHENEY.RAPS.
AURAS.CAGE.FACT
AMOR.TOYS.VICES
.BLAHS.BEETLE
FRI.LEISURESUIT
ABC.ATEASE.TANS
XIS.NARROW.ALEE
```

167 Quite Suitable

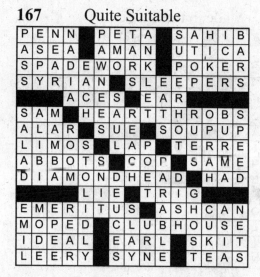

P	E	N	N		P	E	T	A		S	A	H	I	B
A	S	E	A		A	M	A	N		U	T	I	C	A
S	P	A	D	E	W	O	R	K		P	O	K	E	R
S	Y	R	I	A	N		S	L	E	E	P	E	R	S
			A	C	E	S		E	A	R				
S	A	M		H	E	A	R	T	T	H	R	O	B	S
A	L	A	R		S	U	E		S	O	U	P	U	P
L	I	M	O	S		L	A	P		T	E	R	R	E
A	B	B	O	T	S		C	O	D		S	A	M	E
D	I	A	M	O	N	D	H	E	A	D		H	A	D
			L	I	E		T	R	I	G				
E	M	E	R	I	T	U	S		A	S	H	C	A	N
M	O	P	E	D		C	L	U	B	H	O	U	S	E
I	D	E	A	L		E	A	R	L		S	K	I	T
L	E	E	R	Y		S	Y	N	E		T	E	A	S

168 Choices

E	M	T	S		C	H	I	P		W	A	R	N	S
T	A	R	A		L	O	G	E		A	D	A	Y	S
A	U	E	L		O	B	O	E		R	A	V	E	S
L	I	K	E	I	T	O	R	L	U	M	P	I	T	
				A	H	S		N	U	T				
A	S	H	A	M	E		S	L	I	P		A	S	P
C	L	I	M	B		F	O	O	T		O	C	L	E
T	A	K	E	I	T	O	R	L	E	A	V	E	I	T
O	V	E	N		E	A	R	L		L	A	N	C	E
R	E	D		O	N	L	Y		F	A	L	T	E	R
				A	D	S		S	A	M				
	B	E	L	I	E	V	E	I	T	O	R	N	O	T
M	A	R	I	O		A	U	N	T		E	A	V	E
A	D	I	E	U		T	R	E	E		A	P	E	X
T	E	E	N	S		S	O	W	N		P	E	R	T

169 Body Weather

E	L	A	T	E		P	L	A	T	E		D	A	B
L	E	M	O	N		R	A	N	O	N		R	B	I
F	A	I	R	S	K	I	N	N	E	D		Y	A	K
			N	I	C	E		L	A	T	T	E		
R	E	C	R	A	T	E		T	E	E	T	H	E	D
A	L	L	U	R	E		G	E	Y	S	E	R		
L	I	E	G	E		C	R	E	E	S		O	I	L
P	T	A	S		T	R	E	N	D		B	A	R	A
H	E	R		A	R	E	A	S		O	A	T	E	S
			M	I	N	U	E	T		O	R	I	E	N	T
E	M	I	T	T	E	D		E	N	C	O	D	E	S
L	A	N	A	I		E	T	C	H					
C	O	D		W	A	R	M	H	E	A	R	T	E	D
I	R	E		A	L	A	M	O		R	O	U	G	E
D	I	D		R	I	T	A	S		D	E	M	O	N

170 Car Parts

C	O	L	A		S	A	L	A	D		T	H	A	W
A	B	E	L		A	S	I	D	E		R	O	B	E
F	I	F	T	H	W	H	E	E	L		E	R	L	E
E	S	T	E	E	M		S	E	C	E	D	E	D	
			R	A	I	S	E		T	A	T	E	R	
E	L	S		P	L	E	A		E	R	R			
L	A	H	R		L	I	R	A		B	U	M	P	S
S	P	O	O	L		N	R	A		S	N	O	O	P
A	D	O	B	E		E	I	R	E		K	A	L	E
			I	M	P		N	O	R	A		N	O	W
	T	E	N	O	R		G	N	A	T	S			
F	I	S	H	N	E	T		S	T	I	C	K	S	
O	T	T	O		F	I	R	E	E	N	G	I	N	E
O	L	E	O		A	L	T	A	R		H	A	I	R
D	E	E	D		B	E	E	T	S		T	O	T	S

171 Heat Wave

M	A	S	T	S		S	O	R	E	S		O	W	E
E	T	C	H	A		E	N	O	L	A		L	O	X
T	R	A	I	L	B	L	A	Z	E	S		D	L	I
E	I	N	S	T	E	I	N		C	H	A	F	F	S
R	A	T	T	I	N	G		S	T	A	R	L	E	T
			L	E	D		D	U	R	Y	E	A		
L	O	S	E	R		T	Y	P	O	S		M	O	W
A	L	P	S		L	I	N	E	N		H	E	R	E
P	E	I		H	O	M	E	R		C	A	S	E	D
			T	R	O	V	E	S		L	E	B		
D	E	F	A	M	E	S		S	O	L	I	C	I	T
O	B	I	W	A	N		F	I	N	E	T	U	N	E
N	O	R		G	E	O	R	G	E	B	U	R	N	S
O	N	E		E	S	S	E	N		R	E	L	I	T
T	D	S		S	T	U	D	S		E	S	S	E	S

172 Say When

A	M	I	D		G	A	L	A		P	S	A	L	M
S	A	R	I		A	B	E	L		E	N	S	U	E
I	G	O	R		T	O	A	D		T	I	A	R	A
A	I	N	T	G	O	N	N	A	H	A	P	P	E	N
				O	R	E		A	L	E				
A	M	E	N	D	S		C	A	Y	S		T	A	B
M	O	R	A	L		S	O	L	D		S	A	D	E
E	V	E	R	Y	N	O	W	A	N	D	T	H	E	N
N	I	C	K		O	D	E	S		W	O	O	E	D
S	E	T		S	O	A	R		C	A	P	E	R	S
				U	P	S		E	R	R				
T	I	L	T	H	E	E	N	D	O	F	T	I	M	E
A	C	U	T	E		P	O	G	O		E	D	I	T
G	O	N	E	R		I	V	A	N		M	O	R	N
S	N	A	R	E		C	A	R	S		P	L	E	A

173 The Attraction of Opposites

```
B A R T . C O D A . I N F R A
A L O E . H I E D . R O L E S
S L A M . E L L A . A W A I T
S I M P L E S I M O N . M N O
I N S E C T . S M I L E . . .
. . . D A L I . S A I N T S .
I F A T . H A R D K N O C K S
B E R R A . I K E . S N O O T
E A S Y S T R E E T . S S S S
G R O T T O . D R I P . . . .
. . N O U N S . N A M A T H .
W W I . T O U G H C O O K I E
A I S L E . P L E A . B I L L
I N T E L . T U R N . I T E M
T E S T Y . S E E S . L A D S
```

174 Made in the Shade

```
S C A M P . T O M B . C H E F
A L L O T . A R A B . Y A L E
P O O L A C C E S S O R I E S
. D U E . H O O K . D A R E S
. . . S W I S S . S O N . . .
W A L K O N . . S C R O O G E
A G A I N . A R I A . W E A .
D R I N K A D O R N M E N T S
E E N . N E W S . C R E M E .
R E E D I T S . S L I D E S .
. . . U T E . P A N I C . . .
A W O L S . W A C O . I S H .
J E L L Y F I S H B O D I E S
A R I E . A R T E . A L A M O
X E N A . D E E D . R E M I X
```

175 Who's What?

```
W E A R . S P E L L . S T A G
I D L E . P A T I O . C A R T
G E L S . A N T O N . A L S O
W R I T E R D A N I E L L E .
A L E . P E A . T A U N T . .
M E D I C . A U R A . L I D .
. . N O R E L C O . S A C S .
. A C T O R E L I J A H . . .
A S I A . S A V A L A S . . .
O E R . B A S E . M E A N T .
L E R O Y . . P T A . D E E .
. D I R E C T O R O L I V E R
F I F E . A R M O R . B I D S
R E L O . L I E N S . I S L E
I R E S . C O N G O . S E E R
```

176 Parental Guidance

```
J E S S . S A M O S A . A B C
U L E E . C L O R O X . B O A
D O W N T O E A R T H . B O W
D I S T I N C T . A B O N E .
. . . I D E S . D O N A T E D
P L A N E S . B O D D Y . . .
E A V E . L E V E L . U F O .
T H E L I T T L E R E D H E N
E R R . N I C E R . A U T O .
. . . S T R O M . M O T H E R
T A R H E E L . C O N E . . .
I C I E R . C E R E B R U M .
M A D . C A N A D A G O O S E
E R E . O P I N E S . O M E N
R E S . M E T E R S . K E D S
```

177 All Together Now

```
C A T E . S C A B S . A W L S
I B E G . M U S E S . P H I L
G A N G B U S T E R . P I T Y
A B A T E . T A R . J A R . .
R A M I N T O . M U L L A H .
. M O B M E N T A L I T Y . .
F A C E T S . B O N N . G O P
A P A R . A S P . C I N E .
L E N . A I D E . A D A G E S
C R O W D C O N T R O L . . .
O S P R E Y . R E E L E C T .
. . E E S . E P A . S A M O A
A N N A . G R O U P T H I N K
R E E K . A R O M A . A L E E
M A R S . P S H A W . N E S S
```

178 Is Chuck Here?

```
R A D O N . A C L U . S A G S
A L I V E . I R A N . T R O T
F I V E O C L O C K . E L M O
T E A R . A S P E N . V E E R
. . . U A R . . O H E N R Y
M U N S T E R S T W I N . . .
E M C E E . O P I N E . A B E
S P A S . . T E K . A B E T
A S A . S M O C K . S N O R T
. . . S T A R K I S T T U N A
M A R T Y R . . A D E . . .
A G E R . A S W A N . L A K E
N O N E . C H E C K P O I N T
O N E S . A U R A . A P R O N
R Y E S . S E E D . C E S T A
```

179 Related Endings

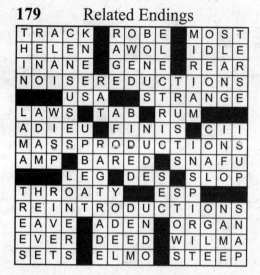

```
T R A C K . R O B E . M O S T
H E L E N . A W O L . I D L E
I N A N E . G E N E . R E A R
N O I S E R E D U C T I O N S
. . U S A . S T R A N G E
L A W S . T A B . R U M .
A D I E U . F I N I S . C I I
M A S S P R O D U C T I O N S
A M P . B A R E D . S N A F U
. L E G . D E S . S L O P
T H R O A T Y . E S P
R E I N T R O D U C T I O N S
E A V E . A D E N . O R G A N
E V E R . D E E D . W I L M A
S E T S . E L M O . S T E E P
```

180 Persistence Pays

```
D R O O P . P A B S T . T O N
R E P R O . E R A T O . I T O
W H E E L . S C R A P . T H U
H A N G I N T H E R E . L E N
O B S . T A O . S K I E R S
. . T I P . C S H A R P
A S S O C . S H U I . A A R E
K E E P O N K E E P I N G O N
C R A G . O Y E Z . L I E N S
. S U M T E R . E L S
A D O N I S . S A T . S R S
B E N . D O N T Q U I T N O W
A R I . S H A M U . M I A T A
T E N . T O S E A . E R R O L
E K G . S T A N D . D E E R E
```

181 Twelve Icons

```
H E N . E M A I L S . S L A M
O V O . M O N K E Y . C O C K
R A T . C A D E T S . H O O T
S N A K E . S I T T I N G S
E S T E E M S . N E R F .
. A D E L A . M I R A G E
A T V . G O L F . P I L O T
C H I N E S E C A L E N D A R
A E S O P . S O R E . A T E
R E E F E R . A M A H L .
. R E A M . S N E E R A T
H O L I S T I C . L E O N I
A X E L . E T R A D E . P I G
R E A L . D R A G O N . E S E
E N D S . R E T A G S . S E R
```

182 At Arm's Length

```
B A W L . B R U T E . I V A N
O H I O . L A P E L . G A M E
W O N T L I F T A F I N G E R
L Y E . O T T O . M O U N D
. H A H S . D E P R E S S
P A R A D E . M O V I E .
I M A M . T O T E S . K I T
S I T S O N O N E S H A N D S
A D S . R O W E D . C O L A
. D A N N Y . B I T T E R
R E F U T E S . M A C S
A L O N E . B A R E . L O G
T U R N S T H U M B S D O W N
E D G E . E E R I E . A R E A
S E E D . E R R E D . B E S T
```

183 Unreal World

```
A L A N . B E A T U P . S P A
R I S E . E L P A S O . L I B
E M I T . H E A D E R . A N Y
A B S T R A C T A R T I S T S
. L U N T . E T H O S
M O D E M . S A C R A .
U P A . B I S T R O . L E A D
F A N T A S T I C V O Y A G E
F L E W . S E N S E D . R U N
. A M O N G . D A N N Y
H E N N A . C O E D .
I M A G I N A R Y F R I E N D
T I M . D I R E C T . D R A Y
A L E . E N I S L E . A I D E
T E D . N E A T E N . S E A S
```

184 An Average Puzzle

```
U H O H . G F L A T . B A N D
L O N I . L O T T E . L U A U
A B I G . E R R O L . A R I D
N O T H I N G S P E C I A L
. B C D E . C A N
N O G R E A T S H A K E S
E R R O R . P O S E . T A G
A N E W . O P A R T . P O U R
L O G . B L O W . F A L S E
G A R D E N V A R I E T Y
. L E S . O L E S
F A I R T O M I D D L I N G
S I N G . E R O D E . E G A D
P A T H . R A R E R . Y O D A
A T I T . S L E D S . S T A Y
```

185 — What a Gem!

```
T A T A   C O L L     A B B A
A B E D   A V I A N   D A R N
N E R D   M E R G E   S K I D
G L I T T E R R O C K   I D O
      O I L S   S K I N N E R
E R R   P L E D   S N A G
B E E P   I L E   D O S E S
B A S E B A L L D I A M O N D
S P I E L   T O M   I D E A
      S T U B   S O P H   A S K
C A T E R E R   R O A R
A D A   B R E A K T H E I C E
L I N K   T W I N E   B A U D
L O C O   H E R O N   A G E D
A S E A   D E B T   R O S Y
```

186 — Seeing Double

```
S T A B   R O B E D   R A R E
O W N S   E M O T E   E B O N
F I N A L F I N A L   P O U T
A G O   A U T O   S O U S E
    T A R T   C O A S T E R
C H A N G E C H A N G E
L O T T E   L A C E S   S O S
A L E S   L A T H S   G N A T
W E D   O U N C E   S A U T E
    S L I G H T S L I G H T
H O S T E S S   T A N G
A V E R S   A V O N   L D S
R E N E   T R I A L T R I A L
E R S E   R A D I I   A N N E
S T E P   A M E N D   E G A D
```

187 — This Will Stop Traffic!

```
T O M E   H A L O   B O N A
H O A X   W A V E R   A N E W
E Z R A   O M A N I   S C A R
R E D C R O S S S O C I E T Y
E D I T E D   T E L L S
    B R O   S E E   O T T
S H O E   O R E   R A B B I
Y E L L O W B R I C K R O A D
N A D I R   E R A   M E R E
E D S   I T A   S S A
    S O U R S   C R E A T E
G R E E N B A Y P A C K E R S
L E V I   E R R E D   I R I S
E D E N   R A I S E   N I L E
N O N E   S T A T   G E L S
```

188 — Take a Hike

```
A B E T   I B I D   H A S P S
M A T E   C O C A   A R T I E
P A C E M A K E R   L I E G E
    D A N   T H E A P E S
S A M   P S S T   I N S P O T
T R A M P O L I N E   E N O
A T R E E   O R O   M O N
B Y C A R   W A S   A N W A R
    H T S   E D O   L E O X I
O U I   T R E A D M I L L S
S T O C K S   S P A S   F E D
B O N A I R E   R E A
O P E D S   R U N N Y M E D E
R I S E S   A N N E   F R E D
N A S T Y   S E E D   M E N D
```

189 — Out in Front

```
L E A R   T R U E D   B A B A
U R G E   H A L V E   U R A L
L I R A   O F T E N   S E L L
L E A D A M E R R Y C H A S E
    S A R A   D Y L A N
F I G H T S   S A T
A T W A R   T H O R   A C T S
T H E H O U S E O F U S H E R
S E N S   P A W N   H E A R T
    A I R   S H A N I A
C A B A L   A C L U
H E A D F O R T H E H I L L S
I S L E   R E B I D   R U I N
N O E L   A B A N G   A L M A
A P S E   L A T K E   Q U A G
```

190 — Wall Street Words

```
A H A B   C A S H   C L O D S
G A M E   A L T O   L I M E S
A L O T   B L U E   E V E N T
S L U S H F U N D   V E N T S
P E R Y E A R   W E S
    A R E   B A R T A B S
W A F F L E   F O R   O B O E
A L I A S   B A A   S C E N T
L O N I   C A R   A N K L E S
L E E R S A T   T I A
    S A P   I M P A S S E
S U S H I   J A M E S B O N D
T R I A L   I R E D   A B E E
A S T R O   L I R A   T E E N
B A S E R   L A S T   E R R S
```

191 — Headwear

S	E	E	N		S	E	D	A	N		T	U	B	E
T	A	P	E		E	L	E	N	A		I	T	E	M
O	R	S	O		P	A	R	I	S		M	A	L	I
I	T	O		C	A	T	I	N	T	H	E	H	A	T
C	O	M	P	A	R	E	D		Y	U	L			
	D	E	B	A	S	E	S		D	A	B	A	T	
O	P	E	N	I	T		D	A	M		G	L	U	E
P	O	R		N	E	L		P	A	R		U	R	N
T	O	B	E		D	I	R		R	E	R	E	A	D
S	L	Y	L	Y		P	E	D	I	C	A	B		
	E	E	N		S	E	N	A	T	O	R	S		
P	O	L	A	R	I	C	E	C	A	P		N	E	T
I	R	A	N		P	O	L	E	D		O	N	L	Y
N	E	M	O		A	L	L	I	E		H	E	A	L
S	O	A	R		T	E	S	T	S		S	T	Y	E

192 — Seasonality

S	P	A	D	E		A	D	E	P	T		P	A	S
A	A	R	O	N		M	A	R	I	A		R	U	T
S	U	M	M	E	R	S	T	O	C	K		E	R	A
S	L	O	E		E	T	A	S		E	S	S	A	Y
Y	A	R	D	A	G	E			S	T	E	S		
			F	A	L	L	F	L	O	W	E	R	S	
C	H	O	R	A	L		L	A	Y		S	O	A	K
R	O	V	E	R		E	A	T		M	O	O	R	E
O	P	E	N		A	R	M		D	U	N	N	E	D
W	I	N	T	E	R	G	A	M	E	S				
			B	A	N	E			A	F	T	M	O	S	T
G	U	I	L	D		O	H	I	O		A	L	T	O
A	P	R		S	P	R	I	N	G	B	R	E	A	K
P	O	D		U	S	E	R	S		A	D	O	R	E
E	N	S		P	A	G	E	T		R	I	S	E	N

193 — Body Language

M	A	J		E	G	A	D	S		A	D	A	G	E
E	P	I		S	M	A	R	T		C	O	R	A	L
S	A	L		S	T	R	A	I	G	H	T	A	R	M
A	L	L	B	E		G	T	I		E	B	B	S	
	S	A	N	D	S		C	F	O	S				
O	N	T	H	E	R	I	G	H	T	F	O	O	T	
R	A	J	A		U	K	R		I	N	N	E	R	
C	R	O		A	M	H	E	R	S	T		E	T	E
A	D	H	O	C		A	U	K		O	B	O	E	
	O	N	T	H	E	O	T	H	E	R	H	A	N	D
		H	E	A	R		R	E	I	N	S			
A	B	B	E		R	D	A		D	O	E	S	A	
P	U	L	L	O	N	E	S	L	E	G		H	O	T
S	T	A	L	K		A	T	O	N	E		I	D	O
E	T	H	O	S		L	A	U	D	S		T	A	P

194 — Saluting 57-Across

S	A	G	S		N	A	G	A	T		T	I	P	S
E	L	L	E		E	T	U	D	E		A	R	E	A
A	L	I	E		R	U	R	A	L		B	A	R	K
L	A	D	Y	O	F	B	U	R	L	E	S	Q	U	E
S	N	E	A	K			E	M	P					
			S	A	S	H		E	S	C	A	P	E	
	R	C	A		P	O	O	H		O	I	L	E	D
D	O	U	B	L	E	I	N	D	E	M	N	I	T	Y
A	T	S	E	A		L	E	T	S		C	D	S	
Y	E	S	S	I	R		Y	V	E	S				
			L	A	T			A	T	L	A	S		
B	A	R	B	A	R	A	S	T	A	N	W	Y	C	K
L	I	A	R		E	M	A	I	L		O	N	E	I
E	D	G	E		S	P	I	N	E		A	D	I	N
W	E	E	D		T	A	L	E	S		M	A	N	S

195 — Linen Store

L	O	A	N		T	A	L	K	S		T	A	L	C
E	L	S	A		B	L	E	A	T		U	L	E	E
D	I	S	H	T	O	W	E	L	S		P	A	C	T
O	V	I		S	N	A	K	E		W	A	S	T	E
F	I	G		K	E	Y			B	A	C	K	E	R
F	A	N	G			S	L	I	E	R		A	R	A
			M	A	E		U	L	L	M	A	N	N	
	T	A	B	L	E	C	L	O	T	H	S			
	S	I	N	A	T	R	A		W	H	O			
E	N	E		T	O	A	S	T		Y	A	W	L	
R	O	T	T	E	N			U	P	S		B	O	O
A	W	A	R	D		B	A	S	I	E		O	R	S
S	P	C	A		B	E	D	S	P	R	E	A	D	S
E	E	K	S		A	T	A	L	E		T	R	E	E
D	A	S	H		T	A	M	E	S		A	D	D	S

196 — Not Against

C	H	A	M	P		L	O	R	D	S		H	A	D
A	U	G	E	R		I	B	E	A	M		E	S	E
T	H	E	L	I	F	E	O	F	M	E		A	H	A
			T	N	O	T	E	S		R	E	V	E	L
C	R	Y		C	R	O		A	S	S	E	N	T	
L	O	O	S	E	D		W	I	T	H	I	N		
A	B	U	T	S		C	O	R	E		A	S	I	A
M	O	R	E	S		A	M	A		A	S	S	N	S
S	T	O	P		S	P	A	N		C	O	A	S	T
			W	O	R	S	E	N		B	A	N	K	E	R
C	A	N	N	O	N			O	E	D		E	T	O
A	N	G	E	L		E	S	T	E	E	M			
B	O	O		L	O	V	E	O	R	M	O	N	E	Y
I	D	O		I	R	E	N	E		I	N	A	N	E
N	E	D		N	E	R	T	S		C	A	B	O	T

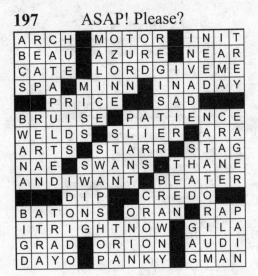

197 ASAP! Please?

```
A R C H . M O T O R . I N I T
B E A U . A Z U R E . N E A R
C A T E . L O R D G I V E M E
S P A . M I N N . I N A D A Y
. P R I C E . S A D .
B R U I S E . P A T I E N C E
W E L D S . S L I E R . A R A
A R T S . S T A R R . S T A G
N A E . S W A N S . T H A N E
A N D I W A N T . B E A T E R
. D I P . C R E D O .
B A T O N S . O R A N . R A P
I T R I G H T N O W . G I L A
G R A D . O R I O N . A U D I
D A Y O . P A N K Y . G M A N
```

198 Zero-G

```
H A R E M . S N I F F . O S S
S A Y T O . H E N R I . L A W
T H E H O L Y R A I L . D Y E
. I N E E D . M A S S E
S C H O L A R . B U S S T O P
C H O P I N . E U R E K A .
H A S I T . E X I S T . N S A
M I T A . W I C C A . O D O R
O R B . D I D O K . C H A N T
. U S O P E N . Z E B R A S
C O S T N E R . B O N E D R Y
O C T E T . T E N T H .
S H E . C H E E S E R A T E R
B R R . R I V E T . A V E R T
Y E S . Y E A R S . L E A S E
```

199 Political Definition

```
S M U . E C H O . T R I E R S
W E T . N O E L . W E L L E S
A L I B E R A L . E V O L V E
M D C I . O R I O L E .
I S A C O N S E R V A T I V E
. N E T . T E L A V I V
H E R D E R . O H S . R I D E
A V O W S . W H O . S T E E R
R I P E . R A M . L A S S O S
S T E E P E N . A A S .
H A S B E E N A R R E S T E D
. P L A S M A . N I L E
A S T U T E . T O M W O L F E
S T A T I C . A R I A . D I D
S E L E C T . R Y E S . E N S
```

200 Texas Transplants

```
T E M P . B A M B A . C O L T
A G E E . O P E L S . O V E R
B A N G . G E N I I . L A N E
. D U L L E S I N D A L L A S
. E L Y . N I E C E .
N B A G A M E . S T E N C H
E R R . N E R T S . N O N O
H U S T O N I N H O U S T O N
I T O R . E T A I L . I T E
S E N O R A . G L E A N E D
. T U N A S . P E N .
A U S T E N I N A U S T I N
F G H I . A L A R M . E N O S
O L I N . L E G U P . U C L A
X I N G . S Y S T S . P A L M
```

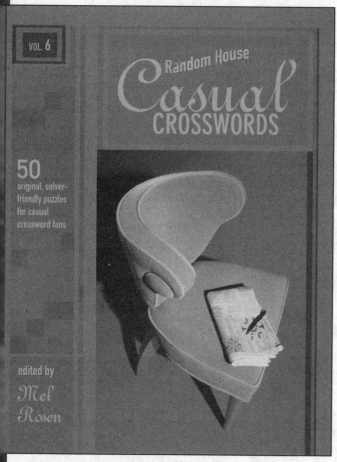

RANDOM HOUSE CROSSWORD ORDER FORM

VOL.	ISBN	QUANT.	PRICE	TOTAL

New York Times Sunday Crosswords

New York Times Sunday Crossword Omnibus
Volume 5 • 978-0-8129-3619-3 ___ $12.95 ___

New York Times Sunday Crossword Puzzles
Volume 22 • 978-0-8129-3645-2 ___ $8.95 ___

New York Times Sunday Crossword Puzzles
Volume 23 • 978-0-8129-3646-9 ___ $8.95 ___

New York Times Sunday Crossword Puzzles
Volume 24 • 978-0-8129-3647-6 ___ $8.95 ___

New York Times Sunday Crossword Puzzles
Volume 25 • 978-0-8129-3648-3 ___ $8.95 ___

New York Times Sunday Crossword Puzzles
Volume 26 • 978-0-8129-3649-0 ___ $8.95 ___

New York Times Toughest Crossword Puzzles
Volume 7 • 978-0-8129-3650-6 ___ $8.95 ___

New York Times Toughest Crossword Puzzles
Volume 8 • 978-0-8129-3651-3 ___ $8.95 ___

New York Times Crossword Tribute to Eugene T.
Maleska • 978-08129-3384-0 ___ $13.95 ___

Los Angeles Times Sunday Crosswords

Los Angeles Times Sunday Crossword Omnibus
Volume 5 • 978-0-8129-3683-4 ___ $12.95 ___

Los Angeles Times Sunday Crossword Omnibus
Volume 6 • 978-0-375-72248-6 ___ $12.95 ___

Los Angeles Times Sunday Crossword Puzzles
Volume 24 • 978-0-8129-3423-6 ___ $9.95 ___

Los Angeles Times Sunday Crossword Puzzles
Volume 25 • 978-0-375-72156-4 ___ $9.95 ___

Los Angeles Times Sunday Crossword Puzzles
Volume 26 • 978-0-375-72174-8 ___ $9.95 ___

Washington Post Sunday Crosswords

Washington Post Sunday Crossword Omnibus
Volume 3 • 978-0-375-72187-8 ___ $12.95 ___

Washington Post Sunday Crossword Puzzles
Volume 14 • 978-0-8129-3491-5 ___ $9.95 ___

Washington Post Sunday Crossword Puzzles
Volume 15 • 978-0-8129-3492-2 ___ $9.95 ___

Boston Globe Sunday Crosswords

Boston Globe Sunday Crossword Omnibus
Volume 3 • 978-0-375-72186-1 ___ $12.95 ___

Boston Globe Sunday Crossword Puzzles
Volume 14 • 978-0-8129-3487-8 ___ $9.95 ___

Washington Post Sunday Crossword Puzzles
Volume 15 • 978-0-8129-3488-5 ___ $9.95 ___

New York Magazine Crosswords

New York Magazine Crossword Puzzles
Volume 6 • 978-0-8129-3526-4 ___ $9.95 ___

New York Magazine Crossword Puzzles
Volume 7 • 978-0-8129-3684-1 ___ $9.95 ___

New York Magzine Crossword Omnibus
Volume 1 • 978-0-8129-3645-2 ___ $12.95 ___

Chicago Tribune Crosswords

Chicago Tribune Daily Crossword Omnibus
978-0-375-72219-6 ___ $12.95 ___

Chicago Tribune Daily Crossword Puzzles
Volume 5 • 978-0-8129-3560-8 ___ $9.95 ___

Chicago Tribune Daily Crossword Puzzles
Volume 6 • 978-0-8129-3561-5 ___ $9.95 ___

Chicago Tribune Sunday Crossword Omnibus
978-0-375-72209-7 ___ $12.95 ___

Chicago Tribune Sunday Crossword Puzzles
Volume 5 • 978-0-8129-3563-9 ___ $9.95 ___

Random House Vacation Crosswords

Random House All Weather Crossword Omnibus
978-0-375-72200-4 ___ $12.95 ___

Random House Autumn Harvest Crosswords
978-0-8129-3622-3 ___ $6.95 ___

Random House Endless Summer Crosswords
978-0-8129-3624-7 ___ $6.95 ___

Random House Fall Foliage Crosswords
978-0-8129-3625-4 ___ $6.95 ___

Random House Four Seasons Crossword Omnibus
978-0-8129-3668-1 ___ $12.95 ___

Random House Harvest Moon Crosswords
978-0-8129-3628-5 ___ $6.95 ___

Random House Snow Day Crosswords
978-0-8129-3483-0 ___ $6.95 ___

Random House Spring Fling Crosswords
978-0-8129-3620-9 ___ $6.95 ___

Random House Springtime Crosswords
978-0-8129-3626-1 ___ $6.95 ___

Random House Summer Nights Crosswords
978-0-8129-3627-8 ___ $6.95 ___

Random House Winter Treat Crosswords
978-0-8129-3623-0 ___ $6.95 ___

Random House Year Round Crossword Omnibus
978-0-375-72201-1 ___ $12.95 ___

Random House Summer Trip Crosswords
978-0-8129-3621-6 ___ $6.95 ___

Random House Crosswords

Random House Casual Crossword Omnibus
978-0-375-72244-8 ___ $12.95 ___

Random House Casual Crosswords
Volume 3 • 978-0-8129-3666-7 ___ $9.95 ___

Random House Casual Crosswords
Volume 4 • 978-0-8129-3673-5 ___ $9.95 ___

Random House Casual Crosswords
Volume 5 • 978-0-8129-3674-2 ___ $9.95 ___

Random House Crosswords
Volume 5 • 978-0-8129-3501-1 ___ $9.95 ___

Wall Street Journal Crosswords

Wall Street Journal Crossword Puzzle Omnibus
978-0-375-72210-3 ___ $12.95 ___

Wall Street Journal Crossword Puzzles
Volume 4 • 978-0-8129-3640-7 ___ $9.95 ___

Wall Street Journal Crossword Puzzles
Volume 5 • 978-0-375-72154-0 ___ $9.95 ___

Specialty Crosswords and Puzzle Refere

Mel's Weekend Crosswords
Volume 1 • 978-0-8129-3502-8 ___ $9.95 ___

Mel's Weekend Crosswords
Volume 2 • 978-0-8129-3503-5 ___ $9.95 ___

Random House Webster's Crossword Puzzle Diction
4th Edition 978-0-375-72131-1 ___ $18.95 ___

Random House Webster's Large Print
Crossword Puzzle Dictionary
978-0-375-72220-2 ___ $24.95 ___

Stanley Newman's Movie Mania Crosswords
978-0-8129-3468-7 ___ $7.95 ___

The Puzzlemaster Presents: Will Shortz's Best
Puzzles from NPR
978-0-8129-3515-8 ___ $13.95 ___

15,003 Answers: The Ultimate Trivia Encyclopedi
978-0-3757-2237-0 ___ $24.95 ___

To place your order, fill out this coupon and return to:
RANDOM HOUSE, INC., 400 HAHN ROAD, WESTMINSTER, MD 21157
ATTENTION: ORDER PROCESSING

☐ Enclosed is my check or money order payable to Random House
☐ Charge my credit card (circle type):   AMEX   Visa   Mastercard

Credit Card Number

NAME   SIGNATURE

ADDRESS   CITY   STATE   ZIP

To order, call toll-free 1-800-733-300

Postage & Handling		Total Books	
CARRIER	ADD	Total Dollars	$
USPS	$5.50	Sales Tax *	$
UPS	$7.50	Postage & Handling	$
		Total Enclosed	$

* Please calculate according to your state sales ta